2010

PRESUMED
DEAD

PRESUMED DEAD

> A TRUE LIFE MURDER MYSTERY

HENRY K. LEE

BERKLEY BOOKS, NEW YORK

THE BERKLEY PUBLISHING GROUP
Published by the Penguin Group
Penguin Group (USA) Inc.
375 Hudson Street, New York, New York 10014, USA
Penguin Group (Canada), 90 Eglinton Avenue East, Suite 700, Toronto, Ontario M4P 2Y3, Canada
(a division of Pearson Penguin Canada Inc.)
Penguin Books Ltd., 80 Strand, London WC2R 0RL, England
Penguin Group Ireland, 25 St. Stephen's Green, Dublin 2, Ireland (a division of Penguin Books Ltd.)
Penguin Group (Australia), 250 Camberwell Road, Camberwell, Victoria 3124, Australia
(a division of Pearson Australia Group Pty. Ltd.)
Penguin Books India Pvt. Ltd., 11 Community Centre, Panchsheel Park, New Delhi—110 017, India
Penguin Group (NZ), 67 Apollo Drive, Rosedale, North Shore 0632, New Zealand
(a division of Pearson New Zealand Ltd.)
Penguin Books (South Africa) (Pty.) Ltd., 24 Sturdee Avenue, Rosebank, Johannesburg 2196,
South Africa

Penguin Books Ltd., Registered Offices: 80 Strand, London WC2R 0RL, England

The publisher does not have any control over and does not assume any responsibility for author or
third-party websites or their content.

PRESUMED DEAD

A Berkley Book / published by arrangement with the author

PRINTING HISTORY
Berkley mass-market edition / July 2010

ISBN: 978-0-425-23593-5

BERKLEY®
Berkley Books are published by The Berkley Publishing Group,
a division of Penguin Group (USA) Inc.,
375 Hudson Street, New York, New York 10014.
BERKLEY® is a registered trademark of Penguin Group (USA) Inc.
The "B" design is a trademark of Penguin Group (USA) Inc.

PRINTED IN THE UNITED STATES OF AMERICA

10 9 8 7 6 5 4 3 2 1

Most Berkley Books are available at special quantity discounts for bulk purchases for sales,
promotions, premiums, fund-raising, or educational use. Special books, or book excerpts, can also
be created to fit specific needs.

For details, write: Special Markets, The Berkley Publishing Group, 375 Hudson Street, New York,
New York 10014.

For Laura and our growing love

ACKNOWLEDGMENTS

This project, my first published book, would not have been possible but for the generous assistance of many people. Many who had followed the Reiser case on my blog at www.sfgate.com/ZBLS had long told me, "You should write a book!" My stock response would almost invariably be a lame, "Just print out the blog!" (I still, of course, would invite interested readers to check it out.)

For suggesting the blog in the first place, I must thank Ken Conner, then metro editor, for assuming that this technophobe knew how to blog in the first place. Trapper Byrne gamely posted my first few posts, which I had sent over by e-mail from my laptop in court. But as my dispatches grew longer and more detailed, he became overwhelmed with all the coding that was involved, on top of his regular editing duties. One day early in the trial, Byrne sent me an e-mail that said simply, "Mercy." So I pleaded with my blog-savvy colleague, Marisa Lagos, for some emergency training. That did the trick. Thanks, guys. And hats off, too, to current metro editor Audrey Cooper, who posts things with lightning speed.

The blog not only was a mirror of the trial, it also served as a conduit that enabled the jury to hear testimony from at least one key witness. Dr. Peter Koltai, who had performed Rory's adenoidectomy, read my blog and had information relevant to the case. Even though Koltai's name had surfaced during the initial police investigation, he had not yet been contacted by the prosecution. At his request, I forwarded his contact info to the DA's office, and Koltai appeared as a witness in the trial.

Naturally, the blog served as a basis for the book, as well as more than nine-thousand pages of investigative material, consisting of police notes and interviews and crime-scene diagrams. I attended every court session in the case and reviewed Alameda County court transcripts from the preliminary hearing and the trial, and federal and state court records, and I conducted numerous interviews in person and over the phone. Conversations and events were also constructed through videos, audio recordings, letters and e-mails.

To my friends at the *Chronicle* who lent their support and constructive guidance: Erin Allday, who deserves special mention for her insightful suggestions; Demian Bulwa, Christopher Heredia, Carolyn Jones, Matthai Kuruvila, Meredith May and Rick Romagosa.

To my fellow authors who showed me this was possible: Claire Booth, Josh Davis, Stephen Elliott, Monte Francis, Paul LaRosa, Don Lattin and Lisa Sweetingham. A heartfelt thank-you to Carol Pogash for her positive feedback and constant affirmation.

To my fellow partners in crime: Vicki Behringer, Kristin Bender, Jamie Colby, Joshua Davis, Jason Dearen, Kraig Debro, Samantha Del Priore, Eric Frick, Jodi Hernandez, Gayane Keshishyan, David Kravets, Michelle Locke, Joan Lynch, Bob Melrose, Chris Metinko, Michelle Meyers, Norman Quebedeau, Paul Rosynsky, Jeff Shuttleworth, Greta Van Susteren and Alan Wang.

To all the legal analysts who provided commentary: Michael Cardoza, Steve Clark, Jay Gaskill and Dean Johnson.

My appreciation also extends to Y. K. and Carrie Tsai and Vanessa "Vee" Kuemmerle.

Had it not been for my agent, Jeff Gerecke, of the Gina Maccoby Literary Agency, contacting me out of the blue one day, this work would not have been published. Thank you, Jeff, for demystifying this whole process for me.

I am honored to be working with Thomas Colgan, executive editor at The Berkley Publishing Group; editorial assistant Niti Bagchi; production editor Stacy Edwards and copyeditor extraordinaire Eloise Kinney. Many thanks to John Pelosi, of Pelosi Wolf Effron & Spates in New York, for vetting the manuscript.

Greg Dolge, Paul Hora, Tom Orloff and Tom Rogers at the Alameda County DA's office were very generous with their time.

William Du Bois and Richard Tamor told me over sushi the challenges of being Hans's attorneys. Daniel Horowitz also provided key details.

Mark McGothigan invited me into his home and showed me many of his Burning Man projects and videos. Sean Sturgeon met with me a number of times to provide his perspective. Anthony Zografos, Shelley Gordon and Peggy Hora took time to chat with me.

Larry Goodman is one of the most personable judges I know, and his openness to the media—much less his decision to allow laptops and PDAs in his courtroom—made reporting on this case much easier. His clerk, Fil Cruz, and court reporter Annie Mendiola made it all effortless. Patty and Katie Goodman are a delight to be around. I was also fortunate to receive help from the many clerks at the criminal division at Alameda County Superior Court.

There are too many members of the Oakland Police Department (OPD) to publicly thank and mention, but Howard Jordan, who is now assistant chief, gave the green light for OPD's cooperation with this book. Personnel from the homicide and communications sections, the youth and family services division and the Targeted Enforcement Task Force patiently answered my questions. Public information officers Roland Holmgren and Jeff Thomason deserve special credit for taking time to discuss the case and to facilitate interviews—all while dealing with a number of other high-profile investigations and department tragedies at the same time.

Alameda County sheriff's sergeant J. D. Nelson and deputies gave me informative walking tours of the Glenn E. Dyer Detention Facility and Santa Rita Jail and explained the booking process.

I also want to thank members of the California Department of Justice's Bureau of Narcotic Enforcement and the FBI for their help.

I am grateful for the assistance of Holly Forbes at the University of California Botanical Garden at Berkeley, who taught me not to judge a tree by its cover. Jan Null at San Francisco State University and Golden Gate Weather Services provided invaluable meteorological data. Andrew Alden's primer on the geology of the Oakland hills was fascinating; his ruminations about the landslide near my house were absolutely frightful. Pilots Rodrigo von Conta and Christopher Freeze lent their aviation expertise to this hapless *Flight Simulator* user.

CNN producer Robert Ade and photojournalist Jeff King graciously spent time obtaining a screen grab from the video of me chasing Hans.

To my buddies in the O.C., Steve and Beth Eppley, Travis Pfahler and Roman Kavianian.

I would not have been able to accomplish this without the love and support of my family. My parents, J. J. and Maureen Lee, had always urged me to write a book. My sister, Brenda Lee, gave me great suggestions, as did Frank and Bonnie Blair. I am especially grateful for the help of my wife, Laura Blair, without whom this book could not have been written. Laura, you are my inspiration and my light.

FOREWORD

In my eighteen years as a crime reporter in the San Francisco Bay Area, I have written about gang shootings, horrific traffic accidents and all manner of incidents that have irreparably changed—or claimed the lives of—the young and the old, the rich and the poor, hardworking citizens and drug offenders, police officers and criminals. I chronicle the heartbreak and pain, telling stories of the horrible things that people do to each other. Why do I do this? This answer is simple, and it comes in the form of these fundamental questions: What would it mean for society if these crimes were just swept under the rug? What if nobody cared? What if victims weren't given a voice, an opportunity—sometimes from beyond the grave—to be heard?

Conversely, it is equally as important to reach out to suspects in crimes. It's standard journalistic practice to give people the chance to defend themselves. To do this, you seek them out, whether it's trying to land a jailhouse interview or, if they haven't been arrested yet, looking for them at their home or work. A good reporter gets all sides of the story and transforms a seemingly one-sided account into a more balanced story, one with proper context.

No matter how far we have come with technology, with things like Facebook, Twitter and MySpace making it easier to contact people instantly, there is no substitute for old-fashioned shoe-leather crime reporting. You try to reach out to suspects directly without going through their lawyers or waiting for the phone to ring. The accused come from all strata of society, but despite their backgrounds, most suspects I approach offer a terse "No comment," hanging up or slamming the door in my face. Others proudly boast of what they have done, almost justifying terrible acts and using the media as a platform. Hans Reiser, a self-described computer genius, did none of that when I approached him on foot in downtown Oakland on September 28, 2006. It was less than a month after his estranged wife, Nina, had vanished after she went shopping with their children. I wanted to see what he knew. I fully expected Hans to either clam up or deny any involvement in her disappearance. I figured I'd thank him and then we'd part ways.

Instead, Hans took one look at me (and a camera crew from a TV station) and took off running—sprinting—down the street. I was stunned for a quick second. Then my reporter's instincts kicked in. I began running after him as police in undercover vehicles gaped in surprise. The chase was on.

PART ONE

>A MOTHER AND HER CHILDREN

CHAPTER 1

> SHOPPING

It was cool and overcast at about noon on Sunday, September 3, 2006, when Nina Reiser pulled her Honda Odyssey minivan away from her home in the Temescal District of Oakland, California. Her children, six-year-old Rory and five-year-old Niorline—Nio, for short—sat in their car seats behind her. It was going to be a busy day. The three of them were going to get lunch and then shop for groceries. The petite thirty-one-year-old mother of two was born in Russia but had readily acclimated to life in the United States and seemed every bit the typical soccer mom. Her English was very good, and she was admired by other parents and her children's teachers for her devotion to Rory and Nio. At five feet five and 115 pounds, with dark hair, brown eyes, porcelain skin and a pretty smile, she turned heads.

Nina was both beautiful and smart. She was trained in Russia as a gynecologist and spoke Russian, English and German fluently. She was busy preparing for the medical licensing exam to become a doctor in the United States. Just two days earlier, Nina had accepted a new job but only after making sure that her hours could be flexible so that she could be with her kids and study. The previous week, she had signed them up for an after-school program at the new school they had started attending.

But now, Nina focused on the task at hand. She drove west on Fifty-first Street and turned right onto busy Shattuck Avenue and entered the Berkeley city limits at Woolsey Street. She continued north for less than a half a mile until the traffic slowed near Oregon Street.

Nina arrived at the parking lot of the Berkeley Bowl, the

city's much-beloved grocery store that was famed for its cornucopia of fresh produce. On any given day, gourmands jockeyed for spaces in the tiny parking lot and then jostled for space in the aisles, eager to snatch up the trimmed baby greens, artisanal cheese and one of six kinds of mangoes. On this busy Labor Day weekend, Nina managed to find a space. The midday clouds gave way to sunshine as she helped Rory and Nio out of the minivan. Nina wore a black-and-white sundress, a necklace with a blue stone and flip-flops. Rory had on a green shirt, and his sister, whose big round eyes and fair skin made her a spitting image of her mother, was wearing a yellow dress. As Nina got a shopping cart from in front of the store, Nio and Rory were excited. They knew they'd be getting their favorite Lucky Charms cereal, which they liked to have on Sundays.

At 12:30 p.m., the three shared an eel roll, soup and pot stickers for lunch at Berkeley Bowl's deli at the front corner of the store and then bought their groceries for the week. Nina checked her cell phone and saw that her boyfriend, Anthony Zografos, had called. At 12:55 p.m., she sent him a text message. "We are at the BB finally and are having lunch. I'm sorry I missed your calls my love. It's great that you stopped to say good-by. Have a fun trip pirates. Love you lots." She called Zografos and his kids pirates, because they liked the ocean and tended to be a bit rowdy.

Nina, Rory and Nio left the store shortly before 2:00 p.m. Now, Nina had to drive to the Oakland hills home of her estranged husband, Hans Reiser. The two had argued over who would have the children for the long weekend, the first since school began, on August 28. He insisted on having them even though it was her turn. So she agreed to split custody that weekend: she would have the kids on Saturday before dropping them off at his home at 2:00 p.m. Sunday. She was running a little late. Records would later show that at 2:04 p.m., she used her cell phone to call Hans at his house, telling him that they had left the Berkeley Bowl and were on their way. Her twenty-two-second call was picked up by the nearest cell site, at Ninth Street and Heinz Avenue, about a mile and a half away from the store.

That would be the last call Nina would ever make. She would never be seen or heard from again.

› By all accounts, Nina Reiser was a devoted mother who structured her life around her children. But behind the scenes, her personal life was in turmoil. Nina was in the middle of a bitter divorce with Hans Reiser, her forty-two-year-old husband and the father of her kids. Each accused the other of being a bad parent: Nina accused Hans of exposing Rory to violent video games and thwarting medical care for him; Hans said Nina was ruining their son by making up illnesses he supposedly had and hiding her penchant for lying under a veneer of being the perfect parent. The tangle of allegations—traded in court papers—was the stuff of soap operas, and their children were caught squarely in the middle. The couple had gone to mediation, counseling and psychological evaluations, but Hans fought Nina every step of the way. "It didn't have the 'War of the Roses' element that some divorces have," one of his attorneys would say later, adding, however, "It takes two to be contentious [and] two to have an argument."

› Hans was used to getting what he wanted. A UC Berkeley student at age fifteen, he was a self-proclaimed computer genius and namesake creator of the ReiserFS file system, which made it quicker to search files in the popular Linux operating system, an alternative to Microsoft Windows. Hans had parlayed his programming prowess into a successful company called Namesys. But he rubbed many people the wrong way, and others in the industry said Hans's file system was as flawed as his personality. He could be obstinate and egotistical, given to composing long-winded statements—treatises, some called them—to explain why he was right on any given issue. Some of his Russian-born employees could scarcely tolerate him.

Before he met Nina, Hans tried his hand at writing a novel and penned poetry in hopes of finding a mate. While working in Russia in 1998, Hans was introduced to a series of women through marriage agencies, which is how he met Nina. A quick courtship—during which Nina became pregnant with Rory—was followed by a hastily arranged wedding in the hills near his Oakland home in 1999. All seemed well.

But Namesys began struggling financially, and after Nio was born, in 2001, the marriage deteriorated. With Hans in Russia most of the year, Nina was left raising two kids on her own. She began having an affair with Sean Sturgeon, Hans's best friend since they were sixteen. As boys, Hans and Sturgeon had bonded over war games and fantasy role-playing games. Sturgeon, who considered Hans his brother, was a colorful character who had been involved in the Bay Area sadomasochism scene—and had dressed in drag to serve as "maid of honor" at the Reisers' wedding. Oddly enough, the affair didn't put as much of a wedge between Hans and Sturgeon as one might think, although it certainly didn't help their relationship. But Hans grew furious at his best friend after he took Nina's side when she filed for divorce, in 2004. Hans accused Nina and Sturgeon of stealing from his company. Sturgeon, who routinely lent Nina money, then sued Hans over an unpaid eighty-four-thousand-dollar loan.

Although Nina and Sturgeon eventually broke up, she was still dependent on him financially—he had put an envelope containing seventeen hundred dollars in her mail slot just two days earlier—and that relationship was now placing strains on her current romance with Zografos, a Greek-born Silicon Valley high-tech entrepreneur with silver temples and a trim physique. The two had met on Craigslist, the popular online community network, where they had placed ads for playdates for their children. Nina, though a responsible and loving mother, had her needs and frequently went outside her comfort zone, browsing Craigslist to meet men, even as she was dating Zografos. Her online search for companionship made Zografos and some of her friends uneasy. They could not fathom why Nina was living so close to the edge.

Zografos was separated from his wife, who two years earlier had accused him of yelling at and threatening their children, causing them to be scared of him. She also said he kidnapped their daughter during a dispute, which Zografos denied. Zografos didn't like Sturgeon and was a jealous boy-friend who'd check Nina's e-mail account, follow her or show up unexpectedly at places she'd be. The day before, Nina and Zografos had talked about breaking up. He wasn't sure if he could have a long-term relationship with Nina, who bore an uncanny resemblance to his estranged wife.

It was the afternoon of Sunday, September 3, when forty-two-year-old Sturgeon threaded his way through the Art and Soul Festival in downtown Oakland. The annual Labor Day weekend street fair featured food vendors, artist booths and live bands on several stages. The air was fragrant with the smells of barbecued ribs, garlic fries and sizzling Cajun turkey sausage. Several streets around City Hall, the Ronald V. Dellums Federal Building and the City Center office and shopping complex were blocked off. It was crowded, and Sturgeon was in a hurry. He had undergone kidney-stone surgery several weeks earlier and wanted to relax in the sauna. Just before 4:15 p.m., Sturgeon opened the glass doors and strode into the exclusive Club One gym, which counted as members District Attorney Tom Orloff, former California governor Jerry Brown and even Oakland Mayor Ron Dellums himself. The denizens of the gym didn't look twice when the downtown power brokers showed up next to them on the machines. People mostly kept to themselves, and that suited Sturgeon just fine. He was in pain and just wanted time to himself. No one had any idea that the man with the startlingly pale green eyes kept guns at his home—and had spoken of killing people.

> Ellen Doren was getting ready to see Nina that evening. Doren, a personal chef, was a native of Moscow and lived in Oakland. Doren, a thirty-one-year-old blond who was also married to an American, met Nina at a Russian-language school for children three years earlier. The couple had kids the same age as the Reiser children. Nina had called Doren at about 10:30 a.m. that day and told her that she'd be lonely now that she had to drop off her kids with Hans. Zografos would be out of town on a camping trip at Big Basin Redwoods State

Park in Santa Cruz County with his kids and his wife. Though still separated, the two were now on better terms. Nina told Doren that she was going to the Berkeley Bowl and offered to buy Doren dinner because she wasn't feeling well. Doren immediately agreed and invited Nina over to her home for dinner at 6:00 p.m.

At 6:10 p.m., Nina hadn't arrived. Doren felt a sense of foreboding. Nina was rarely late, and if she was, she would always call, even if she was behind by only five minutes. Just before 6:30 p.m., Doren called Nina's cell phone and left a message. She again called at 7:00 and 7:30 p.m. The phone rang and rolled right into voice mail. But when Doren called yet again at 9:00 p.m., there was no ring. The call went straight to voice mail.

As he was driving back to Oakland from his camping trip on Monday, September 4, Labor Day, Zografos also tried calling Nina. At 2:30 p.m., he sent a text message. A half hour later, after stopping for lunch off Highway 17 in Scotts Valley, south of San Jose, he tried to call her again. The call went straight to voice mail. Zografos called Nina's home number, and he got the answering machine. He began to worry. If she had wanted to change their plans for that night, she would have left a voice mail or sent an e-mail or text message. When he arrived at his Oakland home at 5:00 p.m., he kept calling.

An hour later, he was anxious as he drove to Nina's home. He found no signs of Nina or her Honda Odyssey minivan, nor did Zografos see the Honda CRX that Hans drove. Zografos went back home. That afternoon and evening, he called Nina's cell phone seventeen times. At 9:00 p.m., he drove back to her house again. Nina usually left a light on. The white, single-story home with green trim was dark. He drove to Doren's house and saw Doren's car but not Nina's. He wondered if one of the kids had become sick and perhaps Nina went to Hans's house. Back home, Zografos typed in Hans's name on Google and found his address. At 10:00 p.m., he drove to Exeter Drive, a winding street up high in the Oakland hills. When that turned up nothing, Zografos drove down Shepherd Canyon Road and Park Boulevard and pulled up to the apartment of Nina's old boyfriend Sturgeon near Lake Merritt, a popular spot for joggers. Zografos felt a wave of disappointment. She wasn't there.

> At 11:00 p.m., Zografos returned to Nina's house and let himself in with a key she had given him. The home was eerily quiet and looked as if it had been frozen in time. Mail spilled from the slot and onto the wood floor of the living room. Along with the catalogs and ads was a "Sorry We Missed You!" notice from the postal service. Rory's Game Boy sat on top of the TV, along with several DVDs, including Disney/Pixar's *Cars* and Dragon Tales' *Whenever I'm Afraid . . . Helping Your Child Cope with Fears!*

Zografos took a few steps into the dining room, which, like many of the home's rooms, was adorned with framed pictures of butterflies, which Nina loved. A Harry Potter Lego box was still on the table in the dining room.

He went into the kitchen and saw two glasses on the table with spoons and leftover milk inside. Hans had found it annoying that Nina was compulsively tidy, refusing to go to bed until all the dishes had been washed. Now, those telltale signs left Zografos unable to shake the ominous feeling in his stomach. *Nina would have cleaned all that up by now.*

Walking into her bedroom, Zografos noticed a huge portrait of a strikingly attractive Nina holding Rory when he was a baby. He saw folded laundry in the room with a shirt of his thrown on top. He tried to look in the garage, but it was locked. There were no signs of Nina. None. Zografos came to the grim conclusion that her house was in almost the same condition as it was the day before. His sense of dread increased when he spotted a closed window Nina usually left open for her beloved Russian blue cat, Basil, who wasn't in the house. Later, Zografos would find Basil at the front door and let the feline in. The knot of worry within him tightened. He thought back to the horoscope he had e-mailed Nina the day before: "Someone will be aggressive with you today, but he can't hurt you."

On Tuesday, September 5, Nina's best friend, Doren, still hadn't heard back from Nina. Doren wondered if her friend had dropped off her kids in the morning and was going to pick them up that afternoon. No matter what may have happened to Nina, Doren was convinced, she'd be there to pick up her children. There was an old saying in Russia: "If you can crawl, you're going to be there." But with each fruitless phone call, that seemed less and less likely.

At 2:20 p.m., Doren went to Adventure Time, an extended day-care program at Joaquin Miller Elementary School in the Oakland hills, where Rory was in the first grade and Nio was in kindergarten. Doren asked to pick Rory and Nio up later that day, but staffers told her that they couldn't release them without Nina's permission. They left a message on her cell phone. At 5:00 p.m., Hans stopped by the school and said nothing about Nina. Oddly, he said he wanted to make sure he was on the emergency contact list. Almost as an afterthought, he told an employee that it would be OK for Doren to pick the kids up. She came to school minutes later and took them home with her.

 As they left work in San Jose, Zografos and a colleague called the Oakland police to see if Nina had been involved in an accident. She tended to drive fast and had been ticketed twice for not wearing her seat belt. But there was no record of her or her minivan. They called the local hospitals, but they didn't have any patients under her name. Zografos called the Berkeley Bowl. "Did you find any car left in the parking lot on Sunday?" They said no. "Did anyone get sick in the store Sunday?" he pressed, his voice betraying worry. Same answer. Swallowing his pride, Zografos called Sturgeon and asked if they could put aside their differences. Zografos asked if it was possible that Nina could be seeing someone else. Sturgeon facetiously replied that it would be impossible that she could be unfaithful to Zografos.

That wasn't the answer Zografos wanted to hear. Now

almost frantic, he went to Doren's house at dusk. Together they decided to call the police. Officer Ed Pressnell arrived at about 9:00 p.m. and took a seat in the dining room. They told Pressnell they believed Nina was supposed to drop off her kids and then visit Berkeley Bowl, although the order of those events would turn out to be the subject of some confusion. Pressnell told Doren to call Hans. At 9:21 p.m., Doren punched in the numbers for Hans's cell phone.

› When Hans answered, Doren wasted no time. "Hello, Hans, this is Ellen Doren, Jacob and Julia's mom. And I'm calling to let you know that I picked up the children today because Nina is missing, and they are here at my house staying over, and I would be happy to bring them to school tomorrow. Is that OK with you?" Doren asked.

"Uh-huh," Hans replied. He didn't sound interested at all about the children.

"I also know that Nina went to your house on Sunday, and to my knowledge, you were the last person that saw her on that Sunday. Do you know anything about what happened next or where she went?"

"I need to talk to my lawyer," Hans replied.

› The next morning at 8:00, Officer Ryan Gill, a member of the Missing Persons Unit in the Oakland Police Department's Youth and Family Services Section, was in his office reviewing Pressnell's police report. Gill spent much of his time reviewing paperwork. It was a far cry from working the streets in some of the city's most dangerous neighborhoods, where suspects routinely ran away from cops or, worse, got into fights with them. In 2003, Gill and a fellow officer were assigned to a Crime Reduction Team when they shot and killed a suspect who reportedly went for one of their guns. "He's got my gun, I can't control him—shoot him!" Gill yelled at his partner. Gill regained control of his weapon, and both officers shot and killed twenty-year-old Terrance Mearis in his East Oakland home. Mearis's family was outraged, claiming the man had been sleeping in bed and had done nothing wrong. The department and the Alameda County district attorney's office determined that the shooting was justified.

Now, the twenty-eight-year-old Gill was sitting at his desk at the Alameda County Family Justice Center on Twenty-seventh Street in Oakland. The three-story structure, which had opened to the public a year earlier in a former county health office, sat in separate quarters more than a mile away from the Oakland Police Administration Building. Officers who were assigned to the center worked with prosecutors, victims' advocates and social service workers under the same roof, saving victims from having to go to different places for assistance. Gill, who had six years on the force, had just been assigned to work with a bloodhound named Jackson, and he was eager for the opportunity. Sifting through reports of missing people was a different but necessary part of police work. Gill knew that some individuals went missing only temporarily. Children wandered off, teenagers ran away and elderly people with medical issues went out for a walk and became disoriented. Others wanted to get away from financial, work or marital problems and clear their heads or just cool off, Gill knew. A few, however, killed themselves, and some of the older people turned up dead from exposure. Some ran off the road and died in car accidents.

Often, a missing-persons case turned out to be just a simple misunderstanding. In 2006, 39,226 California residents were reported missing, of which 17,022, or about 43 percent, were women, according to the state Department of Justice. The majority of those individuals, 82 percent, were described as "voluntarily missing," someone who left on his or her own free will, and many of them returned home. There were only 496 people who disappeared under "suspicious circumstances," in which victims may have been kidnapped by a stranger.

Gill was mindful of these statistics. But the report he had in his hands today seemed different from all the others. Gill had a feeling that something wasn't right. Often, when families seek help for a missing person, the police postpone sending out an alert immediately, knowing that the missing person is likely to show up before long. In this case, the Oakland police didn't hesitate: Pressnell's report described Nina as a missing person at risk, and she had already been missing for more than forty-eight hours. Gill made sure that Nina's name and Department of Motor Vehicles photo were sent out electronically and listed on the missing-persons law-enforcement database and that a "comm order"—what Oakland police called its all-points bulletins—had been broadcast on all dispatch channels.

No one had reported seeing her minivan or crashes with any similar vehicles. He continued looking over the report. Not more than fifteen minutes later, his phone rang. It was Zografos. Zografos explained that he was Nina's boyfriend and that she was supposed to have dropped off her kids at Hans's house on Sunday.

Zografos told the officer that Nina was upset over a messy divorce with her husband and that she had just accepted a job offer with the San Francisco Public Health Department helping Russian immigrants. Nina was also supposed to have taken the medical licensing exam two weeks earlier, but she had postponed it until November 21. The bottom line, Zografos and others told the police: Nina would never just leave her children.

Zografos had his suspicions. He told police and anyone who would listen that Sturgeon, who was bisexual, should be looked at in connection with Nina's disappearance because of their affair and his S and M activities. Sturgeon, who had worked at a recycling center in El Cerrito, a middle-class bedroom community north of Berkeley, was raised in a complicated sexual environment. While growing up, he suffered sexual abuse at the hands of friends and visitors of his mother.

But Nina's best friend, Doren, thought Zografos was a person of interest. He was separated from his wife and was fifteen years older than Nina, and Doren thought he was acting strangely and forcing on people the idea that Nina was depressed. Doren knew that Zografos was prone to fits of jealousy and couldn't stand it when Nina talked to other men.

The police believed that Nina may have fallen victim to foul play. And with Nina's complicated life, the three men she was closest to topped their list of potential suspects: Hans, Zografos and Sturgeon.

Zografos didn't care about whether the police thought he was involved in Nina's disappearance. He just wanted to know where Nina was. He ate, slept and showered with his cell phone nearby, doing his best to maintain his daily routine while at the same time trying to ward off a growing anxiety. He checked Nina's computer and wondered if Nina had gone off with some secret lover she met on Craigslist. Some of the ads she had been reviewing were quite graphic; one was pornographic and showed several sex acts. A bolt of fear shot through Zografos as his mind latched on to a terrifying scenario: *What if one of Nina's "dates" had gone too far and had done something terrible to her?*

> At 10:15 a.m., Officer Gill drove to Nina's house, at the corner of Forty-ninth Street and Coronado Avenue. The bungalow, built in 1924, had a neatly manicured lawn, a pink magnolia tree overlooking the front porch and rose bushes and orange-crested birds of paradise out front. Nina's car wasn't there. Police hadn't obtained a search warrant yet, so Gill peered inside the house. "Home appeared to be in good condition with no obvious sign of struggle," Gill wrote in his notes. "However, note that Zografos has been in and out of this address with his personal key." Officer Gill warned Zografos that despite having the key, he was risking liability by entering Nina's home in her absence.

> Gill contacted a man who was buying a home near Nina's. The man said he saw some "Asian kid" inside the home, working on the computer in the back room the previous Monday or Tuesday.

Gill also checked out a man whose blue Honda had been parked in front of Nina's home. Zografos had never seen it there before.

Gill searched Craigslist for any ads that Nina had placed but found none.

As night fell, with any number of potential suspects to look at, Gill had his hands full. There were still many unanswered questions and possibilities that were swirling in Gill's head, all of which were disturbing. Was Nina kidnapped? Did she get into a car crash in the hills? Was she injured and lying somewhere, helpless, hungry, cold and desperate and frightened for her life? Did she have a tryst with someone from Craigslist? Where was her minivan? It all came down to the basics: where was Nina Reiser, and why was there no trace of her?

CHAPTER 2

> NINA

Nina Vladimirovna Sharanova came into the world on November 3, 1974. She was born in a hospital in Pskov, a town twelve miles east of the Estonian border filled with quaint churches dating back to the fifteenth and sixteenth centuries. Pskov was the center of the very first trade routes with the West. Its role had since been taken over by Saint Petersburg, as Leningrad later became known, 160 miles to the northeast. Saint Petersburg, which had served as the capital of the Russian Empire for more than two hundred years, was nowadays known as the Window to the West. It sits on the Neva River at the head of the Gulf of Finland on the Baltic Sea.

Irina Georgievna Sharanova, who was twenty-six, named her daughter after her mother. Photographs of Sharanova as a young woman telegraphed the dark-haired beauty that Nina would become. When Nina turned two, Sharanova got a divorce from her doctor husband, Vladimir Khashpakyants. Nina went for a time to live with her maternal grandparents as Sharanova studied to become an ob-gyn. When Nina was ten years old, Sharanova married Herman Lavrentiev, a dentist whom Nina would consider her father. She lived with them on Marata Street in a historical and cultural part of Saint Petersburg, a fifteen-minute walk from the main city thoroughfare, Nevsky Prospect.

Nina was close to her mother, who ran a clinic for disadvantaged teenage girls. Sharanova was a "no bullshit person with a wonderful sense of humor," Nina would say later. "My mother knows a lot about life." But Sharanova could be a bit controlling. Nina often confided in her stepfather, who went to all of her school functions. All in all, Nina had no regrets about her upbringing. She would never have any siblings.

When she was sixteen, Nina had a taste of life in America when she studied for a semester at Lincoln School, a liberal arts college-prep day school for girls on Providence's East Side in Rhode Island. The school takes pride in its Quaker roots and values honesty, respect and simplicity. Each October, the leafy campus hosted the Rhode Island Festival of Children's Books and Authors. It was a heady experience for Nina, who met new people and explored the capital city, one of the original thirteen colonies of the United States. She had arrived just as the city was beginning to revitalize its arts scene.

Meanwhile, back in Russia, the era of glasnost and perestroika was just beginning, and a former KGB operative named Vladimir Putin was anointed a top aide to Leningrad mayor Anatoly Sobchak.

CHAPTER 3

> HANS

Hans Thomas Reiser drew his first breath on December 19, 1963, at Providence Hospital in Seattle. As Hans was taking in his new world, the country was still reeling from the assassination of John F. Kennedy in Dallas less than a month earlier.

Baby Hans was the only child born to Beverly Ann Kleiber, age twenty, and Ramon Reiser, who was twenty-one. His name was a combination of those of his great-grandparents. Beverly's grandfather was Hans Kleiber, the noted German-born traditional Western etcher, painter and illustrator known for his portraits of the Big Horn Mountains in Wyoming, where he also served as a U.S. Forest Service ranger and hunting guide. Ramon's grandfather was Thomas E. Martin, who spent twenty-two years as a U.S. representative and senator from Iowa.

The son of Seattle attorney Raymond Reiser, Ramon studied math at Dartmouth College from 1959 to 1960 before ending up at Santa Clara College in San Jose to study philosophy, math and classics. Ramon was dating a woman named Beverly Naughton before he met her friend—another Beverly—who would later become his wife. Ramon met Naughton at a party at the beach in Santa Cruz in May 1962. "She was at that time one of the most socially beautiful women I had ever seen," Ramon said. "She was very intelligent, very sweet." But friends thought Ramon seemed better matched with Beverly Kleiber, who had graduated from a Catholic high school in San Jose and was now studying art at Immaculate Heart College, a private Catholic college in Los Angeles. Ramon agreed with this assessment. Kleiber, whose artistic talents may in part have been in her genes, was unusually articulate about art, Ramon said.

Ramon and Beverly were engaged for eighteen months and spoke about having kids. He wanted eight; Beverly was more comfortable with six. The two married in a Catholic church alongside Ramon's college in February 1963. Hans was conceived the night they consummated their marriage, at the Saint Francis Drake Hotel in San Francisco. The next morning, not knowing about the new life that had already begun inside her, Beverly told Ramon that she didn't want any children at all. Ramon felt betrayed.

Nevertheless, they tried to make the best of it. The couple lived in student housing in Quonset huts alongside the football field of Santa Clara College. After Ramon graduated, they moved to a little apartment above a liquor store on Market Street in San Jose. The rent was thirty-five dollars a month.

They eventually resettled to Ramon's hometown of Seattle, where Hans was born three and one-half weeks after his due date. "He was the ugliest, most wrinkly baby you ever saw," his father said.

Hans was happy as a child. "As a kid, he was everywhere with all the kids in the neighborhood," Ramon recalled. "The kids just loved him." There were no disciplinary problems with Hans. "He was about as easy a child as there ever was," Ramon said.

The family lived in a World War II–era two-bedroom home on Beacon Avenue in the Beacon Hill neighborhood. Some locals, however, dubbed it Boeing Hill because it overlooked Boeing Field, where the airplane giant operated test flights. On clear days, one could see snow-capped Mount Rainier and the Olympic Mountains.

Hans was close to his father. But the elder Reiser spent a lot of time away from home, and Hans missed him terribly. When Ramon went off to medical school and had to stay late, he'd return and Hans would be happy. But when Beverly went somewhere and was delayed, Hans would run to the window, crying, "Where's Mama?"

Beverly later told friends that Ramon always seemed to screw up things. He was constantly coming up with plans that always fell through. Ramon and Beverly separated in the summer of 1967, when Hans was three. By January 1968, Ramon had enlisted in the U.S. Army and was shipped to Vietnam ten months later. Ramon and Beverly had quarreled over the Vietnam War. Beverly didn't feel like it was fair for Ramon to use a student deferment to avoid the war when poor kids were being shipped off to fight. Ramon eventually gave up his deferment and went to Vietnam. Ramon was overseas when he learned his divorce had been finalized in November 1968. Ramon knew that chances would be slim that he'd get custody of his son. Hans would later report that his parents said negative things about each other throughout his childhood. "They were 70 to 80 percent accurate about the things they said about each other. I learned from what they said. It helped me from developing the same flaws. It made me a stronger, better person."

Ramon, meanwhile, became a stronger person and learned a valuable lesson while fighting in Vietnam. In a story he would repeatedly tell his children, Ramon recalled sitting on a dike in the Mekong Delta at 2:00 a.m. when he heard the sound of a rustling bush and immediately found himself face-to-face with a Vietnamese combat engineer. The enemy fighter flipped the safety of his AK-47 at the same time Ramon did on his weapon. "It was the original 'Mexican standoff' deep in the Mekong," Ramon said. Both could have fired, but instead the men exchanged "shit-eating grins," backed away and nodded. When daylight broke, members of Ramon's squad began yelling after they awoke to find that their claymores, or small mines, had been moved by the enemy. Instead of being in their original positions twenty meters away from them, the Vietnamese had rolled them up and secretly placed them under the sleeping troops.

Hans would later say that his father, who retired as an U.S. Army sergeant first class, had been diagnosed as being hypomanic and that his symptoms included compulsive talking and exaggerating everything to an extreme. But in a paper she submitted years later at Georgia Perimeter College, Hans's half-sister Cheyenne Reiser would describe her father as a "great storyteller" whose entertaining tales were all true. As for his Vietnam recollection, "He used it in lectures when he thought we needed an ego check and at times when he thought we needed to understand that there were some people in this world who one shouldn't ever turn their back on," Cheyenne wrote. "My father learned a valuable lesson that day in Vietnam that helped him make it home alive when so many others did not. I'm very thankful he was around to tell it."

Despite it all, Ramon said he had no regrets about his relationship with Beverly. "It was a marriage of intellectual camaraderie," he said. "Beverly permanently changed the way I saw the world artistically. She was brilliant. She opened me up to Picasso and modernists, Rembrandt and so forth. I'm grateful for that part of my life. She was extremely aware artistically and that opened up a part of me that wasn't there."

Hans saw little of his father as he grew up and was often lonely. Ramon saw Hans after returning from Vietnam and tried to maintain contact with his son but grew frustrated over custody issues with Beverly. Beverly forged ahead with her academics, earning her BA in art from Immaculate Heart in 1969.

At age nine, Hans began having more contact with his father and spent two summers with his family in Atlanta, where Ramon later lived. Hans was an only child but had three half brothers and a second half sister besides Cheyenne. Ramon would remarry and go on to teach high school biology, chemistry and math.

Within a year of moving back to California, Beverly met and married Bernard Palmer, who was twenty-two years her senior. Palmer, a native of Utica, New York, was a sergeant and radio operator in the U.S. Army Air Forces during World War II, flying combat missions over Germany. Palmer had been principal of a Jewish high school. He was a high school teacher in Tennessee before coming to San Francisco State in the 1950s to teach college students working for their high-school teaching credential. Palmer was a professional violist who was a member of the Berkeley and Kensington symphonies and the Holy Names and Oakland Civic orchestras.

> By 1976, Hans was thirteen and living with his mother in a three-story, three-bedroom home at 6979 Exeter Drive,

a winding street high up in the Oakland hills just beyond the
outskirts of a neighborhood known as Piedmont Pines. The
home, built in 1968, was nestled amid tall pine, redwood and
bamboo trees and, like many homes in the area, had a carport
built on stilts and a deck. The backyard was so lush with trees
and ferns that it felt as if one were in the middle of a forest.
In decorating the home, Beverly sought to pull the outside in,
invoking nature as part of the design. As she settled in to life
in the hills, she continued her art studies. In 1980, she earned
her master's in art education from San Francisco State University. Her specialty was museum and gallery management.

› Hills residents value their privacy, but Hans went further
than most. Neighbors said he didn't socialize with the kids in
the neighborhood and kept to himself. Neighbor Cheryl Milton used to pick Hans up at a bus stop on Mountain Boulevard
at the base of the hills and offer him a ride home. Although
many kids that age might chatter about their day, Hans would
get in the car and not say a word. "He's in his own little world,"
Milton would say later.

Milton said Hans also had a mean streak in him and used
a bow and arrow to shoot her cat. The feline had to undergo
eight hundred dollars' worth of surgery. Some criminal profil-
ers have argued that childhood cruelty to animals is a significant predictor of future violence toward people.

Palmer gave Hans much of the affection that he received
while growing up, Ramon said. Palmer retired in 1991 and
died of cancer at their home in April 2000. After a service at
Mills College, he was cremated. His death devastated Beverly. Palmer had taken care of most of the couple's affairs.
She was now alone and left to fend for herself. Little did she
know that her golden years would be spent dealing with Hans
and his problems.

CHAPTER 4

> NOT CUT OUT FOR CLASS

Hans's elementary-school years were uneventful. But he began chafing at the traditional educational system and dropped out of school—at the tender age of thirteen—after completing the eighth grade at Montera Junior High on Ascot Drive in the Oakland hills. There, he was one of the fastest runners in gym class. The coach gave the class an incentive: the top seven wouldn't have to run the next week. Hans was always part of that group. "He was one hell of a runner," recalled J. D. Nelson, who was in the same grade as Hans. "I was a decent runner back then, and he smoked me." Nelson would cross paths again with Hans years later.

But although Hans excelled on the field, he wanted nothing to do with the classroom, preferring instead to control his own education and work at his own pace. The teachers insisted that the students sit in neat rows, and Hans couldn't stand it. It didn't matter that the school—whose motto nowadays is "dignity, respect and high academic standards"—seemed to offer a climate that was conducive to learning. Montera and Joaquin Miller Elementary School, which was right next door, were among the best schools in the city, close to home and far from the dangerous streets of the city's flatlands, where violence and death were rife and hardly counted as news anymore.

Hans took some extension classes at UC Berkeley when he was fourteen. He also bought SAT prep books, took the test and scored 1410 out of 1600. Against everyone's advice, he applied to the university, known as Cal, and got accepted at the age of fifteen. But he quickly realized that his writing skills needed some work when he got a D in Rhetoric. "I knew all the vocabulary and I can compose a sentence, but that's different from composing an essay," Hans said later. In an interview with KernelTrap, a computer news Web site, he said, "Berkeley was a lot better than junior high school, but it still involved homework, which deep down in my heart I could never believe in. Reading textbooks, yes, arguing with the professor in class, yes, but homework I could only possess a theoretical understanding of the social purpose of. Such a pity one cannot get a scholarship to go to the bookstore for 10 years and at intervals prove by discussion of it that one learned something."

In 1980, he met Sean Sturgeon, a fellow Dungeons & Dragons enthusiast. Several years later, Hans created a game to compete with Dungeons & Dragons.

In 1984, he was working as a systems administrator at Microsoft Corporation, where his supervisors wanted him to work at least sixty hours a week. Hans was willing to work forty-four hours a week but wanted time off on the weekends to develop what would become his eponymous file system. "We agreed that I should leave," he later told an interviewer. His work with Microsoft never made it onto his résumé, and the reasons why would become clear later. By then he was consumed with building his file system, which would become his life's work.

› UC Berkeley's Evans Hall is an ugly, giant Lego block of a building that sits in a corner of the campus, just north of the landmark Campanile bell tower. Home of the math, statistics and economics departments, it is widely considered to be one of the most depressing buildings at the university, its brutal-ist architecture clashing against the greenery of the Berke-ley hills. No wonder, then, that quite a few students leaped to their deaths from the tenth-floor balcony. When reports of yet another fatal plunge at Evans came crackling over my police scanner in fall 1994, my last semester at Cal, I rode my bike to the building from my Berkeley apartment. I got there before officers arrived and was shocked to see a group of freshmen on an orientation tour headed straight for the body. I pulled aside the student giving the tour, whom I happened to know from high school, and suggested that she take as far a detour as she could from the grisly scene.

When Hans began showing up at Evans in 1988, he stayed far from the top floors, which afforded a breathtaking view of the Golden Gate Bridge and the gleaming office towers of San Francisco. Instead, he rarely ventured beyond the dungeonlike basement, where he would spend hours toiling on computers. Hans had an apartment at the corner of Shattuck Avenue and Kittredge Street in downtown Berkeley, just a few minutes' walk, but Evans was like a second home for Hans. When the administration made it difficult for students to gain computer access at Evans, Hans pushed back. He and fellow student Peter Shipley cofounded the Open Computing Facility, or OCF, in the basement of Evans. The OCF was the first all-volunteer, student-run service group dedicated to free computing for all Cal students, faculty and staff. On his résumé, Hans boasted that he "proposed, solicited and acquired a four-hundred-thousand-dollar Apollo workstation donation which I organized a facility for."

Though the OCF became a success, Hans gained a reputation for being obnoxious and alienating people he worked with. Hans whined when he didn't get his way and tried to take credit for some of OCF's successes when other people did all the work, Shipley said. "*He* learned from *us*," he said. Hans "went out of his way to be mean, petty, arrogant and small minded," someone who knew him from those days wrote on a message board years later. "He acted as if he owned the Open Computer Facility, and that everyone should kowtow to him. Once he booted an undergrad off the system because she had posted a Usenet message that he disagreed with."

In late 1988, Hans went off to New Jersey on a six-month contract job with an army research and development center. He came back expecting a hero's welcome. When none was to be had, he sulked. Shipley tried to put Hans in his place by creating a program that sent five thousand identical e-mail messages, each saying something like, "Don't be a dumbshit" in his in-box. That clogged his machine for several hours and infuriated Hans, said another fellow OCF user, Cimarron Taylor. "He couldn't use his e-mail at all during that time,"

Taylor said. "It was probably the only time I've seen Hans really upset."

Hans had the choice of either losing all the e-mails he had received during that time or painstakingly deleting all of them. Instead, he chose to exact revenge. As Shipley was talking to a friend near the vending machines in Evans Hall, Hans walked over to him and, without a word, wrapped his hands around his waist and lifted him off the ground in what was apparently a wrestling maneuver. Shipley looked over at his friend for some help. The friend, who was significantly bigger than Hans, turned around and gave him a hard stare. Hans immediately retreated and walked away. Shipley filed a report with the campus police, but no charges were filed.

"I'm no saint. I've swung at a few people in my life, but I usually engage in verbal abuse first. In this case, he didn't," said Shipley, who would go on to be part of Berkeley's Dis.Org Crew, a group of self-described amateur trouble-makers and professional security consultants. Shipley is also known by the moniker "Evil Pete."

Taylor said later, "It was certainly an interesting episode, though, because most people who are computer-savvy wouldn't have solved their problem that way. Anyone who really wanted to deal with five thousand e-mails in one file could have easily used this Unix tool to fix it and shrug it off."

While working at OCF, Hans would frequently print out reams of paper that would sit in a huge stack in the basement. He didn't want to bring all that home, so he'd just leave it there. At night, the janitor would throw it all away. The next day, Hans printed out the whole thing again—and again the next night after it was discarded anew. Hans ended up using up all of the toner.

Hans would attend Cal on and off for about a dozen years. In 1989, the OCF board of directors discussed an e-mail sent by Hans in which he complained about being "deliberately excused from the OCF," according to minutes from the meeting that came with the header, "Hans Complains, the Earth Shakes, etc." Hans had worked on a draft of the group's constitution, which said that only students and faculty could be members. "The tone of the message implied that he wished the clauses revised to read something like 'students, faculty and Hans Reiser,'" the minutes read. The board determined that the constitution was sufficient and that the passage was adopted with the understanding that "it was mildly ambiguous to allow for cases such as 'Father' Hans."

Although he certainly started early at Cal, it wasn't until 1992, at the age of twenty-nine, that Hans finally earned his bachelor's degree in systematizing, an individualized computer-science major. His senior thesis discussed differences in the philosophy of computer science and the physical sciences as illustrated by file-system design issues.

Much as he had eschewed a standard education, Hans decided to forgo obtaining a PhD, instead choosing to continue writing his file system. He would later say that he felt his work in the computer field had earned him the same, if not more, respect than he would have received by continuing his education. He also believed that with his credentials, he could have been hired as a professor. Hans would credit his true learning to cafés, bookstores and attending random seminars.

CHAPTER 5

> NAMESYS

Over the next several years, Hans toiled as a programmer at several computer companies. If he chafed at being supervised, he made no mention of it, at least on paper. He worked as a programmer for Premenos Corporation, where he trained operators to perform systems administrator tasks. He boasted on his résumé that a letter of reference "describes me as the hardest-working member of the development team."

He moved to the IBM Almaden Research Center in San Jose as a senior associate programmer but left after a year in 1993 because "economic conditions did not make IBM competitive in pay raises."

In May 1993, he moved on to Synopsys in Mountain View where he worked as a senior technology integrator. He lived in a three-hundred-dollars-a-month room on West Hemlock Avenue in Sunnyvale that was infested with cockroaches. This was around the same time that he read a newspaper article that discussed the fact that Russian programmers were subsisting on only one hundred dollars a month. That planted the seed in Hans. *Why can't I hire them to work for me?* He went to Moscow and began looking for programmers. Years later, he would say that his decision was as much a component of his business plan as it was a grand gesture on his part, and not some quick way to get cheap labor: "I read about the awful conditions for programmers working in Russia and thought it would be nice to help." Not that Hans wasn't struggling himself. He would send papers to conferences only to get rejection after rejection. He would give talks, pitching his ideas. Someone actually fell asleep during one of his sessions. It seemed as if no one in the corporate world wanted to fund the ideas of someone without a track record. In spite of this rejection—or perhaps because of it—Hans became a minor celebrity in his field.

In 1993, Hans launched Namesys, short for Naming System Venture. In the KernelTrap interview, he described himself as architect, project manager, owner and "whatever I can't get another person to do."

> A file system is a way to store and organize computer files and the data they contain to make it easy to locate them. For Hans, his goal was simple: completely revamp the structure of the Linux operating system, which was founded by Finnish software engineer Linus Torvalds, by producing the world's fastest file system, which he named ReiserFS. He would give the source code—a set of instructions about how to build a program—away for free and allow anyone to improve it. Free software was a matter of liberty, not price. This was in line with the creed of the free-software social movement and the values first embodied by the OCF. Besides, free-software developers provide much more expert support and do so at a lower price, Hans reasoned. "I won't describe here how we make money from free software," Hans once wrote, "but it has much in common with what most celebrities traditionally do. Yes, among pear-shaped geeks, I am a celebrity. We are the best in our field, and yet we are in dire fiscal condition. Our work is about more than money."

Put another way, "We are part of a movement to create a free cyber-world we can all participate equally in. Namesys does not oppose copyright laws as they were invented, it opposes copyright laws as they have been twisted," he wrote.

After finding programmers in Moscow willing to work for him, Hans had to work a day job to pay them. It seemed to be a win-win solution: Hans would finally be his own boss, overseeing the work of employees who would now see their salaries triple. He would spend most nights and weekends exchanging e-mails with them about algorithms and building the foundation for his file system. Hans knew that the going was tough. In the Darwinian, cutthroat environment of the computer industry, there was no market for the second-best file system. If it was inferior in any way, the competition would beat him. Hans didn't have to be told that, anyway. His ego didn't lend itself to failure.

ReiserFS was a favorite of many systems administrators because it was faster, eliminated file corruption and made more efficient use of hard-drive space. Many operating systems have files that are placed in a hierarchical, or tree, structure. ReiserFS was unique in that it used so-called balanced tree algorithms that resulted in highly efficient searching. ReiserFS was known as a journaling file system in that it kept a log, or journal, whenever the file system was updated. If a system crashed or a computer rebooted unexpectedly, updates from the journal were still copied to the file system, and a file system consistency check—known in the vernacular as "fsck"—would only take seconds. It was also innovative because ReiserFS was sold separately from the operating system. Novell, a key Linux distributor, began using ReiserFS as its default file system.

In response to questions submitted to the Slashdot Web site in 2003, Hans compared Linux to an ecosystem comprised of both fast-growth and slow-growth vegetation. "The fast-growth vegetation are the people who took what had already been done by Unix, and without changing its design they copied it while making coding improvements," Hans said. "Then there are those who look at Unix, er, Linux, and see something just barely begun that needs a complete overhaul. These are the slow-growth vegetation. Namesys is slow-growth vegetation that got started a long time ago."

But critics sniffed that file operations often became corrupted under ReiserFS, which also struggled on systems with larger files. Hans, however, was convinced that he held the answer to the future of file systems.

In 1996, he told a Synopsys official that he was leaving. "He arranged to more than double my salary to keep me, and this delayed my departure for some time, but eventually the draw of my file system project was too great for me to resist working on it full time despite the wonderful environment they had in the Advanced Technologies Group." Synopsys would not discuss Hans's job performance. If it stood out, cofounder Aart de Geus didn't remember it. To this day, de Geus was not aware that Reiser was ever an employee of the company.

That same year, Hans went to Russia to work directly with his programmers. It didn't work out as he had planned, because they quit en masse, save for one junior programmer "who really believed in the work," according to Hans. The others apparently left because Hans had tried to get them to work as hard and write as cleanly as the junior programmer.

CHAPTER 6

›THE WAR AGAINST MICROSOFT

In August 1997, Hans told people that he was in talks with Sun Microsystems to see if the company wanted to use his file system. Sun apparently wanted Hans to work as an employee with the title of file system architect; Hans preferred working as a subcontractor.

He was prepared to do battle with anyone who got in his way. He didn't hide his distaste for Microsoft, saying programmers there merely implemented the "same feature in twelve incompatible ways in twelve applications."

In October 1997, Hans filed a federal antitrust lawsuit against Microsoft, accusing the Washington corporation of illegally "tying" or including its standard file system with the operating system and preventing users from ordering his file system instead. The intensity with which Hans pursued this litigation would be a harbinger of things to come.

"Plaintiff asks that defendant be required to demonstrate due diligence in arranging that the components of its software systems are separately available to competition from component vendors, so as to avoid creating unnecessary restraints on trade," Hans wrote in the suit, which he filed as a pro per plaintiff, representing himself. His damages? Three months of income, or $37,500.

In a paper he later presented at a conference, Hans likened the controversy to a dealer selling a car with the radio already inside.

"When I bought my '91 Laser from Chrysler, I did not want the manufacturer's radio," Hans wrote, citing a car that would make its way into another colorful story years later. "I wanted my car without the radio, so that I could buy a better quality radio and speakers from a third party. Tying forced me to accept the radio they gave me, and having paid for it, I chose not to replace it. It isn't a bad radio, it's even a decent radio. It may even be the best car manufacturer's radio for cars in that price range, but it isn't the best car radio made. It isn't what I could have had."

Hans noted that economist Adam Smith wrote in *The Wealth of Nations* that the more people there are who participate in a market, the faster a civilization develops. Conversely, monopoly control over entry into the market would have a devastating effect on a civilization.

Microsoft responded to the suit as if swatting a fly. Daniel Wall, an attorney with San Francisco powerhouse firm Latham & Watkins, said that Microsoft was under no obligation to break down Windows 95 into smaller components. "Plaintiff has no right to control how Microsoft designs or markets its products," Wall wrote in a motion to dismiss. In court papers, Wall would use adjectives such as "fantastic," "staggering," "quixotic," "hopelessly confused" and "plainly frivolous" in describing Hans's arguments. He said Hans's figure for damages "appears to be just made up."

The attorney offered an analogy of his own: "It's as if aircraft manufacturers were sued for only offering airplanes with wings, on the grounds that including wings makes life harder for alternative wing manufacturers."

Hans was undeterred. He demanded that Microsoft turn over all relevant evidence in the case. Another Microsoft attorney, Colin Garrett, wrote to U.S. District Judge Susan Illston in San Francisco, who was assigned the case, complaining that since the judge might limit the scope of the litigation, Hans's desire to get the company to "identify and produce truckloads of potentially irrelevant documents at this point would waste both Microsoft's and Mr. Reiser's time." Wall added in another court filing that Hans's references to Adam Smith "should be relegated to the political arena."

In the end, Illston sided with Microsoft and dismissed Hans's complaint in September 1998. She noted that Hans had expressed admiration of several states and the federal government, which had also sued Microsoft on similar issues, for their clear presentation of their positions. As such, the judge made a suggestion: "In light of the complexity of antitrust law, and in particular the vast and complex nature of factual discovery required in such cases, the plaintiff may want to defer to the government's action to achieve the best representation of his interests."

› Less than a month later, Hans pleaded his case with the Ninth U.S. Circuit Court of Appeals in San Francisco. He fumed over the inability of the courts to understand what he was fighting for. "Let us not tell our grandchildren that evil empires never arise in America, no, let us tell them that in America, when evil empires do arise . . . we break them," he wrote in 1999.

The higher court eventually concluded, however, that Hans's case had no merit.

Hans had to have the last word. He filed a motion to impose sanctions, saying he belatedly realized that Microsoft had lied in its court papers. Illston wasn't amused and tersely wrote, "The court will not entertain newly filed motions in a closed case."

PART TWO

> LOVE CONNECTION

CHAPTER 7

›IN SEARCH OF A MATE

The term *mail-order bride* entered the lexicon within the last century. The industry's members prefer to say that they offer an "international correspondence service" or an "online correspondence site," mindful of how important it is to brand their product. Whatever the label, business was good, with a steady drumbeat of women from developing countries advertising themselves in hard-copy catalogs or online.

For many foreign-born women, marrying an American husband ensured better social and economic opportunities. There was also a perception that men from their native countries didn't treat them as well and were less faithful. For years, the market was traditionally dominated by women from Southeast Asia, including the Philippines. But shortly after the collapse of the Soviet Union in 1991, they were soon rivaled in number by women from Russia and former countries of the Soviet bloc.

There were certainly risks involved with such arrangements. A woman whisked away to the United States often found herself isolated in a new land and struggling to start a life with poor English skills and a support system far away. The American man faced the possibility that he was being used just so his new wife could become a permanent resident.

Why would American men want foreign-born wives? For some men, there was a belief that a woman born overseas would be less career-driven than her American counterpart and would instead be perfectly content being a subservient housewife, staying home to cook and to raise kids.

Hans had no qualms about meeting women through

catalogs and dating services. He wanted a wife who would want to have kids with him and not simply use him for a visa. As early as 1991, Hans had told Sturgeon the qualities he was seeking in a wife: she had to be either Russian or Indian, beautiful, well-educated, professional, who he "could conquer." This special woman had to give up everything to bear his children, Hans told his friend. "I will make her mine." Sturgeon told him, "You are far more into what you think is S and M than I will ever be. Because I believe in consent, negotiations, check-ins, after-care, respect, consensual adult fantasy-play between consenting adults."

› But first Hans needed pictures of himself to share with prospective partners. In 1997, Hans went to Sturgeon's apartment on Lakeshore Avenue in Oakland and asked him to do the honors. Many pictures showed Hans without his shirt on. In others, he flexed his muscles and looked at the camera with an inviting smile. In others, he wore a cowboy hat, Sturgeon's black leather jacket over a white tank top and Sturgeon's black pants. Hans wanted to look the best he could to get a woman. "I had everything that he didn't, including the clothes," Sturgeon said later. Hans would come to the realization that he may not have been portrayed in the pictures in the way that he had wanted. "Later, after I sent them out, I realized he had subtly dressed me up as a homosexual, all the while assuring me that this was the latest fashion," Hans would say. "Fashion is not my specialty. I did not get as good of a response rate on those letters. Sean was amused. I let him keep some of the photos." Sturgeon countered years later that Hans had thirty-six pictures to choose from—and had picked the five offending photos himself. Hans professed that he was not homophobic, although he would write later, "I don't think that people with crossed sexual wires in their brains should have society take actions to cause them more harm. I have had many men try to seduce me as a teenager, and I did not hate them for it." He added, "I was unusually pretty in the eyes of homosexuals, not so much so in the eyes of women. Such is life."

In a letter to prospective partners dated August 1997, Hans

introduced himself as a thirty-three-year-old "stereotypical Silicon Valley programmer/entrepreneur" who was writing a novel and working on his own file system. Part pulp fiction, part sci-fi, his novel was about a Muslim theocracy that had been overthrown in a revolution and was now facing an alien attack. "I think that more important than whether my dreams of novels and computer programs are a success is my dream of a family. I earn a good living, but without a family there is a hollow emptiness to it," he wrote.

Hans wrote in his letter that he was a judo student. "If you see minor bruises and small red scrape marks on me in the photos, those are from judo practice," he wrote.

He had some recommendations on how to catch his attention: "The best way to encourage me to fall in love with you is to offer a view of any topic that I have never considered before, and that most people would not have seen. This is what I look for in women, and it does not really matter whether it is poetry, economics or physics that you share your insights on. If letters are not your best media for expressing your uniqueness, say so, and I'll have to wait until I meet you in person."

Hans traded letters with women from a number of countries, including India and Indonesia, but he ultimately decided to set his sights on Russia for a mate. It made sense for Hans. By 1997, he had already traveled to Russia three times to check in on his programmers. Plus, he thought the women in Russia were beautiful.

He admitted that he once came close to marrying a woman from Saint Petersburg, "and yet I don't think she could have interested me by letters; her penetrating perspectives were based on emotional insight into people and situations. But if love is possible by mail, let us try, shall we?"

Hans may have been referring to a woman named Yelena, a beautiful blond whom he later said "got pissed" at him because he brought her to the United States in 1997 only to send her back to Russia on a plane instead of marrying her. Yelena had a gift for talking to other people, but she herself never opened up to him, he said.

In his letter, Hans noted that his personal philosophy "is a mixture of Taoist skepticism and Francis Bacon's scientific method. . . .It is my belief that only half of understanding a philosophy is knowing its teachings, the other half is knowing where to apply them and where not to. No school of philosophy is complete, and yet most schools of philosophy offer something of value if one can but see it. In this I think schools of philosophy are like human beings."

He ended by saying, "I think I would make a good father, like my father was before me."

His letter to potential girlfriends came with a poem in which he described how "the night and I, we have a plan." He implored women to think of the "beauty of the night, and not where my hands go." The poem ended with, "Trust the look in my eyes, and let the night take command."

Hans's letter was sent to numerous Russian women through ANK Enterprises, an Orange County, California, firm that sent the same form letter to each candidate. "Dear [name of woman]: We have the pleasure of introducing Mr. Hans Reiser to you. He is interested in you and wants to meet you through correspondence. We gave him your picture, the information about your cultural and educational background and your address. We hope you will like each other and your correspondence will lead to a beautiful relationship. We wish you a lot of luck and happiness."

Hans received a number of form letters in response. Svetlana described herself as having a "charming face, wick [sic] blond hair, green eyes, good figure and slender legs. I am student. I'm so communicative person."

Anastasia said she was a "very warm, nice, kind, gentle girl. I am a romantic. I like flowers, romantic candlelit dinners, moonlit walks."

Inga, a child psychologist, reported that she had a happy childhood and that if she had a family of her own, "I'll be kindhearted and true." She included her height, weight and breast size.

A woman named Natalie wrote, "I don't have harmful habits and I want have a healthy man. If I'll to met my 'prince,' that I'll got married him. I can to accept him at my home." She apologized if she had any mistakes in her letter, noting, "I want learned the English language very well. I like this language."

In a letter riddled with misspellings, Olga said like every girl of her age, "I dream about romantic, tall man of thirty with buatiful face and atractive smile and full lips."

Perhaps it was Marta who was most forward in her reply: "Of course it's up to you, but if you'd like I would have given a birth for our baby. You're welcome."

CHAPTER 8

> ## HANS AND NINA

Nina, meanwhile, was in the market for a prince. A picture of her and a brief bio appeared in the June 1998 issue of European Connections, which billed itself as the "World's Largest and Most Complete International Introduction Service." She was number 5279. Sharanova would later say that her daughter hadn't explicitly put herself out there but instead agreed to appear in the catalog as a favor for a friend of Sharanova's, who had put it together. In the listing, Nina was described as being a university student who spoke several languages. In the photo, she wore a white buttoned shirt, black pants and hiking boots and was sitting on the ground, kind of on her side, with knees bent. It was a typical modeling-type picture. Her entry was surrounded by photos that were decidedly more risqué, with other women giving sultry looks or posing suggestively. One woman was wearing a bikini.

By 1998, 51 percent of mail-order agencies were for women in the former Soviet Union. But Nina wasn't like most Russian women who appeared in catalogs. She spoke English well, was studying to become a doctor and had already visited the United States once before.

There would be different accounts of exactly how Hans met Nina. In one version, Hans was set up with a woman and went on a date with her only to fall in love with Nina instead when she came to translate. But acquaintances seem to agree that Hans met Nina directly through a marriage agency in 1998. When Hans spoke to Nina over the phone for the first time, he thought that she had the most beautiful voice he had ever heard. She also had the best English of anyone he had met in Russia. In March, he met Nina in person at a café next to a canal in beautiful Saint Petersburg. Her smile lit up the room. Hans's heart danced. He showed her a poem he had written that was about love and having children. It didn't matter to her that he was wearing a cowboy hat, which he'd sport in Russia to flaunt the fact that he was American. He would later say that Americans were quite popular in Russia at the time, almost to the point of being mini celebrities. The brown hat made some of the locals uncomfortable, but to Nina this was proof that he wanted to stand out. Though eccentric, Hans came across to her as an incredibly bright person, one who surprised her with his viewpoints. "Nothing from what I usually hear from other people," Nina would say later. He was the first person she met through a marriage agency, she said.

The two dated in March and April 1998. She took him to her home on Marata Street. Sharanova and Lavrentiev were impressed with Hans.

While in Russia, Hans tended to his programmers in Moscow. He had concluded that it was more effective to ask them in person, instead of by e-mail, why certain things weren't being done. He found that his employees would often ignore the things in the data that didn't make sense. Hans knew from experience that the things that don't make sense are the most important data collected. Again citing Sir Francis Bacon, Hans told KernelTrap that "science is about being a blind man with a stick, and he who most persistently pokes blindly ahead of him contributes the most to our understanding of the universe, though only if he is willing to accept what the poking tells him that he does not want to be true. I am not as qualified or clever as our competition, and we aren't as well funded, but we are much more persistent and rigorous." The blind man with a stick would become one of his favorite analogies.

Nina, meanwhile, became a medical doctor in June 1998 after graduating from Saint Petersburg State I. P. Pavlov Medical University, which was named after Ivan Pavlov, perhaps best known for conditioning dogs to expect food at the sound of a bell. While at the university, she completed a full course of studies in English and passed the qualification exam with a grade of "excellent."

Nina completed her residency in ob-gyn with training in

Kulmbach, a district in Bavaria, Germany. She also completed an obstetrics and gynecology internship program at the Professor Snegirev Maternity Hospital number 6. Sharanova was proud that her daughter was following in her footsteps.

Nina worked at the adolescent reproductive health-care center in Saint Petersburg as part of a team of doctors in a European Union–funded clinic for teens. She helped provide medical checkups, did endocrinological diagnostic testing and STD screenings, conducted ultrasounds and did family-planning counseling. She would later write on her résumé, "About 50 percent of my patients were disadvantaged high-risk patients."

Hans returned to the United States in August 1998, but the two stayed in touch by phone and mail.

Nina came to the United States on November 25, 1998, and met Hans's family. The two were in love, and she told her mother and friends that the relationship was serious. Hans had met his match. He would later tell *20/20* that Nina was like a "well-educated Marilyn Monroe who's a doctor."

> It would have been around January 1999 that the couple's son was conceived. When Nina announced in February that she was pregnant, alarm bells immediately rang in Ramon Reiser's head. Ramon believed Nina orchestrated the pregnancy to guarantee her marriage to Hans and forge a path to becoming an American citizen. There was no way that Nina, an ob-gyn, could "forget" to take birth control, Ramon thought. Hans called his father and said that he had a problem. Nina was pregnant, and he didn't want to abort his first child. That meant he had to get married. But both Hans and Ramon fretted over whether Nina was a plant as part of some plot by the Russian Mafia or rogue elements of the government to seize control of ReiserFS.

Ramon asked what Nina's strong points were. She had a nice smile and eyes and was intelligent, was widely read and had the discipline to be a doctor, Hans told him. What about her most significant weak point?

"Compared to Berkeley girls, she is shallow," Hans said.

"That is a very serious weakness in an intelligent person," Ramon responded. "Do not marry her. You will regret it. Shallowness rarely changes in an adult."

The elder Reiser wouldn't get his wish.

An attorney drafted a prenuptial agreement for the couple. If the two split, Hans would keep Namesys and support Nina financially as she studied to become a doctor in the United States. Nina would keep their child and any others they might have.

But the relationship was doomed from the start. Hans was ignoring Nina's stated wishes that she wanted to be a doctor. And Nina refused to believe Hans when he said that he wanted her to have children and "that's it, to give up everything else," Sturgeon said.

CHAPTER 9

>A BIZARRE CEREMONY

"Dr. Bernard Palmer and Beverly Reiser cordially invite you to celebrate the marriage of their son Hans Reiser and Nina Sharanova, May 15, 1999, 12:30 p.m., at their home, 6979 Exeter Drive, Oakland, CA," the wedding invitations read. "Please read reverse side for directions. Costumes and extravagant clothing encouraged. If the weather is beautiful, we will caravan to a nearby labyrinth for the ceremony. It's an easy walk, but bring comfortable shoes. If the weather isn't beautiful, then the ceremony will be in our home."

Hans and Nina, who by then was five months pregnant, were beaming that day as guests milled about at his mother's home. Hans kissed his soon-to-be wife on the forehead, and she responded with a hug. Hans's mother helped Nina with her hair, which was adorned with a garland of flowers. They both wore traditional Indian garb, and Nina had on sandals.

Everyone then got into cars and drove to Sibley Volcanic Regional Preserve off Skyline Boulevard in the Oakland hills, where the couple was married in a ceremony that could only be summarized as bizarre and unorthodox.

A lot of the details were hashed out at the last minute. At Hans's instigation, Nina asked Sturgeon to be her maid of honor, saying she didn't know anyone in America. So Sturgeon obliged and dressed in drag, complete with makeup, a white spring hat and a diaphanous blouse over a flower dress. His gloved hands clutched a purse. He was dressed this way when he had driven to Walnut Creek only hours earlier to pick up the carrot cake Hans and Nina had ordered. Sturgeon's girlfriend wore a suit and served as best man. "We were both cross-dressed," Sturgeon recalled.

A man hired as an entertainer carried the skull of a bull mounted on a stick and was supposed to be the Minotaur, a half-man, half-bull creature. In Greek mythology, the Minotaur was kept in the center of a labyrinth built for King Minos of Crete. Beverly said she planned the ceremony jointly with Nina, but Beverly's influence is clear. Three years earlier, it was Hans and his mother who put together an interactive multimedia piece on CD-ROM entitled, *Voice Garden: Labyrinth of Love, Labyrinth of Desire,* complete with a Minotaur. "Uncover the echoes of almost forgotten Goddesses in the Labyrinth of Love or journey with your Minotaur past hungering walls, through the Eye of Desire and into the caverns of your heart," according to a description of the piece, which sold for $12.99.

Whatever inspired the ceremony, Hans was ecstatic that day. His hair cut short and clad in a robe, Hans danced around the labyrinth in strange, spasmodic fashion, at one point even assuming a fighting stance. To observers, it was as if he was honing his judo moves. But Sturgeon said later that the two were reenacting a "stylized hunting scene" in which Hans was going after his prey. It was a prophetic moment. Nina smiled gamely and the Minotaur played a tambourine as guests watched the spectacle, apparently unaware that the creature, symbolically at least, feasted on human sacrifices. Among those looking on were Beverly, her hair bright red in the sun, and her husband, a distinguished scholarly looking man with a goatee, bow tie and beret.

› Sturgeon asked his friend, the Reverend D. Mark Wilson of McGee Avenue Baptist Church in Berkeley, to officiate. Hans had angered their first choice, a Unitarian minister, prompting Sturgeon to ask his friend incredulously, "How do you alienate a Unitarian minister?" Wilson, wearing an African robe in honor of his heritage, asked Hans if he would be Nina's husband for as long as they both shall live. "I do," he replied. They were now husband and wife. He was thirty-five. She was twenty-four.

After the guests returned to his home, they were entertained

by a belly dancer gyrating her hips as trance music played in
the background. Hans again began dancing, tracing his feet
across the floor. At one point he fell. A smiling Nina helped
him up, and Hans shrugged and laughed. It didn't matter. Hans
was infatuated. Afterward, he thanked Wilson for performing
the ceremony. Wilson told both Hans and Nina to contact him
at any time if they needed anything.

Sharanova didn't attend the wedding; she wasn't invited,
and there were some financial concerns on her part. But it was
no big deal, because Nina visited her family in Russia two
weeks later. Because she was pregnant, she was accompanied
by Artem Mishin, who trained in judo with Hans. Sharanova
learned that Hans wouldn't allow Nina to call her in Russia
the first month after the wedding because he wanted his new
wife to better adapt in the United States.

In June, Hans filed paperwork with U.S. immigration
officials to sponsor Nina. He wrote that his income the year
before while being self-employed with Namesys was $43,808.
To help support his new wife, he worked for Sun Microsystems. They tried living in the Silicon Valley for a time but ran
afoul of their landlady because Hans liked to walk around the
apartment naked.

› In June and July 1999, the two lived in France, where
Hans had a business contract. In July, Hans was working out
at a Paris gym when disaster struck as he was doing squats
using a machine. One of the safety hooks didn't go in properly, and 160 kilos of weight—or 350 pounds—came crashing
down on his shoulders, driving both his legs out. He broke
both his ankles. The pain was excruciating. To make matters
worse, Hans's insurance company wouldn't cover any medical
care in France. He had to go to Russia, where doctors inserted
metal rods in his legs. He suffered poor circulation and had to
sleep in odd positions as a result.

As Nina prepared to give birth, the couple apparently
forgot one key aspect of their prenup. Strangely, it was written in such a way that the two of them had to sign it before
they got married and then do so again ninety days after the

ceremony. But this never happened. Hans later complained that
he had been deceived about the terms of the prenup and that he
had been in Russia "with two broken legs and had no access
to the document." Legally, the prenup became null and void
on August 15.

Back in the United States, the couple quickly settled into
married life. They lived for a time with Hans's mother and
stepfather on Exeter Drive. The pregnancy was difficult for
Nina, who felt depressed because she was surrounded by
strangers and was far away from her family. To make matters
worse, Hans showed little sympathy. At one point, he asked
her, "Is it hard to be the wife of a genius?" Her Prince Charming, it seemed, was actually a toad.

CHAPTER 10

> RORY

At 10:06 a.m. on September 28, 1999, as the East Bay basked in an Indian summer, Rory Herman Reiser was born at Alta Bates Medical Center in Berkeley. Rory was the name of a childhood friend of Hans, and Herman was in honor of Nina's stepfather.

Rory was fussy and unpredictable as a baby. Hans's behavior was just as difficult, and Nina began having doubts about the marriage. "We were madly in love until our first child was born," Nina later reported. "Hans did not want me to be a doctor in the U.S. He wanted me to have six children and then I could deal with my career. He believed that Russian women would stay at home and devote themselves to their children. He also wanted an educated wife. He wanted me to give up my career and follow him. He didn't want me to study for my exams. I knew that when I married him. We thought we could change each other." It wouldn't be easy. Both had very strong personalities, and both could be very stubborn. It got to the point that neither would give way for the other.

So Nina found herself devoting her time to raising Rory while at the same time serving as the unpaid CFO for Namesys. To her amazement, Hans told her that he thought that it was "OK for only the man to have extramarital affairs and to travel around and maybe have children with other women," Nina said.

> The couple began living in Moscow in December 1999. They stayed with Sharanova until March 2000 and then got their own apartment in the heart of the city. Nina didn't like

the living arrangements, because there were so many people around, from subcontractors and programmers to a cook and office assistants. There was no privacy, and it was all glass doors and no place to take a shower, Nina complained. A friend of Sharanova's who worked as the couple's nanny told Sharanova that the marriage wouldn't last. The friend said Hans yelled a lot and would break things, like dishes, when he was angry. Nina did the best she could to be a supportive wife. Because her penmanship was nice and legible, she prepared the flip charts for his presentations, carefully writing things like "Three Node Types: internal nodes, formatted nodes and unformatted nodes" in big block lettering.

In June 2000, the couple took a trip to Egypt, where they rode camels. Nina became a lawful permanent resident of the United States in August 2000, at about the same time she became pregnant with their second child.

After returning to the United States, they began renting two floors of a three-story home on Marden Lane off Thornhill Drive in the Oakland hills in March 2001. Rent was $2,450 a month. Sturgeon kept a room on the bottom floor and continued to help pay their bills and lend them money.

In another nod to his eccentricity, Sturgeon's checks at one point were printed with his name and "Milkman Dan Rules!" in honor of a character in the comic strip called *Red Meat*. Milkman Dan was known as a "booze-fueled paragon of pointless cruelty and wanton sadism." Sturgeon would later say that Milkman Dan referred to his stockbroker.

› Hans was buoyed that year when the Pentagon's Defense Advanced Research Projects Agency (DARPA) awarded Namesys a six-hundred-thousand-dollar grant to build a file system of the future. This was a major break. DARPA researched and developed concepts that gave the military an edge in combat. Hans nearly didn't get the prestigious grant: security wasn't his specialty, and he saw an article about DARPA's offer for funding almost too late. Officials at the agency even told him that Hans's written proposal was the worst they had ever received.

The going was tough. Hans and his programmers were tasked with rewriting ReiserFS completely from scratch. Hans decided to make four key design decisions that were contrary to the literature and opposed by all his programmers. But luckily, they all worked. Still, Hans's team took too long to finish it. They burned through seven hundred and fifty thousand dollars on top of the six hundred thousand dollars provided by DARPA. Ramon took a break from teaching high school to help with Namesys.

Hans wasn't around at all because he was working all the time, Nina complained to friends. She felt like a caged bird, unable to escape. Here she was, eight to nine months pregnant, driving herself to places and doing errands. Instead, Nina relied on Sturgeon and felt emotionally close to him. He listened to her. And he was right there, living under the same roof. He was the one who found Nina her office assistants and, later, her nannies and babysitters' playdates for the children. He gave her rides to the Russian Consulate in San Francisco to make travel arrangements, took Basil to the vet, helped get the Honda minivan serviced and made her flash cards to help her study for her medical tests.

CHAPTER 11

> NIO

The Reisers' second child, Niorline, was born on May 26, 2001, in the same hospital as her brother. Named after a Dungeons & Dragons character, Nio inherited Nina's bright eyes and soft mouth, which frequently curved into a big smile. Beverly and her artist friend Mark McGothigan came over to the Marden Lane house to visit to see the newborn infant. McGothigan documented the visit with his video camera.

"How old is she now?" Beverly asked.

"Twelve days old," said Nina, appearing relaxed and content.

Nina noted one additional guest that day—D'Artagnan, Beverly's cherished papillon. But the dog was behaving somewhat strangely—and seemingly fixated on the new little creature sleeping peacefully in a baby carrier.

"Sit," Nina warned D'Artagnan, named after Alexandre Dumas' character known as the fourth Musketeer.

But D'Artagnan was still staring at Nio. "No, be good—don't you do that," Beverly told her dog as she bopped it on the head.

"Call the hotline. Animal abuse!" McGothigan cracked.

Nina admitted that this was the first time she'd seen D'Artagnan with that expression. "It makes me nervous!" she said, smiling.

"Is it 'cause his lips are quivering?" Beverly asked.

"He just has this expression in his eyes," Nina said.

"Attack dog!" McGothigan joked.

"A ferocious, French attack dog!" Beverly added.

"His eyebrows are like . . ." Nina said before she placed her index fingers over her eyebrows and pointed them downward.

McGothigan joked that Nio was a "hippie chick from

Berkeley" because she was born in a hospital there. Everyone laughed. From Saint Petersburg, perhaps? "No definitely Berkeley," Beverly said, chuckling.

"It's like, I talked to my grandmother today, and she asked me how do you dress her?" Nina said. "I told her, 'In a diaper!'" Nio wouldn't be naked, she said. The group joked that Rory was the one running around in the nude. As the winters in Russia could be quite cold, Nina got used to doing that in Oakland and tended to overdress him. Beverly quipped that Rory was streaking in revenge.

McGothigan's video then cut to a scene in the house later that same day. It was a unique snapshot of a most unusual ménage. A twenty-month-old Rory smiles and shrieks as he plays with Hans, who is lying on his back, resting and wearing a shirt that reads, "Usenet." A nanny is in the kitchen as Beverly stands nearby. Sturgeon is sitting at a computer, repeatedly tapping on a keyboard. He asks how to reformat a hard drive on a computer. "C colon backslash format," McGothigan says to Sturgeon, who continues tapping. Hans is listening carefully to make sure what McGothigan says is accurate.

Rory shows something to Beverly, who then tells him conspiratorially, "Stick it in Dad's ear."

PART THREE

> CRISIS

CHAPTER 12

›A MARRIAGE CRUMBLES

Things weren't so idyllic when the camera wasn't rolling, however. Hans told his wife that she was "a ball and chain," Nina later said. Hans announced that he would stay in Russia and return to the United States only when he wanted—and that she should stay in Oakland to take care of the business. "He told me that I was not his best romantic interest," Nina said. By June 2001, he had all but permanently moved to Russia. Nina felt abandoned, raising two small children in a new country where she would have to stay in order to qualify for citizenship. It was as if she were a single mother. She felt unsupported emotionally and wasn't able to address her career plans. Sturgeon, sensing her pain, shipped two "Dummies" books to Hans in Russia—one on communication for couples and another about divorce—and told him he was going to need one or the other. Hans didn't seem to care. "Hans would specifically try to isolate her and break her down so she would just do whatever he wanted," Sturgeon said.

The Reisers visited Cyprus for a week in November 2001 with Ramon. The three spent time jet-skiing, paragliding and driving the length of the former British colony, although when Nina was behind the wheel, she drove too fast—and too close to the cliffs—for Ramon's taste. Ramon would later report to his son about strange comments Nina made to him. At one point, she "lost it, rage and fury pouring out, then she suddenly realized she was having absolutely no dominating effect on me so that in the blink of an eye, she changed her eyes from extreme fury to the most adoring eyes of the daughter-in-law talking to the father-in-law she adored, words and face totally changing as fast, but hands, voice, posture, gestures and tempo continuing with rage. It was at best bizarre and disturbing."

Ramon also told his sister, Andree Chicha, who was an attorney in Washington State, that Nina "was scary" in that by all outward appearances, she could be fun, warm, gracious and friendly. But there was a "savageness underneath" that sunny veneer, Ramon wrote from Moscow in a December 1, 2001, e-mail to Chicha. Nina complained that she had varicose veins as a result of having Nio and that children thickened women's bodies and damaged their looks. Ramon also related a disturbing comment he said Nina made to him when they were in Cyprus. "I promised Rory I would never make him have a brother or sister. I would never give him a sibling. And Hans made me break my promise to Rory. I will never forgive him," Ramon said Nina told him. "Rory and I decided that we would not reject Niorline. We would just accept her. But she will never come between us. She will never be more than accepted. She will never be fully part of us. I will keep my promise to him that I had to break." Ramon instructed Chicha to save a hard copy of the e-mail "in case anything serious happens to me or Hans or his children."

Hans came to the United States for a month in February 2002. But when he was home, he was always glued to the computer, either immersing himself in his work or playing his video games, Nina complained. Her resentment grew. Hans derided her as a control freak and a neurotic woman unable to control her violent temper.

Hans and Nina asked Sturgeon to help her and the business out. On March 12, 2002, Hans e-mailed Sturgeon to ask Reverend Wilson to "drop in on Nina and ask her how her marriage is going." Sturgeon was floored. Was Hans really asking his best friend *to ask the pastor* who had performed the ceremony to check on the state of his marriage? Hans knew full well that it was crumbling. The next day, Sturgeon e-mailed Hans, asking if he would only be happy if Nina gave up her desire to be a doctor in order to have his children and continued doing the accounting for Namesys.

Hans replied that they should have someone else do the accounting because "it is not what she wants to be." He added,

"I think that maybe we should set a limit of, say, five children, and then have Nina go back to being a doctor."

Sturgeon asked Hans, "Over the past year I have sensed a deeper sadness and kind of resignation in you. Perhaps I'm wrong? Are you happy?"

In response, Hans e-mailed, "I am not unhappy. That is all I can say . . . I think that Nina knows that my feelings towards her are not deep enough to satisfy me permanently as the only romance in my life, and this is really scary for her. I try telling her she will always be provided for. It is not enough."

From March to May 2002, Hans had no telephone or e-mail contact with Nina. Sturgeon's position as intermediary meant spending more and more time with Nina. He found himself defending her in the face of Hans's angry attitude toward her. "My brother was turning into an even *more* misogynistic, unreasoning and unreasonable tyrant," Sturgeon would say later. As a result, Nina turned more and more to Sturgeon for comfort and advice.

Sturgeon also considered Nina a confidante. She took him for who he was. Sturgeon had spent most of his life "living in the shadows and darkness," he said later. "It was only until Nina's love that I was able to imagine life in the light."

Nina came to his aid when he could not drive because of his medical problems. She answered his questions about medications, helped with paperwork for his ailing grandmother, went with him to the hospital when his father was dying and helped him find "lawful business opportunities." The two would talk late into the night. He taught her how to play Scrabble. They paid respects at street shrines, ate at taco trucks and gave money to the poor. Sturgeon had found a soul mate. He loved how she jumped up and down like a pogo stick when she was excited. "Everything lights up when she's really happy," Sturgeon recalled.

CHAPTER 13

> MATES FOR LIFE

It wasn't long before Sturgeon and Nina began falling for each other. In early 2002, as Sturgeon was showing Nina around an Oakland home he was flipping, he stunned Nina when he started discussing the paints, antiques and exotic plants on the property. "She was looking at me like I was some strange new creature," Sturgeon recalled. "She said, 'Sean, why don't you ever talk about this stuff at all? Why is it that people only ask about the weird stuff?'" Sturgeon told her that was because people chose to ask the wrong questions.

As they went to his BMW parked outside, they stopped and looked at each other. "And then we were looking *into* each other," Sturgeon said. Both of them raised their hands, palms out, their fingers nearly touching. They put their hands down. Nina dipped her head once. "And I smiled, and I inclined my head. And later on, that's when she said she fell in love with me."

In April 2002, as Nina was putting the kids down to sleep, Sturgeon watched from the hallway. A soft light glowed, casting her half in the light, half in the shadow. She sang a Russian bedtime rhyme softly to Rory. Sturgeon remembered that he was suddenly struck with two realizations. "One is, I love her more than I love anybody else on the planet," Sturgeon said, bursting into tears and his face reddening. "I want nothing but for her to be happy. I want her to be a doctor. I want her to be a mother. I want her to serve the people that she desperately wants to."

The other realization was "Oh f—. If they both say no because they want to save the marriage, I will respect that,"

Sturgeon said. "But if she says yes to me, and Hans says no, I'm listening to her. I will not do what Hans has done. I will not cage her, ever. I will never dangle keys in front of a lock that I have shut."

Sturgeon didn't act on his feelings, at least not immediately. Instead, they consummated their love on Sturgeon's birthday, May 8, at his Lakeshore Avenue condo. Mutual friends were appalled. How could Sturgeon betray his best friend? Why would Nina do this? Their coupling surprised even Sturgeon, who had been involved in previous relationships with women but never imagined being seriously involved with one until he met Nina.

The two flaunted their new relationship at times. "I did not approve of the Sean business," McGothigan said, adding if he were in Hans's shoes, he would have killed Sturgeon. But Nina felt secure being with Sturgeon and showed him that he could be in a stable, loving relationship. Sturgeon told her about how wolves mate for life, and after a session of love-making during which they used Ecstasy, Nina looked into Sturgeon's eyes and asked him if he was her wolf. They both agreed that he was. Years later, Sturgeon cried at the memory. "What that means is that the only important thing between mating wolves is the children. The primary thing is you protect your children." That's why Sturgeon would continue to support Nina financially. "I was honor-bound," he said.

"Hand over fist, I supported them before they married, while they were married, when Hans abandoned Nina, when Nina and I were together, when Nina was divorcing Hans and when Nina was with Anthony," Sturgeon said. He had relatively enough to go around from two inheritances, settlements from auto accidents, stocks, a retirement account, loans and "side jobs."

› Sturgeon said their relationship flourished because "we knew each other first as friends, without any thoughts about sex or romance. So we got a chance to actually know each other as two mature adults, who were going through very trying times. This time was a time of fear for everybody because of what? 9/11. The dot-bomb. We were going through extraor-dinary times. There were pressures on everybody. None of this happened in a f—vacuum."

Sturgeon said he made some sacrifices to prove he wanted to be with her, including trading in his BMW 325i for a more family-friendly Subaru. He put two wolf stickers on the back of the car.

He made some more significant changes as well. "I gave up S and M for Nina," he said. Sturgeon acknowledged "try-ing out stuff" with Nina but only with her consent. He added, "It was never about sex. I have plenty of sex." As for Hans, "Nina told me every time she was with Hans, it was rape. He violated her."

Sturgeon later railed at how his love for Nina was warped by others to make it seem as if it was just about some beautiful woman falling for an S and M fancier. "Some people want to make something tawdry out of what we had," Sturgeon com-plained. He said there were some who believed that he was the "bringer of all things unhealthily sexual to an otherwise pristine and proper environment, but that was not the case. Nina and I were simply more open about it."

Even as McGothigan found the affair distasteful, he sup-ported Sturgeon when he launched an informal discussion group known as a Socrates Café. Sturgeon had read Chris-topher Phillips's *Socrates Café: A Fresh Taste of Philoso-phy*, and was inspired by its simple concept: get some people together—anywhere—and ask lots of questions. Beverly and Nina regularly attended with Sturgeon.

In June, Nina went to Russia and told Hans about her and Sturgeon. Nina brought up the topic of divorce, but Hans refused to consider it. Sharanova disapproved of Sturgeon, too. She thought he played too rough with the children and didn't want him to be rearing them.

› By this time, Hans would come back to the United States for a month just once or twice a year. He was extremely busy because business was booming. In 2002, Namesys was bask-ing in success, earning $1.2 million that year.

› In 2003, Namesys's money transfers to Russia drew the suspicion of U.S. Immigration and Customs Enforcement (ICE), which was part of the Department of Homeland Security. An agent came to Hans and Nina's home and asked them questions related to structuring, in which transactions larger than ten thousand dollars were broken into smaller increments to avoid record-keeping and reporting requirements. ICE was suspicious about what they were doing, but Hans explained that he paid his Russian employees in cash.

In 2003, Nina told a woman who lived with them for a time at the Marden Lane house that her life was all messed up. As they talked on the stairs, Nina began crying. She said Hans was never around. The marriage was clearly an unhappy one. She was trying to deal with life and take care of the kids all by herself. Nina said she wasn't happy with Sturgeon either. She confided that Sturgeon had taken her to a sex club in San Francisco where she refused to participate even though she was scared that she might lose him, too. Sturgeon strongly disagrees with this recollection and the implication that he had talked Nina into doing anything she did not already want to do. He said that he, Nina and a female stripper had engaged in consensual activity at a strip club and that Nina, even though she had sought to explore a ménage à trois, got cold feet during a different session involving a female sex-worker friend of Sturgeon's at his Oakland condo. Sturgeon said he did not press the matter.

Nina also went with Sturgeon to All Nations Presbyterian Church on Grand Avenue in Piedmont, a wealthy community ensconced within Oakland city limits. The two also attended "community groups" together, where church members would meet and talk in smaller sessions. It went from one dizzying extreme to the other with Sturgeon, and Nina struggled to come to terms with all of it. Now, while sitting with her housemate, she bemoaned what was happening. "Look at my life. I'm a gynecologist with a truck driver, recycle collector and ex-gay prostitute," she wailed. "I deserve more than that."

Restless and fed up with her love life, Nina spent time looking at Craigslist ads and contemplated going out with people she met online. The housemate urged her not to do that, warning her, "One day something's going to happen to you or your family. There are a lot of crazy people online." She begged Nina, "Don't bring anyone home." Rory and Nio shouldn't be seeing her with different men. Nina knew she was right, but she still wanted to make sure that Sturgeon wasn't still posting things on Craigslist.

From the beginning, Nina didn't want Rory or Nio seeing her and Sturgeon sleeping in the same bed. Sturgeon would leave the house at night after he helped tuck them into bed and read them stories until they fell asleep. But Sturgeon began staying overnight, and the kids saw their mother with him in the covers. This happened, Sturgeon said, because he was on painkillers and didn't want to drive home while under the influence.

› Hans was also confiding in people but in an entirely different way that would speak volumes about his character. While in Russia that summer, he told his mother-in-law that he didn't want a "smart wife." He also complained to Sharanova that Nina was a bad wife and wasn't doing the things that a good wife should be doing. Nina couldn't defend herself, as she was back in the United States studying for her medical licensing exam. Hans said Nina was bringing up the children the wrong way and fumed that the children were speaking Russian. Remarkably, Hans would later accuse Nina of having abandoned her children for two months that summer, even though Sharanova had been taking care of them. Rory and Nio "were really freaking out about being separated from their mother," Hans later said.

In August 2003, Hans and Nina moved again, settling into a home on Jordan Road in Oakland's Redwood Heights neighborhood. It was a three-bedroom English cottage with an art deco flair. It evoked the style of a bed-and-breakfast inn and came with a garden. It was contemplative and peaceful. Rent was twenty-four hundred dollars a month.

In fall 2003, Rory and Nio began attending Grand Lake Montessori, a private school in Oakland's Adams Point neighborhood. Sturgeon, who had attended a Montessori school, recommended the program to Nina. She delighted in helping out in her children's classes, which were given unique names, like Live Oak and Jacaranda. Nio's class was called Camellia. Rory's was called Gingko. Over the holiday break, Nina took care of Squeaky and Fluffy, guinea pigs belonging to Nio's class. For Valentine's Day, Nina brought a beautiful orchid.

In February 2004, as plum trees blossomed and daffodils planted the previous fall sprouted on Oakland's green, rain-soaked hillsides, Namesys, too, was flourishing, converting from a sole proprietorship into a corporation. Hans filed paperwork with the California Secretary of State, listing himself as president. On February 23, Nina's application to become a naturalized U.S. citizen was approved. By then, she had been a permanent resident of the United States and had been married to Hans for three years. Hans reported that Nina stopped sleeping with him when she became a citizen. He wondered if she married him just for the visa.

That same month, Sturgeon, who made money in real estate, loaned Hans eighty-four thousand dollars in the form of a seventy-five-thousand-dollar check and nine thousand dollars in cash. Hans had borrowed nine thousand dollars from Sharanova, and the cash was for him to repay her since he was going to Russia soon. But he never gave it to her, according to Sturgeon. Hans was to begin repaying it on August 1. As part of the deal, Hans had to take three Bikram yoga classes before November, which Sturgeon would pay for. If Hans failed to live up to that agreement, he would have to take two more yoga classes and treat Sturgeon and eight of his closest friends to dinner at Sushi Zone restaurant in Oakland's Chinatown. Bikram yoga is often called "hot yoga" because it is done in a room heated to over one hundred degrees. But the two of them called it "death yoga" because of how they felt after they had taken a class together. "Attendance at a death yoga class means that Hans Reiser appears five minutes prior to each class and participates in each class for ninety minutes (or until death or unconsciousness occurs)," the agreement continued.

Although the terms might have seemed strange, it was a binding contract that made perfect sense to the two men whose lives would continue to be intertwined.

› Things between Hans and Nina, meanwhile, deteriorated further, and she asked him for a divorce in March, shortly after he returned from Russia. He refused. He realized that his father, who had warned him not to marry Nina, had been right all along, because within weeks of becoming a U.S. citizen, she wanted a divorce.

› Despite her marital problems, Nina was still a caring and loving mom and remained on friendly terms with her mother-in-law, who doted on her grandkids. When Beverly visited the Jordan home one spring day, Nina told Rory that he had to eat all his carrots. "Otherwise you will never have enough muscles to go swimming," Nina warned. Rory used his hand to stuff a carrot into his mouth. "Rory? And what happened to using your fork? Use your fork," Nina said firmly. She pushed his plate toward him as he clambered over his chair. "Sit down," she said. As Nina left to do the dishes, a family friend who was there told the little boy not to be afraid of spiders or squirrels. "I'm not scared of nobody," Rory insisted. Nio got off her chair and clambered onto Beverly's lap. Beverly took her granddaughter's arms in hers and they sang "Ring Around the Rosie" together.

› Nina's dedication as a mother was also apparent at Grand Lake Montessori. There was a bright moment when Nio and her classmates decorated butterflies with tissue paper and worked on a Mother's Day project. Nina donated a Polaroid camera and film for the class.

› Hans was also singled out for praise. Sincere Nitonde, Rory's teacher, thanked Hans for bringing big picture books to class featuring jellyfish, fishing trawlers, rescue helicopters, the Empire State Building, castles, oil rigs and steam trains. The children were particularly fascinated by how steam trains operate. It would be the last time Nitonde had anything positive to say about Hans.

CHAPTER 14

› MOVING OUT

The Reisers separated on May 15, 2004, their five-year wedding anniversary. "I don't know what I was hoping," Nina later said. "I thought that if we lived apart, maybe eventually things would get better. I didn't know how things would work out." She worried about how this would affect the kids. She later reported that Hans "sabotages everything I do or offer to do for the kids. I was puzzled at first. I used to tell myself to work harder, try harder and be better. Hans would never approve. It's not good enough, the high standards. Once I realized that Hans had deep emotional problems, I was hurt and angry." The two had an argument about why Rory was having behavioral problems. Nina said the boy, who was also having nightmares and showed signs of anxiety, was overwhelmed and that Hans didn't help matters by letting Rory play violent video games. Hans called Nina a bad wife and told her to go to hell. Nina slapped him. Hans said she hit him with a closed fist.

Nina told Hans to move out, but he refused. So she rented a truck and a worker and moved some of the furniture and his computer to his mother's house. Nina told Hans that she had called his mom about this and that Sturgeon would help him move. Hans told her not to bother. He made suggestions on how to lift the furniture and off he went. At age forty, he was now paying his mom six hundred dollars a month in rent to live with her and D'Artagnan the dog in his childhood home. It was taxing for Beverly. Neighbors reported that Hans yelled at her, and McGothigan said Hans treated his mother as if she were there to serve him. He used her CRX as his own, racking up a couple of traffic citations and putting several dings in it in the process. He took her Honda Civic hybrid and put a dent in that car as well. He could be demanding, obstinate and inconsiderate. He was also a slob, never doing the dishes or cleaning up.

By now, Hans reported that they were $182,000 in debt. Namesys was feeling the effects of the 2000 dot-com bust now that the funds from DARPA had dried up. Hans recognized the vicissitudes of the economy: people would "pay" for or at least invest in free software only if they were flush with cash.

Reiser4 was ready for release that summer. It had to be a success. The new version of his file system, three years in the making, was based on "dancing tree" algorithms, which were superior to the "balanced trees" used by ReiserFS. As a result, Reiser4 was more space-efficient than its predecessor and other file systems. It also featured built-in plug-ins, programs that interacted with a host application, for both encryption and compression. The latter plug-in allowed users to use half the space while increasing performance.

In an online announcement, Hans crowed that DARPA was the primary sponsor of Reiser4, although it didn't endorse the project. Beverly used her computer to create eye-catching images of dancing male and female figures that were evocative of the opening-credit sequences in James Bond films. The only difference was that the images were accompanied by text that could only be appreciated by computer experts. One image showed a woman, her contours clearly visible, sitting with her legs spread on what appeared to be a rocky outcropping and holding a large butcher knife. A bubble coming from her head read, "I can cut bytes off at the end of a file."

› Nina and the children typically went to Russia each summer for vacation. Even though Rory and Nio spent time at a dacha, Hans felt they weren't being challenged in a low-intensity learning environment filled with mosquitoes. Besides, he worried about Russia's air pollution because there were no catalytic converters for cars there and the government was getting less democratic each year.

Late in the evening of May 29, Nina was preparing for her annual trip to Russia. She wanted to spend some extra time with her stepfather, who was ill. Nina told Hans that she and the kids would be gone for two months. Hans was very angry and upset. He didn't want to pay the twenty-four hundred dollars monthly rent if their Jordan Road home was going to be empty. For a while, Hans had suggested that they move back in with his mother on Exeter. "My mother has a large, luxurious empty house that mostly goes to waste," Hans wrote. "I have for a long time endeavored to convince Nina that it is a waste of money for us to live separately from my mom."

He pushed Nina and tried to take her tickets and passports, Nina later reported. Hans accused Nina of kicking him after he found a laptop in her luggage, a computer he had believed she had returned to the manufacturer for a refund. According to Hans, Nina told him that she was planning to sell it in Russia. Hans felt this was theft.

Nina called the police. Oakland police officers Rodney Taya and Bryant Ocampo came to the Jordan Road home at about 12:30 a.m. on May 30. "Husband Reiser was asked to leave, which he complied," Taya wrote in his report. No charges were filed. Hans later said that the police wanted to arrest Nina but he insisted that they not.

› While Nina was in Russia that summer, Hans stewed. He launched an offensive against Sturgeon in July, demanding that he no longer be around his family or the home on Jordan. He accused Sturgeon of being a child abuser, which to Sturgeon was fighting words and grounds for slander. Beverly also did her part to look out for her son's interests. She would later sign a document addressed "To whom it may concern." It said that in summer 2004, Nina "threatened to go to Sweden to live instead of returning to the United States. She also said she would not return until a large amount of money was put in a bank account for her."

But there was no extortion. Nina was entitled to half the money in their primary account, but Hans had blocked her from retrieving any funds, Sturgeon said. On July 29, 2004, she wrote Sturgeon an e-mail while she was in Russia, asking him to "pay the Jordan rent for me" as there was no money in her checking account. "Hans refuses to discuss with me when he might have the money available and also made it clear that my bills are not his priority. The rent is due on August 1. Hans refuses to discuss finances with me and I did not hear from him for the last two days." She promised to pay Sturgeon back on August 20 when she returned. "Thank you. It is such a relief to be able to rely upon you." There was another pressing issue on her mind: because Rory had been acting up, she was taking him to a psychotherapy session the next day.

CHAPTER 15

›"OUR CHILDREN HARDLY KNOW THEIR FATHER"

Oakland family law attorney Shelley Gordon formerly worked as an Alameda County prosecutor. After her first child, a son, was born in 1983, she quit the DA's office because it wasn't offering any part-time positions. She eventually turned to general civil litigation, business and family law and opened her own practice. In July 2004, she was sitting at her desk in her office along Oakland's Embarcadero Cove when her phone rang. It was Sturgeon. He told Gordon that a good friend of his wanted to file for divorce but was still in Russia at the moment. He was shopping for attorneys. "I'm trying to help her pick somebody, so I'm interviewing some people," Sturgeon said. He added, "This may get ugly."

Gordon figured Sturgeon and his friend were understandably nervous about what was to come. "You know, a lot of people feel that way, and there's things I can do to try and have it go smoother, but I don't have any control over the other person," she told Sturgeon. Gordon was confident that this would be a case she could handle. She prided herself at being a good advocate and a leveling influence in divorce cases. "I'm not going to be nasty," she would say. She told potential clients that they may not be happy with her if that's what they wanted.

Gordon spoke to Nina over the phone and exchanged e-mails while she was still in Russia. Nina wanted certain orders in place by the time she was back in Oakland. She was fearful that without those orders, Hans's influence on Rory would cause him to regress. Rory had been a lot calmer that summer while in Russia.

On August 2, 2004, Nina was still overseas when her

divorce petition was filed in Alameda County Superior Court in Oakland. The suit, filed by Gordon on Nina's behalf, cited irreconcilable differences and asked that Nina be granted legal and physical custody of the children. She also asked for supervised visitation on a temporary basis "until the mental health of son is determined." She also asked for child and spousal support from Hans, whom she described as an absentee father.

"Our children hardly know their father because he has been home for only months at a time, three times a year," Nina wrote in her court papers. "Hans came back to stay for an extended period of time this spring, and our relationship deteriorated very quickly, and our son Rory began having horrible nightmares and acting out violently. I saw a rapid and alarming overall [deterioration] in his mental health. He has exhibited signs of post-traumatic stress disorder and dissociative behavior. He was always [a] sweet and engaged child." Now, he was drawing pictures of monsters and soldiers and saying it was a "secret with his dad," Nina wrote.

Whenever Rory had a problem, Hans said it was Nina's fault because she was a bad mother. "He was constantly criticizing me in front of the children" and speaking to them "in the mean and vile way that he has been doing," Nina wrote. "Hans will not accept that any of his conduct has been harmful to our son. He is not willing to accept any limitations on his conduct."

Nina believed that Rory was being harmed by playing violent video games like *Battlefield Vietnam* and *Age of Wonders: Shadow Magic* or being shown war movies like *Saving Private Ryan* and *Blackhawk Down*. "Go to war in new dramatic battle scenarios including leading a squadron of helicopters in an all-out attack on an enemy compound, executing an ambush of enemy soldiers from dense foliage, captaining a PT boat through a dangerous jungle river passage, and more," reads a description of Electronic Arts' *Battlefield Vietnam*, which features loud napalm explosions and blood shooting out of people.

She said Rory has had serious difficulties since he was very young, including high anxiety, eating and sleeping problems,

nightmares, social withdrawal and an extreme aversion
to changes in his routine or switching from one activity to
another. The nightmares would increase after he saw disturbing movies or played those video games, she said. Rory once
commented that he saw something in which a man was looking for his arm on the battlefield. The little boy also asked
one day, "What is the type of wire people use to choke each
other?"

"Since Hans came home this spring, he purposely exposed
Rory to a tremendous amount of extremely violent killing
video games and violent war movies," Nina wrote in her
divorce filing. "This is an activity that Hans does almost
obsessively to relax. Hans believes a child should 'know the
real world' and sees nothing wrong with this behavior. He
doesn't seem to grasp that children are not little adults. Our
son is only four, and I tried everything to get Hans to stop
doing this to him." This included reading various books and
publications about the effect of violent media on children.

When Nina returned from Russia, she paid Gordon a visit
at her office. Nina brought Gordon two watercolor paintings
of pastoral scenes from Russia that a friend of hers had made.
Gordon was touched that this beautiful woman had brought
her a gift on the very day they first met. It wouldn't be the last
offering. For Gordon's birthday in January 2005, Nina gave
her a gift certificate for a massage at a spa.

> Hans and Nina could not agree on anything with respect
to Rory. Nina said she consulted with a neuropsychologist
in Russia when Rory was eighteen months old and was told
that he was possibly autistic. Nina checked with psychologist Meg Zweiback, who told her that Rory needed as much
structure and routine as possible, less stimulation in his environment and fewer changes or transitions. Hans didn't care
for Zweiback's findings. At a session with Zweiback, Hans
insisted that he would not stop showing the videos to Rory
and suggested that Rory should instead work on coping skills.
Zweiback asked if Hans would remove the material from the
house, and Hans replied that he would rather leave than give

up his videos. Hans wanted to take Rory to a male therapist, which he did, and the male therapist also expressed concern about what was happening to Rory, Nina reported.

Rory's behavior in school and at home had improved from 2000 to 2002. He began eating and sleeping through the night and no longer had nightmares. But the problems seemed to return when Hans returned from Russia in March 2004. Nina decided to consult with other child experts because Hans objected to Zweiback. Children's Hospital Oakland referred them to a child therapist, who saw Rory for several sessions. But Hans again objected to that therapist as well.

Hans, acting as his own attorney, filed his response to the divorce petition in September 2004. He said this was a case of "what appears to be a mother spiraling downwards in mental stability." He then threw in an intriguing accusation, saying Nina "is a product of a KGB-dominated society and is the child of someone who works for the KGB."

"There has been domestic violence in our marriage, entirely initiated by the petitioner," he wrote. "On several occasions, she has attacked me without warning. She hit me while appearing very angry and enraged. I did not respond to her. The next day, she apologized but several days later she grabbed my hand, dug her nails into my skin and drew blood, while again appearing enraged."

He adamantly denied that Rory's nightmares were caused by computer games.

To Hans, spending his free time playing games with his son was a natural part of male bonding, similar to going to a football game. Moreover, Rory would also benefit from the hand-eye coordination. Hans wanted to teach Rory not to be afraid of war and accused Nina of reacting negatively to all this with "manufactured hysteria." He wrote that "to Rory, Vietnam has none of the associations it has for adults, just as most of us old folks were ignorant of genocide while playing cowboys and Indians. Helicopters explode. Pretty. Crawling through the grass. Sneaky fun. That is all there is for him. It is only for adults that it is something disturbing." In fact, he said Nina was to blame for showing the children "extensive nature movies—that is, violent movies about animals killing each other." As for concerns that Rory was scared by so-called violent video games, Hans argued that his son would have the same reaction to "Peter Rabbit and other traditional scary children's material." Although he admitted to "maliciously annoying Nina" with his belief that *Saving Private Ryan* was less violent than nature motives, he didn't think it was a good pick. "I am still looking for the right movie with the right values, and not too much intensity, to show Rory as his first war movie," he wrote. "There is no hurry to this."

To Hans, the computer-game issue was 70 percent about Nina pushing him around, 10 percent about his male geek cultural heritage—and his desire to pass it on to the children—and 20 percent his belief that the love children had for games was because it stimulated their development when experienced in moderation. Rory would later say that his dad made him sit in front of the computer for six hours at a time—and told the little boy that it was his job. "Watching a child play such a game reminds one of the enormous amount of spatial skills, counting, reading and strategizing that these games teach, and that we take for granted," Hans wrote. "The games teach in a way that fully engages the kids and makes reading and counting seem relevant to them. Suddenly, numbers and letters are interesting things that they really want to know about."

While Hans was fascinated by video games and played them to unwind, Nina simply needed attention from her husband. But Hans had no time for that. At its core, the argument over video games "is about a husband coming home from work at the end of a long day, and playing computer games for an hour while in the background his wife is going stark raving bonkers over his ignoring her," Hans wrote.

Moreover, Hans said Rory had nightmares long before any exposure to computer games. He said he offered his son an invisible magic sword to defend himself but that Rory wanted magical dynamite instead. "I explained to him that he could learn to fight the monsters in his dreams and blow them up with the magical dynamite," he wrote. "I did this in terms that expressed a quiet confidence that he could handle the job."

Hans railed against Sturgeon in his court papers and other

writings, saying Nina had exposed their children to a survivor of child molestation who is "mentally disturbed and a danger to the children." He described Sturgeon as a "heavy practitioner of sadomasochistic sexual behavior" who uses sex toys. Sturgeon had carved the word "RAGE" on his left bicep and told a then two-year-old Nio when she asked about the cuttings that pain can be "fun." She responded by wrinkling her nose. Sturgeon balks at this characterization, saying he was merely playing a logic game with Nio. "What I actually said was, 'Nio, the sky is pink.'" The little girl would then smile and say, "Noooo." "The moon is in Lake Merritt." "Noooo." "Pain is fun." Same answer. Sturgeon told Hans that he was tortured as a child by men who pulled out his toenails to toughen him, Hans wrote. Sturgeon once told him that he was no longer able to enjoy "vanilla sex" and left Nina books on S and M to read, according to Hans.

"I have come to understand that S and M is transformatively evil," Hans wrote. "It changes the wiring of the brain, and connects pleasure with pain, and love with torture. Sean is now evil, in a way I used to think people only were in badly written fiction. Pleasant, fun, enjoyable, helpful to others, loyal to his friends almost as much as dangerous to them, and evil. It is not just confined to his sex habits, it is now throughout his personality."

Hans said he once sent a letter to Sturgeon speculating about whether marrying Nina was a mistake. Sturgeon showed the letter to Nina, got her high on Ecstasy and seduced her, Hans said. Sturgeon remembered it differently, saying they consensually took Ecstasy.

Hans said Nina may still be involved with Sturgeon and may want his help caring for their children. He was still buying them toys and was not merely interested in replacing Hans as a husband, but as a father, too, he said. Hans asked a judge to prohibit Sturgeon from being in the children's presence. Hans's filing came the same month Sturgeon bought a six-hundred-thousand-dollar John Hancock insurance policy in which he named Nina as the primary beneficiary in the event of his death. Sturgeon's sister was named as the secondary beneficiary. Back in June, Sturgeon had drafted a will in which he wrote that Nina should be given all his property and possessions—including his Lakeshore Avenue apartment, his Subaru and all the money in his accounts—if he were to die. He said his lawsuit against Hans should continue and that Nina "should receive any monies recovered."

Sturgeon wondered why Hans was complaining about him only now. Hans knew full well about Sturgeon's background, including the fact that his father, a Korean War veteran who had worked as an X-ray technician, tried to commit suicide in 1996. Now, Sturgeon was trying to turn his life around. He had been attending church and had a deepening relationship with Christ. Sturgeon believed Hans was using his newfound concerns about Sturgeon being around the children as an excuse in connection with the loan dispute. As recently as June, Hans had asked him to drive the kids to school while he and Nina went to marriage counseling. Now, all of a sudden, Sturgeon was radioactive? Sturgeon couldn't make sense of it all.

Hans said Rory has played "more hours of educational games" than those depicting violence. He did, however, draw the line at *Grand Theft Auto*, in which people can kill cops and solicit prostitutes. "*Grand Theft Auto* is a computer game in which indiscriminate killing earns points, and I think it rehearses evil," he wrote in another court filing. "Many other computer games heavily penalize shooting the wrong person, and I prefer those." He mentioned Oakland's Nut Cases gang, whose members shot and killed numerous people at random in 2003 and had an affinity for *Grand Theft Auto*. He claimed to have spoken to Oakland police officers who were involved in the case, saying they themselves enjoyed playing the video game with their small children. Those cops disagreed with his opinion that the game "teaches bad shooting habits," Hans wrote. "I think they felt the Nut Cases, not the game, were the appropriate focus of the law."

In the filing, which came with numerous subheadings and was riddled with references to Sir Francis Bacon, Aristotle, Ralph Waldo Emerson and the scientific method, Hans said simply that he is being "scammed" by Nina.

But Nina said Hans repeatedly made negative comments

about women in front of the children, belittling Nina and calling her a liar. He derided women in general, calling them bad, stupid and not deserving of legal rights. He also denigrated Russia and Nina's Russian heritage. Hans, in turn, accused Nina of despising his own cultural heritage, "particularly all notions of fighting for honorable causes, and of manhood. This contempt for those who strive for ideals is a common strain in Russian culture and television."

In a memo to Alameda County Superior Court Judge Jon Tigar, who was assigned the case, family court counselor Cris Hodson wrote in September 2004, "Ms. Reiser stated that (the romantic) part of the relationship has ended, although Mr. Reiser feels strongly that Sean is trying to take his wife and children and replace him as a parent. Mr. Reiser has very strong anxieties about Sean, although they still apparently spent time with him and Sean was helping with the children through May of this year. Mr. Reiser insists that the children be kept from Sean. Ms. Reiser agrees to this request. Both parents stated that Sean has not harmed the children."

Hans dripped with contempt for Hodson, other experts consulted in the case and, in what would become a pattern, even his own divorce attorney, Rachel Ginsburg, whom he accused of making errors and misleading statements in his court papers. Ginsburg would be the first in a long line of attorneys who would be hired by Hans to represent him. Through it all, Nina's attorney would always be Gordon.

At about 7:00 p.m. on September 2, the Thursday before Labor Day weekend, Hans picked up Nina, her mother and her kids from the airport after they returned from Moscow. He was already upset that Nina had spent three months in Russia, one month more than planned. But Nina had noticed how Rory had improved over the summer. He was relaxed and no longer having nightmares. Nina said part of the delay was to arrange transportation for her mother to return with her to the United States.

When everyone returned to the Jordan Road home, Hans and Nina got into a heated argument over who would have custody of their children for the weekend, a scene that would be eerily repeated exactly two years later. Nina said Hans was verbally abusive and threatened her, saying "he will make me hurt for the rest of my life." She called the police.

Officer Daniel Gil arrived at about 9:15 p.m. to take a report. "Nina and Hans both stated that no physical violence occurred during the dispute," Gil wrote in his report. "I furnished both parties a resources card and advised them on how to obtain marriage counseling."

The police report was notable for what it didn't say. Although nothing physical happened involving the couple, Hans had tried to forcibly remove Nio. He grabbed his three-year-old daughter by the stomach and pulled her away from Nina. The two had a tug-of-war over the girl. Nina let go and then Sharanova and Hans began fighting over Nio. Hans pushed his mother-in-law away, saying, "This is my daughter, she will leave with me!" Nio became hysterical. On the morning of September 3, she vomited fifteen times beginning at 6:00 a.m. and had to be taken to the emergency room at Children's Hospital Oakland for treatment.

After that incident, their attorneys encouraged Hans and Nina to share the children. Hans had the kids for two weekends, and both ended badly, with Hans telling Nina at the end of the first visit that the children didn't want to see her anymore.

At the end of the second weekend, Hans told Nina that their kids were in a secure location and she shouldn't expect to see them. Nina said she went to their school to pick them up only to have Rory tell her that Hans had instructed them not to go home with her. She took them home, however, and kept them out of school. Hans complained that Nina had "disappeared" them. That fall, Rory and Nio returned to Grand Lake Montessori. Teachers reported that Rory, apparently echoing his father, spoke about how women were bad people and didn't deserve rights in this country. He would say other hateful things, and when asked where he heard it from, the little boy would say his dad told him. Teachers also kept a close eye on Rory because he was undergoing counseling for nightmares.

Hans and Nina were awarded joint physical and legal custody of the kids on September 20. He was ordered to pay fifty-four hundred dollars a month in child support. Hans had Wednesday overnights and alternate weekends with the kids.

In what he called his "child-rearing journal," Hans wrote that on September 22, 2004, "Niorline cried at night for her mommy" and that Rory recently "seems to only have normal bad dreams now, not the paralyzed with fear dreams he had in May 2004 and before. I hypothesize that these are bad dreams without fear."

Two days later, he wrote in his journal of his contempt for a doctor who did not understand how important it was to differentiate between empirical and impressionistic studies. "She is not deeply committed to the scientific method," Hans wrote. "Most significantly, she described herself as very knowledgeable and well-read on the topic, but when asked to cite articles and otherwise demonstrate her knowledge, she completely failed to do so. There is nothing less desirable than someone who lacks an understanding of what they don't know in a proceeding such as this."

An entry for October 2, 2004, noted that Rory slept for twelve hours. "Perhaps he slept badly at Nina's. Talked to Rory; he is having a lot of bad dreams at Nina's."

On October 3, 2004, Rory reported having a dream in which his magical dynamite didn't explode. "He promised to spit at the monster and use his fists," Hans wrote. He would later note that Rory would forget about his dynamite and get scared but then acquire a doom bat friend—demonic creatures from one of his computer games—that he gave the dynamite to. The doom bat would then fly over the monsters and drop dynamite on them, "and he was very excited and happy about it. He had a dream friend. Sometimes victory was his," Hans wrote. But when magical dynamite wasn't the answer, Hans gave his son an invisible magic wand.

Nina believed that Rory needed consistency and a "very safe environment. He needs to thrive. He needs a smaller place, people around him that he loves." She described Nio as "a blessing. She is very functional. Task-oriented. She takes everything that is going on well. She has an ability to stand up for herself. She has a great sense of humor. She wakes up and sings, likes to dance. She does everything with passion." Nina noticed that Hans wasn't as attentive with Nio as he was with Rory. "Deep down, I don't think that he cares about Niorline," Nina said later.

In October 2004, Nina moved into a 1,219-foot, two-bedroom, one-bath home on Forty-ninth Street. That same month, she began working twenty-five hours a week at Franklin Research in Emeryville, a tiny city of shopping centers and biotech firms outside Oakland, and fifteen hours a week on a series of bookkeeping projects at Manzanita Restaurant on Linden Street in Oakland's Temescal District. "Nina did excellent work and was [paid] $25/hour," owner George French wrote in a memo included in the court file.

CHAPTER 16

> POLICE REPORTS

The Reisers came to the attention of the authorities numerous times in late 2004.

On November 29, 2004, Hans was identified in a "suspected child abuse report" filed with Alameda County Child Protective Services (CPS) by employees of Kids' Turn, where counselors helped children deal with the separation of their parents. At one of the workshops, which were ordered by the court, Hans stated matter-of-factly that he disciplined Rory for pushing his sister down two or three steps by "extreme" spanking, consisting of using an open hand on him four or five times, leaving no marks. Kids' Turn employees said Hans had said "old-fashioned punishment" is OK. Rory had made comments that his father "pulls" his sister and that he "hits," the report said. Rory wouldn't provide any more details, said the report, which noted that Nio had "chronic stomachaches." Oakland police officer Jack Peterson also took a report, but no charges were filed in response to any of the allegations.

Hans disciplined the kids by taking them up to a room and telling them to stay there for a time. Rory would have to be convinced that he had done something wrong; otherwise, he might laugh when he was spanked, like all men in the family, Hans said. With Nio, it was different. Hans might say, "Bad!" in a severe tone, and she'd burst into tears. Nio seemed to behave better when she was with her father, Rory would later report. She didn't want to get in trouble with her dad.

Twice that fall, Hans returned Nio to Nina during his scheduled physical custody sessions because the three-year-old girl was running a high fever and Hans didn't know what to do.

Shortly before Thanksgiving 2004, Rory had a dream about hitting a monster over the head with a baseball bat from behind. Hans wrote in his journal, "Wish I had dreams like that!" On Thanksgiving, he proudly reported that the kids were able to sleep with lights out. "Fear of dark is 90 percent cured," he proclaimed.

On December 22, 2004, Oakland police were called to Nina's home. Hans had gone there to pick up the kids. He became angry when he saw presents inside that he believed were from her new boyfriend, Officer Mike Encinias wrote in his report. Hans took the kids to his car, walked back and then shoved her with his right hand, causing her to fall down. Hans drove off with the kids before the police arrived. Nina didn't need any medical attention but said she wanted Hans arrested. In a statement attached to the police report, she noted that the presents were for the kids. Hans was not arrested.

The next day, she filed a request for a temporary restraining order and gave more details about what had happened. She wrote, "Hans became frustrated without a clear reason and appeared very angry when he picked up children from my house. When I asked him what time he was going to bring them back, he pushed me down, grabbed scared children without their warm clothes and shoes and put them in the car. He pushed me down in front of the house with children present and was verbally abusive." She said her elbows were injured as a result and also there at the scene was "a stranger who walked up the street and witnessed what happened."

On Christmas Day, Hans stood outside Nina's home, waiting patiently. Like a paparazzo stalking his prey, he snapped away as Sturgeon drove off in his Subaru. Nina called the police again, complaining that although Hans never contacted her, he was standing just a few hundred feet away from her home. "Resource info provided," Officer Robert Forrester wrote in his report.

On December 26, Nina called the police yet again. It was 3:15 p.m., and Hans had failed to return the kids by noon as required by court order and couldn't be reached. Officer Frank Gysin called Hans and convinced him to return the children to Nina. Within half an hour, Hans did just that.

But Hans was fuming. He filed a crime report of his own the same day, claiming that it was Nina who had violated the court order over the past week. On December 22, Nina and the kids weren't at home when he came to pick them up. "I called her," Hans wrote. "She did not like the way I spoke to her and refused to give them to me." Nina asked a question that Hans said he "chose not to answer." "She then assaulted me in the course of preventing me from picking up my daughter," he wrote. Sturgeon's Christmas Day visit also violated the order, Hans wrote, adding, "I have photos of him driving away from this."

Asked on the form to describe the person responsible, Hans wrote spitefully, "Small, formerly pretty woman." He obtained copies of the police reports, as was his right.

Hans's problems with Sturgeon multiplied on December 30, 2004, when his former best friend sued him in Alameda County Superior Court for failing to repay him the eighty-four thousand dollars. Hans's legal problems were mounting. The same day Sturgeon sued him, Hans hired Hayward attorney Stuart MacKenzie to represent him in the divorce case.

CHAPTER 17

>THE COURT BATTLE

From December 26, 2004, until January 14, 2005, Hans said his children were taken away from him. "Children report that they were told nothing about where I was or when they would see me again. They were anxious," he wrote in his journal.

In January 2005, Hans's custody time with the children was shrunk from Wednesday overnights to just Wednesday evenings from 5:00 to 7:30 p.m. He continued to have every other weekend with the kids.

Hans was also working as a subcontractor for Digeo, a home-entertainment technology provider. In January, Judge Tigar ordered the Washington State company to withhold fifty-four hundred dollars a month in income from Hans in order to pay Nina child support.

In January 2005, a mediator noted that the couple disagreed about everything, including schools, doctors and counselors. It was recommended that the kids be picked up and dropped off at Safe Exchange on Grand Avenue in Oakland and that Hans continue to attend Kids' Turn workshops. At Safe Exchange, one parent would leave the children and the other would pick them up fifteen minutes later. Each visit by a parent cost twenty dollars. Whenever Nina came in that year, she would get down on one knee, put her hands out and both the kids would run to her, according to Ron Zeno, the center's executive director. Zeno remembered Rory and Nio, just like he did every child that came through his doors. This was especially helpful around Christmas, when Zeno dressed up as Santa—an African American one at that—just down the street at Children's Fairyland, a ten-acre park on the shores of Lake Merritt that was a favorite with the Reiser children.

Hans sought to make clear how important he was in the computer industry and how only he could be trusted. He wrote in a court filing in January 2005, "I have a business based on producing the world's fastest file system and giving it away for free and am part of a large and growing free software social movement. I claim [all of Nina's allegations] is pure fraud by a gifted scammer who partially understands the psychological weaknesses of American society and uses them. It also represents the transfer of hatred of the father into hatred of the son and a desire to degrade the son. I challenge her or anyone to reproduce the dissociative behavior in front of me."

He later added, "Male geeks, such as myself, are one of America's most hated cultural minorities. Unlike racial hatred, it is considered socially acceptable to indulge in such hatred."

Also in January, an Alameda County CPS worker received a call from Hans's father, who advised that Nina was dating Sturgeon and that he was into S and M and was hooked on painkillers. Ramon expressed concern that Sturgeon may abuse the children. The allegation wasn't investigated.

On January 19, Hans formally lodged paperwork objecting to Nina's temporary restraining order request. He attached a thirty-two-page declaration—Gordon would call it a manifesto—blasting everyone who disagreed with his views, including psychologists, other "supposed experts" and Nina and Sturgeon.

Hans stopped making the monthly fifty-four hundred dollar child-support payments in February 2005. Nina complained about this and accused him of making her stay dependent on him. She still wanted to study for her U.S. medical licensing exam, get her license and make money. Until Hans and Nina had separated, she had little time or energy to study for the exam in between taking care of the children and working for Namesys.

Acting as his own attorney, Hans responded to Sturgeon's complaint in court papers filed on February 15, deriding it as "uncertain, ambiguous and unintelligible." He said "under no theory of liability is defendant Reiser liable personally for repayment," noting that Sturgeon knew full well that "the majority of the allegedly loaned funds were spent exclusively by Nina Reiser." He noted that the fact that Nina wasn't named as a defendant was "clear evidence of his malicious intent to destroy defendant's marriage and leave the defendant to clean up the wreckage and pay the debts."

In March, marriage and family therapist Denise Smernes conducted a full custody evaluation of Rory and Nio. At a hearing that month, Hans exasperated Judge Tigar by repeatedly asking him questions like, "Do you agree with that?" and "How do you feel about that?" It was as if Hans regarded Tigar as an equal with whom he could freely discuss ideas, as if they were just two guys hanging out watching a game on TV. After all, Tigar, appointed to the bench four years earlier at the young age of thirty-nine, was just over a year older than Hans. But Tigar shot Hans down at the hearing, telling him, "Mr. Reiser, you keep asking me questions. You are going to have a very frustrating morning if you keep it up." Hans did get at least one thing he had asked for: explicit permission from the judge to allow Rory to watch *Jimmy Neutron* and *Sesame Street*. At Gordon's request, Tigar agreed to amend the restraining order by allowing Hans and Nina to e-mail each other directly about issues with the kids, instead of through Gordon.

Despite the court battle, Nina was still there for Sturgeon emotionally. After his grandmother died in March, Nina accompanied Sturgeon to a nearby recreation area, where they buried her ashes and planted flowers in her honor.

As the proceedings wore on, Nina and her mother did their best to create some sense of normalcy for the children. Nina had planned to go to Russia that summer as she usually did, but Hans wouldn't agree to it. So in April 2005, Sharanova came to Oakland instead. Hans would take the kids to places like Kindergym, the Exploratorium in San Francisco, the Oakland Public Library and the Monterey Bay Aquarium. He also took them to dance, drum and robot-building classes. They'd go places with Beverly and her friend Mark McGothigan like the Robot Wars, a competitive mechanical sporting event at Fort Mason Center in San Francisco. McGothigan was "Uncle Mark" to the kids. To Nina, he was one of her closest confidants. In fact, McGothigan told friends that he was in love with her. But he knew that nothing good would come of it. It would only complicate everything, including his artist relationship with Beverly.

Much as the kids enjoyed watching the robots battle it out, Hans seemed to relish the ongoing war with his wife.

Hans wrote a letter to Gordon in April 2005 saying that Nina had failed to send him Namesys accounting data from her laptop. Because of this, Hans complained that Namesys would be unable to perform its tax accounting on time. He demanded that Nina return the laptop, which was company property.

Beverly and Sturgeon had been close, but that was no longer the case now that he had caused a wedge between Hans and Nina. In late April, Sturgeon called Beverly and asked for Hans. But he was on a business trip in Croatia and Italy, giving talks and touting the benefits of "dancing trees" while promoting Reiser4. When Beverly told Sturgeon that Hans was overseas, Sturgeon's concerns were about actual trees. He told Beverly that a large tree had fallen near his house and just missed him. Sturgeon said he "suspected it was Hans with a saw causing the tree to fall," Beverly wrote in a memo that was submitted to the court. Sturgeon later said that he had been joking.

Also that spring, Beverly reported that Sturgeon called and threatened to sue Hans for slander and asked that she throw her son out of the house. "I am concerned about Sean's acts," Beverly wrote in another memo submitted by John Fuery, whom Hans hired that April as his new divorce attorney. Fuery immediately tried to get Tigar to disqualify himself from the proceedings on the grounds that Hans could not get a fair trial before him. Tigar rejected the request, saying it was too late because he had already made a number of decisions in the case. Not surprisingly, Fuery would get shot down by his own client. He tried in vain to convince Hans that it was disrespectful to wear sandals in court.

CHAPTER 18

> HURTING FOR LOVE

Baron Karl Friedrich Hieronymus von Munchausen was an eighteenth-century Russian army soldier from Germany known for regaling people with outlandish tales of derring-do. Although much has been lost to history, he remained an intriguing figure in popular culture for many years. His stories were made into numerous films, the most recent of which came out in 1988 and was called *The Adventures of Baron Munchausen*. In a nod to his flair for exaggeration, Munchausen syndrome was named after him. Sufferers of this psychological disorder, also known as factitious disorder, deliberately cause, fake or exaggerate symptoms in hopes of getting attention.

A related illness is Munchausen by proxy syndrome, in which usually the mother, fueled by a need to meet her own self-serving psychological needs, convinces others that her child is sick by lying and reporting fictitious episodes. The perpetrator is often familiar with the medical profession and fools doctors into ordering unnecessary tests, surgeries or procedures.

> As Hans read the literature on Munchausen by proxy, he became convinced that Nina had the disorder. He thought of the long list of illnesses that Nina alleged Rory had, including traumatic stress disorder, dissociative behavior, sensory integration disorder—marked by an improper response to touch, movement, sights or sounds—borderline autism and poor muscle tone and weak joints. Hans believed Nina was seeking attention because she felt abandoned—first by her father, and then by a husband who was emotionally absent.

Because she appeared so caring and attentive, doctors never suspected anything was wrong, and Hans grew frustrated that they couldn't see what he was seeing—that she was a practiced liar.

Hans thought he had someone in his corner when he discovered that Dr. Herbert A. Schreier, the coauthor of *Hurting for Love: Munchausen by Proxy Syndrome*, was based at Children's Hospital Oakland and was the chief of child psychiatry there. According to Schreier and others, the exact cause of the disorder wasn't known, but researchers have suggested that some factors could include a history of abuse or neglect as a child and major stress, such as marital problems. As the divorce dragged on, Hans became obsessed with the issue, urging his attorneys to see if Nina had been abused while growing up.

Nina had taken the children to Children's Hospital Oakland several times before. In October 2002, Rory put two pomegranate seeds up his right nostril. Nina got one of them out, and she took him to the hospital, where Rory was able to blow the other one out.

A month later, Nio, then one and one-half years old, began walking. But her feet were turning in. Nina was concerned enough to bring her to the hospital to see an orthopedic surgeon. The doctor told Nina that this should correct over time. There was no need for braces or special shoes, Nina was told.

Rory's captivation with his nose continued. This time, he was in day care in September 2003 when a bead got stuck in his right nostril. Nina tried to get it out by covering his mouth and blowing into his left nostril. When that didn't work, she took him to the hospital, where a doctor was able to remove the offending bead.

› By all accounts, Dr. Dorit Bar-Din is a well-regarded pediatrician in Berkeley who has received high marks on the Berkeley Parent Network, an online forum for parents. One parent wrote of Dr. Bar-Din, "Our primary pediatrician is Dorit Bar-Din, who has been wonderful, always willing to take the time to explain in as much detail as we wanted, and she has such a wonderful rapport with kids. I have never felt slighted for asking questions."

Dr. Bar-Din was the Reiser children's doctor. In May 2004, she diagnosed Rory with hearing loss and fluid in his ear. She prescribed antibiotics, which didn't work despite five treatments. That same year, Rory was diagnosed at Alta Bates Medical Center with having sensory integration disorder.

In February 2005, Nina took Rory to Children's Hospital Oakland to see ear, nose and throat (ENT) surgeon Dr. Robert Wesman, who recommended that Rory undergo an adenoidectomy, surgery to put tubes in his ears and to remove his adenoids, structures behind the uvula near where the nose connects to the throat.

Surgery was scheduled for March 1, but it took too long to get the insurance company's authorization, and so it was bumped to March 14. But Rory fell ill with a fever.

Hans called Bar-Din on April 8, saying although he had joint medical custody with Nina, the doctor was not to provide medical care to either Rory or Nio unless he was present. On April 11, Wesman returned a call from Hans, who told him "he did not want any surgery at this time." The surgery scheduled for April 18 was canceled.

Hans said he was very concerned about what he believed was Rory's fear of doctors. He described Nina as a "detached medical professional trained in professional detachment as a technique in dealing with patients, has no trouble finding doctors who share her professional detachment techniques which inadvertently has had the negative effect of instilling in Rory a fear of shots, a fear of doctors, a fear of medical procedures and likely contributed to his past fear of the dark."

Meanwhile, Gordon tried to settle the issue over Bar-Din by drafting a stipulation for Hans and Nina to sign that would allow the doctor to continue treating the children. But on April 22, Bar-Din wrote a letter to Nina saying that she could no longer provide pediatric care for Rory and Nio. "I am accustomed to providing medical care to my patients when either of their parents brings them into my office," Bar-Din wrote. "The only way to insure that your children are not seen unless both of you are present is for the two of you to communicate

openly and regularly. I am not able to act as an arbitrator."
Nina called Bar-Din three times pleading with her to reconsider, but the doctor would not budge.

Wesman wrote Nina a similar letter. "I regret to inform
you that I am not comfortable making medical decisions in
the care of your son Rory Reiser. I would recommend you
contact the ENT department at Stanford or UCSF for further
care." Nina accused Hans of scaring Wesman away, but Hans
noted that the doctor didn't say as much in his letter.

Nina knew that getting Hans to agree with medical decisions would be close to impossible. Now she felt Rory's health
was in jeopardy. He was sick with a high fever and sore throat
from April 28 to May 4 and stayed at home. His surgery, now
set for May 2, was canceled. He got sick again with a low-
grade fever on May 11 and 12. He went to school on May 13
and came back home with a fever once more and stayed home
from school for three more days.

Nina took Rory to see Dr. Peter Koltai, an ENT at Stanford
Medical Center, on May 24 for a second opinion as to whether
Rory needed surgery. Koltai determined that Rory had a forty-
decibel hearing loss—equivalent to plugging one's ears—and
urged Nina to have Wesman do the surgery. But Nina begged
Koltai for him to do it himself because Hans had threatened
Wesman with a malpractice suit. Koltai agreed. But then he
got a menacing call from Hans.

Hans explained to Koltai that Nina had Munchausen by
proxy disorder. Koltai told Hans that it wasn't possible to have
Munchausen by proxy with a forty-decibel hearing loss and
the symptoms that Rory was having. But Hans told him, "If
you operate on this child, I'm gonna bring a lawsuit against
you." Koltai delayed the surgery to consult with the hospital's
social services department. Hans insisted that Rory's enlarged
adenoids could have resulted from an allergic reaction to pets
like Nina's cat or his mother's dog. He also accused Nina of
having used an unapproved medical device to perform bizarre
invasive treatments on Rory. Nina countered that it was a low-
voltage portable laser device commonly used in Russia to
treat inflammation. She said she had showed it to all three
of Rory's doctors and, although none voiced any objection or

concerns, she stopped using it in January 2005. "Of course I cannot practice medicine in this country as I am not licensed," she wrote. "However, I cannot remove the medical knowledge and experience from my functioning as a caring parent."

As Nina fretted over Rory's ears, Hans wrote a memo in which he complained that Sturgeon had brought balloons to celebrate Nio's upcoming fourth birthday on May 26. Hans questioned whether his kids would be Sturgeon's "new recruits" and would be molested by him. "The child victim tends to become the adult victimizer of a child that is the age the adult victimizer was when first molested," Hans wrote in boldface.

Citing Bar-Din's refusal to provide care in light of the conflict, Judge Tigar granted Nina sole legal custody to make medical decisions regarding the children. He cited Nina's medical training as making her "uniquely qualified to evaluate and obtain medical services." Tigar also dismissed Hans's allegations that Nina was practicing medicine without a license, saying, "The court finds that allegation to be unsupported by the evidence." The judge said Nina and Hans would split education and welfare issues, but that was of no solace to Hans. Tigar was siding with Nina on the medical issue just because she had the cachet of being a doctor, he fumed. It was unfair. She was in complete control.

McGothigan said although he believed Nina didn't suffer from Munchausen by proxy, he remained convinced that she went "a little overboard" with some of her children's health issues. She had every right to be concerned because of her medical training, and "it was so natural for her" to diagnose the conditions she believed Rory had, he said. Still, "I think these were just normal kids with fairly normal things growing up," McGothigan said. "She was basically embellishing normal development issues that all children have. I think she was using that as a weapon against Hans."

But Sturgeon countered that it was Hans who was using the kids as weapons against Nina. "The children were of no real interest to him before 7/04," when she got the divorce process rolling, Sturgeon later wrote. "After 7/04 Hans suddenly becomes 'Super Dad,' except he really doesn't."

CHAPTER 19

> E-MAIL WAR

On June 1, Nina asked Hans in an e-mail if he was committed to contributing to their children's tuition at Grand Lake Montessori. Otherwise, they would have to withdraw and possibly consider public schools or other private schools, such as Head-Royce School, the well-regarded K–12 college-prep campus in the Oakland foothills, so long as the "money situation becomes different or we choose to spend what we have on schools rather than legal fighting."

In response, Hans sniffed that Head-Royce "is rumored to be merely decent, not great." He accused Nina of not being the "tutoring kind of personality" like he was and that "they have no internationally famous scientists" like himself at Head-Royce.

He then broached a subject that therapists would later point to as evidence that Hans tended to overidentify with Rory. In psychological terms, Hans's responses to Rory were unconsciously magnified by his own experiences while growing up. "Rory wants to live with me, not with you, I don't know why you choose to ignore that. Don't give him the childhood that I had: let him be raised by a scientist. Leave them with me, and go. You'll be happy and successful . . . You can visit with him when you want and take them on little vacation trips through the U.S. every so often if you want. There are things you can teach them well, I know that." He noted that if she were smart enough to find them, "unemployed Olympians" could be used to teach their kids sports. Instead of McDonald's or Wendy's, Rory would "eat at the table of nationally known chefs if you and Shelley [Gordon] leave me alone to take care of it," he wrote.

On June 2, Nina wrote Hans an e-mail suggesting that the kids either go to a summer program at Grand Lake Montessori or stay at home with a babysitter.

In response, Hans wrote of the babysitter, "Is she into S and M? Lesbian? I don't trust your selectional abilities. Ordinary people cannot educate genius children. It does not work. I remember them trying with me, and it went badly."

The next day, Nina asked Hans to clarify what he meant in an earlier e-mail in which he suggested getting private tutors for the children. To her surprise, Hans replied that he would take Rory to Egypt, "fly some retired Russian national champion in some sport" there and have him train their son four hours a day. Some bright grad student or professor would then spend another four hours a day teaching Rory things like the history of the Middle East. Hans said he would teach Rory how to read himself.

"Cost compared to litigation: far less . . . Cost compared to Head-Royce: less," he wrote. "Quality compared to Head-Royce: it is Chez Panisse compared to Wendy's," he proclaimed in contrasting the hamburger restaurant with the famed Berkeley eatery launched by Alice Waters.

On June 14, Hans and Nina had their first session with another mediator, a psychologist in Berkeley. Hans accused Nina of engaging in domestic violence and of running "scams" on him with her claims of Rory's illnesses. Nina agreed to mediation but not to rehashing their marriage. Hans discussed his concerns about Sturgeon, saying his former friend had threatened to abuse Rory and Nio. Hans complained that the balloons Sturgeon had brought for Nio's birthday were in violation of a temporary restraining order. Nina agreed that it would be better if Sturgeon had no contact with the kids. But she said that the issue was between Hans and Sturgeon and that she didn't want to be in the middle.

At the second mediation session, the next day, June 15, Hans recounted—and Nina did not challenge—that she had hit him on a couple of occasions and during one incident had called the police. Hans saw that as besmirching his honor, as *he* did not hit *her*. He saw this as disingenuous. He spent a lot of time inferring that she intended him harm and that she saw him as weak because he did not retaliate. Nina reassured him that she does not see him as weak. At one point during the session, however, Hans threatened Nina with physical harm, and the psychologist abruptly ended the meeting.

On June 19, Nina wrote in an e-mail to Hans, "I agreed to start mediation hoping that we can move forward and make a mutually acceptable agreement. I will not continue mediation if you keep threatening me. When you give me a hard stare and explain that you are very good at combat and request that I drop domestic-violence charges against you, it very much sounds like another threat. I am warning you that if you are going to communicate with me in this manner, I will have to end mediation and report it to the police. We agreed to keep mediation confidential. However, threats are not part of the mediation process. You don't need to prove to me that you are a strong man. I never questioned it. I respect you as a man and a person but disagree with you regarding some of the important-for-us issues such as parenting. Disagreement does not equal disrespect. Best regards, Nina."

On June 20, Nina e-mailed Hans, saying, "Please don't take it as an offense, but we need to make some major progress on the custody/support issues before we can seriously discuss Egypt, let alone a trip together. My focus is on being able to pay rent and children's school and finally get to the point when I can study to be a doctor and you have Namesys. Nina."

That same day, Hans e-mailed Nina and the psychologist, asserting that Nina lacked sincerity during the sessions because she "smiled at inappropriate moments" and had a history of lying. "The level of lying that Nina engages in is, in American culture, an indication of serious mental instability," he wrote. "We discussed my psychology, but did not discuss hers. I fear she is not willing to share hers in any sincerity."

That night, Hans sent another e-mail to the psychologist and Nina. "Nina, I think that Rory needs to be acknowledged to be somebody special, and then he will have the will to be so. It is really important to him—don't underestimate the importance of honor to a five year old. He had a powerful sense of honor before he could talk, much less now. As his parents, we cannot indulge his every request to respect his honor, so we need to be careful to find some aspects of his honor that we can openly acknowledge and recognize. He needs that, and if you want him to love you again, you must allow him his honor."

Hans and Nina had two more sessions with the psychologist, on June 21 and 22.

After the June 22 session, Nina proposed that she yield to Hans any community interest in and designate sole ownership rights to Namesys, including all file systems if (1) Hans agreed that Nina would have sole legal and physical custody of the children and be allowed to return with the children to Russia or (2) Hans paid six thousand dollars a month in family support to Nina for three years, during which time she would continue to live in the Bay Area and pursue licensing as a doctor in the United States. Afterward, spousal support would cease, and child support would be determined by state guidelines.

Hans did not agree with either proposal. As a counterproposal, he said he would pay for the children's school tuition, their clothing and medical insurance and pay four thousand dollars a month in family support for three years.

Nina did not think Hans's counterproposals were enough to allow her to continue her medical studies or become self-supporting. The psychologist suggested that they check with their attorneys "to determine if Nina's proposals provided a basis for negotiating a mutually acceptable solution towards each recovering financial viability and the division of their community assets."

On June 24, Nina wrote Hans, "Hans, do you understand that it's not appropriate to talk to a child who s/he wants to live with? It HURTS them. Rory wants to live with BOTH of us. Not with just you. Do you know that after coming back from you he throws tantrums and cries how much he loves me? He does it because you create loyalty conflicts for him. He loves BOTH of us. It is our job to explain to him why we can live together in a way which won't hurt or give him a negative impression about either one of us. There are many very honorable reasons why some men do not live with their children. Of course, I will never tell the kids something like 'Daddy does not love you; he abandoned you and sold you for his business.'

Even if it was true, I would NEVER do it because it HURTS the KIDS and I care about them. We can include what we tell the kids in the agreement if you would like."

In response, Hans wrote, "You don't get it. I don't lie. I was not asking you to lie. I was asking for a reality, one in which he lives with me most of the time so that I can supervise his education, which I hope will not be the alienating fiasco that mine was. You can't discuss with him why he needs to read the great scientists, the original with him, like I can. You can't give him the world-class scientific education that I can because you are not an internationally famous scientist. There is a difference between the way the best in the world teach and what he gets at GLM [Grand Lake Montessori]. You can't even appreciate how alienating it is for him to be tutored by people not as smart as he is. You cannot understand that while YOU need a classroom setting to study, he needs anything but. You don't understand that what he will need in 6–24 months is to be left alone most of the day with an hour or two of talking about what he reads and supervised selection in what he will read. What he needs is an education . . . unlike other children. . . . Once he's over the reading hill," Rory will have been educated more than any school could teach him, he wrote. "Other children aren't like that. He is. You cannot raise him effectively any more than my mother could raise me. Don't put him through that. I hated school just like he does. It was such a waste of my time. And, oh, what I might be today if I had been left to my father to educate. You can teach him other things, but not to be a man. He needs to be a man. You think he needs to be a woman, but . . ."

Hans continued, "You find the man you are looking for, and he will not make you orgasm. Such a pity that I only understood at the end what you needed sexually. Oh well, there will be a next wife. I hope she is just less extremely female, or at least I think I hope it. A pity you are not here now to talk to late in the night like we used to when we needed to get up early."

In response, Nina wrote, "You are creating a situation which leads us to prolong conflict and disputes over the company. Why do you do it?"

Hans replied, "I do it. . . . The problem here is that you think you can smile at me and I will forget. Those who anger slowly, cool slowly Nina."

On June 29, Nina wrote Hans an e-mail marked, "This is confidential for your eyes only and is for settlement discussion purposes." "Hans, you have asked me several times to honor our prenup. Before marriage, we agreed that you'll get the business. I'll get the kids and you help me with becoming a doctor. You now propose that I/we split custody 50/50, you won't help me become a doctor and you get the business. Do you see the inconsistency?"

In response, Hans wrote, "You don't want the kids except as a bargaining chip. They interfere with your career. Give them to me 2/3 until you become a doctor, and it will be much easier for you to become a doctor. Why do you want to make Rory and I unhappy? Why do you want to send Rory to bed most nights with an acid stomach? I don't want Rory to live with me because I need him. I want it because he needs me. What you propose satisfies my rights and needs but it does nothing for him. Think of him a little instead of thinking of us. I never expected him to want to live with me. It was a complete surprise to me that he did. His needs must come first. Do you agree? It so happens that what you need to become a doctor (which is to only have the children 1/3) corresponds to what they need and want. Let your needs and theirs be satisfied. Let our children grow up to become wealthy and privileged. That means let me stop fighting and start making some money. And let them grow up with private tutors and making childhood friends in Silicon Valley as it becomes ever wealthier in the next twenty-five years. You know the amazing thing is that we settle this, then during the next ten years I will start moving in the circles of the very wealthy in Silicon Valley because of the fame from my work. (Actually, if I could just get a break from this divorce and have the time to do it, I could already start moving in the elite social circles in Silicon Valley.) And so even though our kids will only be moderately well off, their friends are likely to be very wealthy, and when they get into young adulthood they will absorb some of that wealth I am sure. Let them have these social advantages you and I never had. Your terms are in your interest and not in their interest. Propose some more moderate proposal please if your heart is not in going back to Russia. Even your attorney does not think six thousand dollars a month is reality based. Let's find a potted plant to mediate and discuss things, OK? Why do you think I will settle for what you are proposing? Because you love the children more than you hate me."

On July 2, Hans wrote Nina, "I don't think you are evil because you are shrewd, I think you are evil because you cannot help what you are."

On July 15, Nina asked that Hans be held in contempt of court for failing to pay medical expenses and the costs of summer school and a babysitter. Hans was making more than ten thousand dollars a month but was paying nothing, Gordon wrote. The attorney provided an overview of Hans's intransigence to date over everything, from refusing to agree on a psychologist or evaluators. Hans flatly rejected anyone who he believed had a bias against violent video games, and doctors linked to UC Berkeley counted among them. At least two potential evaluators had decided not to take the case after speaking to Hans. After Smernes was appointed, Hans sought to disqualify her and asked that Dennis Robles be appointed. When his motion was denied, Hans took Rory to see Robles anyway. Robles said he saw no signs of any problems with Rory, Hans reported.

Gordon wrote that Hans refused to enroll Rory at Joaquin Miller in his neighborhood even when it was better than the one where Nina lived. Hans suggested taking the kids to a third-world country where tutors who were leading experts in their fields could teach the children.

In short, "Hans has refused to agree on summer programs, or really ANYTHING AT ALL concerning the children," Gordon wrote.

CHAPTER 20

> POLICE: GET A GUN

The Oakland Police Administration Building sits on Seventh Street near Broadway alongside smog-choked Interstate 880, adjacent to a courthouse and a jail. In the 1860s, the street corner was part of the city's original downtown, where visitors in suits and petticoats disembarked from the Central Pacific Railroad station to visit the shops nearby. The old station still stands, but the passengers are long gone, replaced by clients at a bail bonds office handing over money to spring their loved ones from jail.

Nina walked into the cavernous marble lobby of the police station on the afternoon of July 20 with Rory and Nio in tow. The three waited for forty-five minutes, but Hans failed to show up to pick up the kids. Nina asked the desk officer to make a note that Hans never came. Nina called Beverly, but she didn't know where he was, either. Nina later learned from her mother-in-law that Hans hadn't had an emergency or any other reason to have missed having the kids that night. Hans would claim that he had asked his mom to call Nina to arrange for a later pickup and that Nina didn't answer her cell phone.

Oakland police officer Ben Denson was in the twilight of his career, having served twenty-seven years in a department that had also counted his two brothers as members. Denson witnessed a number of exchanges of Rory and Nio while working the patrol desk in 2005. Hans would play with his children for about fifteen minutes, tossing them up in the air and swinging them around. Nina would give her kids a big hug before leaving them with their father. "My impression was that she was a caring, loving mother," Denson later recalled.

But the enmity between Hans and Nina was palpable. "It was almost an ever-present thing," Denson remembered later. "They rarely talked for any length of time, but when they did engage in face-to-face conversation, it was my impression—this is what I observed—[Hans] displayed hostility toward Nina, and I would call it barely restrained aggression."

Although the two never came to blows, Hans seemed particularly upset during one visit and loomed over her. "He never put his hands on her but, you know, I could tell by the way he was looking at her, there was menace in his eyes. It was very hostile," Denson said. Hans didn't care if the police were right there

That's when Denson gave Nina some chilling advice: "You need to get yourself a gun."

PART FOUR

>NEW PROSPECTS

CHAPTER 21

> ANTHONY ZOGRAFOS

In a way, Anthony Zografos found himself in a situation similar to Hans. His wife of ten years had filed for divorce in 2004, saying he yelled and scared their two children and denigrated her in front of them and others. If the kids acted up, Zografos overreacted, imposing long "time-outs" or demanding that his son write an essay on why he appreciated his father, she wrote in her filing. When she tried to intercede, Zografos yelled at her to "stay out of it," telling her that she didn't know how to properly discipline their son.

She accused him of kidnapping their four-year-old daughter in October 2004 during a dispute in which the two had argued over the children's U.S. and Greek passports. Zografos denied that he had tried to kidnap his daughter. Zografos said his wife had taken the passports away, and he wanted them back. He came to her house and said he wanted to take the kids to the movies. But his wife and her friends prevented him from taking his son. He left with his daughter, prompting his wife to call police. He immediately returned with his daughter when an officer called him on his cell phone. The girl was very clingy and had trouble eating after the incident, her mother reported. Two weeks later, he came to her home uninvited, saying he had the "absolute right" to do that and stay whenever he wished.

Like Hans, Zografos had also attended UC Berkeley. But any similarities ended there. Hans was a geeky American computer expert who was now losing his once-trim physique. Zografos was a handsome, foreign-born entrepreneur with an exotic Greek accent. He seemed to be quite a catch for Nina.

Nina had placed an ad on Craigslist seeking playdates for

Rory and Nio. In the summer of 2005, she got a response from Zografos, whose son was nine by that time and his daughter seven. Nina and Zografos exchanged e-mails for a while and soon agreed to meet July 31 at a café near College and Claremont avenues in Oakland. Zografos was stunned by her beauty when he met her in person—and struck by how she looked a lot like his estranged wife. "I thought she was gorgeous. She was very well-put together," Zografos said later of Nina. "I thought, 'a single mother of two kids does not look like that.'"

The two bought coffee, but Nina took only a sip, if at all. Nina said she wasn't looking for a relationship. She didn't mention Sturgeon, whom she was still dating at the time. Zografos told her that he wasn't looking for a companion, either, as he was going through a divorce. "But I'll make an exception for you," he thought to himself. They left with plans to get their kids together.

During the divorce proceedings, Hans's programmers rallied on his behalf, even as they complained that their pay wasn't ideal. "We produce free software," programmer Vladimir Saveliev wrote in August 2005. "Hans is not always to pay us well for this, but we have understood that he pays what he can, and the production of free software is more charity than business, so we are willing to sacrifice major portions of our life for a good cause at not the best rate of pay that could be gotten." Saveliev reported that some employees even had to loan Hans money from the salaries that were owed them.

McGothigan said the Reisers' divorce was a "train wreck, start to finish," adding, "Nina really tried to clean him out. I thought that was mean-spirited of her. I thought that she could have been a little more gracious." But Sturgeon was quick to defend Nina, saying that the blame fell squarely on Hans, who "assaulted Nina and spewed insane megalomaniacal hate in words and ink for years."

Nina complained to Hans in an e-mail on August 24 that they could be using the money they were spending for Safe Exchange on the kids. She suggested continuing to exchange the kids at Oakland police headquarters or having his mother serve as an intermediary.

Hans responded that he preferred Safe Exchange to the

police station. And he told her that it wasn't safe for her to be around his mother. "She is probably the only person I know that you could physically beat up," he said in an e-mail. "She might be tougher mentally, and maybe that might overcome her physical disadvantage in a fight with you, but I will not risk her safety." Hans invoked World War II. "It is June 1941, and you are the Nazis, and you think we will not suffer the necessary amount to defeat you. We will."

He wasn't finished. "Children are not people you care about, for you they are just tools you use to obtain societal importance and leverage over men. You don't care about anyone, which is why you are so perfect in imitating niceness. If Sean, or any other man, wants you, he should pay for you. You cost much more than you are worth in my view. Best of all would be if you paid for yourself. Give it a try; you'll be a better person in ten years if you do."

> Hurricane Katrina made its second landfall as a Category 3 storm on August 29, 2005. The levee system in New Orleans failed disastrously, flooding most of the city and forcing a million people in the metro area to flee. Images of poor Louisianans pleading to be rescued from their rooftops and jamming into the Astrodome were seared into the nation's consciousness. Firefighters from the Bay Area and across the country converged along the Mississippi coast to help.

On Labor Day weekend 2005, Sturgeon and Nina decided to do their part by organizing donations via Craigslist and church and from others in the alternative community. While Sturgeon drove more than forty hours to New Orleans, Nina stayed behind in Oakland, helping with communications. In an e-mail to volunteers on September 5, 2005, Nina introduced herself as "Sean's girlfriend" and said she'd be posting regular updates from him. Sturgeon was overwhelmed by Nina's selflessness. Consumed with stress over custody evaluation tests, here she was, helping others left stranded by a natural disaster, manning the phones and serving as a point of contact. This only deepened Sturgeon's feelings for Nina, whom he regarded as his beacon.

But Nina proved to be the light in two men's lives: she soon began dating both Sturgeon and Zografos.

In early September, Zografos and his two children joined Nina, Rory and Nio for a trip to the Renaissance Faire. "She looked unreal, unbelievably good," Zografos recalled. In the parking lot, someone saw Nina and the four photogenic kids walking toward the fair's entrance and commented, "What a good-looking family!" Zografos, who had been lagging behind the group, felt left out. He ran up to join them and said with a smile, "I'm with them!"

It felt so right. Zografos was taken by Nina, whom he found irresistible. And everywhere the two went, people assumed that they were a couple. In November, Zografos told Nina, "You know what? I mean, wherever we go, everybody calls us like a family, right? I mean, we're just like a couple." He asked her if she wanted to have a relationship with him. Nina was hesitant. The divorce was ongoing, the custody issue was still up in the air—and she was still seeing Sturgeon.

Zografos and Nina were still just friends that September when he went over to her house to watch a movie. The next thing he knew, her door opened, and in walked Sturgeon. "Who the hell is that?" Zografos wondered. Nina said, "Hi, Sean." Sturgeon responded, "You should have told me that you had company," and left. That would be the first time Zografos heard the name Sean. It would be far from the last.

Nina told Zografos shortly after that incident that Sturgeon was into S and M, was addicted to pain pills as a result of surgeries to repair a 1997 shoulder injury and that she could not have a relationship with Sturgeon for those reasons. He had a lifestyle that was unacceptable to her, and their relationship wasn't working, she told Zografos. Still, Nina continued to see Sturgeon.

On the night of September 7, Hans called Alameda County's child-abuse hotline to report his belief that Nina had Munchausen by proxy disorder based upon his own research and knowledge about how people with the disorder behave. Nina believed Rory, then five, was suffering from traumatic stress disorder and dissociative disorder because of playing too many violent video games. Hans told screener U-Sef

Barnes that Nina's allegations were nonsense and that Rory was simply affected by the ongoing divorce proceedings. Hans said his son was normal, mentally healthy and brighter than most boys but a little lazy when it came to schoolwork.

Hans said Rory was taking two different medications leading up to his ear surgery, which was now scheduled for September 9. Hans told Barnes that Nina failed to give Rory his medication for two days and was therefore "medically negligent" during that time. Nina later wrote in an e-mail to Hans that she had run out of medication and that in any event, the doctors had told her to stop giving them to Rory before his surgery—which again had to be rescheduled.

Hans was on the offensive. On September 8, his attorney, John Fuery, filed a cross-complaint against Sturgeon in Alameda County Superior Court, accusing him of alienating the affections of his children and Nina and of working with her to steal Namesys assets. He said the money Sturgeon claimed was still owed him actually belonged to Namesys. Hans wrote in court papers that he didn't want to continue to pay for funds that were stolen from him. He said he refused to be "forced to finance my wife's adulterous relationship and be indebted to Sean."

Among the grounds he listed for the suit were intentional infliction of emotional distress, loss of consortium, intentional interference with prospective business advantage, embezzlement, extortion and civil conspiracy.

Sturgeon's actions were aimed at proving to Nina that he was "a better man" than Hans, he charged. "Sean did willfully and intentionally conspire with my wife and others to try to induce my wife to steal my business and clients and he did attempt to convince her to do so by drugging her, seducing her and conspiring with her to steal my business and clients. Sean did influence, cajole, manipulate, conspire and intentionally act to steal money from my business individually and in concert with my wife and others to steal from me individually and to steal company assets."

Hans also attacked the "death yoga" agreement he had signed with Sturgeon and accused him of forcing him to participate in an "illegal and possibly fatal activity," saying it had the purpose of "slowing down one's heart to the point of death." With Hans "out of the picture" from death yoga, Sturgeon would then "take over as my wife's spouse and my children's 'real' father," he wrote.

As if she didn't have enough to deal with, Nina learned that the children were still playing the *Shadow Magic* video game. In a September 11 e-mail, she wrote Hans, "I wanted to remind you that *Shadow Magic* is one of the games which we specifically discussed during mediation with Dr. Hodson, the evaluation with Mrs. Smernes and court hearings and that children should not be allowed to play this game. It has also come to my attention that your secretary has been ordering copies of credit-card statements in my name. I would like to discourage her to do so because it is illegal. I have provided you with all the documents you have requested so far. If you need more papers please submit a request through your lawyer and I will provide whatever is needed promptly. Take care, Nina."

On September 12, Nina sent Hans an e-mail about why Rory's adenoidectomy, now six months overdue, was required. She noted that lymphoid tissue in the adenoids grow not because of allergies, as Hans believed. "If it was, all the asthmatics would have large adenoids, but they don't. Adenoids and tonsils in small children get enlarged because of a unique upper respiratory infection." Their son's problem "has to be cured surgically," she wrote. "I know you seem to believe that he is absolutely allergic to dogs and cats because you are, but Rory is not you and is not your clone, and allergies have different mechanisms in different people."

On September 14, Nina blasted Hans in an e-mail for discussing details of Rory's surgery instead of leaving it up to a nurse using child-appropriate books and materials. "You have completely disregarded this and gave Rory information which is not accurate and not even appropriate and ethical in these circumstances," she wrote. "Telling Rory that some patients can die from poorly given general anesthesia and using as an example the fact that Russian government used poisonous gas on terrorists and hostages in a Moscow theater was inappropriate. Telling Rory that a doctor will cut his head open during the surgery was inaccurate. Why do you do this? Do you really think that it helps Rory?"

Rory needed therapy because of Hans's anesthesia comment, Nina said.

"Hans, I don't think that we both should be present at the medical facility with Rory at the same time. Last time I saw you, you were verbally abusive and called me a thief and a liar during several hours of mediation. I don't want to create a hostile situation in the hospital with Rory present. I also think that asking a child who he wants to go home with him after he has surgery is a bad idea. It will create a loyalty conflict for him and add stress on the day of the surgery." But the surgery, which had been rescheduled for September 16, was canceled yet again to let the attorneys sort out the issues.

> Zografos had his camera in tow on September 25, when he and Nina went to Head Over Heels Gymnastics in Emeryville to celebrate Rory's sixth birthday, which would actually be three days later. Nina had on the same sundress as the first day they met. She wore a big smile as she brought a cake to the twenty-thousand-square-foot gym, which had been adorned with balloons and decorations. Rory and his friends romped around on trampolines, swung on ropes and jumped into a seven-foot-deep foam pit. Rory did the "crab walk." Nina smiled and tended to the kids, at one point jumping with them on the mats barefoot.

The gym, located within a stone's throw of the famed Pixar Animation Studios, played music that was quite outdated, including 1980s hits like Debarge's "Rhythm of the Night," Kenny Loggins's "Footloose," Michael Jackson's "Billie Jean" and Whitney Houston's "I Wanna Dance with Somebody." Nina was probably having too much fun to notice that Pat Benatar's "Love Is a Battlefield" was playing in the background at one point.

The kids were having a blast.

Zografos zoomed in on Rory and asked him how old he was.

"Six," he said.

"Are you sure?" Zografos asked.

"Yeah."

"Show me six," Zografos challenged.

Rory held up seven fingers, and Zografos called him out on it.

"I'm six," Rory insisted.

"OK, if you insist," Zografos said.

The kids sang "Happy Birthday" to Rory as Nina beamed.

On Rory's birthday, on September 28, his class at Grand Lake Montessori had a birthday circle. Nina told the children about each year of his life. Rory brought a gift to the class, a book entitled, *Biggest Ever Book of Questions and Answers*.

Sincere Nitonde, Rory's teacher, adored Nina. Nina always asked how Nitonde was doing, knowing that the teacher was from Africa and was in California alone. When Nitonde got an ear infection, she asked Nina about what kind of medications she could take. Nina gave Nitonde a gift of wooden dolls that stacked inside each other.

By then, Nitonde had nothing good to say about Hans. She had seen him throwing a child up in the air at the school, and it wasn't Rory or Nio. "I told him that it wasn't safe to swing her around or throw her up in the air," Nitonde said. Hans was not happy. He had some unkind words for her in response. Hans would later complain to the administration, accusing Nitonde of not being a capable teacher, that Rory had been bored in her class and that he didn't trust her. It wasn't long before Nitonde would physically move closer to other teachers in the yard when they saw Hans driving up in his car. She was terrified of him. Others at the school had noticed his anger and hostility to the point that Helen Campbell, the head of Grand Lake Montessori, decreed that no teacher would meet Hans alone.

In October 2005, the same month Rory finally had his ear surgery, Hans filed a crime report with Oakland police against Sturgeon. "Sean Sturgeon has been attempting to blackmail me using IRS-related threats. He has been going through my mail. He is mentally decaying and on drugs (Vicodin). He wants to be around my children. Please send an officer to talk to him. The blackmail is an effort to get me to allow him around my children. He is dangerous. He is heavily into S and M.

He should not be around my children. He used to be an S and M pimp and prostitute." Once again, on the report, under physical description of the responsible, Hans got creative. "Pale complexion, ugly," he wrote. Sturgeon said the allegations were false and that the police never contacted him.

Smernes, the child-custody evaluator, wrote in November 2005 that Hans's "motives and sudden claims that Mr. Sturgeon was 'dangerous' are suspect. This evaluator is not concerned with Mr. Sturgeon's reported sexual practices among adults." Smernes noted that Rory and Nio were "delightful, creative, sociable children. Despite their parents' difficulties, Rory and Niorline show many signs of having been parented well. They are very resilient, as children often are, and display minimal behavioral concerns despite the intensity of their parents' conflict."

At a hearing on December 5, 2005, Hans and Nina agreed to waive trial and adopt Smernes' recommendations. Nina achieved sole legal custody for all matters, including medical, educational and welfare issues. She was granted a one-year civil restraining order whereby Hans would stay one hundred yards away from her. "The parties may communicate by e-mail concerning the children," Judge Ronni MacLaren wrote in her formal order in January 2006. "Also, the parties may communicate by phone to report any emergencies concerning the children. In exchange, Petitioner agrees to withdraw her request for the temporary domestic violence restraining order to become a permanent order." The judge ordered Hans to pay one thousand dollars a month in child support, retroactive to March, 50 percent of child care and medical costs for Rory and Nio and their tuition at Grand Lake Montessori. Nina dropped her request for a contempt charge against Hans, who was represented by his new attorney, Linda Cox-Cooper. The children were not to have any contact with Sturgeon. Because of this decision, Nina broke it off with Sturgeon. Sturgeon felt that she had broken her word. But no matter what happened, he would always be her wolf.

As for Hans, it seemed as if no one attorney would always be there for him. By the end of December, Hans had dropped Cox-Cooper. In came Greg Silva, his fourth lawyer.

Now that the custody issue was settled, Nina told Zografos that she wanted to have a relationship with him. The two began dating several days before Christmas. Nina told Zografos about her situation with Hans. Nina liked to call Zografos "Tiger," and the two enjoyed trips together to Lake Tahoe, where they bundled up while riding a Ski-Doo. It was Nina's first time on a snowmobile. She could barely get it to move. Then, as they came to the first turn, she floored it. The next thing Zografos knew, they had tumbled off into the snow and the snow-mobile had landed on top of them.

Zografos and Nina became inseparable. Hardly a day passed that the two didn't see each other. Each day, the two spoke on the phone at least a half a dozen times and sent each other at least a dozen e-mails or text messages They usually were not together on Tuesdays, when Nina took Rory and Nio to Russian lessons.

Despite the fun they had, there was still an uneasiness in Zografos. Nina was still hanging around Sturgeon and other people at the same time. The people she hung out with were "worlds apart from me," Zografos later said.

Then there were her kids. Zografos was uncomfortable with the fact that both of them called their mother a liar and said she wanted to steal their dad's money. They called her a control freak and said she had lied to a judge. Zografos didn't know what to make of this.

Although Sturgeon was ordered not to be around Rory and Nio, he was still very much in Nina's life. In January 2006, Zografos was at Nina's house watching a movie. All of a sudden, Sturgeon came in the door. It was a repeat of what had happened four months earlier. Sturgeon couldn't believe it. Sturgeon walked over to Zografos and asked him, "Where's your son?" Zografos had no idea why Sturgeon was referring to his son, but silently, he seethed. Keeping his cool, Zografos calmly replied, "My son is at home." Nina pulled Sturgeon outside. The two had some kind of discussion. When Nina returned, she showed Zografos the key she had taken from Sturgeon. "That was it. I took the key from him," she said, promising it wouldn't happen again. It wasn't until later that

Zografos learned that Nina had told Sturgeon that she had planned to hang out with Zografos and his son.

Hans and Nina continued to battle over logistics in court. Nina wanted to insulate their kids from the process as much as possible. In an e-mail on January 18, she wrote to Hans, "I suggest *Hoodwinked* at Grand Lake Theater to accommodate Nio, who does not want to watch *Duma*. Want to meet at 5 for chicken noodle soup at Pho Place on East 18th? Miss Saigon is closed on Wednesdays. I'd like to make an argument that all our meetings and outings remain confidential and are solely for the purpose of establishing civilized relationships between kids and us and cannot be used for any legal purposes. See you soon and have a good day. Nina."

It irritated Zografos that Nina still had a connection to Sturgeon. On the weekend before April 15, Nina told Zografos she was going to take some time to help Sturgeon with his taxes. Exasperated, Zografos told her, "Whatever. Go do his taxes." Later that day he went to pick her up, and she wasn't there. But soon Nina and Sturgeon pulled up together in a car. They got out with plants in hand. Zografos was upset. He wondered why Nina told him that she was doing taxes instead of gardening with Sturgeon. Sturgeon said he quickly got out of the car and was walking toward his vehicle when Zografos shouted at him, "You got a problem with me?" Sturgeon stopped and walked back to Zografos and replied, "Yeah, I got a f—problem with you, but it'll be in June when it gets resolved, when Nina will make a decision as to who she will be with." Sturgeon got right into Zografos's space, and Nina got upset. "This is what you're leaving me for?" Sturgeon growled before leaving. Nina confronted Zografos afterward and asked why he had challenged Sturgeon. Zografos said he saw the opportunity to try to clear the air, and he took it. But Nina thought Zografos was acting like a bully, according to Sturgeon.

CHAPTER 22

›REVAMPING THE SYSTEM

Hans, meanwhile, was convinced that the county's family court system was placing his children in harm's way. In December 2005, he had launched a one-man campaign, standing outside the Alameda County Administration Building in downtown Oakland and asking people to sign his petition to overhaul what he deemed was a broken system. He met county supervisor Gail Steele during this effort. Although the supervisor did not sign his petition, the two had a ten-minute chat. They immediately bonded. Steele, whose grandchildren were about the age of Hans's kids, had a soft spot for children who were at risk, were in foster care or were caught in the juvenile justice system. Each year, she organized a tree-planting memorial for children who had lost their lives to violence. And every time a child was murdered, she asked that county flags be lowered to half-staff.

By January 2006, Hans had developed a rapport with Steele and was giving suggestions to her on how to get her grandson to come visit: show him how to cook candies and desserts. He also gave her a recipe for making marshmallows. "If you sprinkle in a few drops of food dye, they can do a beautiful swirl," he wrote. "Another important trick is to not beat the marshmallows to where they are as hard as the store-bought ones. As I found out accidentally as a child, they actually taste better if they are a bit gooey."

Now, nearly four months later, Hans sought out Steele again. On April 28, he donated two thousand dollars toward Steele's reelection campaign, even though he owed twelve thousand in child-support payments and his Patelco Credit Union account balance was only eight hundred and twelve dollars. Hans tried to cover up the payments, which Steele hadn't solicited, by using money orders. He needed Steele desperately. It didn't matter that he didn't live in her district, which included the cities of Hayward, Newark, Union City and parts of Fremont in the east San Francisco Bay Area.

Hans may have given Steele money and tips about how to handle children, but he could have benefited from a little bit of both himself. Teachers noticed that when Hans brought the kids to school, sometimes their hair wasn't combed and they hadn't been bathed or he forgot to pack their lunch, even after being reminded to do so. Rory would report that he had candy in the morning, and Hans was told not to do that.

Nina was having no such problems when it came to preparing the kids for school. In celebration of Easter, Nina, Marni Hunter, whose daughter was in the same class as Rory at Grand Lake Montessori, and other parents helped the kids create Easter bags, dye eggs and decorate cupcakes. The parents also threw a surprise bridal shower for one of Rory's teachers, Deserae McClindon. The children made a wedding gown for her out of toilet paper and toasted her with apple cider. They then had an Easter egg hunt in a campus garden tended to by Helen Campbell, the head of the school.

In April 2006, Hans went to a party for Grand Lake Montessori parents in the Oakland hills. A group of them was making small talk when Hans made a strange remark. He said Nina and his family were a "financial burden" and that he'd be better off financially if he didn't have to take care of them, according to Clare Conry-Murray, whose son was best friends with Rory. Hans wasn't joking. The parents were aghast at the vehemence of his remarks. Conry-Murray remembered how Nina had said Hans was "not that nice of a guy," and Hans's comments at the party "sort of confirmed she was right," she said.

Conry-Murray said she brought her son over to Nina's house on Forty-ninth Street, and Nina, without hesitation, offered to babysit him. "I managed to get some grocery shopping done. It was typical of her," she said. "She already had two kids she was watching all by herself, and she was helping me."

Nina came to Conry-Murray's son's fifth birthday party that spring at Tilden Park in the Berkeley hills. When the party was over, Andrew Conry-Murray and his wife were busy getting things cleaned up. By then, they had welcomed a second boy into their family. Nina took their infant son and held him, cooing to him to make him laugh. She took a group of kids on a little hike nearby to give the Conry-Murrays a chance to clean up. "It was just another example of what a good person she was," he said.

Clare Conry-Murray never saw Hans the first year that their kids attended Grand Lake Montessori. "The second year, I saw him like a handful of times," she said. "I thought it was strange because our kids were basically best friends, but he didn't ever say hi to me."

She said she noticed that Rory "was a little bit troubled." In class, he would rearrange things, putting things where they didn't belong. Yet he'd be proud, as if he'd accomplished something. Monica MacDonald, a teacher at the school, noticed that some of the behavioral problems she had seen in Rory in 2004 had returned. He told her to "Shut up" and said, "I don't need to listen to you, you're a woman and women shouldn't have their rights in this country." MacDonald said later, "They were odd remarks for a six-year-old." Rory also drew pictures with "a lot of guns and a lot of dead people and violence," she said. Asked about the pictures, the boy told teachers that this was what he saw while playing video games at Hans's house.

Hans further alienated himself when he accused Nina of falsely claiming that Rory had weakness in his fingers, causing him to have problems learning how to write. In an e-mail he sent to school officials, Hans said the real reason for any calligraphy problems was that Rory thought writing "is boring and uninteresting and does not want to learn it. I told him not to grip the pencil too tightly and to relax and enjoy what he is doing."

Hans paid a visit to Rory's class and told Rory that he would give him a root beer if he did his cursive. To his surprise, and with McClindon watching, Rory told Hans that his wrist was sore. Hans worried if he could have been wrong. Hans took

Rory out into the hallway to have a little talk. "Would it be better if we did it a different day?" Hans asked. "Yes," Rory said, and his father said they would. But then Rory asked if he could still have the root beer. "On that different day, when you do your cursive," Hans told him. But Rory said he wanted the root beer. Hans asked him if he wanted to do his cursive today after all, and Rory said yes. He wrote cursive nonstop for almost an hour, with a break for pencil sharpening.

In a May 5 e-mail to the school, a triumphant Hans wrote about his classroom visit. Hans had long dared Nina, therapists, psychologists—anyone—to reproduce Rory's problems right in front of him, as if his son were a lab rat at the center of a scientific experiment. Now Hans had taken matters into his own hands by interrupting his son in the middle of class and commandeering and observing him like a guinea pig. But it was worth it. Hans now had irrefutable proof—by way of empirical data that he so cherished—that Rory was normal.

"I asked Rory to do cursive for forty-five minutes straight without any pause. I assume you will agree that is sufficient to completely dispel any possible notion that he has any weakness of the grip. He did it on the first attempt. I must say, he completely despises learning cursive now, but he did it in hopes of settling the issue. I think there is no task in this world he dislikes more, perhaps not even cleaning his room." Hans was proud of what he did and was expecting some kind of thanks.

Instead, Campbell responded in a terse e-mail that same day to memorialize her displeasure with Hans having used his son as a prop. "Please refrain from visits where you become the director instead of the observer," she wrote. "The classroom setting is not appropriate. You are welcome to schedule visits where you follow your children's interests by observing politely and not disrupting the classroom or the teachers from their activities."

> On May 8, Gordon filed a contempt citation over allegations that Hans had not paid his fifty-fifty share of $3,515.89 in uninsured medical expenses. Naturally, Hans denied the

allegations and threw it all back on Nina, accusing her of racking up exorbitant charges with sprees at stores like Bloomingdale's. "Nina's general approach to life in America is, if it is on the shelf in the store, she should have it," Hans wrote.

His divorce attorney, Greg Silva, deposed Nina beginning on May 25, 2006. Over the course of several sessions that summer, the attorney grilled her about her financial circumstances. Hans wanted Silva to ask her about much more and barraged his attorney with the questions he wanted asked: What were details of her sex life? Did she engage in S and M? Was she molested as a child? Did she have any abortions? Was she a paid whore? Hans had similar questions for Sturgeon. Did he hit Nina during sex and, if so, did she like it? Did they engage in S and M? Was he molested as a child? Did he and Nina have sex in church? His questions bordered on the obsessive.

In June 2006, Hans returned Nio to Nina with a rash, which was caused by his failure to properly bathe her. He had previously noticed an inflammation on Nio two years earlier.

That same month, Nina pulled Rory and Nio out of Grand Lake Montessori. Hans wasn't paying her child support, and she could no longer afford the tuition.

On July 4, Nina and her kids went to Russia for their annual vacation. During the trip, they visited the Crimea along the beautiful Black Sea coast. Sharanova gave her daughter a gift, a gold ring with four green stones. It looked like a butterfly. Nina's biological father worked as a doctor in the resort city of Sochi, but she didn't visit him. Nina confided in her mother that she didn't think she would marry Zografos, because she thought he would return to his wife. Zografos's wife had written Nina an e-mail saying she had ruined their marriage, even though Zografos and Nina had gotten together after his estranged wife had filed for divorce. Zografos's wife warned Nina that he would leave her, too, when she got older.

Hans kept busy that summer, trying to change the family law system. He sent an e-mail to Supervisor Steele on July 10, one that would later haunt those involved in the case. He outlined a "methodology study proposal" in which the family law system could be revamped by the Alameda County

Board of Supervisors, with input from Dr. Herbert A. Schreier at Children's Hospital Oakland. Hans railed at how unfair it was to be falsely accused of domestic violence. "What effect does this have on the psychology of falsely accused men?" he wrote. "Does inaccurate punishment damage the psychology of those punished and increase the likelihood of later real domestic violence?"

He said Dr. Schreier, an expert in Munchausen by proxy disorder, should solicit input from the public, such as civil rights groups and "news venues that take an interest in the judiciary (e.g., *The Bill O'Reilly Show*, the *San Jose Mercury News*, etc.)."

Nina and the kids flew back to Oakland via New York's JFK International Airport on July 23, 2006.

Under an agreement reached over the summer, because Nina had custody of the kids during the three weeks she was in Russia, Hans then had custody of the kids for the next three weeks, from July 24 to August 14. Afterward, they would have the kids for alternate weeks.

Hans plowed ahead with his plan and met with Steele and members of her staff at her office on July 27.

Nina, meanwhile, wanted to get her finances in order. She met with bankruptcy attorney Darya Druch on August 9. Nina wanted to file for Chapter 7 as quickly as possible. She now owed $83,000 on her credit cards, of which $75,000 was joint debt with Hans and the remaining $8,000 was personal debt. She listed $62,740 in assets, including a $7,000 bank account, a $3,500 account with her landlord, $40 in cash on her person, artwork, $1,000 in jewelry and her 2001 Honda Odyssey with a blue-book value of $16,000. Nina said she had an interest in Namesys but didn't think there would be anything there for her. The two set up a meeting for September 20 to discuss filing the bankruptcy petition.

Nina applied for several jobs that summer. In response to ads she found on Craigslist, she sent out a letter and résumé expressing interest in becoming a San Ramon Health Center director, program director at the Golden Castle Adult Day Health Care Center and program manager for the National Kidney Foundation of Northern California. She also considered a position as project manager for the San Francisco Health Plan.

On August 10, Nina walked into the Ocean Park Health Center in San Francisco. She had seen an ad on Craigslist for a job at the San Francisco Department of Public Health to help Russian-speaking immigrants as part of a project called "Let's Be Healthy." As project director, she'd be responsible for creating healthy-lifestyle activities for the immigrants, such as putting together walking groups and cooking classes as well as developing a media campaign encouraging immigrants to change their diets or lifestyles. "Desirable qualities include a Masters in Public Health or related field, and a Russian-speaker or experience with Russian-speaking newcomer community," the job description read. Nina was particularly excited about this position. She met with Patricia Erwin, a project manager with the public-health department, and Mary Jo Williams, associate executive director of Bay Area Community Resources.

> Beverly was worried. Her grandkids would be going to Joaquin Miller Elementary School for the first time in a couple of weeks. On August 11, she left Nina a voice-mail message on her cell phone. "Hi Nina, this is Beverly. I think it would be wise if you took the children back before school started on the 28th so they'll arrive at school on time and suitably dressed, et cetera. Hans just doesn't have much of a sense of those things. And I can provide you with the—they asked for utility bills and documents showing the address; I can provide those for you—but they, they asked for a bunch of other documents to have anything to do with immunizations and all of that stuff, which I, you need to take care of, because I know Hans won't do it. So anyway, could you give me a call back? Bye-bye."

Nina loved her home on Forty-ninth Street. But she wanted a bigger place and at the same time wanted to save money. On August 12, she responded to an ad on Craigslist and expressed interest in a shared-housing arrangement, although she admitted that she had never lived in that kind of a situation with kids. She described herself as "professional, divorced, with excellent references, MD from Russia trying to get licensed in the U.S. My kids are well-behaved, but active, they live with me 75%." She said she wanted to find a place in an Oakland neighborhood like Montclair, Rockridge, off Piedmont "or any other nice area."

On Monday, August 14, Gordon sent an urgent fax to Silva, saying Hans believed he had the kids again that week. But Gordon said that conflicted with the schedule that had been set back in May when Silva deposed Nina. Gordon said this week was Nina's turn to have the kids and that Hans would have the kids the week of August 21, specifically beginning at 4:00 p.m. the Sunday before until 4:00 p.m. Sunday August 27.

"I would appreciate if you could speak to Hans about this, making sure the parties don't have to have any unpleasant scenes," Gordon wrote. "Nina picked up the kids from science camp today and will continue to have them this week."

School would begin Monday, August 28, and that week Nina would have the kids. Hans apparently had plans for a trip and didn't think missing the first day of school—a new one, at that—was a big deal. But Nina and Gordon disagreed strenuously and even threw him a bone by allowing him to be there for the important milestone. "Nina and Hans can both enjoy this big occasion, but please make sure he understands that he cannot extend his vacation to include the first day of school," Gordon wrote to Hans's attorney.

According to the schedule, Nina would have the kids Labor Day weekend.

On August 16, Silva responded to Gordon's contempt motion, saying Hans was complying with the payment schedule that the parties had agreed to. Silva said the contempt claim "is not only inappropriate and unfair but underhanded and deceitful."

That same day, Sturgeon asked to dismiss his suit against Hans after Hans agreed to pay him ten thousand dollars.

As Silva waged war with Gordon, Hans hatched plans for a ballot measure to change the family law system. On August 19, Hans e-mailed Steele to propose that a new Custody Evaluation Department—completely different from family court—oversee child-custody evaluations. If this "institutional framework," one "designed to reduce issues of bias," was successful in Alameda County, then other states and countries could replicate the new system, Hans wrote the supervisor. He suggested that they get endorsements from Ron Dellums, who had been elected Oakland mayor two months earlier, and "other prominent members of the black community. When I was collecting signatures, I found that support among the black community for auditing for discrimination was quite high, higher than any other demographic. There are advantages to living in Oakland." He wrapped it up with a burst of optimism, believing that he was on the cusp of a revolution. "Supervisor Steele, as I look at it, I think this could end up being more important than my two decades of work in computer science, if you decide to back it," he wrote.

He ended by flattering the supervisor. "I enjoyed talking with you," Hans wrote. "It is rare that I meet someone I so immediately like and respect."

On the same day Hans e-mailed Steele, Nina went to the IKEA store in Emeryville to buy a one hundred dollar coffee table. She exchanged the table several days later.

On August 25, Hans pleaded not guilty to the contempt charge before Commissioner Taylor Culver, who told him that he could face jail. Trial was set for October 11. At that hearing, which Nina didn't attend, Hans appeared to have gained weight. He was also cocky, Gordon thought. It was as if Hans believed he had gained an advantage in the battle, something Nina's attorney didn't see. Because he was in court, Hans canceled a dental appointment for Rory that day in Oakland. Nina had to reschedule two things that day—she set up a new dental appointment for Rory for October 9, and she opted not to take one of several medical licensing exams that day. She decided to wait until she could get a new job lined up. Nina figured it would take three years for her to pass all the exams.

On August 28, the first day of school, Nina wrote a Patelco check for $497.52 to cover six weeks of after-school care for Rory and Nio at Adventure Time at Joaquin Miller school. Nina picked up her kids on Mondays, Tuesdays and Thursdays. Hans picked them up on Wednesdays. Nina and Hans would alternate pickups on Fridays. Whoever would have the kids for the weekend would then drop them off at school on Mondays.

On August 29, Nina went back for a second interview with the San Francisco Public Health Department. This time she met with staff members at the Chinatown Health Center. They liked her and felt that they'd get along with her.

That same day, Beverly steeled herself for the eight-hour drive to Burning Man, the sprawling weeklong bacchanal held each year in Nevada's Black Rock Desert. She hitched a ride with fellow artist Milton Fabert. She had already been to Burning Man many times before with her good friend Mark McGothigan, who had left the day before. Beverly already had her work showcased at gallery shows around the globe, including in Japan, Canada, Germany, the Netherlands and Argentina. But here at Burning Man, it was a whole world unto itself. They would be surrounded by like-minded, nonconformist artists at a retreat that culminated in the torching of a four-story wooden man. The event billed itself as a "temporary community based on radical self-expression and self-reliance."

Beverly had first met McGothigan at Burning Man 1998, when they worked on a project called "Nebulous Entity." At Burning Man 2004, Beverly, McGothigan and Fabert created a "video installation" underneath the structure called "Black Hole of Desire." The project allowed people to "record their desires" for later playback on a round video projection screen mounted on a 10 foot by 10 foot wall. "We are using the metaphor of a black hole—a dense force drawing all matter around it inexorably into it—to portray the human capacity to relentlessly desire, never reaching a point of stasis," according to a description of the piece.

The theme for Burning Man 2006 was "Hope & Fear," and Beverly and McGothigan created the "Hopeandfearometer," a video voting kiosk that asked two questions: "What makes you glow?" and "What dangers do you delight in?" Participants pushed a red or green button, and two computers recorded their hopes and fears for the future. The collected responses were then played back in a "cacophonous medley of random hopes and fears." Beverly and McGothigan marveled that all the electronic systems functioned well even in the hot desert. They were proud to be one of ten featured art installations in the Pavilion of the Future, an art deco palace located right underneath "the man."

On August 30, Hans placed an angry phone call to the Department of Child Support Services to contest a notice he had received in the mail stating that he owed $12,161.08 in child support. Hans demanded a hearing.

By that day, teachers at Joaquin Miller school saw that Rory was having trouble fitting in. In class, he was unfocused and couldn't produce any work. He cried at least three times that week because he couldn't do something, such as thinking of an imaginary animal and drawing it. At lunch, instead of playing with the other children, he kept to himself, walking around with his backpack on and holding a multiplication table, trying to memorize it. Hans showed up at the school that day and told Rory's teacher how to instruct him. She told him that even though Rory was able to memorize the multiplication table, he was too young developmentally to apply it. Instead, she was teaching the kids addition and subtraction as a basis for other math. Rory would later boast that he was the smartest in the class.

On August 31, Nina was offered the San Francisco Public Health Department job. Nina was ecstatic. Her immediate plans for the future seemed to be on track. That day, she signed in at the Kaplan test preparation center in Berkeley to continue studying for her medical licensing exam.

She accepted the job the next day, Friday, September 1. Patricia Erwin, project manager with the Newcomers Health Program at the public-health department, offered Nina a salary of about forty-nine thousand dollars a year, but Nina said she was a single mother and needed more. They agreed on fifty thousand dollars, as well as Nina's request for flexible hours, which would allow her time to pick up her children. The job included health benefits, sick leave and three weeks of vacation the first three years. She agreed to come in September 7 to fill out some paperwork and to get fingerprinted. She would have a meeting on September 15 before reporting for work on September 21. Nina met Doren for coffee and happily told her about the new position. "Everything in her life except for the custody battle was going really well, and she was the most happy, of course, about the new job offer that she had received," Doren remembered. "She was very, very excited."

CHAPTER 23

> LABOR DAY WEEKEND

Although Nina was buoyed by the new job, her spirits darkened when Hans insisted that day, September 1, that it was his turn to have the kids Labor Day weekend. Nina thought otherwise. Silva's office faxed a letter to Gordon, saying although the parents alternate weeks in the summer, Hans had alternate weekends during the school year. School had started on August 28. "Last weekend was technically Nina's weekend but she and Hans exchanged weekends (she already took her weekend switch). Thus, this weekend is Hans's weekend," the letter said. "Hans plans on picking up the children today."

About 1:00 p.m. that day, Nina called Zografos. She told him that Hans was insisting that it was his weekend to have the kids. Nina thought it was her turn because the kids were with Hans the previous weekend. Nina didn't know what to do. Zografos gave her two suggestions—have the attorneys work it out, or talk to Hans and ask to split the weekend. Nina didn't want to bring the attorneys in. That would require an expense. Nina hung up. An hour later, she called Zografos and said Hans had agreed to split the weekend and that she'd drop the kids off at his house on Sunday.

That morning, Yasmin James, an associate of Silva's, left a message with Shelley Gordon, saying there was a problem. That afternoon, Gordon listened to the message and went down the hall to get a drink of water. Several minutes later, she sat back down at her desk and then saw that James had left another voice-mail message saying that Hans and Nina had worked it out.

Hans called Supervisor Steele's office four times over the span of about an hour that afternoon. Hans made one call at

4:35 p.m. that lasted sixteen minutes. A minute after hanging up, he called her office again and was on the line for six more minutes. Neither Steele nor any member of her staff recalled talking to him that day. Steele felt awful, especially when she realized that Hans had left numerous messages with her office earlier in the week. She never heard from Hans again. She wondered if things would have turned out differently if she had called him back.

At 5:00 p.m., Nina took her kids to soccer practice. Marc Prager, Doren's husband, took their kids to the same practice and saw both Hans and Nina there. They were talking and walking to the parking lot together.

At 11:00 a.m. on Saturday, September 2, Zografos drove his kids to Nina's house and dropped them off before doing a quick errand. While Zografos was gone, Nina went on her computer to browse personal ads on Craigslist. On the site, both women and men were reaching out for a mate, often with the sophomoric prose typical of such endeavors. One woman, a forty-seven-year-old from San Francisco, wrote, "How I long to be your passion, to have my pheromones drive you to me with primal urges, seducing me with your exploring gaze." A thirty-seven-year-old single dad posted several sexually explicit images and said he was looking for a "fun naughty woman to play with. Please let me know if you are feeling a bit horny and would like to enjoy yourself some today. Thanks."

After Zografos returned, the six of them piled into her Honda Odyssey and drove to the Montclair Village shopping district, where Nina took Nio to Top Dog and Zografos took the other kids someplace else. They then went to the beach in Alameda. They stayed there until about 5:30 p.m. Zografos took his kids back home for a quick shower and then drove them back to Nina's house an hour later. The six of them walked five blocks to Pasta Pomodoro on College Avenue in Oakland's Rockridge District. There, Nio munched on crayons, which Zografos found disturbing.

That night, Nina called her mom in Russia to tell her about the new job. She was excited about it, telling Sharanova that it was a good fit given her medical background. Nina then said she had to get off the phone to get the children ready for bed.

As the children slept, Beverly and McGothigan and nearly thirty-nine thousand other revelers were three hundred and thirty miles away, cavorting on an ancient lakebed known as the playa. At about 10:00 p.m., a seventy-two-foot wooden effigy was set ablaze.

On Sunday, September 3, the final day of her known existence, Nina told her mother in a phone call that she was very happy about the new job. Her supervisors were really accommodating to her, it fit her schedule and there was insurance. But Nina was worried that she would be unable to pay the rent on her house and said she might have to move. Her stepfather urged her not to move because it was a very good house. Sharanova and Lavrentiev offered to loan her one thousand dollars. Sharanova said she would contact the bank to make arrangements and would call back the next day. But it would be the last conversation the mother and daughter would ever have.

Zografos, meanwhile, was getting ready for his family camping trip. He took his kids to a Safeway store. Zografos's wife preferred a different Safeway and went there. He called Nina at about 11:30 a.m., but she didn't answer. He decided to drive to her house. He rang the bell but got no response. He was leaving a message on her cell when she opened the door. Her hair was still wet. "I was in the back," she said. She invited him inside. Rory was playing computer games. Nio was in her room playing. There were puzzles and children's books on the dining room table. Zografos said he'd be back at about 5:00 p.m. the next day, Labor Day, and he and Nina made plans to meet about 5:30 p.m. for a dinner and movie. He kissed her and turned to leave. He had no way of knowing that Nina had only hours left to live.

PART FIVE

>THE INVESTIGATION

CHAPTER 24

> MISSED CALLS

On Monday, September 4, Ellen Doren figured Nina was spending the day with Zografos. Hans had the kids that day, and they didn't have school because of the holiday.

Sharanova tried several times to reach Nina that day on both her home and cell phone. "My dear, dear, dear little Nina. I cannot reach you by phone," Sharanova said in Russian in a voice-mail message. "I will call you later regarding the bank issue."

In another voice-mail message, Sharanova said, "My dear daughter, you're not picking up either telephone line. We need to speak."

Zografos also repeatedly tried to reach Nina on her cell, only to get her outgoing message. "Hello, you have reached Nina Reiser's voice mail. Please leave me a message, and I will get back to you as soon as I can. Thank you."

"Hi, it's me," Zografos said in the fourth message he left for Nina. "I'm afraid something is wrong and I hope it's not bad. But anyway, I'm worried about you. Can you give me a call when—when—if you get this message? Don't worry about what time it is. I'll probably be here waiting. OK. And I hope everything's OK. And I'll talk to you soon. OK. I love you. Bye."

On the morning of Tuesday, September 5, Hans took his kids to Joaquin Miller Elementary School. In a remark that would be dissected later, Hans told Rory that he would be picking them up that afternoon. It was Nina who usually did that on Tuesdays.

A worried Doren showed up at Adventure Time at about 2:30 p.m. to see if Nina had showed up. A staffer picked up the phone and called Nina. She left a voice-mail message on her cell when she didn't answer. "Hi Nina, this is Claudette from Adventure Time. I have Ellen Doren here to pick up Niorline and I didn't get any message from you or her dad. Niorline's saying that she's supposed to go home with you. Can you please give us a call? I'm going to try to reach Dad and see if he gives permission for her to go with Ellen. OK, thank you. Bye."

At about 5:00 p.m., Hans showed up at the school, looking nervous and appearing hyper. He moved his body from side to side and didn't make eye contact with employee Natalie Potter. Rory saw his dad and ran over to him, but Hans ignored him. Hans said he wasn't there to pick up the kids. Instead, he wanted to set up a meeting to discuss the school's enrollment policies. He didn't say anything about whether he had received the call from Adventure Time.

Hans left the school after writing down the wrong cell phone number on a form that listed people to contact in case of emergency or disaster. It was one digit off. Instead of (510) 316-6306, Hans wrote (510) 316-6036. Potter asked if the children could be released to Doren. "Yeah, yeah, that's fine," he said with a dismissive wave of his hand before leaving. He never asked about Nina.

At 5:04 p.m., he called Nina's cell phone, the reason for which would be disputed later. The call lasted for only six seconds

At 5:15 p.m., Doren returned to the school. Nina wasn't there. Staffers called Nina's cell phone, but it went into her voice mail. Doren picked up Rory and Nio and took them to her home on Capricorn Drive in the Oakland hills. She fed them, and they played for a while. She tucked them in for the night and then went to bed. She had a fitful sleep.

At about 9:00 p.m., Hans got into his mother's Honda Civic hybrid and picked Beverly up from her friend Mark McGothigan's house, on Simson Street near Mills College in Oakland. Beverly and McGothigan had arrived back in Oakland from Burning Man seven hours earlier. Hans looked tired and didn't say anything about Nina being missing. Hans told them that the Honda CRX had a dead battery and that was why he was driving the hybrid. Beverly asked her son where the CRX was and he wouldn't tell her.

At 9:21 p.m., Hans's cell phone rang while he was at McGothigan's house. It was Doren, asking if he knew where Nina was. His statement to her that he needed to talk to his lawyer left her reeling. He didn't ask one question about his kids. She handed the phone to Officer Pressnell. Hans told the officer that it was OK for Doren to keep the children overnight and said that he'd pick them up from school the next day. He refused to say anything else to the officer and referred him to his divorce attorney, Greg Silva. In a little more than five minutes, the call was over.

Hans and his mother drove home. He then did something that was uncharacteristic for him: clean. At about 10:00 p.m., neighbor Jack Stabb was watching a tape of the Giants losing to the Reds. His wife, Cheryl Milton, wanted him upstairs at about that time, so Stabb went outside to water the plants on his deck before going to bed. That's when he saw Hans hosing off the driveway for about a half hour. Even though it was warm, Hans was dressed for winter, wearing what looked like a hooded hunting jacket. It was odd, even for Hans.

The next morning, Wednesday, September 6, Stabb, a building contractor, got into his truck, which was emblazoned with his name, and started to leave. He glanced at Hans's driveway. It didn't look as if he did a good job cleaning up. There were still leaves on it, and the garden hose was still out. Stabb didn't understand Hans. He really didn't like him, either. Hans tended to think that certain parking spots on the narrow street were his. He would tear out of Exeter Drive in his car. The two had exchanged words from time to time. And it didn't help matters that the cat Hans had shot with a bow and arrow years ago had belonged to his wife. Milton also reported something strange: that same week, she tried to speak to Hans in front of her home. Hans wouldn't talk to her and looked down at the ground while bending slightly at the waist. He seemed to be hiding his face from her.

That morning, Hans told his mother that Nina was missing. He said he didn't tell her the night before because he knew she was tired and would be upset. It didn't matter. Beverly was plenty upset when he told her that day. Beverly asked him some questions, but Hans didn't seem to have any information. She called McGothigan, sounding very upset, and said that something terrible had happened—Nina was missing. McGothigan felt like he had been run over. One of his best friends had suffered a stroke before Burning Man. Now Nina was nowhere to be found. He felt like he was trying to cope with two unrelated disasters.

Doren left Hans a voice mail at about 11:40 a.m. Sounding friendly, Doren offered to take Rory and Nio for a playdate. Zografos e-mailed Hans asking about Nina and also offered to set up a playdate. Hans never responded to either Doren or Zografos.

Doren and others continued to try to get ahold of Nina throughout the day. "Nina, where are you?" Doren said in their native tongue. "This is important."

"Nina, this is Shelley," Gordon said in a message. "I'm panicked about your whereabouts like your friends are. Hope you're OK. Bye."

Sturgeon, Nina's ex-boyfriend, checked in. "Hey Nina, Sean here. Uh, please give me a call when you can. Uh, where you at? We're looking for you, and we're worried. Please give us a call—either me or Anthony or Ellen. Love you. Bye."

Sturgeon left a second message that evening. He assumed that Nina and Zografos might have had some kind of disagreement. "I hope you're OK," Sturgeon said. "Obviously, you're still going through stuff with Anthony that I didn't know anything about. I don't know what's up with you. I didn't understand about Anthony still being—well, I don't understand what Ellen was telling me. I understand what Ellen was telling me; I guess all I need to say is if you actually get this and you just have—needed to get away from everything for a while, when you can, call me. And I won't say anything about it to anybody. If you've just gone away for a while to try to get your head together, I understand. I love you. Bye."

Hans left no messages. If he was truly concerned about the welfare of the mother of his children, he wasn't showing it.

Beverly, meanwhile, was trying to make sense of why

Hans kept on using her hybrid, leaving her stranded in the Oakland hills.

On the morning of September 7, four days after Nina had vanished, Hans used the hybrid to take the kids to school. Hans then drove to the law office of noted criminal defense attorney William Du Bois near Sixteenth Street and Telegraph Avenue in downtown Oakland, around the corner from City Hall. Du Bois had been recommended by Silva, who didn't have to look far: both attorneys served on the board of directors of the Alameda County Bar Association.

Hans walked into Du Bois' eleventh-floor office at the Latham Square Building, a historic Beaux-Arts edifice in downtown Oakland that had a sweeping view of the Berkeley and Oakland hills. Framed posters of Malcolm X and Muhammad Ali knocking out Sonny Liston hung on the walls, the message to any would-be clients patently clear: the gloves were off. Hans told Du Bois that his Russian-born wife was missing and that she had passports for her native country. Du Bois' first impression of Hans was that he seemed to be a normal guy, maybe "sort of funny looking." Hans's first impression of Du Bois was that he was a "very likable, avuncular gentleman." Du Bois didn't think there was anything sinister going on. The police would naturally look at Hans as a suspect. All that had to be done was to look out for Hans's interests and make sure he wasn't being railroaded. Du Bois agreed to represent Hans and told him that he wanted him to talk to the police right away, if only to clear his name.

Officer Gill called Hans's cell at 9:51 that morning. "Mr. Reiser, this is Officer Gill, G-I-L-L, with the Oakland Police Department Missing Persons Unit. I'm conducting an investigation trying to locate Nina Reiser. I believe she's your— either your ex-wife or your wife that you're separated from. I'm just trying to find out if anyone knows where she's at. If you could give me a call back at (510) 587-2528. I see in the report that you left your attorney's phone number. I'll try giving him a call and see if he has any information. Thank you. And I'd appreciate a phone call back. Have a great day. Bye."

Gill then called Silva at his office in Alameda. Silva said he was only representing Hans in the divorce and declined to any answer questions about him. Silva told the officer that Hans had retained a separate attorney—Du Bois—for "this case." Gill asked him what he meant by "this case," as this was just a missing-persons report and it was not a crime to be missing. Silva said he didn't know why Hans had retained Du Bois and told Gill to contact Du Bois with any more questions. But Du Bois was in court in Modesto that whole week. Silva said he had spoken to Du Bois, who had said he would call the Oakland Police Department (OPD) when time allowed. Gill felt he was getting the runaround. The average person would do everything in his or her power to find a missing person, and Hans sure wasn't lifting a finger. It should have been a team effort, and they weren't getting any help from a key player.

To cover his bases, Gill left a message on Nina's cell shortly before 11:00 a.m. "Ms. Reiser, this is Officer Gill with the Oakland Police Department. Just trying to get ahold of you. I'm investigating a report that you're missing, so if you get this message, call me back. It's very important. (510) 587-2528. And let me know that you're OK. And if you'd like, give me your location and we can meet, and I'll interview you and close the case. Hopefully, everything is well."

Shortly after noon, Youth and Family Services lieutenant Kevin Wiley told Gill that homicide sergeants Bruce Brock and Tim Nolan were available as the investigators "on standby," responsible for handling all the murders in the city that week. There was no proof that Nina was dead, but the police had to be prepared.

At 1:00 p.m., Officer Herb Webber called with a promising lead: a woman said she had seen Nina at the Walgreens drugstore at Fourteenth and Broadway in downtown Oakland. The missing mother purportedly had told the woman that she had dropped off her car and was on her way to work in San Francisco. But the police later learned that the woman spotted by the tipster had actually been Zografos's estranged wife. Coincidentally, Nina was supposed to have gone to her new job in San Francisco to submit her fingerprints for a background check. Zografos called Nina's new bosses and told them that Nina wouldn't be coming in. There was an emergency.

Webber and Officer Hamann Nguyen went to Nina's house on Forty-ninth Street at 1:45 p.m. After finding the front door locked, they went into the backyard through a wooden gate from the side of the house. They found a window halfway open in the rear bedroom. Webber called Gill, told him that the house was unsecured and asked if he should do a protective sweep of the home. Gill checked with Brock, who said yes. Webber was told to go ahead and do it. No warrant was required because of "exigent circumstances"—the possibility that Nina could be alive in the house and in need of immediate help. The window crank was close enough to open the window completely. Webber called out "Oakland police" and climbed inside, followed by Nguyen. Webber, a former U.S. Army forward observer, drew his gun. His senses were on heightened alert. But the house was empty. Gill called Webber's cell and told him that Officer Shan Johnson and sergeants Brock and Nolan would be joining them at the house. Together, they searched a detached garage and the attic and found nothing.

Brock told Gill that Du Bois had left a message, saying his client would talk by appointment only. "I have information on where you should do a search warrant and what to pick up," Du Bois said. But the attorney said he'd be out of town the next week on the case in Modesto and would be available by cell phone.

Gill tried calling Du Bois' cell phone that afternoon, but it was malfunctioning and wouldn't accept voice mail.

Du Bois got a hold of Gill at one point and promised to make Hans available for an interview. But Du Bois said he couldn't do that immediately because he was out of town.

Later, instead of calling Gill, Du Bois left a message with Oakland homicide sergeant Brian Medeiros, telling him that he was representing Hans. "I know he'll be a suspect as they always are in these cases," Du Bois said. He repeated that he was out of town but would make his client available for an interview. As a frustrated Gill tried to buttonhole Du Bois, he also tried to determine who had picked up the kids from school that day. He didn't know at the time that Beverly had done so. He called her house and left a message asking her to call back.

CHAPTER 25

> OAKLAND POLICE

That afternoon, Oakland police broadcast a "be-on-the-lookout" (BOL) alert on the radio: "BOL for a missing person, possible victim of foul play," a dispatcher intoned from the radio room on Edgewater Drive, on the opposite side of Interstate 880 from the Oakland Coliseum. "Nina Reiser, female white, 31, DOB 11-3-74, 5'5," 114, black hair, brown eyes, last seen wearing a black summer dress with a blue stone necklace. Good physical and mental, associated vehicle 4-Union-Boy-Boy-4-9-1, 2001 Honda van, tan with damage on right-side door. If located, conduct well-being check. The time is now 1543, channel's clear." The alert was broadcast every two hours on the Patrol 1, 2 and 3 police radio channels. Patrol 1 was for the West and North Oakland officers, Patrol 2 for the central part of the city and Patrol 3 was for East Oakland.

In fall 2006, the Oakland Police Department had only seven hundred officers, of which two hundred were assigned to patrol a city of seventy-eight square miles and 397,000 people. Violent crime spiked upward that year, yet there were still only ten homicide investigators—the same number in San Jose, which had one-third less murders. There was an overwhelming backlog of cases that had to be investigated. It still ate at the rank-and-file that there were more officers assigned to internal affairs than to homicide, which was the result of a federal consent decree imposed on the department after the "Riders" misconduct probe in 2000, the worst scandal in recent history. Three officers were arrested and accused of beating suspects, planting evidence and falsifying reports in West Oakland. The defense fought back, saying the officers had simply been following orders by the chief and then mayor Jerry Brown to cut down on crime. Two criminal trials ended in mistrials, but a $10.5 million civil settlement cast a pall over the force and led to numerous reforms. A fourth ex-officer, the alleged ringleader, remains a fugitive and is believed to be in Mexico.

The department was already chronically understaffed to begin with, but Officer Shan Johnson of the Youth and Family Services Division didn't think enough resources were being put into the Reiser case. Some of his superiors seemed to think this could be a "filer," something that could be closed out with a perfunctory search and a police report that would be filed away and forgotten. Johnson, an eight-year veteran, knew that every possible lead had to be investigated aggressively and quickly. He urged that a surveillance of Hans be put into place as soon as possible. If Hans had injured Nina and was holding her captive somewhere, every hour was critical—it could mean the difference between life and death. And if he had killed Nina and hidden the body, it was possible that he could lead a tail straight to it. Department officials signed off on the operation.

In one of Johnson's first official department photos, his hair came down to his neck. It was a fitting look for a man who had traded his skateboard for a surfboard and then a badge. Johnson eventually got his hair cut and landed in the Special Victims Unit (SVU), investigating sexual assaults committed by predators, pimps and even political scions like Ignacio De La Fuente Jr., the namesake son of the president of the Oakland City Council. Tall and angular, Johnson sat in the front row of the gallery and made small talk with reporters before De La Fuente Jr. was led into court.

Fellow SVU officer Mark Battle couldn't be more different than Johnson. Battle was an intense aikido expert who relished working in the shadows. He was a former loss prevention officer at Saks Fifth Avenue who nabbed shoplifters. In his first department photo, Battle's hair was short. But now he had a beard and mustache, and his hair was tied in a ponytail. Battle had honed his skills working as an "under," or undercover officer. Like many Oakland officers who are eager for action and proactive, Battle had seen his share of controversy. In September 2000, Battle was rushing to help other officers chase a fleeing suspect when he crashed into a woman's car at an East Oakland corner. The city paid $2.75 million to the woman, who was left permanently disabled, in what was Oakland's largest lawsuit settlement at the time.

Now, Battle and Johnson were partnered up and assigned to conduct a surveillance of the home where Hans and Beverly lived. At about 7:00 a.m. on September 8, they drove up to Exeter Drive in separate cars. Johnson drove his undercover minivan past the house and saw Beverly's gold Honda Civic hybrid parked in the carport. He parked his car south of the home. At about 8:00 a.m., Johnson slumped down in the seat to avoid being seen as Hans sped past him in the hybrid.

"He's moving," Johnson said into his cell phone to Battle, who was parked on the other side of the house. Johnson lost sight of the car as Hans made numerous turns in the twisty streets of the Oakland hills. Anyone who didn't drive these narrow roadways on a daily basis would easily be confused by the endless Y intersections and hairpin curves snaking through the neighborhood. The officer then lost his cell phone connection because of poor reception, which was also a constant source of aggravation in the area. Battle soon spotted the car at the Joaquin Miller Elementary School, on Ascot Drive. Hans was apparently dropping off his children, because the car was empty. Battle soon spotted Hans walking back toward the car. His head was shaved, and he had a scruffy beard. He was wearing a light T-shirt, sweatpants and a fanny pack. Battle watched as Hans got back in the car and drove to a corner of the parking lot. He stayed there—parked with the engine idling—for several minutes. He appeared to be looking for signs that he was being followed.

Hans then drove to the Montclair Village shopping district and pulled into a parking spot near Mountain Boulevard and La Salle Avenue, the street where he kept a post office box for his business. He walked to Peet's Coffee, bought a cup and read a newspaper. He then got back into the hybrid and drove onto southbound Highway 13, which traced the much-feared Hayward Fault. The officers followed him as he merged onto eastbound Interstate 580. He got off the freeway at Ninety-eighth Avenue and then immediately got back onto westbound I-580, in the opposite direction. It soon became clear that he was driving in a manner commonly referred to as counter-surveillance, backtracking, speeding up and slowing down repeatedly in hopes of revealing or shaking any cops following him.

He continued back onto Highway 13, exited on Mountain Boulevard and then reentered the highway in the opposite direction, going only 10 mph. He again merged onto I-580 and then took the Estudillo Avenue off-ramp in San Leandro. He pulled to the curb on MacArthur Boulevard, just off the freeway. He then made a series of turns on quiet residential streets. Battle and Johnson decided to end their surveillance. They didn't want to risk Hans seeing them. Hans eventually ended up at Du Bois's office, where he paid the attorney a five thousand dollar retainer.

As Hans was driving erratically, Officers Julio Pinzon and Michael Weisenberg went to Beverly's home at about 9:40 a.m. They were nervous about her dog, D'Artagnan, but it stopped yapping. "This is a nice house you have here, ma'am," Pinzon told her.

"Very beautiful house, ma'am," Weisenberg agreed.

"Oh, thank you," Beverly said.

She told them that she was an artist who was at the Burning Man Festival during the Labor Day weekend. She came back on Tuesday and learned the next day from Hans that Nina was missing. Weisenberg asked if she had discussed the disappearance in any detail with her son. She said no.

"Do you have any idea where she might have gone?" Pinzon asked.

"I can't imagine her leaving the children," Beverly said. She suggested that the officers look at Sturgeon as a possible suspect in the case, because he had had an affair with Nina.

She went back to how unusual it was for Nina to be gone. "That would be so atypical of her to leave the children. Something must have happened to her."

She acknowledged that Hans and Nina were incompatible as a couple. Beverly said there was no clothing, mail and other things belonging to Nina at the home now. Beverly rejected the officers' request to take a look around, saying, "I just feel intruded upon." She also said no to them searching the garage for the same reason and noted that a car would not fit in there.

At the end of the forty-minute visit, the officers asked Beverly to sign a piece of paper saying she had made a taped statement. She got confused. "I don't understand what this is," she said.

"That means that besides taking notes, we also had a tape recorder so that in case we miss something—" Weisenberg said.

"OK, but you should have told me that," Beverly interrupted.

"I'm sorry, ma'am," Weisenberg said. "I thought you saw the tape recorder on the table."

"No."

"Oh, I apologize."

Johnson and Battle went back to Joaquin Miller Elementary School at about 10:30 a.m. and showed their police IDs to the staff before taking Rory and Nio into protective custody. Police had feared that Hans would grab them and run. As the children were driven to the Family Justice Center on Twenty-seventh Street in Oakland, Nio spontaneously said, "My dad says my mom tells big lies." Already, the divorce had made its sad mark on the children, and now their lives were in a state of upheaval. The police were haunted by the grim likelihood that the kids would be dealing with far more long-term effects.

CHAPTER 26

› CPS

Bertha Nevarro knew she had to be careful when questioning the children. She was part of the Child Abuse Listening, Interviewing and Coordination Center (CALICO), where workers were trained to be sensitive in dealing with minors who were frequently caught up in situations beyond their control. The challenge was to elicit as much information from the kids without tainting their memories or traumatizing them even further. Nevarro wore a pink shirt, and the children were interviewed separately in a second-floor room filled with pink dolls, teddy bears, crayons and books.

A restless Rory kept changing positions on a couch and fiddled with his shirt as Nevarro gently asked him about his mom. Speaking with a child's lisp, Rory said his mother lied to the courts, about him being scared of "teenager computer games" and that he had a weak wrist. Both claims, he said, were "false."

Nevarro asked how he knew his mom said those things.

"My dad told me," he said.

Asked about the day he last saw his mom, Rory said he remembered that his parents talked at his dad's house while he and Nio played "educational and non-educational software."

Later, as his mother was leaving, "she asked us to give her a hug," he said.

"When your mom asked you for a hug, how was she?"

"Happy."

"And then what happened next after you gave her a hug?"

"She left and then she drove her car somewhere. But I don't know where because I wasn't there."

Later, Nevarro asked, "Do you have any recent secrets with your mom?"

"No."

"What about your dad?"

"No." He paused. "Only one."

"What secret's that?"

"That I'm not telling any policemen anything about my dad."

"How come?"

"Like they might try to track him down or something."

"Why would they try to track him down?"

"Because policemen sometimes can be mean sometimes."

"How do you know that?"

"My dad told me."

He said his father knows judo, "but he's not as good at the sweep-foot roll as me."

His precociousness was quite evident. He surprised Nevarro when he told her not to eat M&Ms because they contained "hydrogenated vegetable oil."

In her interview, Nio also said her mother's belief that Rory was afraid of video games was "not true." Nevarro marveled at this beautiful little girl who called her mom Nina. Looking at Nio was like looking at Nina. Nevarro tried to pin down what happened on which days, but the children were inconsistent in their answers.

After their CALICO interviews, Rory and Nio were taken by car to an Alameda County assessment center outside Oakland. During the ride, they did not ask any questions about where they were going or why they couldn't return home. A child-welfare worker asked them about school, and they talked excitedly about their new teachers and their previous school, Grand Lake Montessori.

Pinzon and Weisenberg, meanwhile, went to Sturgeon's second-floor condo on Lakeshore Avenue. He was very cooperative and allowed them to check the home. Sturgeon admitted that he had had an intimate relationship with Nina and that she broke it off because of the issue over custody of the children. He said he cared very much for Nina.

Shelley Gordon was in a cab in New York City and headed

for a hotel when she got a call on her cell from Zografos that day. He sounded relieved. He told her he believed Nina had been back at her house because things had been moved around. He had no idea that the police had been inside a day earlier. Zografos asked her to call Nina's cell to reassure her that if she was worried about anything, things could be straightened out.

"Hi, Nina. This is Shelley calling. I'm—excuse me. It's Friday. I'm in New York City. I've been in touch with Anthony and Ellen all week because everybody's so worried about you, and Anthony says that he thinks that you're OK and that you're back. And I want you to know that whatever is going on, we can work it out, we can figure out how to handle it. And it's not something that's going to be—ruin your fight for the children. So please call me. I will be back on Tuesday, and I have my cell phone, and I want you to call me. I've been very worried about you, and I hope you're OK. Bye-bye."

Beverly made the first of several calls to Child Protective Services (CPS) asking that the kids be placed with her. She explained to social workers that her son wasn't at her house. The reason he was avoiding the police was because he didn't want to be picked up by officers until he could go to the police station with his attorney for an interview, she said.

That evening, Hans went into the Barnes & Noble bookstore on Shattuck Avenue in downtown Berkeley. He had his trusty black fanny pack wrapped around his waist as he browsed. Hans preferred it to a backpack because it was more functional and, he believed, was the preferred choice of engineers. He found two books that he wanted and made his way to the front counter. Hans smiled and made small talk with employee Sandra Starr Rudd. He grabbed a magazine on a shelf, glanced at it and thought better of it, putting it back. He reached into his fanny pack and handed Rudd $40 in cash for the $28.25 purchase. He didn't give her his Barnes & Noble member card. He didn't want the police tracking his purchases, in no small way because of what they were about: inside the green plastic bag Rudd had handed him was *Homicide: A Year on the Killing Streets*, a behind-the-scenes look at the Baltimore police homicide squad, by David Simon, the former *Baltimore Sun* reporter and creator of the acclaimed television show *The Wire*. The other book was called *Masterpieces of Murder*, which featured "the best true crime writing from the greatest chroniclers of murder." Hans strode purposefully out the front door. He had some reading to do.

CHAPTER 27

> MONTCLAIR

Montclair Village is a compact shopping district alongside Highway 13 at the base of the Oakland hills. The enclave along Mountain Boulevard prides itself for its woodsy, small-town feel as well as its restaurants and chichi boutiques offering seven hundred dollar strollers, truffles and fine wine favored by many "Montclair moms" and retirees. Each year, residents elect the Montclair Pet Mayor, and each Sunday, purveyors of the best organic vegetables hawk their wares at the farmers market. But the tranquility of the neighborhood was disrupted on Saturday, September 9, as the first news reports surfaced that Nina was missing. Zografos, Doren and others put up missing-persons flyers throughout Montclair that morning. The posters, tied with yellow ribbons, were a jarring contrast to those advertising the annual Montclair Jazz and Wine Festival set for the next day. Residents saw the flyers while strolling with their children and dogs and stopped in their tracks. The woman in the picture was familiar to them. They had seen her at the store or at soccer practice or at the school picnic. Parents realized that their kids knew Rory and Nio. Her disappearance became the talk of "the hill," as residents called Montclair, and quite a few people were freaked out, all but jolted from their comfortable existence in a normally quiet part of the city. What happened to her? If they thought the flyers were ominous enough, within hours a grim discovery would unnerve them even more.

> "2-John-11," a dispatcher keyed the mike from the Oakland police radio room at 11:24 that morning.

"2-John-11," rookie officer Erica McGlaston responded on

the radio of her Ford Crown Victoria. Sitting in the passenger seat of the black-and-white was her field training officer, Kevin Kaney. McGlaston had graduated from the Oakland Police Academy in June, and Kaney, a firearms expert, was teaching her the basics of street patrol, a requirement before she could work solo.

"2-John-11, inquiry match on a missing persons vehicle, Fifteen forty-eight Fernwood Drive, 1-5-4-8 Fernwood, a 2001 Honda, license plate 4-Union-Boy-Boy-4-9-1, comes back to Nina Reiser, a missing person since 5 September."

"2-John-11, 904," McGlaston replied, using the Oakland police code acknowledging the call. Cars were found abandoned or illegally parked all the time in the city. But this was no ordinary car.

McGlaston and Kaney met up with Chris Bunn, the resident on Fernwood who had called the police. Fernwood was a heavily wooded street carved alongside Highway 13, less than a mile from Montclair Village. For at least five days now, a tan Honda Odyssey minivan had been parked along the retaining wall on the 1500 block of Fernwood. "What was unusual was that most people don't leave a car there day after day," Bunn said. "And I began to notice that the car was just sticking around day after day. My neighbors were thinking the same thing." No one on the street recognized the vehicle. The rear license-plate frame read, "Namesys" and "Trees Are Fast." No one had any idea what that meant.

Homicide sergeant Bruce Brock came to the scene in jeans and sneakers and inspected the minivan with the officers. The vehicle had dried mud on the tires and the wheel wells, which intrigued the officers. There had been no rain recently, so they suspected that the minivan had been driven on a road that was either unpaved or poorly maintained. All the doors were locked and the windows were up. Ominously, there were groceries spilling out of plastic bags in the back of the minivan, as if someone had been driving it recklessly. A tan purse was on the floorboard of the passenger seat. But the keys were nowhere to be found.

A tow-truck driver came to the scene and used a Slim Jim to open the driver's side door. The smell of rotting food wafted outside.

Officer Bruce Christensen, who was cross-trained as a crime-scene technician, pulled a cell phone from the purse. The flip phone was in the open position and its battery was detached, but still in the purse. Police wondered if Nina had been trying to use the phone when she was violently interrupted. It was not altogether improbable. Years later, a masked gunman using Craigslist to lure potential car buyers robbed a man on that very same block of Fernwood. It was a relatively isolated street, yet close enough to Highway 13 for a quick escape. The spot was also a few turns away from Doren's house on Capricorn Drive. Could Nina have been attacked by a random stranger while on her way to see her friend?

But the circumstances reeked of suspicion from the start. The investigators knew that the location of cell phones could be pinpointed if they were on—even when no calls were being made—but not if they were turned off or if the batteries were removed. No random attacker would take the time to remove the battery from a victim's cell phone, and most certainly Nina wouldn't have done that herself. Christensen dusted the car for fingerprints. As the officers scoured Nina's minivan, they concluded that neither robbery nor carjacking could be a motive for stashing the vehicle. Nina's purse still had money inside.

Ron Sites, Frances Roelfsema, Cindy Gigliotti and Lisa Fitkins of the Alameda County search-and-rescue team came to the scene with three tracking dogs and one cadaver dog. Their dogs were given scent samples from a comb from the purse, glasses found on the floor near the driver's seat, a cell phone charger from the cigarette lighter socket and a compact from the center console. The canines and their handlers searched the area, but the dogs all came back to the van. This meant that Nina never left the vehicle. Someone else had parked it on Fernwood. The Odyssey was put on a flatbed tow truck and followed by police to the Eastmont police substation in East Oakland, where it was secured in a locked facility.

As days passed with still no signs of Nina, Zografos continued to leave messages on her cell phone, giving her running updates on the police investigation with the fervent hope that she was following along somewhere.

"I'm just letting you know that the police found your car, and we're all hopeful that very soon you'll give us a sign that you're OK," Zografos said in a message.

The police had finally found Nina's minivan, but they still had not located two cars used by Hans: the 1988 Honda CRX hatchback and the 2003 Honda Civic hybrid. Beverly owned both cars and primarily drove the hybrid. She wanted to know where her cars were, too.

At about 8:45 a.m. on Sunday, September 10, Hans walked out of the Kragen Auto Parts store on Hesperian Boulevard in San Lorenzo with blue shop towels and isopropyl alcohol. He went back into the store and bought a $15.99 siphon pump at 9:30 a.m. A short while later, Beverly's phone rang. It was her son. He said he was at the Fresh Choice restaurant at the Bayfair Mall in San Leandro and asked her for a ride. Beverly was exasperated. She and a friend, Todd Britt, went down there looking for the CRX. Instead, they found her hybrid parked on a side street. Now she was angry. She didn't want to take the car back to her house because Hans might take it again. So she and Britt drove it to McGothigan's house, where they parked it in a carport on his hillside property, put a Club lock on it and surrounded it with other cars so it couldn't be seen from the street. They didn't want to hide it from police; they wanted to hide it from Hans. But he wouldn't be anywhere near the house—nor Oakland, for that matter. That night, Hans drove the CRX to a Motel 6 in Fremont, twenty-two miles south of his hometown and far from the prying eyes of the police. He plunked down $45.35 in cash and spent the night.

On Monday, September 11, short blurbs about Nina's disappearance appeared in local papers. Beverly went to an Enterprise Rent-a-Car along Oakland's Broadway Auto Row and rented a white Chevy Malibu that day. She would drive the Malibu that entire week, at the same time that posters with the title "MISSING ADULT" were popping up throughout Oakland's Temescal and Montclair neighborhoods as well as along busy Lakeshore, Grand and Piedmont avenues.

Across San Francisco Bay in San Mateo County, Redwood City police officer Eric Stasiak was on duty at about 7:30 p.m.

on September 12 when he saw a Honda CRX make a U-turn on El Camino Real at Madison Avenue right in front of a SamTrans bus. Stasiak pulled the car over and walked up to it from the passenger side. Hans was behind the wheel. He looked nervous and apprehensive. Stasiak told him why he pulled him over. "I'm sorry, I miscalculated," Hans said. Stasiak didn't notice anything unusual about the car, other than it was dirty, with things strewn all over it inside. Stasiak gave Hans a ticket for failing to yield the right-of-way, an infraction, and sent him on his way. Hans continued south and ended up spending the night in the CRX at the Saratoga Springs campground near San Jose, fifty-one miles away from Oakland.

On Tuesday, September 12, the *Oakland Tribune* and *San Francisco Chronicle* ran the first full-length stories about Nina's disappearance. The articles noted that she went missing after dropping off her children at Hans's house and that her minivan had been found, but police did not release details to the public or press about the precise location of the vehicle or the fact that the groceries were jumbled.

That day, Oakland police criminalists Shannon Cavness, Todd Weller and Waliana Wong and police evidence technician Anthony Camacho went to the Eastmont substation to examine Nina's Honda Odyssey more completely.

They found numerous plastic bags from Berkeley Bowl. There was again the strong odor of spoiled food.

A number of items served as proof that Nina had short-term plans and hadn't chosen on a whim to leave her family and life behind. In the center console was an envelope with an undelivered twenty-one hundred dollar Patelco check, dated August 31 and addressed to Anthony Britto, Nina's landlord. There was a dental-office reminder for Rory's rescheduled appointment at 10:30 a.m. on October 9, 2006, and a card from a skin-care business on College Avenue in Oakland—just blocks from her house—that said "Your next appointment is September 27, 2006."

There was also the minutiae of everyday life inside her vehicle: Altoids, Orbitz gum, an iPod Nano, a handicapped-parking placard, a FasTrak transponder that allowed her to zip through Bay Area bridge tollbooths, a rosary, a necklace, a water bottle, CDs, a CD case, an ad featuring 80 percent off at a clothing store, loose change, an umbrella, a flowery bag, a flashlight, pens and pencils, vehicle registration and tools including pliers and a razor blade with no blood on it.

In Nina's purse was a $144.48 receipt, dated 1:55 p.m. on September 3, showing fifty-one items she bought from the Berkeley Bowl, including heirloom tomatoes, bread, chicken, Bartlett and Bosc pears, sour cream, yogurt, milk, butter, eggs, bananas, Lucky Charms, English muffins, and Sabarot lentils. There was also $94.07 in cash, one euro, a bracelet, a hair scrunchie, an August 2006 earthquake-preparedness form from Joaquin Miller Elementary School, her cell phone with its battery detached, her driver's license, credit cards and Blue Shield insurance cards for her children. Police also found a fortune cookie strip that read, "If you had your life to live over again, you'd need more money."

The groceries matched up with the receipt. There was also a second Berkeley Bowl receipt from the store deli for $15.18 dated 12:38 p.m. September 3, 2006. Some leftovers from the deli were also found.

Other books found in her car were *Parent Power! A Common-Sense Approach to Parenting in the '90s and Beyond; Kill as Few Patients as Possible; The Best Advice I Ever Got; First Things First;* and *For Your Own Good: The Roots of Violence in Child-Rearing.* In the center passenger area were children's books, including *The Runaway Bunny,* and some kids' books in Russian.

There was a stuffed animal found crammed into a cup holder.

Several dark red stains on the outside and inside of the car were tested, but all came back negative for blood. The police concluded that there was no evidence of a crime in the minivan.

On that day, Officer Michael Weisenberg returned a phone call from Beverly. She asked Weisenberg if her son was a suspect in the case. Weisenberg knew that now Beverly and possibly her son were aware that police were conducting a criminal investigation into Nina's disappearance.

› I also knew that this didn't seem to be your average missing-persons case. I had channeled my childhood fascination with cops and sirens into a job as a crime reporter at the *Daily Californian* student newspaper at UC Berkeley, where I studied psychology. After I convinced my parents that medical school was nowhere in my future, I landed a job at the *San Francisco Chronicle* in 1994 and ended up covering crime in the East Bay. My beat included virtually everything east of San Francisco, in Alameda and Contra Costa counties and far beyond, such as the Scott Peterson case when the first court hearings were held in Modesto. By the time the Reiser case came around, I had this creeping intuition that something bad had happened to Nina—and that there would be no happy ending. The first thing I did was to review the Reiser divorce file at the René C. Davidson Courthouse in downtown Oakland. I quickly got a sense of just how toxic their relationship was. I left messages with the attorneys. I also called Hans's house. A woman I later identified as Beverly answered the phone and said, "I hope they find her" when I asked about Nina. Beverly hung up after I asked more questions.

Top Oakland police officials huddled that afternoon to discuss their next steps. They had no idea where Hans was, nor Nina, and still had no clue where Hans's mother's two Hondas were. The investigators mulled over some ideas, like pulling insurance policies, wills and trusts; getting records for Hans's and Nina's cell phones; and placing tracking devices on cars linked to Hans. They knew that some murderers would return to where they dumped the body to see if police had discovered it. The police needed as much help as they could get: there were many places where Nina's remains could have been hidden. In the East Bay alone, there were countless mountains, parks, lakes, ravines and woods extending hundreds of square miles. To the west was San Francisco Bay and, past the Golden Gate Bridge, the white-crested swells of the Pacific Ocean. She could be anywhere.

The police got their first inkling of how much the media would be interested in this case when Gill got a call from a producer at ABC News's *Good Morning America*. Up until then, the police had received calls from just the usual local reporters. But *Good Morning America*? This was now national news. The public's fascination was understandable. The story was riveting: a beautiful Russian doctor and mother of two had mysteriously disappeared, and suspicions were falling on her computer-genius husband. It was a tale of intrigue, deception and betrayal—just the kind of story that made rapacious producers and editors salivate even more.

The media onslaught was also affecting Grand Lake Montessori. A newcomer could easily miss the school, tucked in a corner of Chetwood Avenue right at the edge of the overpass to Interstate 580. But TV trucks found it with no problems and descended on the school in droves, unannounced. School officials scrambled, barring reporters from entering the campus in hopes of protecting the children from the media spectacle. Parents were urged by e-mail to keep a lookout for Nina, and teachers spent their lunch breaks passing out missing-persons flyers.

"To be part of the GLM community during this time was to witness surreptitious hallway conversations among parents who knew the Reisers, whispered in a sort of code language that developed to keep our children from knowing what we were talking about," parent Jennifer Pahlka wrote on her blog, Pahlka Dot. After all, what could be scarier to little kids than the prospect of losing one's mom or having her go missing?

At Joaquin Miller Elementary School, which the children had attended for only eight days, school staff also barred the media.

The media attention—fueled by pictures of the missing doctor from Russia—would only get bigger the next day.

CHAPTER 28

> THE CITY

Oakland is a city that conjures up images of violence, murder and mayhem. While San Francisco had flower power and was crooned about in romantic ballads, Oakland was its ugly, poverty-stricken stepchild across San Francisco Bay, forever synonymous with the Hells Angels and bursts of bloodshed like the 1973 murder of its school superintendent by the Symbionese Liberation Army and the crack-cocaine epidemic that led to a record one hundred and seventy-five homicides in 1992. It got so bad that when a city police officer strangled his wife, he spray-painted the word "WAR" on the side of her car and left it in a seedy neighborhood, convinced that her slaying would be chalked up as just another drug-gang execution.

In recent years, the city saw a number of nationally publicized cases that would forever be burned into the public consciousness: the shooting of unarmed passenger Oscar Grant by a BART transit police officer led to riots and the eventual arrest of the officer on a rare murder charge. Four Oakland police officers were shot and killed by a parolee in two distinct bursts of gunfire on the same day, the single deadliest loss of life in the department's history. The headlines were not for the squeamish: innocent children, cut down by errant bullets. A woman killed and dismembered her sister to steal her money and stuffed the body in a freezer. Two thirteen-year-old boys, one a murder victim, the other the suspect. A ninety-seven-year-old woman slain, the city's oldest resident to fall victim to homicide. It was gory crimes like these that prompted outsiders to shake their heads at this tableau of fear and lawlessness that was Oakland. Despite the bloodshed, the residents of Oaktown, as many called the city, came to resent this typecasting. The writer Gertrude Stein once famously said, "There's no there there," which has been widely misconstrued as a comment disparaging Oakland. In fact, she had simply been lamenting the fact that her childhood home had been torn down. Even so, as a counterpoint, a sculpture at the Oakland City Center is simply titled, "There."

In reality, there is much "there" there. Oakland is California's eighth-largest city, a major West Coast port and the proud home of the Oakland A's, the Raiders and the Golden State Warriors. It is comprised of distinct neighborhoods, from the gritty streets of the Fruitvale District, where fruit vendors hawk their wares, to the trendy shops and restaurants in the Rockridge District. Oakland's revitalized downtown featured coffee shops, tapas bars and upscale lofts. The city's wealthiest pocket is in the Oakland hills, a virtual oasis from the hardscrabble streets that make up the city's flatlands just a short drive down. A look at a map of crime patterns in the city shows that the bulk of the violence erupts at its two ends. West Oakland, filled with rundown Victorians and liquor stores, was plagued by drug-related shootings in enclaves with names like Lower Bottom and Ghost Town. East Oakland, stretching from the central part of the city to the San Leandro border, fared no better, with many residents of predominantly African American neighborhoods living in fear of gang warfare yet unable to move, trapped in the Hobbesian nightmare of the inner city.

Running alongside the Hayward Fault, Highway 13 is a physical representation of the deep economic divide separating the hills from the flatlands. Residents of the hills were largely immune from the types of murders and robberies that dominated headlines and sullied the city's reputation. Hills residents dealt mostly with burglaries, wayward wildlife, solicitors and other relatively minor nuisances. But violent crime is certainly not unheard of in the hills. And when it does occur, the media has an insatiable appetite. Critics would sniff that reporters didn't care about so-called low-rent murders, with criminals killing each other in poor neighborhoods. To some extent, that may be true. But anything that was unusual or any kind of event that happens infrequently, regardless of where it happened, was bound to get the media's attention.

That was the case in May 1998, when Dan Dean returned to his home on Florence Avenue off Highway 13 in the Upper Rockridge neighborhood and found the body of his pediatrician wife, Kerry Spooner-Dean, thirty, on the kitchen floor. Two knives were still lodged in her chest. Reporters descended on the area to interview concerned neighbors. Within two weeks, police arrested Jerrol Glenn Woods, a fifty-year-old carpet cleaner from Vallejo who had spent most of his adult life in prison. Spooner-Dean had hired him to clean the carpets at her home. Woods was convicted and sentenced to life in prison without the possibility of parole. It was a story that captured the media's interest because of a number of factors, not the least of which involved race and class: a white woman in an affluent neighborhood had been brutally murdered by a black man with a criminal past. But it also underscored the dangerous reality of inviting a stranger into one's house for a simple service call.

Now, eight years later, the relative tranquility of the Oakland hills would again be shattered. But as the law-enforcement juggernaut reared its head, it became exceedingly clear that no stranger was responsible.

CHAPTER 29

> EXETER DRIVE

Armed with a search warrant, Oakland police showed up in force at 7:00 a.m. on Wednesday, September 13, to search 6979 Exeter Drive. The warrant, signed by Judge David Krashna, gave police the authority to seize "items or articles of clothing or the items, soiled with blood and or semen, cutting instrument(s) and or cutting instrument soiled with blood, blood samples and items of physical evidence that are consistent with an assault by stabbing or cutting, photographs and measurements of evidence collected, firearms and or ammunition, any and all items or objects, which may show that a physical altercation occurred at (the home)."

The warrant authorized a search of the home, the Honda CRX and the Honda Civic hybrid. But neither car was there when the police arrived. Instead, the white Chevy Malibu that Beverly had rented from Enterprise Rent-a-Car was parked in the driveway. Grant had asked the police at San Francisco International Airport to look for the CRX in the parking lots—which was standard practice in the event Hans had taken a flight overseas—but they came up empty-handed. Officers had also checked with Hans's mechanic, but the car wasn't there, either.

Gill asked Krashna to seal the warrant. He didn't want the media to screw up the investigation. The police had to deal with enough publicity and didn't need more to jeopardize the integrity of the case.

Lieutenant Kevin Wiley and Officers Gill, Bruce Christensen and Jesse Grant were dressed in full police uniforms. Sergeant Tom Hogenmiller and Officers Mark Battle and Shan Johnson were clad in blue jeans and raid jackets with

"Oakland Police" written in the back in yellow block lettering. Criminalists Cavness and Weller, from the crime lab,
wore long white lab coats. Weller was in his element. He
seemed eons removed from his time at the Sigma Phi Epsilon
fraternity at Dartmouth College in New Hampshire.

The investigators took stock of the trilevel, 1,836-square-
foot house, which was cut into the hillside and dwarfed by
redwoods. The driveway and garage opened up to the top
floor of the home. The group walked down a set of steps
that took them past a towering cypress tree and down to the
front courtyard and deck, which led to the front door. As they
approached the entrance, the officers were startled to see a
scary-looking ceremonial Balinese mask hanging on a wall
outside. To the right of the door was a full-length stained-
glass window made by Beverly. Gill knocked on the door, and
Beverly answered. She said she didn't know where Hans was.
Police did a protective sweep of the house to make sure that
Hans wasn't there. There was no sign of him. Beverly told
them that she had hid her Honda Civic hybrid at her friend
Mark McGothigan's house, on Simson Street in Oakland, so
that Hans wouldn't find it. She said she had found her car at
the Bayfair Mall in San Leandro, where Hans had dumped it
because he thought he was being followed by the police.

Among the officers at Beverly's home was Jim Saleda,
who had served thirteen years in the U.S. Navy and fourteen
years in the Army Reserve. Saleda was deployed to Iraq from
2003 to 2005 as a cavalry scout, conducting reconnaissance
and surveillance. Marine reservist James Beere also served in
Iraq, where he narrowly missed getting cut down by an AK-47-
wielding insurgent and was awarded the Bronze Star with a
Combat V, for Valor, for a series of heroic acts, including dis-
arming roadside bombs. Back in Oakland, as police officers,
Saleda and Beere fought another battle, going after pimps and
human traffickers and coaxing teenage prostitutes to get off
the streets. Saleda let his beard grow and wore his grayish-
white hair long. Beere had a light beard. Like Battle, Saleda
and Beere knew how to fade into the scenery.

As police searched the Exeter Drive home that morning, Beverly left and went to McGothigan's house. Saleda

and Beere followed her there and quickly realized that they weren't the only ones adept at camouflage. Even as Beverly and McGothigan pointed in the direction of the Honda Civic hybrid, they still couldn't see it. It was wedged in the carport, which sat on top of a small hill on McGothigan's property, away from the street. The side door was so close to the carport wall that whoever parked the car would have had to exit through the passenger side. The car was towed away. Police found what looked to be bloodstains and soil-type matter on the right front passenger seat and pine needles and a small branch between the two child seats in the back. There was also a pile of women's clothing.

Back at Beverly's house, the first thing officers saw as they went inside was an exquisitely decorated living room with a parquet floor. The space was adorned with a shoji screen, a Japanese throw pillow, bamboo sticks, Oriental lamps hanging from the ceiling, Chinese paintings, an Indian painting on cloth and a large branch made to look like a tree, extending from a vase to the ceiling. Beverly had long been enthralled by Asian cultures. She had studied Chinese brush painting and had completed graduate work at the California Institute of Asian Studies in San Francisco. Her home was as much a place to live as it was an eclectic, if not somewhat discordant, collection of artifacts.

Upstairs, Beverly's bedroom featured a light green and burgundy color scheme, with drapes that matched the comforter and a rug. A blue pet bed for D'Artagnan sat on the floor near the head of her bed. Another upstairs bedroom had bright red shutters that matched the baseboard. Beverly kept the same bull's skull and tambourine that had been used at Hans and Nina's wedding in that room.

Police evidence technicians meticulously took pictures of each room in the house. Christensen drew a diagram of the home. TV and print photographers, in turn, had taken up positions outside the house, documenting the search.

Police found bloodstains on a pillar and a couch in the living room. They also found a bloodstain on the light switch in the crawl space in the basement. A later analysis could not match the blood to either Hans or Nina. Also in the basement were several items used for digging, including a Ridgid shovel, a Structron shovel and a pickaxe with a yellow handle. But they appeared brand-new and never used. Police decided not to seize the three tools and instead took pictures of them.

In the basement bedroom where Hans spent most of his time, they found more apparent bloodstains, including under the mattress lying on the parquet floor. The officers noticed that someone had removed disks and the hard drives from a computer. They believed Hans had taken those items away in anticipation of a search warrant. A file cabinet was partially open and had no hanging files inside. A set of patio doors opened into the backyard.

When Alameda County search-and-rescue K-9 handler Shay Cook was brought to the home, Bishop the cadaver dog showed interest in the ground floor under construction, sitting next to an exposed beam in a crawl space. The dog also alerted to a closet in the corner of an upstairs bedroom. But Kody, a yellow shepherd-Lab mix being handled by Frances Roelfsema, didn't show any signs of interest. The handlers told police that dogs were trained to different levels of detection.

As the search came to an end that day, it was clear that Nina wasn't at the home. And there were still no signs of Hans. But Wiley, without elaborating, told the *Tribune* that police knew where he was but were unable to contact him. The latter part may have been true, but Wiley's first assertion was based on a faulty assumption. Police had been told a day earlier by U.S. Immigration and Customs Enforcement (ICE) that Hans had fled to Frankfurt, Germany. Police told Beverly that day that her son had gone to Germany, implying that he was on the run.

But Gill was startled that afternoon when Seng Fong of Alameda County CPS called and said that Hans had in fact been in family court just moments ago—in downtown Oakland. Hans, represented by attorney Cheryl Hicks, was seeking custody of the children. At that day's detention hearing, Alameda County Commissioner Nancy Lonsdale had ordered Rory and Nio be removed from the custody of Nina and Hans. Another hearing was scheduled for the next day.

Gill wanted an explanation as to why he had been told

that Hans was out of the country. He called Wiley, who soon confirmed that there had been a mix-up: immigration agents reported that it was a Hans J. Reiser who flew to Germany, not the Hans from Oakland, whose middle name was Thomas.

That night, Zografos, hoping to draw attention to the search for Nina, appeared on *On the Record with Greta Van Susteren* on the Fox News Channel. He talked about Nina's minivan being found with groceries inside.

"Does that suggest to you that she dropped the kids off and at least went to the grocery store?" Van Susteren asked from her studio in Washington, D.C.

"Well, that suggests to me that someone driving Nina's car went grocery shopping sometime after she dropped the kids off," Zografos said. He—and everyone else—turned out to be wrong.

The search of Hans's home was reported the same day online in the *Oakland Tribune* and the *San Francisco Chronicle* and led the local newscasts that night. Police weren't done searching, however, so Officers Saleda and Battle stayed at the home overnight to provide scene security.

On that day, police refused to term Hans a suspect, but Deputy Chief Howard Jordan pointedly told the *Chronicle*, "As far as we know, he was the last person to see her at the home." The implication from the stories was clear: Hans had the motive—and the mind-set—to do harm to his wife.

The next morning, September 14, residents of Oakland awoke to find the story splashed in the pages of the *Tribune* and the *Chronicle*. "Man's home searched—wife is missing," read the headline for the story I wrote with Jim Herron Zamora. Both newspapers reported details about the Reisers' bitter divorce battle. My story in the *Chronicle* went further by identifying Sturgeon by name and referring to his affair with Nina. Speaking through a painkiller-induced haze, at times answering my questions with questions of his own, Sturgeon told me that Hans had made a lot of "irrational" accusations against him. "He has shown increasing signs of mental instability," Sturgeon said.

Police continued to search the Exeter home for that day.

Judge Krashna had signed an amended warrant to give officers the authority to search Beverly's rented Chevrolet and to seize whatever remained of Hans's computer equipment as well as his bank statements and travel documents.

As police scoured the home, the custody hearing for the children resumed at a court building at 600 Washington Street in downtown Oakland, adjacent to police headquarters. Hans did not show up, but Hicks, his family law attorney, made clear that he would contest the kids' detention. Gill wanted to share his suspicions with Commissioner Lonsdale, but the defense was there, and he wasn't about to reveal anything that could get back to Hans. The case was continued until September 18.

Du Bois said later that Hans didn't go to the hearing because he was upset about the search of his house. Hans told his attorneys that they needed to tell the media that the reason for his no-show had to do with the day of the week. Hans feared that he'd be detained that day, a Thursday, and if he was booked into jail, he would have been stuck there all weekend. Prosecutors have forty-eight hours to charge a suspect. But if they had arrested him on a Thursday, they would have had "48 hours plus a weekend," Hans reasoned. He had a point. The DA *did* have two *working* days to decide whether someone in custody would be formally charged. But police had no evidence to arrest Hans at this point.

Undercover officers followed Beverly after the hearing. Because police were now searching the Chevrolet, she was driving a red Toyota Camry she had rented from Hertz. They tailed her as she drove through the Webster Street tube that dipped below Oakland's Inner Harbor, connecting Oakland to the island city of Alameda. She parked at the Mariner Square Athletic Club, which was right near the exit to the tube, at 3:00 p.m. As Beverly swam laps inside, the officers planted a tracking device on her rental car.

Meanwhile, Judge Barbara Miller signed an order authorizing a pen register on Hans's cell phone, which would reveal which numbers he dialed, how long the calls were and where he was when he was on the line. But the police wouldn't be

able to actually listen in. The judge also signed search warrants allowing police to search Nina's home and to order Cin-
gular Wireless to release records for her cell phone.

Back at Exeter Drive, police wrapped up their two-day
search at 7:00 p.m. Officer Kwang Lee locked the house, and
everyone left.

CHAPTER 30

›FORTY-NINTH STREET

On September 15, Officer Shan Johnson called Nina's landlord, Anthony Britto, for help getting into her house on Forty-ninth Street. Britto was unavailable but said he could have his cousin deliver a key. Shortly after noon, police and a federal immigration agent got the key and served a search warrant at the house. Officers looked for anything that could help establish a DNA profile for Nina. They opened the medicine cabinet in her bathroom. There were two SpongeBob SquarePants toothbrushes, one purple and the other light blue. They took a contact-lens case and razor from the bathroom and women's underwear from the laundry basket above the washing machine.

Police also seized five passports—three U.S. passports in the names of Nina, Rory and Nio and two Russian passports belonging to Nina and Nio—as well as $1,980 in cash and a laptop computer.

Officer Grant saw the portrait of Nina and Rory on her bedroom wall and found it slightly unsettling. No matter where he walked in the room, it seemed as if Nina was staring at him. But it also stirred him and the other officers to action. They knew they had to figure out what happened to her.

Nina's refrigerator was decorated with family snapshots held in place by penguin magnets, representing happier days. Rory proudly holding a toy castle; Nina beaming with Nio in her ballet dress; Rory on a scooter, his sister on a bike with training wheels, Nina with her hands on their shoulders. Nio had scrawled, "I [heart] Mom" on a piece of paper. There was also a calendar on a dry-erase board with meals written for each day. One of the kids had written "Lunch!" with a red marker in big letters. For breakfast, it was Greek yogurt on Monday, waffles with maple syrup and honey on Tuesday, oatmeal with eggs on Friday, pancakes on Saturday and Lucky Charms on Sunday.

Nina's bookshelf was filled with test-preparation books for the U.S. Medical Licensing Examination and medical texts, like *Gray's Anatomy* and *The Merck Manual of Medical Information*. Kids' books lined the bottom shelves, including *My First Dictionary* and *A Hatful of Seuss*.

After the search was completed, Johnson met with FBI agents Martha "Marty" Parker and Terry Shannon. Police wanted help conducting polygraph examinations of Zografos and Sturgeon. Shannon said it would be necessary for the police to reinterview both men and get a firm denial of their involvement before they were given a polygraph test. The tests were scheduled for four days later.

Johnson and Grant were well suited as partners. The boyish-looking Grant, a seven-year veteran, had big ears and was a full head shorter than the lanky Johnson, but the two shared a mind-set and were close friends off duty. Grant had been a groomsman at Johnson's wedding earlier that year. Another guest was retired Oakland missing-persons sergeant John Bradley, whom they greatly respected. When an eighteen-year-old woman named Kristen Modafferi went missing in 1997, Bradley and his partner diligently investigated and quickly honed in on a suspect. But there was no concrete evidence to tie him to her disappearance, and he was never arrested. Modafferi was never found.

Johnson and Grant didn't want their case to languish without a resolution. They knew that they had to examine everything they could to find out what had happened to Nina. They went to Berkeley Bowl, where a security manager gave them five CDs showing activity at the store from 1:00 to 2:00 p.m. on September 3. Another officer was assigned to review the CDs. One had fleeting images of what appeared to be Rory, Nio and Nina at the checkout stand 13 shortly before 2:00 p.m. That meant that Nina had gone shopping at the store before she went to Hans's house, and not after, as everyone had originally believed.

Gill was still frustrated that Du Bois wasn't calling him back directly. Gill knew that Du Bois had all his contact information. Yet on September 15, Du Bois left another message with the Oakland police homicide squad, this time with veteran sergeant Lou Cruz. "Give me a ring. I have something to talk to you about," Du Bois said.

CHAPTER 31

›THE VIGIL

On the night of September 15, at 7:00 p.m., about fifty friends and concerned Montclair neighbors held a vigil for Nina at Montclair Park, alongside Highway 13. Marni Hunter, whose daughter had been in the same class as Rory at Grand Lake Montessori, was among those in attendance. She had seen a missing poster—one of thousands posted throughout the area—on lampposts in Montclair Village during the Jazz and Wine Festival.

Organizers decided to pass out yellow carnations instead of candles. It was fire season, and residents of the hills were particularly wary of the dangers, especially in the wake of the 1991 Oakland hills fire, which destroyed several thousand homes and killed twenty-five people.

After the tumultuous events of the past week and a half, the vigil was a chance to redirect the attention to Nina. Even as the vigil was laced with sadness, there was a sense of hope that she would be found. The flowers from the gathering were taken to Nina's house, a visible reminder of their wish to bring her home.

I went to the vigil to see if Hans would show up and whether the police were there. It was dark, and I was a little nervous. Would he come and join the group? Would he be arrested? Would there be an ugly scene?

I peered into the far corners of the park. I wondered if he was sitting in the bleachers at the ball field or maybe loitering near the duck pond or maybe surveilling the scene from a rented Cruise America RV that was parked on Moraga Avenue on the outskirts of the park.

But Hans never showed.

Deputy Police Chief Howard Jordan and the department spokesman, Officer Roland Holmgren, both showed up in uniform. Their appearances were striking. Jordan, an eighteen-year veteran who had previously commanded the SWAT team, had a clean-shaven head and projected an air of dignified authority. He looked like a trimmer, younger version of actor Laurence Fishburne in the *Matrix* movies. Holmgren, a U.S. Marine veteran who stood six feet five, served on the SWAT team on top of his regular duties acting as the public face of the Oakland police. At times, Holmgren would be involved in a hostage standoff and then immediately switch roles by briefing the media while still wearing his tactical gear.

I saw Officer Kwang Lee in plainclothes at the park, holding a yellow carnation just like everyone else. We knew each other but I recognized his undercover role and studiously ignored him. Everyone there wore pictures of Nina adorned with yellow ribbons.

"I feel happy because of the community that showed up today to give their hopes to Nina and, so in that way, I feel grateful," Doren told me and a TV reporter. "Otherwise, of course, I feel very sad. I feel empty inside not to have my best friend with me."

Asked if she was surprised that Hans didn't come to the vigil, Doren said, "I really didn't know him that well. Sure, I thought he would be here."

So did the police. Besides Lee, Sergeant Tom Hogenmiller and Officers Jim Saleda and Mark Battle had taken up positions around the park. Unbeknownst to those at the vigil, they had a search warrant, signed a day earlier by Judge Miller, to collect a DNA sample from Hans by swabbing the inside of his mouth to get skin cells. They also wanted to attach a tracking device to his car. It was a bust, and the police left the park disappointed.

That same night, Jordan went to a studio not far from police headquarters for a live appearance on *On the Record with Greta Van Susteren*, his second time on the show that week. All the deputy chief could see was a camera on the other side of the room. He didn't realize at first that another host, Catherine Herridge, was filling in for Van Susteren.

"I hope you're not disappointed," Herridge said into his ear-piece. Jordan said he was not.

Herridge asked why the police waited ten days before searching Hans's home. Jordan said they had to develop enough probable cause before a judge could sign a warrant. Asked if Hans was cooperating, Jordan said he personally spoke to Hans's attorney that day. "We are in the process of making arrangements for Hans to be interviewed by our detectives."

It would again be wishful thinking.

CHAPTER 32

> NATURAL SUSPECTS

On Saturday, September 16, friends passed out flyers at the Lakeshore Farmers Market. The Reiser children's soccer league had a moment of silence for Nina.

That afternoon, Officer Johnson called Zografos, who said he wanted to come over right away to the Family Justice Center to talk. Zografos immediately focused on Sturgeon, noting that Nina had borrowed money from Sturgeon. Knowing that Doren had voiced suspicions about him and his jealousy, Zografos said it was Nina who gave him the passwords to her cell phone voice mail, home phone voice mail and Yahoo e-mail. Zografos told Johnson that she gave them to him to prove that she had nothing to hide.

Johnson asked Zografos how many times he had gone inside Nina's house since she was reported missing. Zografos said about twice a day. Asked if he had taken anything from the house, Zografos said he had taken a checkbook and credit-card statement at Gill's direction and that he also took one of her laptop computers, Basil the cat and a bowl of tadpoles and their food. In a surprise move, Zografos told Johnson that he had changed his mind about taking a polygraph test and refused to take it. Like Gill had warned him earlier, Johnson told Zografos not to enter Nina's home again unless the police gave him permission. Johnson and Grant then drove to Zografos's home, off Highway 24 near the tunnel that connects Alameda and Contra Costa counties. There, Zografos turned over Nina's toothbrush, the laptop, two keys to her house, her checkbook and a file folder with her MasterCard statements.

It was clear from the beginning that the police were focusing their attention on the men in Nina's life. Police naturally focus their suspicion on the boyfriend or husband, and research bears this out. Women who were separated from their husbands reported higher rates of violence than those who were married, divorced or never married. In cases of murder, about one-third of all female victims were killed by an intimate— defined as a current or former boyfriend or husband—from 1976 to 2005, according to the U.S. Department of Justice's report *Intimate Partner Violence in the United States.*

In a search warrant outlining his request for all child-support records pertaining to Rory and Nio, Gill summarized the bitter custodial disputes between Hans and Nina. Gill wrote, "Based on my training and experience, I know that the above mentioned custodial disputes often become very volatile, and occasionally cause persons to act out in a violent manner such as domestic violence, assaults, assaults with deadly weapons, or even homicides. I also know from training and experience that persons who are expected to pay large sums in accordance to court-ordered child support also occasionally resort to the crimes listed above."

Hans knew that the police would automatically consider him a suspect. After visiting Du Bois at his office in Pleasanton on September 16, he set out to do some damage control. He sent an e-mail to his Namesys employees at 6:30 p.m. while at a nearby copy store. The subject line read, "Nina." "As you will probably hear, Nina has disappeared," he wrote. "As her ex-husband, statistics require the police to investigate me in depth. I cannot comment on the matter, as my attorney says he will quit the case if I do so to anyone without his presence. It is my hope that you will all be insulated from this matter. However, I will be difficult to reach at times, I am sure you understand."

Hans's choice of words was curious. Hans knew full well that his divorce hadn't been finalized. His description of himself as Nina's "ex-husband" made it appear as if he were referring to Nina in the past tense. Whatever the reason, Hans took pains to distance himself in more ways than one. That evening, he enjoyed a sushi dinner in Pleasanton before driving east forty-two miles in the CRX to Manteca, in California's

Central Valley. He spent the night in the car, in the parking lot of a bar next to some RVs.

> Her once vibrant eyes filled with sadness, fifty-seven-year-old Irina Sharanova arrived in Oakland from Saint Petersburg on September 17. She was convinced that something terrible had happened to her daughter. As Sharanova settled in at Ellen Doren's house, trying to block images of Nina suffering a horrible fate, Hans stopped at a 7-Eleven in Manteca to buy a $10 calling card and paid a visit to California Self Storage, where he got a U-Haul printout that detailed a proposed $28 one-way trip from Manteca to Oakland. After arriving back in the Bay Area, he went back to the same Kragen Auto Parts store in San Lorenzo that he had visited a week earlier and paid $4.99 for a forty-piece socket set.

Also on September 17, police again interviewed Sturgeon, this time at the Family Justice Center. He told Weisenberg and Johnson that he had loaned more than two hundred fifty thousand dollars to Hans and Namesys and helped pay Nina's legal bills in the custody case. Sturgeon said he eventually agreed that Hans didn't have to pay him back the eighty-four thousand dollars that he sued him for, because he had made peace with Hans. Sturgeon commented that being bisexual, he never thought he would settle down with a woman. But he fell in love with Nina.

Sturgeon said he drove around looking for Nina, including Montclair Park and the Sibley volcanic preserve where Hans and Nina had gotten married. He said Nina would do anything for her children and would have never left them. Sturgeon said he was getting different stories about the status of the relationship between Nina and Zografos. Sturgeon said he was under the impression that Nina only wanted to be friends with Zografos. In fact, Sturgeon said Nina had told him in June that she had broken up with Zografos. Citing what Nina had told him, Sturgeon told the officers that Zografos once wanted to beat him up. As for Hans, Sturgeon said he believed he was paranoid and that his life now consisted primarily of his company, judo and video games.

When the interview with Sturgeon was over, Weisenberg met with Lieutenant Pete Sarna and members of the state Department of Justice to go over their game plan. First on their list: they wanted to tap Hans's phones.

Johnson, meanwhile, went to Doren's house to take another statement. Doren said Zografos had "uncoded" Nina's passwords to her e-mail and became upset when she opened a new account. To preserve her privacy, Nina told Doren to call her instead of using e-mail. Zografos would follow Nina and pressure her to tell him where she was all the time, Doren said. She said Zografos told her that the first night after he knew Nina was missing, he went through all her e-mails going back to 2000. Zografos seemed to be "acting like a victim" and focused on feeling sorry for himself in the wake of Nina's disappearance, Doren said. How could Zografos focus on how this was affecting *him* when everyone was trying to find Nina? Doren wondered.

Doren reported that while in Russia, Nina had cried a couple of times, fearful that Zografos might return to his wife. Doren said she saw an e-mail that Zografos's wife had sent to Nina. The week before she disappeared, Nina told Doren that her relationship with Zografos was fine and that she didn't have any plans to break up with him.

As for Hans, he was becoming more difficult for Nina in the weeks leading up to her disappearance, Doren said. Hans disputed that the Labor Day weekend was Nina's turn to have the kids. Hans told Nina numerous times to leave the country, give him the children and that she was in the way.

CHAPTER 33

> CAT AND MOUSE

On the morning of September 18, Hans awoke in the CRX. He was parked near a reservoir near Euclid Avenue in North Berkeley. But Oakland police had no idea where he was. In fact, they hadn't seen him in ten days. They still didn't know where the CRX was—or Nina, for that matter. They wanted all that to change. That day, officers launched a full-scale surveillance of Hans, using undercover officers on foot and in cars. They dubbed it "Operation Find Nina Reiser." About a dozen officers using Nextel phones in the "group talk" mode were riding in "covert vehicles," ordinary cars outfitted with police radios. Officers Jim Saleda and Mark Battle set up surveillance outside the Exeter home.

On that day, there was a daylong child-custody hearing at the court building on Washington Street in downtown Oakland. Sharanova and Beverly attended. At one point, Hans came up to Sharanova in the hallway and said, "I wish that the circumstances were better. Good luck." The battle lines had been drawn.

During the noon break, plainclothes officer Gino Guerrero watched as Beverly, Hans and his friend and fellow judo expert, Artem Mishin, went into a restaurant on Washington Street and had lunch.

I ventured to the courtroom that day. Outside in the hallway, I immediately recognized Guerrero and Officer Larry Robertson in plainclothes and sitting unobtrusively on a bench in a corner. It was clear the department was sparing no resources in trying to find Nina, as Guerrero and Robertson were among the best of the best.

A respected undercover officer, the grizzled Robertson

had the look of a Hells Angel, with a white beard, mustache and ponytail. He typically wore jeans, a baseball cap and a hard stare. He was known as "Dirty Rob" among members of Los Carnales, a Harley-riding cop motorcycle club that also counted Officers Saleda and Beere and gang unit sergeant Randy Brandwood as members. They liked to have fun, but Robertson, a former "Officer of the Year," meant business. He never smiled in pictures, even at cop functions. The story went that no one would dare flirt with his wife, a striking, blond Alameda County prosecutor, for fear of incurring Robertson's wrath.

Robertson's menacing look contrasted sharply with that of Guerrero. His slightly disheveled look and hangdog expression evoked images of Eeyore. With a penchant for plaid or checkered shirts and blue jeans, the twenty-year veteran was ideally suited for undercover work. He didn't have to grow his hair long or wear a beard. He automatically blended in, especially in the working-class neighborhoods of the mostly Latino Fruitvale District.

When Hans, Beverly and Mishin returned to court that afternoon, Officer Johnson played the straight man as Guerrero and Robertson lurked in the shadows. Johnson contacted Beverly in the hallway and asked for her help in finding Nina. Beverly didn't answer directly. She referred Johnson to Du Bois. Johnson reached out to Mishin and also asked him for his help.

As Judge Pro Tem Janet Sherwood listened to the attorneys' arguments that afternoon, a nondescript Cessna 182 taxied from the KaiserAir facility at Oakland International Airport's North Field. Gleaming in the sunshine, the plane maneuvered onto Runway 27-Right. Within moments, the single-engine aircraft was cleared for takeoff. The San Francisco skyline was straight ahead as a state Department of Justice pilot pushed the throttles down. The plane, its lone propeller a blur in the windshield, accelerated smoothly down the runway before lifting gently into the sky. It made a climbing right turn over San Leandro Bay and pointed briefly toward the Oakland hills before banking left to "follow the Nimitz northwest," as air-traffic controllers called Interstate 880, named after Admiral Chester Nimitz.

On board was Oakland police officer Leo Sanchez, who had a picture-perfect view from his lofty perch. Ahead of him were the skeletal cranes at the Port of Oakland, ready to service the giant cargo ships laden with goods chugging through San Francisco Bay from the open ocean. To his left was San Francisco, his hometown, and to his right was the city that he helped protect. Today, his job was to focus on just one person: Hans. Sanchez was naturally suited for his role as the eye in the sky. A member of the department's Targeted Enforcement Task Force, Sanchez had previously served with the security police in the U.S. Air Force Reserves. As a state Department of Justice pilot handled the controls, Sanchez peered through special gyroscope-mounted binoculars that pointed through a large Plexiglas window on the side of the plane. Circling at about five thousand feet, Sanchez could easily see anything within a half-block radius, down to the color of a bag someone was carrying. To talk to officers on the ground, Sanchez pushed a button on the floor of the plane. Constant contact was critical today.

Back on the ground, Hans was having some problems communicating with the judge. Sherwood handed down her ruling, and it wasn't what Hans wanted to hear. She ordered that Rory and Nio remain in the custody of CPS and be held in foster care. At about 5:45 p.m., Guerrero watched as a dejected Hans, Mishin and Cheryl Hicks, Hans's family law attorney, left the Washington Street court building.

Hicks expressed surprise that the police hadn't arrested Hans. Her client began walking up and down Washington. "As he was pacing, he was looking in all directions," Guerrero recalled. "His head was constantly moving all around, as if looking for somebody or something." Hans then walked to the corner of Sixth and Washington and again his head swiveled around. The group then walked together to the corner of Seventh and Washington streets, where Hans and Mishin then split up from Beverly.

The two men walked a block to Seventh and Clay streets,

where Mishin began looking at the undercarriage of his brand-new BMW M3. The undercover units were convinced that Mishin was looking for tracking devices. Mishin got in from the driver's side, and Hans sat in the front passenger seat.

Mishin drove north on San Pablo Avenue as police tracked his every move from the air and by car, keeping constant radio contact. Mishin made several evasive maneuvers while driving through Berkeley, making numerous turns off the busy thoroughfare. "At one point we were northbound on San Pablo and the vehicle made a left turn on a side street and then it made a right turn, went to the next block, made a left turn, went to the next block and made a right turn and eventually ended up on Gilman Street, where it turned east to San Pablo," Guerrero remembered.

With Sanchez high above them giving directions, the cops tracked Hans and Mishin as they approached the city of Albany on San Pablo and made a right turn onto Solano Avenue. At one point, Mishin drove so slowly that he caused a minor traffic backup. The two parked and took a circuitous path on foot, ducking in and out of a wine store before ending up at Fonda, the trendy tapas restaurant on Solano Avenue, as the sun started its drop toward the horizon. Undercover Officer Eric Karsseboom slipped inside and secretly watched them eat. At 7:35 p.m., Hans and Mishin left the restaurant and walked back to the BMW, where Mishin again checked under his car before the two got back inside.

Mishin drove south on San Pablo Avenue. At the corner of San Pablo and Ashby avenues, the police realized that there were now two identical BMWs next to each other stopped at the light. When the light changed, one BMW continued south on San Pablo. The other made a right and parked behind an AC Transit bus at the corner of San Pablo and Ashby avenues in Berkeley. It was almost right out of a movie, where the bad guys would try to throw off the police by using decoy vehicles. Which one to follow?

Guerrero and Officer Jason Sena saw Hans getting out of the BMW that was behind the bus. The officers watched for the next half hour as Hans walked seemingly aimlessly around the neighborhood, stopping frequently to look in all directions. He would stop at street corners, talk on his cell phone and look over his shoulder to see if he was being followed. He took a meandering stroll along Acton, Mabel and Carrison streets. He didn't know that the cops were tracking his every move.

At 8:15 p.m. at the corner of Acton and Carrison, Hans walked past a Honda CRX—the same car that the police were looking for, and the same one that Hans had claimed had battery problems. Five minutes later, he got into the Honda and drove away as the officers rejoiced. This was just the break they needed. Was Nina's body in the car? If not, was he going to take them to her body? Sanchez watched from the plane as Hans drove south on Market Street, got onto Highway 24, merged onto Highway 13 and then exited on Park Boulevard. He parked the CRX on the 2400 block of Monterey Boulevard, just a stone's throw from Highway 13.

What was most striking about it all was where the CRX was parked: as the crow flies, it was about three miles from Hans's house. Nina's Honda Odyssey was also found on a street alongside the same highway, also three miles from his house.

Sanchez watched through the gyroscope as Hans, inexplicably, walked away from the car four times, opening and closing the trunk. He walked back and forth on Monterey before turning onto Park Boulevard.

At that point, a blue taxi pulled up to the corner of Park and Mountain boulevards, and Hans stuck his head through the window to talk to the driver. Shortly after, the taxi took off. "He's in the cab!" one of the officers radioed excitedly. The plane began following the cab overheard. Sena and Guerrero caught up with the cab as it headed down Hegenberger Road toward the Oakland International Airport. This was it, they thought. Could Hans be getting ready to get on a plane— for real this time—and disappear?

Battle and Saleda, who had spent all day parked outside the Exeter house and were now driving down the hill, weren't so sure. They were prepared to expect the unexpected. When they heard that the cab was moving toward the airport, Battle drove in the opposite direction—back up the hill toward Hans's house. It was a smart move, because at about 9:20 p.m., lo and behold, the officers saw Hans sprinting up Snake Boulevard, against the flow of traffic. He had not gotten into the cab at all.

They watched as Hans continued running as Snake turned into Shepherd Canyon Road, a street that sliced through the Oakland hills and was heavily wooded on each shoulder. He alternated between a fair jog and a brisk walk, all the while looking all around him and to the sides—and apparently carrying leftovers from Fonda. He even looked at Battle and Saleda as they passed him in their undercover car. He was moving pretty fast up the road, which followed the path of an old railroad grade and ran through a canyon that was bounded on either side by house-lined ridges. "He was going [at] a good tilt," Saleda remembered. "In my best shape as a Scout in Iraq, I wouldn't have kept up with him."

Battle and Saleda pulled off onto Gunn Drive, got out of their car and hid in the bushes. They saw Hans continuing up the hill at a good clip. He was still looking around him in all directions. That same night, Goli Fahid, a resident of Exeter, also thought she saw a man running up the hill. As she approached him in her car, he started running. Fahid knew she recognized him from somewhere and thought for a while. Then it hit her. *That man looks a lot like my neighbor*, Fahid thought.

The officers drove to Exeter and saw Beverly's rented Camry parked out front as they passed the house. They parked their car up the street and got out on foot. By the time Saleda went into a neighbor's yard and looked in Beverly's driveway, the Camry was gone. They later found the car at McGothigan's house, on Simson Street. Beverly had gone there to pick up a computer. But Hans, once again, had vanished.

Targeted Enforcement Task Force officers Larry Robertson and Omega Crum, meanwhile, went up to the CRX that Hans had abandoned on Monterey Boulevard. They realized that the front passenger seat was missing. That was the most significant discovery yet, and to the police it meant only one thing: Hans must have transported Nina's body in the CRX and then tossed the seat because he had gotten blood on it.

That's why Hans was trying to hide the car. The officers took pictures of the CRX and left, but not before Crum stuck a tracking device on it. The police may have finally found Hans's car, but Nina was still out there somewhere.

CHAPTER 34

> WIRETAPS

On the same day that the Oakland Police Department (OPD) was following Hans around, the alphabet soup of law-enforcement agencies was only thickening. The U.S. Immigration and Customs Enforcement (ICE) reported that they had enough to file a structuring complaint against Hans. (The federal agency, however, later said Hans was not yet arrestable because agents still had to conduct interviews.) The FBI said it had opened up a kidnapping case, which would be helpful if Nina had been taken across state lines.

But the most important development came that day when Alameda County Superior Court Judge Jon Rolefson secretly authorized wiretaps on Hans's home and cell phones, signing off on an application written by state Bureau of Narcotic Enforcement (BNE) agent Michael Fanucchi. BNE's entry into the case signaled how unusual the case was becoming. There weren't many wiretaps done in Alameda County, save for a couple of homicide cases and a few narcotics investigations. Wiretaps were time-consuming and complicated. But it had to be done in this case. Fanucchi, a former Sacramento County probation officer, was brought in because drug cops have the most experience with wiretapping.

"I believe there is probable cause to believe there exists an immediate and substantial danger to the life or limb of Nina Reiser," Fanucchi wrote in an affidavit in which he described both Hans and his mother as "possibly being involved with these crimes."

The BNE agent noted, "I believe persons who are involved in such violent crimes, specifically as in this case, a kidnapping and/or murder, will talk about their crime or talk about their involvement in the crime by utilizing telephones, specifically their cellular telephones and hard lines. They will talk to co-conspirators, family members, friends or make statements that may provide information related to the investigation." Fanucchi had no idea how prophetic those words would be.

He continued in his affidavit, "Suspects involved in these types of crimes may need to make payment arrangements to those who assisted them with the crime. It is also common for these types of suspects to tell stories and change their stories to family, relatives and other people who may be involved with the crime."

District Attorney Tom Orloff had to personally request the wiretap from Presiding Judge George Hernandez. The DA's application was filed with Judge Rolefson by Deputy District Attorney Paul Delucchi. It was Delucchi's father, the late Judge Alfred Delucchi, who oversaw the murder trial of Modesto fertilizer salesman Scott Peterson, whose wiretapped calls to mistress Amber Frey helped lead to his conviction for murdering his pregnant wife, Laci, and their unborn son.

Paul Delucchi gave the police explicit instructions on how the wiretap would work. All officers had to sign in on a log sheet before monitoring calls. No recording machine could be left unattended or on automatic. And perhaps the most important limitation to the electronic eavesdropping—any time there were phone calls between Hans and his attorney, the police had to shut off the recorder or "minimize" for two minutes. They could then listen in again for up to thirty seconds, then repeat the process if it was still a so-called privileged conversation. They could only listen to calls that were deemed legally pertinent. Delucchi warned that failure to properly minimize calls could doom the case—all wiretapped calls could be thrown out, plus any evidence obtained as a result of those calls.

With the judge's legal go-ahead, a group of officers began rotating shifts in a "wire room" on the fourth floor of Oakland police headquarters, listening to and recording all of the calls Hans made and received.

Although a tracking device had been placed on the CRX, police decided to tow the car at 10:30 a.m. the next day, September 19. Saleda took digital photos of the car and made a

point not to touch anything inside. Giving the car a visual
once-over, Saleda also noticed that the front passenger seat
was missing. There was a roll of heavy-duty green plastic
trash bags in the back of the car. There were numerous articles of clothing, a backpack and many pieces of trash inside.
A tow-truck driver arrived, and Saleda told him to put on
gloves so as not to disturb any evidence. The CRX was put
onto a flatbed truck and towed to the Eastmont substation,
joining Nina's Honda Odyssey. There, the tow-truck driver
used a Slim Jim to open the car door.

Battle and Saleda then went back to the 1500 block of
Fernwood Drive, where Nina's minivan had been found. They
then checked all possible routes from there to Hans's house,
trying to see if any businesses had external security cameras.
They only found a couple of ATMs on Mountain Boulevard.

The officers then got a list of all the cab companies that
operated in Oakland. They wanted to see which cabbie had
been called to the area the night before. They wanted to know
if Hans had summoned the taxi to the scene, only to send it
away.

That same day, Weisenberg and Grant went to McGothigan's home, on Simson Street in Oakland. Beverly's friend
said she had told him that Nina was missing on September 6,
the day after they returned from Burning Man. Beverly told
him she was concerned that Sturgeon may have set up Hans
and might be involved in Nina's disappearance. McGothigan
also said that Sturgeon had bragged about beating up a person
who had tried to mug him.

CPS worker Seng Fong called Hans shortly after 2:00 p.m.,
asking to meet with him to discuss what they should tell the
children. Hans asked her to call Dr. Schreier, the Children's
Hospital Oakland expert on Munchausen by proxy disorder,
to get his input. "He's generally thought of as extremely competent," he said.

At about 3:00 p.m., Officer Grant drove to Doren's house,
on Capricorn Drive in the Oakland hills, to interview Sharanova. He was assisted by a Russian translator employed by
the FBI. Sharanova said she learned that there were problems

in the relationship through a family friend who had worked as a nanny for the couple. The two would get into arguments, the friend reported. Sharanova said she spoke to her daughter on the phone on September 1, 2 and 3, the day she disappeared. Nina told her about the job offer and revealed that she was considering moving in with Zografos, who was known to be a jealous and suspicious person, Sharanova told the officers. Nina reported that she had told Hans that he needed to move on and find himself a woman. Hans told Nina sometime between August 29 and September 1 that he would never stop trying to get revenge against her. When Sharanova first heard that her daughter was missing, she immediately suspected that Hans had done something to her.

At about 3:30 p.m., during a wiretapped call, Ramon called his son and, in his raspy voice, railed that someone was leaking information to the press, because "people don't normally go through court records and divorce stuff and all that." I knew this to be false, as I routinely pulled these kinds of records for stories in which spouses were suspected. Ramon urged Hans to have his attorney read a press release that Hans was drafting. Ramon knew his son could be "bombastic."

Ramon again called to give some fatherly advice at about 4:15 p.m. In a voice-mail message, Ramon urged that his son make a public plea for help in his press release, asking anyone who may have seen Nina or her car to call the police. He suggested that Hans mention that his children miss their mother very much. Ramon warned his son not to talk about Nina, Namesys or Sturgeon as the press might "hang you by the balls." Ramon was clearly worried about Hans's planned press release, because he told his son to make sure there was "perfect wording" on it.

That day, Hans was busy with his Patelco bank accounts. He visited the Oakland branch at Twenty-second and Webster streets and deposited a check for $12,000. Another $7,447 was also deposited into his account. An employee recognized Hans, telling him that Patelco staff had "heard what had happened." Hans acted as though he did not know what the employee was talking about.

‹ The Mormon Temple is one of Oakland's best known landmarks. Perched on the foothills off Lincoln Avenue just below Highway 13 and up the street from the Head-Royce School, the 170-foot-tall building features five golden spires surrounded by colorful gardens lined with palm trees. The temple's white granite walls are so striking—and swathed in light at night—that pilots and air traffic controllers use it a visual checkpoint before landing.

At 9:12 p.m. on September 19, Hans was using the temple as a place of refuge. Officer Andre Rachal was in the wire room when he monitored a phone call Hans made from his cell phone to his mother. Hans was very upset. The cops had towed his wheels—with all the evidence inside.

"Hello?" Beverly asked.

"Hi, Mom. Um, can you get me at the Mormon Temple? I'd like to talk with you about something. OK?"

"At the Mormon Temple?" an incredulous Beverly asked.

"Uh-huh," Hans said, as if it was only natural that he'd be there.

"Hans, we're trying to set up this, this, um . . . why do I have to pick you up there?"

"Mom, could you just do it, OK?" Hans said plaintively.

Beverly went to do something before coming back on the line. "All right, uh, I'll—I'm going to come over and get you," she said.

"OK, thanks."

Rachal immediately called Officer Jason Sena. Sena had a laptop computer that was linked to the tracking device that police had placed on Beverly's rented Camry. Sena confirmed that the car traveled to the area of the Mormon Temple and then returned to Exeter Drive.

Officer Grant scanned the page that came off the fax on the morning of September 20. There was the confirmation he was looking for: the registration form showing that Zografos and his wife were indeed at Big Basin Park during the Labor Day weekend. Grant also received the license-plate log for all the vehicles that came into the park. The officer would later receive from Zografos a CD of pictures he took, proving that he and his family in fact had gone camping.

Zografos may have been cleared as a suspect, but he was still acting suspiciously to Doren and her husband, Marc Prager. Prager told Officer Johnson that morning that Zografos was convinced that Nina had met Sturgeon for a rendezvous on Fernwood Drive, where her minivan was found.

Oakland police drove two of Nina's computers, a flash card and a digital camera to the Silicon Valley Regional Computer Forensics Laboratory in Menlo Park. The lab specializes in examining digital evidence for criminal cases, including terrorism, child pornography, violent crimes, theft of intellectual property, Internet crime and fraud. FBI Agent Parker, whose agency had a close relationship with the lab, asked that Nina's items be examined pursuant to a search warrant.

> Hans and his mother had a supervised visit with Rory and Nio at a social services building on Broadway in downtown Oakland. Hans tape-recorded the visit and whispered to Nio that social workers and lawyers were making money from them being in foster care. Hans later whispered something to Rory. When Alameda County child-welfare worker Seng Fong asked Rory what his father had said, the boy said it was a secret. While waiting for Sharanova and Doren to arrive, the kids read a book that included sample furs of different animals. When Nio spent a little longer feeling one of them, Rory became upset, pushed his sister and grabbed her in the face. He called her stupid and an idiot for not knowing her multiplication tables. Fong, who had been sitting in between the children, had to mediate the situation, telling them to spend an equal amount of time with the book.

When Sharanova and Doren arrived, Rory repeatedly hugged Doren and read to her. Doren brought notes from her children for Rory and Nio as well as toys and clothes. They played with the toys as if they had never seen a toy in their life.

Undercover officers tailed Hans and Beverly as they got into the Camry near police headquarters. They spotted him as he went into Du Bois' office in downtown Oakland at 1:00 p.m. Less than two hours later, they watched as he walked two blocks to the office of his family court attorney, Cheryl Hicks. Ten minutes later, he walked to the Patelco Credit Union on Twenty-second Street and withdrew five thousand dollars.

At 5:00 p.m. Hans called *Oakland Tribune* reporter Jason Dearen, who had been gently persuading the computer programmer to provide a comment. "Hi Jason, I just wanted to confirm that my attorney offered you a statement and you guys turned down the opportunity to print it, is that correct?" Reiser asked.

"No, no, that's not what I was told," Dearen said. "I was told you guys turned it down."

Hans fell silent.

Dearen repeated, "That's what I was told. Is that not correct?"

Hans laughed. "Maybe I need to get you and my lawyer in the room at the same time," he said.

After hanging up, Hans got onto an AC Transit bus at Seventeenth Street and Broadway.

He called his mother again at 5:03 p.m. He told Beverly that he was on a bus in Berkeley and was going to the downtown YMCA to work out. The two discussed what they wanted to do for dinner. Beverly said they could have leftovers from last night. "We can have dinner here, Hans," she said. "It's cheaper." Hans asked his mom to pick him up in front of the YMCA at about 6:30 p.m. He suggested that they "swing by Whole Foods" afterward so that they could get breakfast and lunch for the next day.

"But Hans, don't be late, because I really hate sitting there waiting," Beverly said. They went to the Whole Foods Market at Ashby and Telegraph avenues in Berkeley and bought a tri-tip roast, two cheeses—sharp cheddar and Bucherondin, from French goat's milk—grapes, apple juice and apple pie.

› Nina was to have met with her bankruptcy attorney on September 20. She was supposed to have started her new job in San Francisco the next day. She didn't show up on either date.

> On September 21, Beverly, fed up with being her son's chauffeur, made another trip to a rental car agency. As she drove the Camry, with Hans in the front seat, undercover police and BNE agents were not too far behind. The agents tailed mother and son as they made their way to Budget Rent a Car on Mission Boulevard in Hayward. They were supposed to have picked up a Chevrolet Cobalt. But they left together in the Toyota. The officers followed them as they drove on westbound Interstate 580 back toward downtown Oakland, but not before Beverly got off the freeway on Fairmont Drive in San Leandro and then got back on.

"Cop behind you," Hans told his mother at one point. State BNE agent Brad Bautista was listening as he intercepted a message Hans left on the voice mail of an associate in Massachusetts. Hans said he had a new Yahoo e-mail address. The police believed Hans suspected his phones were tapped and would be communicating by e-mail to thwart the wiretap. Police later learned that Hans used the account to contact Du Bois, among others. Officer Weisenberg inadvertently read an e-mail between Hans and Du Bois. At the direction of the DA's office, investigators assigned Sergeant Rodney Grimes, who was not directly involved in the case, to go through and redact the privileged e-mails.

That morning, the police had a big meeting on the second floor of Oakland police headquarters to see what had been done and what next steps had to be taken. They used the line-up room where cops met at the beginning of their shifts. Deputy Chief Jordan, head of criminal investigations, Captain Jeff Loman, Lieutenant Ersie Joyner and Sergeant Bruce Brock of homicide, Lieutenant Wiley and Sergeant Tom Hogenmiller of youth and family services, Special Operations Group commander Lieutenant Pete Sarna, intelligence sergeant Gus Galindo and Officers Gill, Johnson, Grant and Weisenberg were all there. So were state BNE agents Fanucchi and Brent Burwell, who reported to their supervisor Carl Estelle, a former Oakland officer. Even after leaving the force, Estelle still worked closely with the department. There is a saying among former Oakland cops: "Once OPD, always OPD." Three months earlier, Estelle and Oakland police sergeant Randy Wingate, a respected SWAT officer, had shot and killed a Vallejo murder suspect near Oakland's Highland Hospital. Now, both Estelle and Wingate were on Hans's trail.

Fanucchi told the group that the wire room was generating a number of calls, including those from Ramon to Hans. Ramon used a router phone in Washington State but actually lived in Georgia, Fanucchi reported. Hans "blows up a lot" and is quick to hang up on people, Fanucchi said. Hans was using pay phones and reading newspapers about the case. The police noticed that he was still working out, enjoying good food and carrying out his life as normal—and apparently not lifting a finger to look for his missing wife.

Sarna was a respected veteran who oversaw the gang, intelligence and department task forces as head of the Special Operations Group, whose logo was a stallion's head with two lightning bolts. He was instrumental in bringing "shot spotter" software to the city, in which gunfire could be automatically tracked through GPS technology. Sarna suggested that officers talk to Assistant District Attorney Tom Rogers about a possible arrest. Joyner said the cops should catch Hans on video acting nervously because it would be "very powerful in courtroom settings." No one at that time could predict how true that statement would become.

Hans ended up renting a red 2002 Ford Escort that afternoon from North Bay Car Rental on Ninety-second Avenue in East Oakland.

Police decided to return to Nina and Hans's neighborhoods to check with residents to see if they had seen or heard anything unusual around Labor Day weekend. Residents on Exeter were asked when they last saw Hans, Nina or Beverly and if they had ever seen Hans running in the area, exercising or practicing judo.

On September 21, Rory and Nio were placed in the care of Doren, who would now be responsible for their medical and educational needs pending ongoing child-custody hearings.

On September 22, Officer Grant went to Doren's house and met with Sharanova, with whom he had developed a rapport.

The plan was to have Sharanova make a "pretext" call to Hans to try to get him to say something incriminating.

As Grant watched, Sharanova called Hans at 11:54 a.m. No one answered. She left a message in accented English. "Hans, hi. This is Irina. I'd like to talk to you. I'd like to know what happened, and I do not understand why, why you don't want to connect with me. Could you please—I'm so sorry," she sighed. "Could you please help me to find her. Maybe you know something about her. I'd like to know everything. It's very important for me." She was desperate and hoping that her son-in-law would have some shred of decency to give her answers. "And when you visit in Russia, we have a good relationship, and I hope for your help. I'd like to understand what has happened. And I hope that you call me back as soon as you can. Thank you, bye."

Several minutes later, a call came into Doren's home. There was no one on the other line.

Sharanova left another message at noon. "Hi Hans, this is Irina again. Unfortunately, I forgot to say phone number where I am staying now." She recited Doren's phone number. "Thank you, bye."

Sharanova then relayed to Grant something disturbing she had heard from Rory: Hans had told him that it would be better if Nina left and never came back. The little boy said his father had also said that Nina had stolen money from him. Doren also reported that Hans told Rory that his mother was gone—and that Hans wished Rory never had a mom. Hans told Rory that Nina used him as a tool to get money from Hans. Both Doren and Sharanova said they had heard Rory say many times that girls were idiots.

Grant then interviewed Rory himself. The boy said that "although it is hard to catch a Russian in lies," he believed he had caught Nina making a lie. Rory confirmed that his dad had told him that Nina was a liar and that she lies to get money from his father. Rory said his mom had lied about Rory being afraid of teen-rated video games and did so to get money. But then Rory abruptly changed his opinion of his mom. He said she was a really honest person and that he had only caught her in one lie. He couldn't provide any details.

As Grant was busy with the interviews, Oakland police

criminalist Shannon Cavness called shortly after noon with a major break in the case: the blood on the pillar in Hans's home was from a woman—and Nina's DNA could not be excluded from the sample.

Beverly spoke with a child-welfare worker that day. They scheduled a home-assessment visit for September 29 to see if her Exeter home would be suitable for placing the children. Beverly said she didn't have any concerns about her son caring for the kids and described him as a devoted father. Hans may do things differently, but it didn't mean he wasn't competent, Beverly told CPS. She said she had her own life and wasn't dependent on what her son thought. She said Hans wanted the kids out of foster care, and if they could not be with him, then he wanted them placed with her. Beverly said her son was no longer in the home but was in the process of moving out.

About a half hour before Sharanova tried to call Hans, Beverly got a call from a friend. She talked about consulting with an attorney to try to get her cars back and discussed how it didn't seem as if she would be getting custody of the children. "I think I'm tainted by Hans," she said. Later, she added, "The prospect of having my grandchildren raised in foster care is just horrific." She told her friend that she didn't know what was going on beyond what was in the newspapers.

Shortly before 6:00 p.m., Officer Johnson called the Exeter home. Officer Rachal was listening in from the wire room. Johnson reached Beverly and asked her to participate in a massive search for Nina that was planned for the next day. Beverly said she had a prior engagement. Johnson then asked if Hans would be available. Beverly said she had been trying to reach him, but his voice mail was full. Beverly asked what the search would entail, and Johnson said they'd be searching for Nina and anything related to her disappearance. Beverly asked Johnson if he believed Nina was somewhere in the hills. Johnson said anything was possible.

After Johnson hung up, Beverly's friend called. She told him that she was "living in hell." She noted that Johnson had asked about Hans taking part in the search. "It would be a stupid idea for him to help," the friend told Beverly. "What if he finds the body in the hills?"

Hans poses for a picture at his friend Sean Sturgeon's home in Oakland. Hans wanted to send pictures of himself to prospective wives.
Courtesy: Alameda County Superior Court

Nina in Russia at about the time she met Hans.
Courtesy: Alameda County Superior Court

Hans and Nina on their wedding day in the Oakland hills. Nina was five months pregnant with her son at the time.
Courtesy: Alameda County Superior Court

Nina and her son, Rory.
Courtesy: Alameda County Superior Court

Nina and her children. She and Hans rarely agreed on parenting techniques, and it would become a contentious issue in their divorce.
Courtesy: Alameda County Superior Court

Nina with her boyfriend, Anthony Zografos, during a trip in the snow. The two met on Craigslist while both sought playdates for their children.
Courtesy: Alameda County Superior Court

Groceries from Berkeley Bowl, including perishables like fruit and dairy products, and children's books were found in Nina's minivan.
Courtesy: Alameda County Superior Court

The Honda CRX driven by Hans was found with its passenger seat missing. Hans later said that he removed the seat to make the car more comfortable to sleep in.

Courtesy: Alameda County Superior Court

Billboards with Nina's picture appeared throughout the East Bay, asking anyone with information to call the Oakland police.

Courtesy: Alameda County Superior Court

Oakland police search the home on Exeter Drive in the Oakland hills where Hans lived with his mother.
Courtesy: Alameda County Superior Court

Oakland police officer Mark Battle in a living room full of Asian paintings and artifacts. Hans's mother, Beverly, was an artist who had studied Chinese brush painting. A bloodstain on the pillar in the foreground was later determined to contain DNA belonging to both Hans and Nina.
Courtesy: Alameda County Superior Court

While under police surveillance, Hans runs at full speed from the media while carrying a telescope. It is a birthday present for Rory, who turned seven that day and was in protective custody. The author, pictured at right, is chasing Hans.
Courtesy: Alameda County Superior Court

Booking photo of Hans. Police arrested him even though Nina's body had not been found.
Courtesy: Alameda County Superior Court

LEFT:
Prosecutor Paul Hora in his office. He had fretted over whether he could prove Hans had murdered Nina.
Courtesy: Author photo

RIGHT:
Defense attorneys Richard Tamor (left) and William Du Bois outside the René C. Davidson Courthouse in Oakland. They argued that there was no proof that Nina was dead, let alone murdered by Hans.
Courtesy: Author photo

Superior Court Judge Larry Goodman presided over Hans's trial. He grew frustrated with the defendant numerous times.
Courtesy: Author photo

CHAPTER 35

› SEARCHES IN THE HILLS

At 6:30 a.m. on Saturday, September 23, search-and-rescue teams gathered at a command post at the Trudeau Training Center, at 11500 Skyline Boulevard. It was a massive operation that had to be coordinated through the state Office of Emergency Services. Participating were search-and-rescue teams from Alameda, Contra Costa, Marin, San Mateo and Santa Clara counties; California Search and Rescue; California Rescue Dog Association; and Oakland and East Bay Regional Park police. Searchers adopted the "abduction protocol," whereby a kidnap victim was snatched and then dumped within an hour of being taken. They were told to look for possible dump sites two hundred to three hundred feet off roads, at turnouts and along trails. Any possible clue was logged in real time at the command post, and police would immediately respond to check it out.

At 8:00 a.m., teams began scouring the Oakland hills by foot and on horseback and with cadaver dogs. The area they'd be searching was massive and was broken into four sections.

"This was the last general area that she was believed to possibly come to," Oakland police public information officer Roland Holmgren said at one of the parks being searched, choosing his words carefully as he was interviewed on camera. "Talking with friends and family members, we also know that she loved to go hiking, loved parks, loved this area. So it would be a disservice for us not to fully engage and search this area."

Sadly, the Bay Area had seen its share of massive searches for missing women. Some of the same searchers were on hand several years ago, looking for Laci Peterson in the waters of the bay. East Bay Regional Park police Lieutenant Dave Dubowy, who headed up his department's team to search for Nina, was the one who greeted Modesto police in April 2003 as they arrived by helicopter at Point Isabel in Richmond to examine Laci's body.

There were numerous potential items of evidence found on that warm day, when temperatures rose to as high as eighty-one degrees. Officer Grant found a rock and a car floor mat, both of which were stained red. Officer Saleda took pictures of the items, which were found fifty meters south of a road sign. Grant took a picture of a bra strap that he found south of a gate that closes off Pinehurst Road from traffic. Also found that day and booked into evidence were cigarette butts, sweaters, a yellow rope wrapped in silver duct tape and a sandal with a snakeskin strap. They also located bones, but it was confirmed they were from an animal.

Someone also found a car seat in the bushes off Redwood Road. But it was wider than a standard CRX seat, and police decided not to collect it as evidence. Officer Weisenberg was flagged down on Redwood Road by a man who said he had heard digging noises coming from the brush at about 2:00 p.m. on September 17. A cadaver dog searched the area but found nothing.

There was interest by a dog, however, in a bulldozer on an empty lot on Thorndale Drive. The owner of the property arrived and offered to help in any way he could. Searchers on horseback reported that they doubted anyone would be able to carry a body up two hundred feet near the equestrian centers and then drop it over the edge.

Many teams reported the same hazards: sharp thorns from blackberries making passage impossible, steep hillsides, poison oak and fast cars on the roads. Some searchers encountered bees, clouds of mosquitoes and huge spiders. But none of them found Nina.

CHAPTER 36

›PHONE CALLS TO MOM

Hans listened to Sharanova's voice-mail messages that morning.

"Irina asked me to call her," Hans told his mother after the first message played.

"Irina asked you to call her?" Beverly repeated.

"Yeah," he said.

As search crews scoured the hills, Hans was on a mission of his own. He drove from one Patelco branch to another, making cash withdrawals. At 12:16 p.m., he went to a branch in San Leandro, just outside Oakland, and withdrew one thousand dollars. He then drove further south to a Hayward Patelco and withdrew another thousand dollars at 12:54 p.m. Next, he went to a Patelco in Fremont and got an additional one thousand dollars at 1:47 p.m. While in Fremont, he also transferred funds from one account to another.

He then got into the Ford Escort he had rented and drove to Reno.

At 8:36 p.m. that night, Hans called his mom.

"Anything interesting going on?" he asked.

"Oh, nothing really," Beverly said, laughing. She said she had plans with a friend to go to the Asian Art Museum in San Francisco because "it was just kind of lonely in the house."

"Well, what can I say. With me not in the house it will increase your chances of getting custody."

"I hope so," said Beverly, sounding unconvinced.

Hans gave a number of reasons—excuses, investigators would later say—as to why it probably wouldn't be a good idea for him to talk to Sharanova. But Beverly said he would be making a mistake if he didn't talk to her because it would make him look guilty. Beverly told her son to at least tape-record a conversation with her.

"Why don't you meet with Irina?" Beverly asked.

"Mother, she will say that I threatened her—she's done it before."

"Well, then take your tape machine with you and tape the whole meeting."

Hans said Sharanova was lying about him at child-custody hearings. He said his previous divorce attorney, Rachel Ginsburg, had warned him never to meet Nina alone. "I'm so sorry I didn't believe her," he said of Ginsburg. "She was right."

Hans recounted the tussle over Nio in 2004. "And, you know Irina engaged me in a tug-of-war with Niorline."

"Niorline?" Beverly sounded surprised.

"Yeah!" Hans said this with an "as if" tone. "Both Nina and Irina. First it started with Nina. Then she handed it, uh, then she handed it, uh, Niorline to her mother so she could go call the cops. And you know who won the tug-of-war? They won the tug-of-war. So they won the tug-of-war, I'm a black belt in judo. What does that tell you, Mom? They were pulling so hard on Niorline's arm that I was afraid that Niorline's arms were going to be damaged. And then I tried to pull Niorline away from Irina without hurting Niorline. And finally I had to give up."

Beverly told Hans about "some sort of memorial service for Nina" that was going to be held the next day at a church in Berkeley. The police could not have engineered the conversation any better, which they in fact had not. If Nina was truly not dead, as he would later suggest, Hans did not challenge his mother with her reference to a *memorial* service.

There was a long silence on the line before Hans finally said anything. "What do you say about a woman who convinces all these psychologists that my son has all these problems?"

He then referred to testimony at the child-custody hearings suggesting that Rory had to be protected from him. "It's pretty rotten," he said.

"Actually, the children really love you," Beverly said.

"They do," he agreed. "I'm a better parent than Nina ever

was." He paused. "Or ever will be." Another pause. "Or ever could be."

He continued, "She doesn't like tutoring people. You know what she likes? She likes sitting around with the other parents and talking about how much—what wonderful parents they all are, but not actually taking time to teach the kids anything. I mean, you sit there and go through storybooks, but you know, it's a lot of work to teach kids things. Nina was just never willing to put in the work. Never mind that was her role in our family, never mind that I was providing for her, never mind that I was giving her eighty-five hundred dollars a month—well, actually, I think she spent more than that—you know, giving her this immensely comfortable lifestyle, she couldn't be bothered with teaching the kids anything. And our kids should have been far, farther along, given their intelligence and their education, than they are. And as soon as I got some real time with them this summer, their education took a sudden spurt ahead."

"Well, I still think you should talk with Nina's mother, because it makes you look hostile," Beverly said.

"Well, maybe you should tell the press that Nina and her mother have a history of making stuff up about me. And that's why I don't talk to them." It wasn't clear if *them* referred to the press or Nina and her mother. "Maybe lying isn't OK. I'll say this much for Irina—at least when she lies she's not able to look me in the eyes and doesn't look very convincing, whereas Nina, when she lied, it was just absolutely believable, just absolutely unquestionably believable, when Nina lied. I don't know why Nina's mother isn't as good of a liar as Nina. Well, I guess Nina was something special, even for Russians." He sighed.

State drug agent Fred Doran, monitoring the twenty-five-minute call from the wire room, noted that Hans was using the past tense.

A minute after hanging up, Hans called her back, at 9:03 p.m. Doran was still listening. This fourteen-minute call would later be used as ammunition in the case against Hans, his own words making him appear to be a remorseless killer justifying his actions.

"Hello?" Beverly answered.

"Hi, Mom."

"Yeah."

"Yeah. I just want—you know, I just realized that I never really spoke to you much about the divorce, and you know, I had wanted to go to a mediator. I tried to talk Nina into a mediator, and you know, I guess Nina decided that wouldn't be enough fun, so she did this traumatic-stress-disorder-due-to-violent-computer-games thing. And you know, it was more than that, because you know Nina, Nina kept doing it after it was to her disadvantage. I mean, it's finally got to a point where it was to her legal disadvantage to come up with this stuff. And she really was nuts, mom. She really was."

"She really was what?" Beverly asked.

"She really was nuts. She really was Munchausen by proxy disorder, and you know, she came up with these illnesses because she hated me. And Rory was the proxy for me, so by discovering that he was borderline autistic, that was her way of degrading me. And you know, Rory—you know, I was really surprised when, you know, the kids asked me about custody, and I explained about how, you know, custody gets divided out. And Rory said that he wanted to live with me, and not live with me, you know 50 percent of the time, but live only with me. And I think that's because he understands Nina. And he understands that she doesn't mean well by him, and he understands his mother, who wants him to be sick and who wants him to have things that are wrong with him, doesn't really like him on some deep conflicted level. And there's also some truth to what my father said, which was that Rory didn't want to impose on Nina. And, I think he understood that his existence was an imposition on Nina.

"Um, and then you know, she would do things like, she would, bought this really fancy laptop, and then she told me that, 'Oh that was a warranty replacement.' And we got her on the deposition on that one, uh, but we never presented it to the court, but you know, the proof that it was a lie. And she stole, stole stuff and took it to Russia, and she stole money. And you know, at the time that, at the time that, you know, I was asking guys to take pay cuts from $5 an hour to $3.75 and from $29 to

$9.66 or whatever it was that I paid them, um, she was spending money like crazy. She was increasing her expenditures because she had been told that the amount of money that she got during the, after the divorce was required by statute to be enough to maintain the lifestyle that she was accustomed to, so she figured she should make her lifestyle as fancy as possible and that would get her more money, you know, and she's doing this while the company is going bankrupt. And she concealed all kinds of money—I'll never know how much—both before the divorce and after the divorce.

"She did things like she would kick me and then call the police," Hans said, referring to the May 2004 incident. "I mean, she kicks me, and then she knows that because she's a woman, called the police. Well, and actually, in that case it didn't work. In that case the police offered to arrest her. The police wanted to arrest her, and I had to talk them out of it. And so I told them that because it didn't bruise me and it wasn't violent, so they shouldn't charge her. Was that a mistake. You know, I would advise any man getting a divorce, if your wife ever kicks you or hits you during the divorce and then calls the police, you need to let her get arrested, because—"

"I know, but nobody wants to have the mother of their children arrested," Beverly broke in.

"Yeah, well being decent is a mistake, a mistake I paid for heavily. Boy, would things have gone better if she had gone to jail instead of to Russia. Wouldn't have had to have her ransom, you know, that whole business where she tried to get a bank account set up for herself before she came back, and she threatened to not—you remember she threatened to not come back, and threatened to go to Sweden instead. You know, unless she got money, fortunately, I knew better than you do that she was bluffing on that one. You know, she's just—she didn't just abuse me. She looked for every possible way to screw me and did it. And the fact that I had been a good and generous husband just seemed like weakness to her. That's all she could understand it as."

"Well," Beverly began.

"And then this last bit about Rory's front teeth being too large and therefore he might need orthodontic work, and all of this sensory diet that she got from [a therapist], and she convinced all the teachers at Grand Lake Montessori that Rory had weak wrists rather than that he was bored, and because of his weak wrists and poor muscle tone, he couldn't learn how to write, or he needs special therapy."

"You know, but Hans, as awful as these things are, it's still sad, whatever it is that's happened to Nina," Beverly said.

"Well, yeah," he replied.

"I mean, no matter all these things that she did, she didn't deserve whatever it is that's happened to her." There was a long pause before she added, "Don't you think?"

"I think my children shouldn't be endangered by her."

"Well, I still think—"

"The whole thing is sad."

"What?"

"Because all I ever wanted was to be nice to her and give her an opportunity to come to the United States and, you know, for the opportunity to have some children."

"Still, Nina didn't deserve whatever it is that happened to her," Beverly said, trying to elicit some kind of sympathy from her son.

"And neither did I, and neither did Rory," Hans answered.

"Well, hopefully we'll somehow get through all this."

"It's just sad, you know, and the whole, the court system made it so much worse than it had to be, just so much worse."

"Well, that's true."

"And then they—you know, these lawyers just systematically drained us of everything we had. And Shelley Gordon took advantage of Nina's being nuts and used it to make money. And I don't think for one minute that Shelley Gordon thought that Rory had traumatic stress disorder due to violent computer games, but you know, Shelley actually had the nerve to tell me that I deserve it. I guess if you're male, you deserve anything." (In an interview later, Gordon said she disagreed with Hans's assertions. "My job was not to assess Rory. My job was to help Nina get the professional help she needed based on the professional recommendations she had previously received with regard to Rory," Gordon said.)

Beverly asked her son if he was getting his e-mail at a café.

He replied that it might be hard to reach him but to go ahead and e-mail him. Beverly reminded Hans about the child-custody hearing scheduled in four days.

"I love you a lot," Hans said.

Beverly laughed. "Good. Bye-bye," she said, and the two hung up.

Late that night, Beverly watched *Matrix Reloaded* on DVD. It featured an action-packed chase scene, parts of which had been filmed several years earlier right near Du Bois' office at the corner of Sixteenth Street and Telegraph Avenue. Crews had also filmed at the nearby Webster Street tube, through which a surveillance team had secretly followed Beverly as she went to the gym. Beverly had no idea that within days, there would be a real-life chase through the streets of Oakland, and her son would be right in the crosshairs.

> On Sunday, September 24, friends and family of Nina took up spots on the red carpet inside the tiny, ornately decorated Saint John the Baptist Russian Orthodox Church in Berkeley. The blue-domed church, frequented by many Russian immigrants, sat just down the street from where Nina had gone shopping at Berkeley Bowl. Father Kirill Hartman, his white beard and traditional vestments adding more gravitas, led the group in prayer for her safe return, speaking in both English and Slavonic. It may not have been a true memorial service, but Sharanova was overwhelmed with emotion. "It's very hard for me, because she was very close to me," she told reporters afterward on the church's front steps. She was barely able to get the words out.

Immediately after the service, Doren, Zografos and dozens of others conducted their own search of the hills. They fanned out in several parks, including the Sibley volcanic preserve, scanning steep brush- and tree-covered slopes. Zografos handed out red flags and pink tape for searchers to mark any items they found. Searchers were told that they weren't looking for a body but rather clues that would bring them closer to finding Nina. This search also produced nothing of evidentiary value. Nina's friends were still torn between disappointment and relief. If her body wasn't found, didn't that mean she could miraculously show up alive and well somewhere? Although no one was saying so publicly, everyone knew that as each day passed, the chances of that happening grew smaller. Zografos told reporters that he was confident that Nina would be found. The only question, however, was what condition she would be in when that happened. He broke down and cried.

On that day, Hans was in the Sierra Nevada. Shortly before 5:00 p.m., he made three withdrawals of five hundred dollars each from a U.S. Bank ATM in Truckee.

During the search, Doren grimly pulled out her cell phone to call Officer Grant. She had smelled a foul odor on the 9600 block of Skyline Boulevard.

> On September 25, Johnson and Weisenberg went to Doren's house to interview Rory and Nio. Rory told them that he thought his mother was "lost in Oakland." When Weisenberg asked the boy why he could be so sure, he replied, "Why would she be lost somewhere else when she said nothing about leaving the house?"

The boy added that it was possible that his mother was working on some kind of surprise for him. "Maybe she didn't want to tell the future to me," he said. "I think she often does that, she didn't want to tell the future unless it's something that, uh, that is exciting."

He confided to them that "only my dad makes her mad" and that she said "he's grumpy when he talks to her." He added that although his father made "thousands of bucks," she "wants more than my dad even has." Rory said his dad "pays actually the most attention to me," while his mother spent most of her time "getting something ready to make or working" or "making her bed."

Weisenberg asked Rory to put on a "memory hat" and to try to remember what happened on the day he last saw his mom. Rory said he remembered giving her a "squeeze-hug" and that he didn't want to kiss her because he thought cavities could spread. Hans told him not to be on the same floor in which he was talking, Rory said.

He said he if he found shoeprints, he'd follow them to his mom. "I'll tell you a little clue," he told the officers. "She has black hair. She's tan. And black eyes." She "kind of" looked like him, he said. "She doesn't often wear dresses. She often wears skirts or pants," he offered.

Nio told the officers that she didn't remember the last time she saw her mother. But she did say that her parents argued and that one day they were at a garden at the top of the Oakland hills when both her mother and father shouted. Nina accused Hans of not listening, and Hans at one point dropped Rory's fold-up bed on the sidewalk. But when they pressed Nio for details about when she last saw her mom, it was clear she would be of no help. She didn't remember going grocery shopping. She was more interested in playing with a toy, showing off her loose tooth and talking about a "horrible ski class" that she took near Lake Tahoe.

Grant, meanwhile, drove to the 9600 block of Skyline to check out the rotting smell. He suspected that the odor was that of propane or sewage. While looking around, Grant happened to witness a domestic dispute, and an Oakland park ranger, Kent McNab, came to cover him on the call. McNab also told Grant that the foul odor had been wafting in the air off and on for several years and was most likely coming from a faulty sewer line at the nearby Chabot Space and Science Center. It may have been the same smell that Oakland Fire Inspector David Davis noticed on a roving fire patrol days earlier, driving with the windows down. He had reported the strong pungent odor of decomposing "something" near the 9400 block of Skyline, near Castle Drive.

Convinced that it wasn't Nina's body, Grant then took soil samples recovered from Nina's minivan and drove to McCone Hall at UC Berkeley. Dr. Hans-Rudolf Wenk and staff researcher Tim Teague of the Earth and Planetary Science Department performed an X-ray diffraction analysis to identify the mineral composition. They told Grant that it was more compatible with granite or beach sand. That ruled out the East Bay hills, which were made of volcanic material like basalt and andesite.

Wenk said later that Grant had proved to be a meticulous

investigator. "He came to my office a couple of times, and I even introduced him to my mineralogy class. Students were impressed to see an application of mineralogy in a criminal investigation," Wenk said. Grant, in fact, felt right at home at Cal, as he had earned his undergraduate degree in sociology from the university.

› On that day, the Carole Sund/Carrington Memorial Foundation committed a five-thousand-dollar reward for tips leading to the safe return of Nina. If it was determined that a homicide had been committed, then the money would be provided for information leading to the arrest and conviction of whoever was responsible. Sund's parents, Francis and Carole Carrington, started the foundation after a reward they posted led to a key break in the case of their missing daughter, Carole Sund, her daughter, Juli, and their friend, Silvina Pelosso, near Yosemite National Park in 1999. Tragically, the women were later found murdered, and motel handyman Cary Stayner was convicted in the case, but the Carringtons resolved to help families in similar circumstances. The foundation's executive director, Kim Petersen, was a familiar face to anguished relatives who were missing loved ones, including Laci Peterson's family in Modesto. The foundation's five-thousand-dollar reward in Nina's case was in addition to a ten-thousand-dollar reward already in place for tips.

CHAPTER 37

›SCOURING FOR CLUES

Members of the Oakland police crime lab pored over the CRX at the Eastmont substation for two days. They had the authority to search the car by a warrant that was identical to the one used for the Exeter home. But it outlined another, chilling reason for the search: police wanted to look for "ransom notes, ropes, tape, wire, medication or any other instrument or item which could be used to tie, bind or render a person defenseless, immobile or unable to give consent."

Inside the car was a virtual treasure trove of evidence, which gave the police a clearer picture of what Hans had been up to over the past several weeks. The car was in poor condition. Where the front passenger seat would have been was a metal bracket, four bolts that fit the holes in the front floorboard and a socket wrench with a 12 millimeter socket attached and packaging from a forty-piece socket-wrench set.

The floorboard in the passenger area was soaked with water, as if someone had tried to wash away evidence. Police were more confident than ever that Hans had used the CRX to take Nina's body somewhere.

The driver's seat upholstery was torn, exposing an interior metal bar and padding at the left shoulder and headrest. There were food items inside, including two Styrofoam takeout boxes, an empty Arizona green tea bottle, a box of Wheat Thins with some crackers inside, an empty box of Good & Plenty candy, four V-8 tomato juice containers, a nearly empty tin of Planters mixed nuts and a partial loaf of bread.

On the front passenger floor was a sleeping bag, a North Face Cat's Meow sleeping-bag stuff sack and an REI dome tent. The stuff sack had a bloodstain on it measuring one by three inches.

Also found was a Northern California atlas, a siphon pump, a September 13 *Oakland Tribune* newspaper article with the headline "Police search home of missing woman's spouse" and a September 8 receipt from Barnes & Noble listing the two murder books he bought. There was also a map of the Stockton area, which convinced the police that Hans had used it to scout out locations to dump Nina's body.

The entire rear cargo area, including the cover and carpeting that covered the spare tire, was missing. Inside the spare-tire well area was a white plastic bag with a toothbrush and toothpaste, shaving cream, a disposable razor and blue shop towels.

Other items found in the car included many receipts, including one from the Patelco Credit Union, another from Target for Hanes fleece underwear and one from the Motel 6 in Fremont.

There was also an ad from StoragePRO, located alongside Interstate 5 in Stockton. In red pen, Hans had written "$109 + half off first month" next to a picture and description of a ten-by-fifteen-foot "two bedroom apartment" space with one hundred and fifty square feet. He also wrote $169 next to a description of a ten-by-twenty-foot "two bedroom apartment with appliances" space with two hundred square feet.

In the glove compartment were insurance and registration cards with Beverly's name on them and the traffic ticket Hans had received from the Redwood City police officer on September 12.

On the rear bumper were stickers that read, "Practice Random Kindness & Senseless Acts of Beauty" and "Jazz KCSM," from a local radio station.

> On the morning of September 27, Hans was supposed to be at a child-custody hearing in Oakland. Instead, he was a no-show because he was driving his CRX back from Reno. Along the way, he checked his voice mail on his cell phone and listened to a message from his dad. Ramon told him not to throw away any receipts, as they would indicate what time he did things like buying gas or books or had a meal. Ramon told

Hans to keep a good log of what he did, much as a police officer does when investigating somebody. Hans left a message for CPS worker Seng Fong and reminded her to consult with Dr. Schreier. Around noon, he stopped to get gas in Roseville, just outside Sacramento. He also swung by a local Target store to buy a twenty-seven-dollar AT&T phone card.

Back in Oakland, Beverly went to the hearing without her son. McGothigan called that evening and asked how it went. "Terrible," Beverly responded. No decisions were made, but the chances of Hans getting custody of the kids appeared slim to none. "I don't think there's much hope," she told McGothigan.

Weisenberg, meanwhile, who had received approval from Judge Miller to examine Hans's and Nina's bank records and credit reports, also got the judge's approval to secretly obtain the credit report of Beverly and Sturgeon. Weisenberg wanted to find evidence that would either incriminate or eliminate Sturgeon. As for Beverly, Weisenberg was suspicious of her, echoing concerns by Fanucchi. Among the things Weisenberg cited in his request for a search warrant was Beverly's August 11 message in which she asked Nina to take the kids on the first day of school because Hans couldn't be depended on to do that. "I asked Palmer if she had ever made a call like that to Nina Reiser and she stated no," Weisenberg wrote. "It became apparent to me that Palmer was willing to be untruthful about her son and her own activities to law enforcement." He added, "She may have further knowledge of Nina Reiser's whereabouts. In addition, she may be involved in her disappearance after the fact and may be assisting additional persons in concealing the crime."

Gill still hadn't heard from Du Bois directly. The two men had been playing phone tag for weeks. The police felt Du Bois was stringing them along, repeatedly promising in phone messages that Hans would be interested in talking to them. But still no interview had been set up. From the police standpoint, it was not a crime to go missing, and so Hans should have been far more willing to sit down with them to help find Nina. As Officer Weisenberg noted in a search warrant affidavit, "Despite custodial differences, when a member of [a] family, broken or not, is missing, all parties involved commonly provide whatever assistance is necessary to find the missing person; therefore your affiant and Ofc. Gill believe that it is unusual that Hans Reiser is uncooperative in giving information to the Police Department regarding Nina Reiser's disappearance." Gill had had enough. On September 27, Gill wrote a letter on City of Oakland letterhead and sent it to Du Bois by registered mail. Even though their offices were a mere ten blocks away from each other, the point had to be made. "We both have attempted to contact each other throughout this investigation, but have only been able to pass messages to each other," Gill wrote. "I would like to arrange an interview with your client, Hans Thomas Reiser, as Mr. Reiser is most likely eager to assist in this investigation."

Gill couldn't be more wrong.

Hans didn't care much for authority, whether it was battling Microsoft or his wife or thumbing his nose at police. Years ago, he had installed a radar detector in his trusty 1991 Plymouth Laser. In July 1998, he made a report with San Francisco police when the device and his cell phone were stolen during a break-in on Howard Street in the South of Market neighborhood. Hans also had a bumper sticker that read, "No, you may not search my car, my person or my residence." He also owned a shirt that read, "A gun in the hand beats a cop on the phone every time." Some of this was tongue-in-cheek, but within those quips there were kernels of truth as far as Hans was concerned. And his mind-set would presage the way he behaved as the police closed in.

From the beginning, Hans fretted over the fact that he was being followed. Had he known at the time that the police had at one point contemplated using NASA satellite imagery, he probably would have hit the roof. But Parker, the FBI agent, told Gill that because of domestic-spying laws, NASA was barred from taking pictures of people or locations on consecutive days. And images could be used to develop leads but couldn't be used in court.

On the night of September 27, Hans paid forty-five dollars for a room at another motel, the E-Z 8 in Fairfield off Interstate 80 in Solano County, forty-five miles from home.

Hans felt he had every reason to be paranoid about surveillance. Ramon had warned him that the KGB could be targeting him to avenge Nina's disappearance. He told his son not to assume that it was the police who were following him.

Ramon was right in that respect. But he had no reason to expect that it would be another element altogether that would be following his son: the media.

CHAPTER 38

› "THEY'RE CHASING ME!"

On the afternoon of September 28, Oakland police were again following Hans near their headquarters on Seventh Street downtown. There was another child-custody hearing at 1:30 p.m. at the same court building nearby. Behind closed doors, Alameda County Commissioner Nancy Lonsdale denied Hans's custody request after listening to what police had to say.

NBC reporter Jodi Hernandez and cameraman Eric Frick had heard about the hearing and were waiting for Hans when he came out. When Frick walked up to Hans outside the Oakland police building, Hans, carrying a large blue box, turned on his heels and darted inside. But Frick wasn't going away. Hans emerged from the building, saw the cameraman and again turned his back before taking off running down Seventh Street.

Hernandez called me at about 2:30 p.m. "The police are following him," she said, the urgency in her voice evident. Hernandez was a standout TV reporter, one who took the extra step and didn't follow the pack. She was the first Bay Area reporter to land a sit-down interview with Scott Peterson after his affair with Amber Frey became public. In 2001, she also landed a one-on-one talk with Gary Condit, the congressman from Modesto who had an affair with Washington intern Chandra Levy before she was found dead in a park. Condit was scrutinized for years until police arrested a Salvadoran immigrant in her slaying. "I want to be first," Hernandez said. "I really thrive on the big story. It's a challenge."

When I answered Hernandez's call, I was sitting at my desk a block away at the *Chronicle*'s East Bay Bureau, on

Ninth Street in the historic Old Oakland District. This was it, I thought. The arrest is going down. I disappeared through the back door of my office, dashed across the parking lot and ran down Washington Street. I passed CityTeam Ministries, a homeless shelter where Sturgeon had volunteered his time. In no less than ten seconds, I was at the corner of Seventh and Washington streets, within sight of the police building. Hernandez met me at the intersection.

We spotted Frick running with his camera down Seventh Street and tried to catch up to him, but Frick soon stopped and said that Hans, who was wearing a white shirt, dark jeans and his fanny pack, had rounded the corner and was still running. We then learned from one of the surveilling officers, Sergeant Randy Wingate, that Hans was walking toward us on the sidewalk of Fifth Street. Hernandez, Frick and I set up a position behind a fence at the corner of Washington Street, where we couldn't be seen.

As Hans walked up, we pounced. Hernandez called out to him, "Hans, where are you—why aren't you talking to police?"

We didn't get an answer. Hans took one look at us and began sprinting at a full clip down Fifth Street. And he was very fast. Almost instinctively, I decided to chase him. A brusque "no comment" is what reporters are used to. But Hans was running like a racehorse right out of the starting gate, as if his life depended on it. He was carrying a big box with something sticking out of it. I wanted to know where he was going and why he was running. I had on me a metallic police ticket book I use as a reporter's pad and a bulging folder of crosswords and sudokus, which I brought everywhere in case I got stuck in line somewhere or had to wait for cases to be called in court. It didn't make for optimum running conditions, but I did my best. Then I got worried. I turned my head in a quick runner's glance. Where were the cops? Would they see me and go after me instead? Was I getting in the way somehow?

I had no time for more questions. As Hans continued running, I picked up speed. As he rounded the corner onto Broadway, I was right on his tail. He threw open the door to the Alameda County social services building and ran inside at full speed, with me right behind him. Sheriff's deputies Kevin Tracy and Michael Woodfolk looked up to witness the spectacle of a man barging in, carrying some bazooka-like object sticking out of his arms and being chased by some Asian guy.

"They're chasing me!" Hans yelled.

"Who!?" asked Tracy.

"The media!" Hans hissed. "The judge told me not to talk to the media. I want this guy to stop following me!"

Not a problem. By then, I had already turned on my heels and left. I was certain that Hans, or I—or both of us—were going to get shot or something.

Tracy said as much when he told Hans, "You running in here with that box—I don't know what that is."

I later learned that the object Hans had been carrying was a Galileo telescope that he had bought that morning at Fry's Electronics in Concord. It was a present for Rory, who turned seven that day. Hans was visiting his children that afternoon at the social services building. They were being cared for by Ellen Doren.

Away from the prying eyes of the media, Hans met his mother inside the building. Beverly brought a book about King Arthur for Rory. They also brought Rory a birthday cake, lit the candles and sang "Happy Birthday" to him.

Ten minutes into the visit, Rory asked his father about going somewhere, and Hans said they couldn't go.

"Why not?" Rory asked.

"Because the courts won't let us," Beverly said.

His words hushed, Hans started to explain to Rory what the court said, and Beverly started to speak loudly. Child-welfare worker Seng Fong believed Beverly was doing this to mask what Hans was saying.

"You're not supposed to be discussing the case with the children," Fong warned them.

"Oh, OK," Beverly said.

Hans told Rory that if he wanted to know why they couldn't go, he should "go ask her why she won't let us go." Fong wasn't sure if Hans was referring to her or not.

Hans then made another inappropriate remark, telling Nio in a soft voice that she and Rory "have to stick together and not fight, because they are trying to say when you fight, they try to blame it on me." As Hans said this, Beverly again started speaking to Rory in a loud voice to mask what Hans was saying.

Fong was having no more of it. She told Hans, "This conversation violates the terms of the visitation. If I have to warn you one more time, I'm going to end the visit." Hans looked at Fong but didn't respond. There were no further problems.

I decided to see what Hans would do after he visited his kids. At about 4:00 p.m., when his visit was supposed to be over, I again set up a stakeout point, this time on the Broadway side of the social services building. Soon I spotted Hans and his mother walking out and quietly ran up to them on Broadway as they walked underneath the Interstate 880 overpass. The roars of passing traffic masked my approach. Just as I got behind Hans, I called out in an authoritative voice, "Mr. Reiser." Without even looking behind him to see who it was— for all he knew, I could have been a police officer—he bolted away again. Beverly, wearing a puffy green coat, said nothing to me but kept on walking as Hans continued running.

Hernandez rejoined me at this point. We finally caught up with Hans on Seventh Street near the police station as he was walking with Beverly and his family law attorney, Cheryl Hicks. At last, he didn't run. Hernandez and I gave him our cards and explained that we just wanted to get his side of the story. Hicks told us simply, "He wants his children back."

Ruddy, round and balding, the mustachioed Lieutenant Wiley broke into a smile as he watched much of this media circus unfold. As amused as he was, there was evidently some nervousness on his part about a plan to detain Hans for a DNA sample that afternoon. Although the police now had him in plain sight, it would certainly be embarrassing if TV crews shot video of Hans running away from the cops, leaving them to eat his dust. Wiley told Lieutenant Pete Sarna to "hold off on the swab." Sarna didn't think that was a good idea. "It might be a good idea to put a little more pressure on him now," Sarna told Wiley.

Late that afternoon, I returned to my office and switched on the evening news. To my astonishment, I realized that Frick's camera had been rolling during my little adventure hours earlier, because there I was on the television screen, chasing Hans down the street.

CHAPTER 39

> CHAOS

All that hand-wringing over whether to swab Hans for DNA became moot at about 5:30 p.m. Hans was walking on the 600 block of Twenty-second Street when he was stopped by Officers Cliff Bunn and Gerardo Melero, members of the gang unit. The decision was made to go ahead and get the DNA sample from Hans. The officers stopped and searched Hans and his fanny pack. Inside, they found $8,960 in cash, a passport and numerous other cards and paperwork.

They also found a Treo cell phone with its battery detached—the same way Nina's cell phone was found when police recovered her minivan.

Officers Shan Johnson and Jesse Grant were trying to find a friend of Hans's near the UC Berkeley campus when they got word that Hans had been detained. They jumped into their car and rushed over to the scene.

On the street, Johnson explained to Hans that they had a warrant to get a DNA sample and to take photographs of him. The officer had obtained similar swabs from Beverly and Sharanova in the previous few days. Beverly did so reluctantly on September 25 after saying she wanted to talk to her attorney. Now, Hans was saying the same thing. "I want to consult my attorney," Hans said. The officers told him an attorney wasn't necessary and that the Miranda warning didn't apply. They asked him if he had eaten anything in the last fifteen minutes. "I want to consult my attorney," Hans repeated. They told him they wanted to take photos of him, and Hans agreed to be taken to the police station.

They led him inside through a squeaky back door. They ended up at the Criminal Investigation Division on the second floor, where Hans didn't seem to be interested in the investigation or ask if they had made any progress finding Nina. Instead he chatted with them, asking them what kind of "cons" they enjoyed. He mentioned three-card monte, which involved sleight of hand. The officers felt he was trying to flaunt his intelligence, but they bantered with him nevertheless, trying to build rapport. They later wrote a note to themselves to research the game. There had to be some reason why he brought this up.

Was Hans sucking them in somehow and playing them for fools? If they were the "marks," was there some "outside man" also involved? Was Hans going to somehow disappear again?

The officers knew that Hans was antsy and was asking for his attorney. They tried a backdoor approach by commenting that they were interested in Nina's well-being, but Hans wouldn't bite. "You are asking me a question without my attorney," he said. They told him again that Miranda—the famous "you have a right to an attorney" warning—didn't apply because they had a warrant. He told them he understood they were just trying to do their job.

As Grant began fumbling around with a digital camera, Hans joked, "I was wondering what was so fascinating about my body." The police, hoping to find evidence of injuries on his body, asked him to take off his shirt so they could take a picture of his chest. They then asked him to take off his pants, while leaving his underwear on. Hans said he was short on underwear because he had problems doing his laundry lately. Hans then took off his pants, and the police realized that he wasn't wearing any underwear at all. He smelled bad, as if he hadn't showered for days. Grant took pictures of Hans's entire body, both clothed and unclothed. He took photos of Hans's face from the left, right, front and back and close-up shots of his back, arms, shoulders, hands, genitals, buttocks and legs. Hans had two red marks on his chest and back, but they could have been small cuts or pimples.

Grant was mindful of the seriousness of it all and tried to be respectful of Hans because he was getting undressed. The officer needn't have worried about sparing Hans's feelings, however. At one point, as Grant was crouched near the ground and preparing to take another picture, Hans suddenly blurted out, "You're about to experience chaos." Before Grant could make sense of what that meant, Hans farted—right in the officer's face. The nerve of this guy, Grant thought. The mother of his children was missing, and here he was making jokes and passing gas?

But Grant still had to remain professional. After the air cleared, Grant put the detached battery in the phone. It fit perfectly.

Grant took an inventory of Hans's fanny pack, taking pictures of everything inside, including the $8,960 in cash; a business card for California Self Storage in Manteca; a "frequent diner rewards" card at Tomatina restaurant in Alameda; a business card from the Sundance steakhouse in Palo Alto; membership cards from Barnes & Noble, Borders Books, Blockbuster, the Exploratorium and 24-Hour Fitness; Oakland and Berkeley public library cards; several phone cards; a Citibank card with Nina's name on it; Visa cards in his name; and a Namesys business card identifying him as the owner-operator.

Also crammed into his fanny pack was a three-page printout labeled, "Statement from Hans Reiser," which was also copied by police.

He began the statement by blaming the system for removing the children from his custody.

"At the time of her disappearance, my wife and I were engaged in a bitter custody battle over our children, a battle that brought great sadness to our children. With her disappearance, there are some who are increasing the stress on our children even more by taking them away from their parents and grandparents."

He said Nina "matches the textbook description for Munchausen by proxy disorder, a mental illness in which women invent illnesses in their children, but of course no one involved by the court had the time for reading the textbook when it was handed to them."

Rory was a perfectly normal six-year-old boy who could only get attention from Nina if there was something wrong with him, according to Hans. His son was subjected to strange therapies that included rolling him in a carpet, he said.

Hans described himself as a "well-known scientist" and offered a unique proposal to show that Rory didn't have any of these illnesses. "I offer to prove before any member of the media or the legal system anytime anywhere that Rory has not one disability other than being yellow-green color blind that I cannot cure by the offer of a six-pack of [Henry] Weinhard's Root Beer as his reward for completing the task in question."

He complained that his children had stayed in a foster home where they slept on plastic-covered mattresses, where people yelled at them and where Nio got a burn "that will probably scar her face permanently." Hans was referring to an accident that happened when Nio was leaning over a lamp and Rory pushed her head down so that her chin hit the light bulb, according to Alameda County CPS. The foster mother put cream on Nio's chin.

Hans ended his statement by saying, "I may be a danger to the worldview of some, but I am no danger to Rory and Niorline. My children are innocent. Let them out of jail, please." The investigators shook their heads at Hans's moxie. Hans seemed unable—or unwilling—to recognize the fundamental paradox in this case: can a man capable of murdering his wife still be a loving parent?

But for Hans and his mother, the issue was clear-cut: "He desperately wants his children back," Beverly told Hernandez and Frick on camera that day. "He hasn't been accused of anything. He's not even a suspect, and yet they took the children away. He wants his children back."

As Hans was being detained, his judo friend, Artem Mishin, called and left him a message at 6:30 p.m. "Hey, Hans, this is Artem. Hey, I was just calling to find out how it went yesterday. I read an article in the newspaper that said you didn't show up in court. But I was just curious what's happening. Did you get the kids back or what's up? Give me a call. Let me know. I'm worried about you, man. OK, talk to you later, bye."

When they were done taking pictures, Johnson finally got a swab sample from Hans. He thanked the officers for their professionalism and for a "job well done." He then asked to be taken to his mother's house. NBC cameraman Frick was again there and had his camera rolling as Hans, covering his face with a piece of paper, was whisked away by Officer Grant in an unmarked police cruiser.

Beverly called Hans's cell phone at about 7:00 p.m. Her friend, Barbara Lee, was over at her house for a steak dinner, and Hans was nowhere to be seen. "Hi Hans, it's Mom. I'm wondering where you are. The food is ready. Bye-bye," she said in a voice-mail message. She had told Lee that Hans would be there. Police later confirmed that Lee was "not *that* one," referring to the U.S. representative in Congress.

Hans showed up minutes later in a police car. He went inside the house, told his mother what had happened and immediately called Du Bois.

As Hans fretted about what had happened, Beverly asked him, "Are you sure you want to carry so much money around with you, Hans?" Hans said yes, and Beverly replied, "Why? Maybe you should leave some here."

Beverly then got on the phone and called another friend, asking her if she could be a character witness for Hans at his child-custody hearing. The woman said she would, and Beverly handed the phone to Hans.

Hans told the woman that the authorities were trying to argue that "I can't be trusted to take the kids to the doctor, that I have an explosive temper, that—oh what else—um, that I don't bathe the kids frequently enough. The whole thing is pretending that it's not about something else."

"They seem to be putting out some kind of impression on television that you are hiding from the police," said the woman, sounding concerned. "Would you say that you're keeping a low profile and you're avoiding them—but you're not really hiding from the police, right?"

"Well, they picked me up today at the hearing—after the hearing," Hans said. He laughed. "I don't know. There's a limit to how hard you can hide from the police when you show up for hearings."

He added, "The police have a lot of tactics that the black community knows more about than we do, and I'm—we're sort of starting to discover why the black community has its attitudes, and they make a lot more sense than they look like at a distance."

As Hans groused about police tactics, Officers Gino Guerrero and Andrew Barton were right outside the house, sitting in separate undercover vehicles on the street. They waited patiently as Beverly and Lee chatted while drinking their second glass of wine and eating chocolates. The phone rang shortly after 10:00 p.m. McGothigan was on the other line. Beverly was about to invite him over, but Hans interrupted her. After conferring with her son, Beverly told McGothigan that she had to give Hans a ride to downtown Oakland.

Guerrero and Barton watched as Beverly and Lee emerged outside at 10:20 p.m. Lee took a drag on a cigarette as the two women took D'Artagnan for a walk. They passed by Barton's car once and then doubled back. They then walked past Guerrero's car on the other side of the house. It appeared as if they were on a recon mission.

And sure enough, Hans would be on the move yet again that night. He still had to pick up his rented Ford Escort, which he had left parked in downtown Oakland. He had been heading to the car earlier in the day but was instead picked up by the police. At about 11:00 p.m., Guerrero and Barton watched as Lee pulled away from the house in a maroon Nissan Maxima. Barton got part of the license plate and tried to relay it to the other officers, but again the poor reception in the hills proved to be an obstacle.

Suddenly, Hans came jogging out of the house and approached the driver's side window. The car stopped, and Lee got out and got back in on the passenger side. Hans climbed into the driver's seat and the two drove off toward Highway 13.

He again began driving erratically, pulling over for no apparent reason, speeding and making sudden turns. The officers lost him but later saw him driving south on Martin Luther King Jr. Way and Twentieth Street near the Greyhound bus station in downtown Oakland. Hans knew he was being followed, but the officers continued tailing him anyway, having been instructed not to let him slip away. They made no secret of it, driving so close to him that the tactic was called "bumper locking." At 11:40 p.m., Hans stopped the Nissan near Twenty-fourth Street and Northgate Avenue, close to a tangle of freeways known as the MacArthur Maze and several blocks from where Hans had been detained. He then got into his rented Ford Escort. Lee, meanwhile, drove off in the Nissan.

With police on his tail, Hans drove through numerous traffic lights while driving north on Broadway into North Oakland. He then drove into Berkeley, heading west on Ashby Avenue before getting onto eastbound Interstate 80 toward Richmond. Two exits later, Hans got off I-80 at Gilman Street and then got back onto the freeway in the opposite direction. He continued onto the Bay Bridge and waved at an undercover officer near Yerba Buena Island, where two parts of the span meet at a tunnel. The game continued as Hans got off at the Fremont Street exit in San Francisco. He again began running red lights—with police watching—in the Financial District. There had been taunting on both sides, but by now the officers, concerned that he might cause a crash, had seen enough. At 12:30 on the morning of September 29, they pulled him over.

"Are you going to follow me all night?" Hans demanded. The officers warned him about his driving and let him go.

Hans got back onto the Bay Bridge—with the officers still following him—and headed back to the East Bay. He took the University Avenue exit off I-80, got some gas and then parked the Ford at Eighth Street and Hearst Avenue in West Berkeley. He pulled a blanket from the trunk and hunkered down to sleep. Police debated whether to get a search warrant for the Ford Escort but decided not to. They knew Hans would likely get another car—which would be unknown to them—if they towed the only car he had. They'd be back to square one.

Just as the sun began to rise, at about 7:00 a.m. on September 29, police were still watching as Hans slept in the rental car. After a day of ratcheting up the pressure on Hans, "He now seems completely demoralized," Lieutenant Pete Sarna told Lieutenant Kevin Wiley, adding, "We will probably go to breakfast with him in a little bit."

About an hour later, Hans got up and drove a few blocks to Sixth Street and University Avenue. He got out, used a pay phone near the corner and then drove to Whole Foods Market at Ashby and Telegraph avenues, where he used the restroom and spent thirty dollars on food. Police continued to follow him as he made a series of stops in downtown Oakland: Du Bois' office, a Patelco branch, where he moved money from one account to another, and an Indian restaurant. At 3:00 p.m., he went into the 24 Hour Fitness on Webster Street and stayed there until 6:15 p.m., when he walked a few blocks to a pay phone near the Nineteenth Street BART station. He went back to the gym and emerged at 7:40 p.m. He drove to Durant Square, a food court a block south of the UC Berkeley campus that students dubbed the "Asian Ghetto" for its cheap ethnic food. He used another pay phone near the Bank of America at the corner of Telegraph and Durant and then stopped at another restaurant nearby. He got back into the car and returned to the same Barnes & Noble bookstore on Shattuck Avenue where he had bought the two murder books. He bought some more books and then drove a few blocks to Ashby Avenue, where he again made a call from a pay phone. At 8:30 p.m., he got back into the car and drove to Telegraph and Haste Street near People's Park. He used a pay phone outside Cody's Books, the venerable Berkeley institution that had closed its doors for good two months earlier.

At one point he called his mother. "Hi Mom, it's Hans, uh . . . I'm doing well and being followed by an enormous number of policemen but, uh, doing well," he said. "They're polite. I'm polite to them. Actually, all things considered, we have a good relationship. Uh, and so I just called to let you know that I'm alive and well. I know you're worried, so I gave you a call. Take care." He returned to the Ford Escort at 11:00 p.m., took out the sleeping bag and went to sleep.

As Hans spent that morning at his attorney's office, Oakland police officer Roland Holmgren, the department spokesman, and Deputy Chief Jordan addressed the media. Jordan confirmed that police detained Hans and obtained a biological sample through a search warrant.

"Mr. Reiser was cooperative. He was not questioned. His attorney was not present, and he was released without any further incident," Jordan said. His statement was probably only half accurate. Hans was cooperative to the point of submitting to the DNA sample, but only because he had to under court order. But beyond that, he refused to talk to the police.

In response to questions, Jordan said the sample was needed to compare some of the evidence police had recovered during a search of Hans's home.

Asked if Hans was a suspect, Jordan replied, "He is not a suspect now because we really don't, we don't have a crime." A reporter noted that Du Bois appeared to believe that police were considering Hans not merely as "a suspect" but "the suspect." Jordan smiled and said, "Well, that's the perception of the attorney, but our case hasn't changed, and we have not categorized him as a suspect."

Jordan said police had to detain Hans for the sample because he declined to turn himself in voluntarily to get that done. "We knew that consent was not going to be possible, so we got a search warrant because it makes our case a lot more solid."

Jordan made clear that there were still a lot of unanswered questions. "We're looking at every possible scenario. Every potential lead is being followed," he said. "We're not sure what happened to her, you know, if there was foul play or not. We haven't gotten to the point where we can say definitely that this is what happened."

Later that day, Hernandez asked Du Bois about when Hans would be interviewed. Du Bois said he had offered to have Hans talk with police the week Nina disappeared, and the department blew him off. Du Bois also said he would reconsider the request to have Hans talk to police if they disclosed what evidence they had. Hernandez e-mailed Jordan and asked if they would do that. "No, tell him to call me and stop negotiating his client's surrender through the media. He has my number," Jordan responded by e-mail.

That night, I appeared on Greta Van Susteren's show. I had appeared numerous times on live TV by then, having gotten

my feet wet with a flurry of appearances on cable news programs during the Scott Peterson case and other high-profile
crimes. I always jumped at the chance to appear on these
shows, if only to help put the *Chronicle*—and lowly print
reporters—on the map. Plus, being on TV gave me a chance
to shake the dust off my Men's Wearhouse suit, put on a tie
and look halfway decent, and I mean halfway quite literally:
because the camera only shows guests from the waist up,
viewers had no idea that I was wearing my jeans while on
national television.

Guest host Jamie Colby asked me if I saw comparisons
to the Peterson case. "Well, in fact, yesterday, he ran away
from me as I was trying to get him to comment," I said. "He's
certainly not attended the vigils, like Scott Peterson did, but
there's a lot of information that would suggest that he has
some information, but police don't have that. They do want
to talk to him. And it's just another case of a woman whose
husband is acting strangely."

Colby thanked me and then addressed former LAPD
detective Mark Fuhrman, who had worked on the O. J. Simp-
son case, asking for his views on why Hans was refusing to
talk to police even as he submitted to giving his DNA. "Interviews, they sometimes turn into interrogations, which sometimes turn into confessions. But if you're innocent, you have
nothing to fear," Fuhrman said, from a different studio. "You
can explain anything that's in the vehicle. If you have something to hide, then you certainly don't want to talk to a trained
interrogator."

Colby brought the segment to an end. "Even the reporter
that we had on, Henry Lee, was saying that this particular
gentleman, Hans, had run away from him. Mark, thank you
very much."

On Saturday, September 30, criminalist Shannon Cavness
had more news to report: the bloodstain found on the sleeping-
bag stuff sack in the CRX was likely that of Nina. Gill called
Joyner, who said to hold off on any arrest until the DA was
consulted. Gill also called Wiley, who said he would put an
end to the twenty-four-hour bumper locking of Hans and prepare an arrest warrant.

> That evening, Hans again believed he was being fol-
lowed. But this time, Hans didn't think it was the police, but
rather two Russian-speaking men who seemed to be taking an
interest in him. One guy seemed to be holding himself oddly.
They might be trying to kill me. I'd better tell the police, Hans
thought. He figured he'd just look for one of his tails. Police
had followed him everywhere in the past couple of weeks,
to the point of watching *The Guardian* with him in a theater
when the movie, starring Kevin Costner as a Coast Guard rescue swimmer and Ashton Kutcher as his trainee, premiered
that weekend. Hans and an undercover officer even chatted
about the film in a theater restroom. But now, he didn't see
any officers around. *Where are the cops when you need them?
Strange how these Russian guys showed up just as the cops
disappeared.*

He went to a pay phone in Berkeley and called the Oakland
police radio room shortly after 8:00 p.m. He told a dispatcher
that he wanted to speak to "Sergeant Ryan Gill," mistakenly
promoting the officer in the process.

"My name is Hans Reiser, and the police have been following me for several days, and so I think they'll want to talk
to me," he said. The dispatcher tried for several minutes to
explain that Gill wasn't available. She added that they had no
knowledge of anyone following him, because all they did in
the radio room was send black-and-whites to calls. "You feel
like you're being tailed by the police?" she asked.

Hans laughed—cackled—at the absurdity of the question.
"My name is in the newspaper, OK? I'm not being paranoid,"
he said, chuckling heartily. "Ask your boss whether there's a
Hans Reiser that they're looking around for, that they've been
tailing."

"Hans, I'm not trying to be disrespectful to you or anything like that, but I know a black-and-white car doesn't follow people around here," the dispatcher said.

"Uh, I didn't say a black-and-white was following me
around," Hans replied. He again asked to be transferred to
Gill or whoever was available. "I have a particular reason for

it," he said. The dispatcher said she couldn't transfer him, and he again erupted into peals of laughter before finally giving up. He said he would ask his attorney to get in touch with the police.

The dispatcher then left a message with Gill to report the strange conversation. "I just received a call from Hans Reiser. He sounded very 922," she said, using the Oakland police code for drunk.

CHAPTER 40

> TIPS

The search for Nina continued.

On October 1, Erik Hoffman, the husband of a sheriff's deputy in neighboring Contra Costa County, joined Lieutenant Wiley, Sergeant Hogenmiller and Officers Johnson and Grant on a search in the Oakland hills. They drove to some streets off Shepherd Canyon. Hoffman had known Reiser from school and said he knew of some caves and old train tunnels in the area that should be searched. They took a look around but couldn't find any tunnels—which had long been sealed off—or any evidence related to the case. As they were beating the bushes, Hans discovered a device attached to the Ford Escort. Curiosity got the better of him. He crawled underneath it and used a screwdriver to take off what turned out to be a battery cover. He took a picture of the device and had a private investigator look at it. It was a tracking device—and not a bomb, as Hans had feared. Satisfied that he wasn't about to be blown up, he paid $155 and checked into the Durant Hotel, a block south of the UC Berkeley campus.

> On October 4, Oakland police called a press conference to announce the arrest of Earl Stefanson, a forty-one-year-old roofer, in the killing of his girlfriend, Leslie Lamb, thirty-six. They said Stefanson had tortured and beaten Lamb in his soundproofed home on Coolidge Avenue before dropping off her lifeless body at Highland Hospital in Oakland on the night of August 26. Homicide sergeant Tony Jones described the case as something found in the movie *The Silence of the Lambs*, a comparison made all the more chilling because of

the victim's last name. Investigators said blood from Lamb and apparently two other victims were found in the home.

It wasn't long before police received the usual complement of crackpot tips from people convinced that Stefanson had also killed Nina and that it could be her blood that was in his home.

"Wonder if Earl Stefanson and Sean Sturgeon knew each other from the S/M environment? Or Nina Reiser and Earl?" a woman e-mailed from Copenhagen, Denmark.

"Perhaps they could run a rapid DNA test to eliminate the chance of a correlation," another woman suggested in an e-mail.

A self-proclaimed psychic asserted that while Nina's DNA must be in Stefanson's basement, her body would be in San Francisco Bay. Although the woman didn't say so explicitly, everyone knew that Scott Peterson had dumped his pregnant wife, Laci, in the bay after claiming to have gone fishing for sturgeon.

Another woman, a mother of four from San Jose, said she had the ability to "see" or "feel" the last few moments of a victim's life. She, too, believed that Nina had been dumped in the water like Laci had, although she made no reference to Stefanson.

"Look, I know you folks are going to pass this around the office as the tip from the nutcase," she wrote in an e-mail. "So I'll get right to the point. Nina's body was wrapped in plastic garbage bags and (I want to say) dumped off one of the bridges after he killed her. I'm not sure how he accomplished it. Maybe he made it seem as though his car was stalled (hood up, blinker on, etc.). I just know her remains will be found in or near the water."

There were other tips as well, some plausible and others more far-fetched. A former neighbor said Hans had anger-management problems and would yell at his mother or some-one else. The woman said the last time she saw Hans, "he looked psychotic." She speculated that he could have driven to the city's Embarcadero or Port of Oakland, swung the passenger side door open and pushed the unbolted seat—with Nina still strapped in—directly into the water.

Adam Richter, who knew Hans from their days at UC Berkeley, e-mailed from China to say that the two had once had a conversation about Eastern European organized crime and that Hans had once told him of a professional kidnapper in Russia who "made a point of making sure that nobody knew where he slept at night." Hans had told him about some investors trying to hire away his employees, whom he feared would steal his file system. The tipster said he was also concerned about Ramon Reiser because he was a U.S. Army soldier who had served in Vietnam.

On the same day the media's attention was focused on the "Silence of the Lambs" case, Hans was back in court for another child-custody hearing. Commissioner Rhonda Burgess ordered him not to whisper or to have any private conversations during visits with his kids.

On October 5, Hans and Beverly visited the children at the visitor's center on Broadway in downtown Oakland. Doren had brought the kids there. Beverly brought art supplies, toys and books. Rory seemed more excited than Nio to see Hans. Nio reluctantly gave her a father a hug, only after he requested it.

Hans brought with him study materials about civics and the structure of the American government and immediately launched into a lesson with Rory as Nio played with Beverly. But Rory soon lost interest. Hans grew agitated and began pacing around the room and looking out a window. But he later returned to the lesson and discussed with Rory how each branch of government was supposed to supervise the other.

At one point, Rory snapped, "Why can't the president just make things the way they're supposed to be?"

Hans spoke of how others took over the reins of leadership if the president was incapacitated. But while reading from the Constitution, he repeatedly used the words *die* and *dead*, and that didn't sit well with CPS.

Hans complained about Joaquin Miller Elementary School even though Rory said things were going well at the school. Rory would be better off doing a distance-learning course through Johns Hopkins University, Hans said.

Also that day, Gill called Beverly, saying the police were

done examining her Honda hybrid and that she could pick it up the next day.

On October 6, Hans left a message for Seng Fong and asked if CPS could pay for Dr. Schreier's consultation because not only was he nationally renowned, "he's also expensive. If you can't pay for him, then I'll pay for him, but if you can pay for him, that will be very desirable."

CHAPTER 41

›"YOU'RE JUST A WALKING CALAMITY"

On the evening of October 7, UC Berkeley graduate Greg Iskander and his wife were among the sellout crowd of 72,516 at Memorial Stadium who watched Cal's 45–24 victory over Oregon during the homecoming game. They were driving home at about 9:00 p.m. in their Nissan Altima, headed south on Telegraph Avenue, when a man in a red Ford Escort traveling in the opposite direction made a left turn in front of them on Carleton Street across from Andronico's Market. There was no time to stop. Iskander collided into the Escort's right side, causing it to spin around.

The impact of the crash activated both air bags in the Nissan. But aside from a small chemical burn to his wrist, Iskander and his wife weren't hurt. A man he would later learn was Hans came out of the Escort and asked if they were OK.

"I'm sorry. I didn't even see you," Hans said. He repeatedly apologized.

Iskander told him, "It's OK. That's why they have insurance."

Hans seemed sincere enough. But something about him seemed off. It was as if he was high on something. He began to freak out. "I can't believe this is happening," Hans kept saying. "Why is this happening? It's not even my car. It's my mom's car."

Hans gave Iskander his name and home phone number. When Iskander asked to see his driver's license, Hans suddenly became uncooperative. "No, I'm not going to give it to you," he said. "I've given you everything I'm required to give you by law."

But Iskander persisted, saying that he couldn't be sure if Hans gave him his true name.

"Look, I promise you, I've given you the right name," Hans said.

"Well, if that's the case, then I'll have to call the police," Iskander said. He took out his cell phone and started dialing.

That's when Hans abruptly said that he was leaving. He got into the Escort and began driving south on Telegraph, now heading back in the direction he came from. But then he suddenly stopped, backed up and got out of the car. He walked up to Iskander and his wife.

"Are you guys married?" Hans asked.

Flummoxed, Iskander and his wife of six years looked at each other for a moment. Yes, they replied.

"Well, I hope it works out for you guys," Hans said. Without another word, he got back in the car and drove away.

The Iskanders didn't know what to make of all this. Then it got even stranger. As Iskander was on the phone with the police, an unmarked Ford Crown Victoria with a surveillance team inside pulled up, not more than a minute after Hans had driven away.

"Are you OK?" one of the officers said. Iskander said yes, and the officer said, "Well, the local police will be here shortly." Then they took off.

What the hell is going on? Iskander wondered.

Hans called his mom early the next morning, October 8.

"The rental car got hit. It got hit and both cars were totaled."

"Was it your fault?"

Hans didn't answer for a while.

"Hans, whose fault was it?" Beverly pressed.

Hans sighed. "Let's discuss it in person. I'm still not quite sure what happened."

Beverly again asked what happened. Hans said, "Well, nobody got hurt, but two cars were totaled."

"How did it get totaled?"

"We'll discuss it in person," Hans said. When Beverly began to protest, Hans added, "We're not going to discuss it over a tapped telephone."

Beverly complained that Hans was going to drive up her insurance rates again and that she wouldn't able to afford it. Hans said he'd be losing his license because his driving record was so bad. "You know, I'm just not driving normally these days," he admitted. "Just one more disaster. I'm sorry, Mom."

"Well, Hans, you've got a lot to be sorry for lately," Beverly said.

"Yeah, that's true," Hans replied.

"Hans, how could you create so many calamities?" Beverly asked. "How can you do this? I mean, you're just a walking calamity."

That day, friends of Nina held a playdate at Montclair Park. Children were given thirty-five yellow balloons to release, one for each day she had been missing.

That night, Hans went to the Burning Man decompression party, a rollicking twelve-hour street event near Indiana and Mariposa streets in San Francisco. But he couldn't find his mother and McGothigan and left. He left a message at his mother's house. "It's not really my kind of a place. Take care," he said.

At about 6:00 p.m. on October 9, Beverly called McGothigan and asked if Hans could sleep in his camper—the same one they had used while at Burning Man—until Hans could get a place for himself. Beverly said she needed to prove to the children's case worker that he wasn't living with her. She wondered if McGothigan would write a letter saying that Hans was living in the camper.

CHAPTER 42

>A CHEMICAL SEARCH

An hour later, at about 7:00 p.m. on October 9, Oakland police converged on the Exeter home, armed with a warrant to search the residence for a second time. But now they were accompanied by homicide sergeant Bruce Brock and eighteen FBI special agents and members of the bureau's vaunted Evidence Response Team. They told Beverly that they would be using chemicals, a process that came with some safety hazards.

Publicly, police did not say why they were searching the house again more than a month after Nina disappeared. But the new search warrant affidavit that was approved by Judge Miller six days earlier was telling. Gill wrote: "Affiant believes that the assault on Nina Reiser would cause trace amounts of blood and/or saliva to have become embedded on the clothing of her attacker(s), as well as the interior of any vehicle for which she was transported within, and within the flooring and spattered on the walls of 6979 Exeter Dr. I believe that based on the amount of time for which Nina Reiser has been missing, I believe that ample time has been allowed for the cleanup of any visible biological evidence. Based upon the continued investigation which has developed the discovery of new evidence, affiant believes through the use of chemical application, and illumination with alternative lighting source, additional trace evidence that was not initially discovered at the original service of the above noted search warrant of 6979 Exeter Dr., will be discovered within 6979 Exeter Dr."

Beverly agreed to give her house key to Sergeant Jeff Ferguson so that police could open the door. She asked when she could get her CRX back. Brock said he'd look into that and get back to her. Brock asked whether the CRX had any damage on it, and she said it was old and ratty. Brock then asked if the car had a front passenger seat. Beverly laughed and said, "Of course there is." She left and went to McGothigan's house.

The FBI team treated the house with Luminol, which detects traces of blood invisible to the naked eye, even if it's been cleaned or removed. The chemical emits a striking blue glow when it encounters the iron found in blood. The effect is most noticeable in the dark, which was a primary reason why the investigators came at night. The criminalists got a positive reaction on the entire living room floor, although there was nothing specific. But they did get a darker, more distinct glow when they sprayed an area rug and the back of the front door. Investigators decided to seize two area rugs from the living room, a computer from Beverly's office and the entire front door, which was painted black in front.

Jack Stabb, who had seen his neighbor hosing down the driveway shortly after Nina disappeared, flagged down an officer during the search of Beverly's home, saying that people in the neighborhood had recently seen Hans skipping and clapping in the roadway, "acting as though he got away with something."

But Hans had some support in his corner from the "other Jack" on Exeter, Jack Clauson, a resident of the street for twenty-five years. In that time, he had never seen or heard anything amiss, like loud noises, screaming or shouting. There was nothing that would suggest that either Hans or his mother were angry, mean, nasty or given to socially unacceptable behavior. In early October, Clauson signed a letter in support of giving custody of Rory and Nio to Hans.

While at home in Oakland, I saw a television news report about the search and drove up to the scene. I had to check a map to make sure I didn't get lost on the winding streets in the hills. As I approached the home, I could see that the street was blocked off. I stuck my head out the door of my Jeep Cherokee and greeted Oakland homicide sergeant Bruce Brock. He was in no mood for pleasantries. He told me I had to go back down the street.

I parked farther down on Exeter, got out of my Jeep and

walked back toward the home. Brock again blocked me. "But Channel 7's up there near the yellow tape," I protested, upset that reporter Alan Wang had been doing live shots from virtually right outside the house. "I don't care," Brock said. "You have to move back." As I walked back down, frustrated, I passed ponytailed Officer Larry Robertson, who was on foot back to the house. "Dirty Rob" actually made a friendly comment and smiled. I went home and filed a story, still frustrated that I wasn't able to get close to the Exeter residence.

That night, in a phone call at 11:00 p.m., Hans and his mother discussed the "chemical search" of the house.

"What's a chemical search?" Hans asked.

"Presumably, they spray chemicals around and try to find DNA and stuff like that, I guess," Beverly said. "I have no idea."

Hans sighed. "O-kaaaaaaay. OK, um. Well, I'm sorry you've been dispossessed of your house again."

"Well, they're supposed to be finished by around midnight, and I'm going to go back. But he said they do it with chemicals that are very toxic. The people who do it are all suited up. So that leads me to wonder if I'm gonna—my house is going to be full of toxic chemicals."

Hans didn't seem to be be listening. He complained that the system was playing games with him. "These guys play so many games. If they weren't playing games, I'd have my kids," he groused. "The whole thing is a game—well, game is the wrong word. It's something less nice than a game. You understand what I mean?"

"Hans, it's no fun having your house filled with all those chemicals."

"Yeah, I know. I'm sorry, I've created one more burden on you."

"You certainly have. You've created a lot of burdens lately, Hans."

"I know. I'm sorry."

Beverly came back to her home at 11:30 p.m. She was not happy about having her home searched again, in no small part because it was now full of chemicals and missing the front door. She was especially vexed when she saw the police removing another computer. When did living in her home become such a Kafkaesque nightmare? The police stopped short of reminding her that it was her son who had put her in this situation.

"All that I can tell you, Ms. Palmer, is that we're trying to gather evidence for hopefully locating Nina Reiser, and unfortunately we've been forced to the point where we have to do search warrants to continue to try to find her," Gill told her.

"But that computer wasn't even here when she disappeared," Beverly protested.

Gill patiently repeated himself. "We have been forced to take steps in order to try to get more information," he said. "This is one of the steps we take in order to get more information."

Gill asked Beverly if she wanted them to board up the house.

"Well, at least something has to be done," said Beverly, clearly peeved. "I can't leave it open all night."

Two workers from the city corporation yard came and boarded up the front entryway. The police and FBI left at about midnight.

CHAPTER 43

> PICNIC BAG

At about 1:00 a.m. on October 10, Kamala Stuart, McGothigan's housemate, heard a knock. She opened the door and there was Hans.

"Is my mom here?" Hans asked.

"No, she went home," Stuart said.

"Can I sleep here?" he asked. Stuart shrugged and said sure. She gave him a blanket and pillow, and he disappeared into McGothigan's office to sleep. Back at home, Beverly stayed up until 2:00 a.m. mopping the floors.

At about 7:00 a.m., McGothigan had a business call to make. He went to his home office and found the door closed. Puzzled, he pushed it open, startling Hans, who flew up from the ground from a deep sleep. Hans got dressed and came out of the office. Stuart offered him coffee, but he declined. She made him hot cereal, which he ate. He worked on his press release on his laptop on McGothigan's kitchen table. Hans also asked McGothigan to get Beverly to come to the house—without telling her that he was there.

McGothigan called Beverly and told her she needed to get dressed, hurry up and come over right away to pick up her "picnic bag."

Police believed McGothigan knew that Beverly's phone was being tapped and was using some kind of code phrase to alert her. Picnic bag? The police thought McGothigan was trying to get Beverly to remove items of evidence from his home. Lieutenant Joyner hurriedly called Weisenberg to tell him about the intercepted call.

There was no more waiting. It was time to get Hans Reiser.

CHAPTER 44

> CLOSING IN

Officers had with them an arrest warrant addressed from the People of the State of California and signed a day earlier by Judge Miller.

To any law enforcement officer in the county of Alameda:
Proof by affidavit, having been made before me on this date by Officer Ryan Gill, Oakland Police Department, Youth and Family Services Section, Missing Persons Unit, Oakland, California, this court finds that there is probable cause to believe that the offense(s) of Murder (187PC) was/were committed on or about September 3, 2006 by Hans Thomas Reiser; 12/19/1963; 5-07, 160 lbs.
Wherefore you are commanded to arrest Hans Thomas Reiser, 12/19/63; 5-07, 160 lbs, 6979 Exeter Dr., Oakland, California 94611 and to bring said person forthwith before the Superior Court, County of Alameda, State of California. Defendant may be admitted to bail in the amount of: no bail.

As police mobilized, Beverly showed up at McGothigan's home, on Simson Street. She spoke to her son in the living room. Beverly asked him about her car. They talked for a short while before Hans told her, "Let's talk outside." They stood near a large art structure out front, a figure called *Surfing Man* that McGothigan made out of carpet tubing.

Sergeant Randy Brandwood and Officers Gino Guerrero, Doug Keely, Jad Jadallah, Eric Milina and Jason Andersen pulled up to the house at about 11:00 a.m. Andersen spotted Hans outside, talking to his mother. "That's Hans!" Andersen exclaimed. Hans sported a light beard and mustache and was dressed all in black, including a shirt with an astronomy design on it. He did not resist as Andersen placed him in handcuffs and put him in the back of a police car. The officers searched him and found two sums of money in his possession: $5,790 and $2,018.

Both McGothigan and Beverly were detained.

Officers had a warrant to search McGothigan's house, given that he had agreed to hide her hybrid and Hans had checked his e-mail there. McGothigan made sure the police produced a copy of the warrant. He joked to the officers that they could search all they want because he didn't have any bodies sticking out from anywhere. As a legion of cops scoured his property, McGothigan felt like he was stuck in a bad cop show. Both McGothigan and Beverly were taken in separate cars downtown to be interviewed.

Officer Bruce Christensen, the crime-scene technician, took photos of McGothigan's home and each room. He took a picture of the laptop on the kitchen table. The press release Hans had been working on was clearly visible.

Under a subheading entitled, "Protecting the Children," Hans had written, "There is something about protecting children that attracts the very worst sorts of people, at least as much as it attracts the best."

Hans complained about divorce attorneys and the family court system. "If they're telling people what they want or at least expect to hear, and they are lying, they aren't the good guys. Prior to meeting divorce lawyers, I have to tell you I have never met a demographic group before with the majority of persons who enjoy hurting others. In the name of protecting the children, family law suspends every constitutional right that matters. Many of you may read this and think that it is an exceptional case for the courts to grant sole custody to someone alleging traumatic stress disorder from violent computer games."

Hans wrote that the public has a choice: "They can either believe that I'm a paranoid, unbalanced individual, or that our court system is susceptible to sweet, adorable little white housewives like Nina, whose eyes are filled with admiration for our wise public servants."

Christensen also took a picture of the screen of a desktop computer in the office where Hans had been sleeping. It was a Yahoo search page showing news headlines about the Reiser case, including the search at the Exeter home a night earlier. "NEW: Police, FBI search Reiser's house again" blared a headline from the *Oakland Tribune*. "Home of missing woman's husband is searched in Oakland," read a headline from the *Chronicle*.

Search dogs combed McGothigan's property. Denise Blackmon and her dog, Gilly, scoured the home, as did Shay Cook and Bishop, the same dog that had searched Exeter.

That afternoon, the Oakland Police Department held a press conference at the Emergency Operations Center at Sixteenth Street and Martin Luther King Jr. Way to announce Hans's arrest. The gathering was held blocks away from police headquarters, where police were busy with interviews and were able to shield their witnesses from distractions.

Sergeant Michael Poirier, chief of staff for Chief Wayne Tucker, introduced Deputy Chief Howard Jordan, head of the bureau of investigations. His head shaved bald and wearing a suit and striped tie, Jordan strode to the podium and read a prepared statement to confirm that Hans had been arrested.

"We believe that based on circumstantial evidence, as well as statements and other evidence, that Hans Reiser murdered Nina Reiser," Jordan told the throng. "We have not located her body. However, we are working diligently to locate the body. Our investigation has gone from a search and rescue to a search and recovery. We have presented this case to the district attorney's office and anticipate that charges will be filed shortly."

Jordan said that during the course of the investigation, officers served more than fifteen search warrants for various types of evidence, which he declined to discuss. He thanked the men and women of the Oakland Police Department and allied agencies, including the FBI, the state Department of Justice, the Alameda County sheriff's office, East Bay Regional Park police and U.S. Immigration and Customs Enforcement.

Most reporters tend to ignore the laundry list of thank-yous that police feel compelled to give at press conferences. I considered myself to be part of that group. We wanted to get to the nitty-gritty, the unsavory details—namely, what led to Hans being arrested when there was no body?

Officer Ryan Gill was next to speak. But his remarks didn't add too much, either.

"During the course of our investigation, Hans Reiser has made himself unavailable to elaborate on Nina Reiser's activities while at his house or where she had gone to after she had arrived at his house. Evidence has been collected which has determined that Nina Reiser has been murdered by Hans Reiser," Gill said.

Homicide lieutenant Ersie Joyner opened his remarks, as was his practice, by offering the department's condolences. He said he recognized this was a difficult time for Nina's family. Turning to the investigation, Joyner said police had looked at all aspects of Nina's life. "All avenues led us to Mr. Reiser being responsible for the death and disappearance of Ms. Nina Reiser," Joyner said. "At this point, we believe that Mr. Hans Reiser acted alone."

Joyner said police believed Nina's body "is still out here in the Bay Area. It's very important that we find the body to determine the cause of death, the time of death, things of that nature."

Joyner then opened it up for questions.

Ethan Harp of NBC 11 News asked why Hans was arrested now, when there was still no body. Wouldn't that be a risky move as far as any prosecution?

That's a very good question, Joyner said. Investigators had to go to great lengths to be able to prove that Nina had a lot of contact with her family and that "all traces of her being alive or having any contact ceased the day she went to Hans's house," Joyner said.

"We have biological, trace evidence to prove that a crime has occurred. It is our strong belief, supported with the evidence, supported with our statement, that we believe Ms. Nina Reiser is deceased," Joyner added.

Some of the reporters were clearly skeptical about the

department's decision to arrest Hans without Nina's body. Was the DA's office on board with all this? It was a valid question. In some cases, police have been known to arrest suspects on probable-cause warrants, without any input from prosecutors, only to see the DA refuse to file charges because the evidence was just too flimsy.

Jordan made it clear that this wasn't the case here. "We've been consulting and working with the DA's office for quite a while on this case," he said. "We've had several meetings, including meetings today, and we feel very strongly that the DA will file charges against him and that we will prosecute this case with or without a body."

Jordan fielded one last question about how Hans was arrested as a suspect at the exclusion of any others. "We looked at everyone we thought could have been responsible and in the end, we circled back to Hans Reiser," he said. "OK? Thank you."

Zografos was among those who attended the press conference. He wept as he listened to what the police had to say. Wiping away tears, he abruptly left.

Shelley Gordon told me that day, "I guess that the police are not expecting to find Nina alive. I'm very sad about that, terribly sad. I just pray for the children."

At 11:15 a.m., Hans was put into a windowless, eight-by-eight-foot interview room at the Oakland police homicide section, a drab room with blue walls on the second floor of police headquarters. It was where investigators toiled under harsh fluorescent lights, their shelves brimming with bulging folders, each one a sad chronicle of another life lost. Hans's body odor was again noticeable as he declined Sergeant Brock's offer of water at 1:00 p.m. Homicide sergeant James "Mo" Morris checked in on Hans every half hour. Morris, a former U.S. Army paratrooper who was also a minister at a West Oakland church, took Hans to the restroom at 3:00 p.m. and offered him a sandwich. If the police had planned to let Hans sweat it out, letting him cool for hours, he wasn't biting. Hans declined the sandwich, saying, "I'll wait until 7:00 p.m." He still wanted to be in control.

As Hans was being escorted to the restroom, I was at my

desk at my Oakland office a block away, leaving a message for Beverly seeking comment on his arrest. I did not know until later that the cops had listened in to my call. I also didn't know at the time that at that very moment, Beverly was sitting alone in another windowless interview room at the homicide section, waiting for the police to talk to her.

McGothigan was also brought in for questioning and placed in a third interview room.

The investigators talked to McGothigan first. McGothigan told Officer Weisenberg that it was possible that Hans could have been responsible for Nina's disappearance. But McGothigan also stated that he didn't think Hans had it in him. McGothigan reported that he had asked Hans twice in recent weeks if he had anything to do with Nina's disappearance. Hans said he couldn't answer that on the advice of his attorney.

Beverly told homicide sergeant Tim Nolan and Officer Grant that her son "plays it close to the vest" and didn't tell her until September 6 that Nina was missing. He refused to tell her where the CRX was, but that wasn't unusual in itself. This type of behavior infuriated her, but there was nothing she could do about it. She said she didn't notice anything unusual at her house when she returned from Burning Man, although Hans didn't want her to go into his room in the basement, for some reason. She also reported that Hans, strangely enough, had bought the children new towels while she was away. Hans told her that the children had raised a stink about the old towels, which were green and maroon, so he bought them new ones, which were yellow and white. "He didn't—he didn't usually buy household things, but he bought things for the kids," Beverly said.

Beverly said she didn't participate in the search for Nina because she was allergic to poison oak. She also said Doren and Sharanova were hostile to her, so she didn't feel as if she could have taken part anyway. She reported that her son ran the trails at Skyline Gate at Redwood Regional Park, a 1,836-acre wilderness with thirty-eight miles of hiking paths.

Hans stayed in the interrogation room until shortly after

6:00 p.m., when Sergeant Brock and Officer Johnson went inside. They tried to ask him questions, but he had lawyered-up long ago. He cut them off and said, "I would like to speak with my attorney." Hans would later say that Brock and Johnson threatened to send his mother to jail unless he confessed.

At 7:30 p.m., Gill and Johnson took Hans to the Glenn E. Dyer Detention Facility, an austere, 176-foot high-rise jail run by the Alameda County sheriff's office. Even though it was a quick walk from Oakland police headquarters, Gill and Johnson still had to follow protocol by driving him in through a sally port off Seventh Street. They parked and walked him to a locked gate. After being let in, Gill and Johnson pat-searched Hans and sat him on a metal bench. He was again searched by a sheriff's deputy. His money and personal property were placed into plastic bags, and the intake deputies went through a screening form, making sure he hadn't been restrained, pepper-sprayed, Tasered or hit with a baton. After he went through a metal detector, Gill and Johnson left. Sheriff's deputies then walked Hans inside the jail. His information was inputted into a computer. He stood against a wall and was photographed, and his fingerprints were scanned by a machine that checked him for any outstanding warrants. He was then subjected to a series of questions. Do you have a psychiatric disorder? Are you suicidal now or in the past? Have you been exposed to or have a contagious or communicable disease? If he had answered yes to any of those questions, he would have been transferred immediately to Santa Rita Jail, across the county in Dublin, which provides mental health and medical services.

Hans answered no to all the questions, and so that meant he would stay at the Glenn E. Dyer Jail. He was assigned a person file number of BFP563. He was taken to a jail cell and strip-searched by deputies wearing gloves. They told him to squat and bend over to make sure he wasn't hiding any drugs, weapons or other contraband. He was changed into jail clothing and locked in an eight-by-ten-foot cell, with no bail allowed.

Now that Hans had been arrested, the police shut down

their wiretap operation. From September 18 to October 10, police intercepted 627 calls on Hans's cell, of which 19 could be used as evidence. A total of 399 calls on Beverly's home phone were intercepted, of which 37 were deemed of evidentiary value. The rest were either hang-ups, privileged calls with Du Bois, Silva or Hicks or "non-pertinent" calls, those that had nothing to do with criminal activity. In all, there were 1,026 intercepted calls, although that number counted some conversations twice, such as when Hans used his cell to call his mother at her house.

On October 11, as the Bay Area was still swathed in darkness, Oakland police sergeant Gus Galindo and Officer Andrew Barton of the intelligence unit were 2,475 miles away in Atlanta after arriving on a red-eye flight from Oakland. They picked up a rental car and stopped briefly at a hotel to freshen up before driving to Sandy Springs, Georgia, a largely white, wealthy community just north of Atlanta. They met up with Sandy Springs police investigators and drove to an apartment where they thought Ramon Reiser lived. But the apartment manager said Ramon hadn't lived there for a month. Galindo reached Ramon on his cell phone and learned that he was in fact in Birmingham, a two-and-one-half-hour drive from Atlanta. The officers squeezed back into their small rental and headed west on Interstate 20. Ramon called them twice as they were en route to see where they were. He told them he had reserved a conference room on the third floor of the Birmingham Public Library and would be standing under a tree awaiting their arrival.

Back in Oakland that morning, a throng of media showed up at the corner of Telegraph and West Grand avenues. With a large billboard with Nina's picture and promises of a fifteen-thousand-dollar reward as a backdrop, Zografos joined Sharanova to announce that eighteen billboards were being put up urging the public to call in with tips. Clear Channel donated eight signs in Oakland, and CBS Outdoor donated nine signs in Oakland and one in Berkeley along Interstate 80. The billboards advertised a Web site, www.ninareiser.com. Plans for the billboards had already been in place before Hans was arrested. Nevertheless, they would still be put up. They still had to find Nina.

"My entire relationship with her will continue forever. I still hope—a glimmer of hope—that Nina is alive and we'll see her again," Zografos said, his face quivering as he addressed reporters. "But regardless of whether this is a search-and-rescue or search-and-recovery operation for the police, Nina is still missing—we've got to find her."

In halting English, Sharanova, her face etched with pain, told reporters, "I wish Nina never met Hans." She noted that "Nina did everything she could to keep the children away from Hans." She confirmed that Hans was not returning calls. "I also called him, but he didn't answer," Sharanova said.

As Zografos and Sharanova addressed the media, Galindo and Barton finally met up with Ramon at the Birmingham library. Barton had eavesdropped on a call Ramon made to Beverly several days earlier and was now able to put a face to the scratchy voice. But as the officers began talking with Ramon, they quickly realized that it was difficult to get a straight answer from him. Over the course of more than three hours, the white-bearded Ramon, blinking from behind black-rimmed glasses, rambled about different subjects that had nothing to do with Nina's disappearance. Ramon did say, however, that he didn't know what had happened to Nina, nor had he been told. Ramon noted that Hans had never shown any interest in police or military stuff, such as books about police interrogation techniques. Hans had told him to "watch his back" and to warn his siblings that people could be coming after them because Nina was missing. Ramon also claimed that Nina had threatened to leave Hans when she found out there was no money for her. She also feared the Russian Mafia, according to Ramon.

Back in Moscow, Namesys programmer Alexander Lyamin wrote on a Linux Kernel discussion list shortly after Hans's arrest that his employees were "rather shaked [sic] and stressed at moment, although I can not say we didn't seen it coming." As for Namesys's future, Lyamin wrote, "We will just buzz along as usual, chunking out patches and going through review, while

pursuing existing business opportunities to get some funding."
In the long term, Lyamin said the company "will do fine" if
everything went the way they hoped it would. "If it goes bad,
that is where it becomes tricky. We will try to appoint a proxy
to run Namesys business."

CHAPTER 45

›THE DA WEIGHS IN

On the morning of October 12, Assistant DA Tom Rogers formally filed a murder charge against Hans in Alameda County Superior Court.

"The undersigned, being sworn, says, on information and belief, that HANS REISER did, in the County of Alameda, State of California, on or about September 3, 2006, commit a felony, to wit: MURDER, a violation of section 187(a) of the PENAL CODE of California, in that said defendant(s) did unlawfully, and with malice aforethought, murder NINA REISER, a human being."

As is customary in Alameda County, the murder charge wasn't designated as first or second degree; that would be left up to the jury to decide. Rogers did not file any special circumstances—such as murder committed while lying in wait or in the course of a kidnapping—that would have made Hans eligible for the death penalty. The authorities had no idea what led up to the slaying. Nor could they say conclusively how she had been killed—stabbed, bludgeoned or strangled—without her body. The relatively small amount of blood evidence didn't seem to support the possibility that she had been shot. There were so many unknowns, but all they could say for sure, with any conviction, was that Nina was dead and that Hans had killed her. Still, there were a fair number of people in the legal community who believed that Rogers, in filing the murder charge alone, had already bitten off more than he could chew.

It was undisputed that the vast majority of cases handled by prosecutors weren't whodunits. They know who did it most of the time. It was more like a "what is it?" The DA could aim high and charge someone with murder, knowing that it could be pleaded down to a lesser charge, like voluntary manslaughter, after considering a defendant's mental state at the time of the killing. "It's a safety net for the DA," Rogers said. "When it's a complete 'I didn't do it,' we say you're playing without a net—you could get a complete 'not guilty,' which is very hard to live with. So we either plead those cases or not even try them. So this one, even though I felt it was a strong case, it's one we don't normally try. The body wasn't the issue. It's a circumstantial case—and we don't try anywhere near as many circumstantial cases as we do 'what is its,' where there's no issue as to the person actually having done the homicide. It's just, what the mental defense is or is it self-defense, something to mitigate the actual infliction of the mortal wounds."

Du Bois would later tell Rogers, whom he had faced at trial numerous times in the past, that the prosecutor was like the baseball manager "who calls for the suicide squeeze," asking the man on third to run for home even without knowing whether his batter could deliver a sacrifice bunt. Was the DA's office really willing to stick its neck out for Hans without knowing whether it would prevail? Was it going ahead with the case—and just hoping that Nina's body would surface later?

But Rogers had faced such doubts before. Rogers had prosecuted Fremont serial bomber Rodney Blach for a three-day wave of explosions in 1998 that terrorized the police chief, a city councilman and a family against whom he had a grudge. The case against Blach was largely circumstantial, and it appeared that Blach had a solid alibi that put him nowhere near Fremont at the time of the blasts. But after being asked to take a look at the case, it was Rogers who concluded that Blach had used Casio watches as timing circuits that delayed the pipe-bomb explosions--by six months. The federal Bureau of Alcohol, Tobacco and Firearms (ATF) had initially discounted that theory after finding watches that could only be set a month in advance. And it wasn't until after Blach was charged that Rogers was handed a treasure trove of evidence: a tip led investigators to a San Jose storage locker filled with chemicals, gunpowder and bomb-making books.

An up-and-coming prosecutor named Paul Hora fended off defense efforts to suppress the key evidence.

> On the day that Hans was charged, I obtained a copy of a probable-cause statement written by Officer Gill, outlining the grounds for Hans's arrest. It made for an eye-opening read and ran for several pages. Most statements were no more than one or two paragraphs long. The court filing mentioned publicly for the first time the murder books Hans had bought at Barnes & Noble and the fact that the passenger seat from the CRX was missing and the floorboard was soaked with water. The seat was still there when he was pulled over by the Redwood City police officer on September 12. On the day Nina was last seen, she and Hans were heard by their children using "not nice words," the statement said. The groceries found in Nina's minivan were "in such disarray that it appeared that it was a result of the vehicle being driven rapidly and possibly recklessly," it said. Finally, "trace amounts" of Nina's blood were found in Hans's home as well as in the CRX, the statement said.

That afternoon, a crush of media gathered on the sixth floor for Hans's arraignment at the Wiley Manuel Courthouse, which was attached to the jail where he was being housed. Newspaper and TV reporters milled about. Photographers clicked one shot after another as Beverly, wearing sunglasses, entered the courtroom while accompanied by two women. Doren arrived separately with Sharanova.

The air was electric, the mood tense. Reporters commented to each other how Hans was now being represented by not only Du Bois, but also Daniel Horowitz, a scrappy East Bay attorney and well-known TV legal analyst. It was a bit surprising, if not jarring, to see Horowitz in court. Almost exactly a year earlier, Horowitz had returned to his expansive hillside property in the Contra Costa County city of Lafayette to find his wife, Pamela Vitale, brutally beaten and stabbed to death. The killer, a brooding teenage neighbor named Scott Dyleski, had been sentenced to life in prison just sixteen days before Hans's arraignment.

Horowitz didn't want to take the case at first. After Nina went missing and attention turned to Hans, a neighbor of Hans had asked Horowitz if he was interested in representing the computer programmer, and he said no. After all, here was a guy whose wife had disappeared and was presumed dead—and murdered—by him. "The way it read in the press, it seemed like he did it," Horowitz said later. It just hit too close to home, and Horowitz didn't want to be in the unseemly position of defending a possible cold-blooded murderer. But then Du Bois called. "I got a high-publicity case and I need to know how to handle the media," he told Horowitz. "I think we can work well on this case."

"Tell me about it," Horowitz said. When Du Bois was done, Horowitz signed on. "It was clear to me that he was either innocent or it was not premeditated," he said.

Horowitz introduced himself to Hans for the first time in a back room of the courthouse on October 12. "I know who you are," Hans replied. It would have been hard to miss Horowitz, who in recent years had become one of those ubiquitous talking heads on television, providing legal commentary on CNN, MSNBC, Court TV and just about any outlet that wanted him. That afternoon, cameras were allowed to film the scene as the defendant, wearing a red jumpsuit emblazoned with the words "Alameda County Jail" on the back and his hands shackled to his waist, emerged from a holding area and was brought into court. He turned to take in the packed courtroom and made brief eye contact with his mother before taking his place beside Judge Trina Thompson Stanley. He was greeted by Du Bois and Horowitz, who shook his hand, leaned in and said something to Hans, who laughed in response. Reiser did not enter a plea. Within moments, the arraignment was over. Hans was ordered to return to court on November 28 and was taken to Santa Rita Jail, where inmates were transferred post-arraignment. The color of his jumpsuit signified that he was being held in a single cell for his protection.

Now it was time to face the media.

"We don't feel numb anymore. We just feel—now we feel angry and we want justice," Doren said as Sharanova stood at her side. "And I think now we're faced with two choices—either

Hans had something to do with it, or he knows somebody that had something to do with it, and in either case, it's time to come out with the information."

Sharanova repeated what she had said a day earlier: "I wish Nina never met him."

Beverly spoke briefly with the defense attorneys and did not address reporters before leaving.

The defense gave their spin with an impromptu press conference in the hallway.

"Anybody can be charged with a crime," Du Bois said. "The evidence that I have seen in the statement of probable cause in support of custody is relatively flimsy." Nevertheless, Hans "knows that this is a severe problem and a solemn undertaking," he said.

Horowitz also attacked the probable-cause statement as if it were a dime-store novel with a threadbare plot. He was back in his element, by all appearances the same pugnacious criminal defense attorney as he was before. He was ready for a fight. "When you read it, you'll see that their case is much weaker than what they said it is, and when we get to court they'll have to put up or shut up," Horowitz said, offering a tidy sound bite for the evening news.

He scoffed at the fact that his client had purchased the two murder books. "Anybody being pursued and followed around by the police might want to read a book whose focus is on improper police tactics," Horowitz told me before the hearing that day. Police were "leaking sensational information that may not even be accurate," he groused. To the defense, all that talk about Hans's odd behavior was just window dressing to make him look as sinister as possible. Where was the proof?

CHAPTER 46

> JAILED

The Ohlone Indians were the first inhabitants of what is now known as the Tri-Valley, thirty-three miles east of San Francisco. Much of the land was granted in 1835 to Jose Maria Amador as payment for serving as administrator at nearby Mission San Jose. The hamlet known as Amador's Ranch sat in the middle of a triangle of land comprised of the Amador, Livermore and San Ramon valleys. The area grew slowly until World War II, when the U.S. Navy built the Camp Parks Military Reservation to house ten thousand servicemen. The reservation was adjacent to Camp Shoemaker and the original Santa Rita Jail, which opened in 1947. Tract homes advertised as "city close, country quiet" began appearing in 1960, and with development came crime and the need to house those responsible. The jail became severely overcrowded. Charles Plummer, the hard-charging, take-no-prisoners Alameda County sheriff and former chief of police in Berkeley and Hayward, was tasked with building a state-of-the-art facility.

The new "megajail," built at a cost of $172 million and also named Santa Rita, opened in 1989. Since then, the area has seen skyrocketing growth, with the sprouting of the Hacienda Crossings Shopping Center—built on the site of the old Santa Rita Jail—sleek office buildings, cookie-cutter townhouses and new tracts whose residents may not have known at first that they had four-thousand neighbors nestled in the foothills, most of whom were clad in "Santa Rita yellow" (unless the inmates were in protective custody, in which case their jumpsuits were red). It wasn't something Realtors or the city of Dublin advertised.

A quarter-mile wide by half a mile long, Santa Rita

features eighteen housing units sprawled over 113 acres. It boasts a rooftop solar electric system and a fleet of robotic vehicles that carry containers of laundry, supplies and food. Morbidly, the carriers resemble coffins, and it is eerie for visitors to see the six-feet-long boxes seemingly moving about by themselves along tiny ruts in the ground.

Under different circumstances, Hans may well have appreciated the technological aspects of the jail. But his focus was somewhere else. About a week after his first court appearance, Du Bois and Horowitz paid him a visit. To see Hans, the attorneys had to walk down what Horowitz called the world's longest bowling alley, a narrow corridor of concrete walls stretching hundreds of feet. After an interminable walk, they finally reached a set of metal doors. After being buzzed in, they walked to a small, steel room designed for attorney-client meetings.

On this day, Du Bois and Horowitz sat in flimsy plastic chairs near a metal table and waited. Soon they saw Hans through a glass window being escorted by sheriff's deputies. He was led inside with his hands shackled in front of him. Hans appeared frail. His eyes darted back and forth, as if he was taking everything in. But then his face broke into a broad smile. "Thank you for coming," Hans said.

The attorneys invited Hans to tell them everything he wanted them to know. For the next forty-five minutes or so, Hans laid out his story. He spoke deliberately and precisely and made good eye contact. He had handwritten notes with him. Horowitz could see that this was a brilliant computer engineer who didn't come off as your everyday criminal. "He was a very remarkable human being in an equally remarkable institution," Horowitz said.

Horowitz would visit Hans at least two more times in jail. Life at Santa Rita was difficult for Hans, who had been placed in administrative segregation. That meant spending twenty-three hours of the day alone in a cold seven-by-nine-foot cell with a stainless steel combination toilet-sink and a mattress two inches thick. Deputies didn't care if he was some genius computer programmer. Here, he was just another inmate with a number and a regimented life, where deputies told you what to do, where to go and when to do it. Some inmates complained that the deputies talked down to them or were rude. Breakfast was at 5:00 a.m.—earlier if you had to be in court in the morning.

"The jail conditions were literally breaking him down physically," Horowitz said. "He was looking more and more haggard and exhausted."

Horowitz would not say what Hans discussed, citing attorney-client privilege, but noted that "he talked about his kids repeatedly."

At a child-custody hearing on October 19, Hans asked Commissioner Burgess to have his children visit him while in jail. Not surprisingly, his request was denied.

At the jail, Hans had access to a phone for up to an hour at a time, once every several days, unless there were other inmates waiting. Hans used that time to call his mom—the clamor of the jail sometimes drowning out his words—and press her to act as his surrogate researcher. Beverly would pick up her phone and hear a recorded voice saying, "This call may be recorded or monitored. I have a collect call from—" and then Hans would announce, "Hans Reiser" before the voice continued, "an inmate at an Alameda County sheriff's jail." Because his time on the phone was limited, Hans usually dispensed with any pleasantries and would immediately give Beverly a series of instructions. He told her to call his attorneys to press his case and to try to reach the children to make sure they knew they were loved. Hans's requests overwhelmed Beverly at times. After he asked her to find the mailing addresses of the *New York Times* and the *Wall Street Journal*, a befuddled Beverly asked how she would be able to do that. Exasperated, Hans told her to go online.

He asked Beverly to contact a Web site that would be sympathetic to those who were fighting lies about the dangers of computer games.

"They don't like people who make up stories about problems with computer games, at this particular Web site," Hans told her. "There's a reason I've chosen them."

CHAPTER 47

›THE PRELIM

Just because Hans was in custody didn't mean that police could rest on their laurels. The investigation continued in earnest, and within days Deputy District Attorney Greg Dolge was assigned the task of handling Hans's preliminary hearing, also known as a preliminary examination, or prelim for short. Dolge would be in charge of laying out just enough evidence at a "mini-trial" of sorts to convince a judge to hold Hans over for a full trial before a jury. The case could have been brought to a grand jury, and had that happened, Du Bois would not have had the chance to cross-examine the people's witnesses. Now, at least the prosecutors could get a preview of the defense's strategy.

Dolge seemed to be the perfect fit for the Reiser case. A youthful forty-one, Dolge lived in the Oakland hills in between Snake and Shepherd Canyon roads and ran in the neighborhood. He knew the Montclair neighborhood and the schools the Reiser children attended. Dolge's two kids, in fact, were a couple of years behind Rory and Nio. This case had unfolded right in his backyard.

Dolge had traveled an unlikely path to law. After he graduated from UC San Diego, a friend from college who worked in the entertainment industry as a writer inspired him to move to Hollywood. He worked as a production assistant and stage manager on such shows as *Golden Girls*, *Empty Nest* and *Herman's Head*. But Dolge got tired of it all. He had always thought of being a lawyer. He leafed through an LSAT prep book and found himself, at the age of thirty, going to UC Berkeley's Boalt Hall School of Law. After a stint at the

San Diego DA's office, he moved back up north to become an Alameda County prosecutor.

It was literally straight out of central casting for Dolge. He was now in the big leagues, working for an office with one of the best reputations in the state, the same one that produced U.S. Supreme Court Chief Justice Earl Warren and U.S. District Judge D. Lowell Jensen, for whom Dolge had worked as an extern.

Dolge was relieved that Hans hadn't entered a plea on October 12 and invoked his right to a preliminary hearing within ten days. Had Hans done so, that wouldn't have given the prosecutor much time to prepare his case.

Dolge knew he had a formidable warhorse of an opponent in Du Bois, a sixty-three-year-old former Alameda County prosecutor who had been practicing law since Dolge was only four. As a former DA, Du Bois knew all the prosecutors and their tactics. But Dolge had gone up against Du Bois before in court and had an idea of what to expect. "I knew him well enough," Dolge said. "I think he's got certain tendencies and, perhaps, weaknesses."

Dolge wouldn't elaborate. But other lawyers say Du Bois is not the most organized. As the Oakland police had discovered, he could be difficult to reach because he was always stuck in court somewhere. "Bill's a very bright guy, very quick on his feet. He's also very volatile in the sense that something will pop up in his mind during an examination or he'll go off on a tangent without having thought through why he's doing it," said one veteran Bay Area attorney who didn't want to be named at the risk of offending a colleague.

Du Bois was also saddled by a tremendous workload. He is one of the busiest criminal defense attorneys in the East Bay, having gained a reputation for aggressively defending his clients. A graduate of the University of Oregon and UC Hastings School of Law, Du Bois spent his first six years as a prosecutor with the Alameda County DA's office. He then switched sides in 1976 and would go on to handle more than one hundred serious felony trials. He had three murder convictions overturned on appeal and one murder acquittal in recent years. "Where others see defeat, he sees the opportunity to defend," reads his Web site. He relished going to battle with the government's attorneys. Juries may not have liked the defendants whose lives hung in the balance, but they at least seemed to tolerate this well-spoken gentleman with glasses and a quick wit. He was a likable guy, full of stories and colorful tales. He spoke of being "related distantly" to civil rights activist and NAACP cofounder W. E. B. DuBois. Both were descendants of the French Huguenots who came to the United States more than two hundred years ago. "When my father found out, he was catatonic for two days," Du Bois joked. "We revived him, however. He lived for several years thereafter."

Du Bois tended to please people to a fault. He accepted nearly everyone who walked in his door or gave him a call. Naturally, they promised to pay him. But the well would invariably run dry, and sometimes, a week before trial, Du Bois would start wondering if he should have withdrawn from the case. Oftentimes, it was too late.

With Hans, Du Bois jumped in quickly because it was a high-profile case. Money didn't seem to be a problem, as Hans agreed to give his attorney a stake in Namesys.

The bottom line was, Du Bois enjoyed being in the limelight. Du Bois had defended Jose Merel on charges that he was among several men who murdered Newark, California, transgender teen Gwen Araujo in 2002 after learning that she was biologically male. Merel was sentenced to fifteen years to life in prison for second-degree murder but not before Du Bois pledged to the *Hayward Daily Review* that he would bring "enthusiasm, initiative and inventiveness" to the trial, which drew national attention. It didn't matter if his clients were distasteful or accused of a terrible crime. That was the nature of the job.

"The way one thinks about criminal defense is the same way an ER doctor thinks about a body rolled in the door from an ambulance," Du Bois said. "He doesn't sit down and say, 'Does this guy deserve saving? Let me look at his life and see what kind of person he is before I perform any procedures.' He looks at the body and says, 'What are the medical problems? What can we do to rectify them, to solve them, to cure the patient?' The same thing is true with criminal defense.

You look at a case and say, 'How can we best assert a defense, consistent with the rights provided by the United States and California Constitutions?' And that's where you put your emphasis."

"Bill's reputation is that he's very good on his feet in the courtroom," said District Attorney Tom Orloff. "He's often pretty entertaining. He's a smart guy and very experienced. Bill was a very good prosecutor."

Du Bois, in fact, was known as an aggressive prosecutor. He was the talk among the office when he charged a defendant with *attempted* drunken driving because he was fumbling with the keys and trying to start the car. "Bill was famous for overcharging," said Assistant DA Rogers, his eyes crinkling as he smiled.

Du Bois and Orloff used to share an office when they were prosecutors. The two had plans to be partners in a civil law firm. But Orloff ended up staying, and Du Bois set out on his own. "The DA's a fun job, if you don't need money and don't mind working for the government," Du Bois said. "I didn't care to work for the government under the circumstance of it being a huge bureaucracy. I was a child of the '60s. I wanted to be on my own. It had nothing to do with prosecution or defense. I still would love to prosecute. It's fun. It's the most fun you could have with your clothes on. You have tons of evidence, everybody loves you and usually you're on the right side of things."

Orloff would certainly agree with that assessment. A career prosecutor since 1970 who has been district attorney since 1995, Orloff was well respected in the community and studiously avoided the limelight, never grandstanding at press conferences or using his position as a stepping-stone to higher office. In fact, when he spoke at all—even when he personally prosecuted a San Leandro cop-killer—it would be in a slow monotone, in the deliberate manner of someone who had seen enough in his years to rarely get excited about anything. But as the Reiser case unfolded, Orloff's reputation would take a hit. Senior Deputy District Attorney Angela Backers filed a gender discrimination lawsuit against Orloff, accusing him of failing to promote her and making derogatory remarks about women in the office. A judge eventually threw out the suit, and the four-term district attorney emerged unscathed—unless one counted a story in an East Bay weekly that zinged Orloff for his habit of illegally smoking smelly cigars in his office.

For his part, Orloff said defense attorneys like Du Bois played an important role in the criminal justice system. "I view the role of the defense attorney, more than anything else, as they hold our feet to the fire and make sure we do everything right," he said.

> By October 23, the reward for tips in the case had grown to twenty-five thousand dollars, thanks to donations received through www.ninareiser.com. "We plead with anyone with information that may help police locate Nina to come forward," Zografos said. "It is the right thing for the community, Nina's friends and family and most importantly her children, who are faced with the prospect of never finding out where their mother is."

Nina's thirty-second birthday, November 3, 2006, passed empty and heavy. It was supposed to have been a day of celebration, but instead the mystery of her absence continued for the sixty-first agonizing day. There was some solace for Sharanova, however, when she obtained physical custody of Rory and Nio five days later and would now be in control of their medical and educational needs. But that Thanksgiving, as families gathered together to count their blessings, there was only pain and disappointment for those who kept Nina in their thoughts and prayers. They still had no tangible evidence to indicate that she might still be alive.

On November 28, Hans returned to court, shackled and again clad in the red jail jumpsuit, because the notoriety of the case made it necessary to keep him in protective custody, away from other inmates. He pleaded not guilty—and surprised everyone by asking for his preliminary hearing to start within ten days. He wanted his day in court as soon as possible. Judge Stanley scheduled the hearing for December 11. Ramon and Beverly sat in the courtroom gallery and showed no emotion. But Doren, sitting next to Sharanova, wept.

Things seemed to be moving quickly as far as Hans was concerned, but Zografos, who had publicly thanked the Oakland police for their diligence in arresting Hans, was now irritated at them, saying they weren't doing enough to find Nina. "I think that's unacceptable," Zografos said.

Ramon contacted CPS worker Seng Fong that day, saying he had proof that Rory could extend his arms, rebutting a report that said he couldn't. It was almost a carbon copy of what Hans had done when he wanted to prove that Rory could write cursive. Ramon suggested that the previous tester may not have done the activity in a fun fashion and didn't have any experience with kids. In contrast, Ramon told Fong that he had the proper credentials and could serve as guardian for the kids because he was a teacher, could speak multiple languages and had an IQ in the top 3 percent. His intelligence had been passed on to his grandson, as Rory was able to read a pamphlet on lead poisoning, Ramon boasted, as if that was something to be proud about.

Horowitz withdrew from the case that day, saying Hans couldn't afford to pay him.

But Du Bois was still on board, and he held court again with reporters after the hearing. "No case in the history of California, based on circumstantial evidence of murder, has featured an investigation which ran such a short period of time. They have to prove not only that she's missing, which we all know, but also that's she dead, which we don't know."

Du Bois added that there's no evidence that her death was "caused by a criminal agency." Hans had a number of theories of where his wife could be, including "all around the world," Du Bois said. For all he knew, she could be somewhere on the Black Sea, enjoying a Stoli vodka, according to the attorney.

With all the focus on Hans and Nina, Doren redirected reporters' attention on Rory and Nio. "The people suffering right now are the children," she said.

But the public's attention shifted back to Nina when about fifty people searched for her on December 2. Search teams looked in areas that hadn't been checked before. But there were still no signs of Nina or her body.

Although it would have been ideal to find a body for the purposes of the criminal proceedings, it wasn't required. Decades ago, juries would have been hard-pressed to return guilty verdicts without a body unless a defendant confessed. The bulk of homicide cases resulted in a body, but nowadays prosecutors can proceed in a homicide case without many things, such as a confession, a motive or a murder weapon. But juries in bodyless cases could be skeptical. Sometimes they refused to convict if there was still a chance that the purported victim could be out there somewhere, hiding and very much alive. The worst nightmare for a prosecutor would be an acquittal in a no-body case, followed by the discovery of the body or other evidence that only later cemented the defendant's guilt. The double-jeopardy clause in the Constitution barred the DA from trying someone a second time. So the DA had to tread carefully and make sure that the circumstantial evidence was solid, as it were.

"If you don't have a body, you have to circumstantially prove the person is dead," said District Attorney Tom Orloff. "And it just depends on what circumstantial evidence develops."

There had already been many so-called "no body" cases that had been successfully prosecuted across the country and in the Bay Area.

In Contra Costa County, prosecutors won a first-degree murder conviction in 1994 against a man who kidnapped and killed a U.S. Navy civilian worker whose body was never found. In 1986, a man was convicted in San Mateo County of murdering his former fiancée, whose skeletal remains were found fourteen months after the trial ended.

At the time Hans was arrested, Mario Garcia was being tried on murder charges in the October 2005 disappearance of Christie Wilson, twenty-seven. The two had been caught on videotape leaving a casino in Placer County. Wilson's body was never found. The trial was moved to Sacramento because of pretrial publicity, and a jury there eventually convicted Garcia of first-degree murder. He lost his appeal.

Now Deputy DA Dolge had to convince a judge—not a

jury—that there was enough evidence to send Hans to trial. The bar was relatively low at the prelim level. In an ordinary case, a prosecutor would call some witnesses and lay out enough evidence—but not all of it—to show that there was enough probable cause to show that the defendant should be tried.

But this was no ordinary case, and the judge assigned to Hans's prelim was no ordinary judge.

Judge Julie Conger stood out among her colleagues on the Alameda County Superior Court bench. While the bulk of her fellow judges were former prosecutors, she had served in the county public defender's office before working with famed criminal defense attorney Penelope "Penny" Cooper in Berkeley. Another graduate of Boalt Hall at UC Berkeley, Conger was elected to the bench in 1983. It wasn't long before she was lambasted by prosecutors for what they felt were rulings that leaned heavily toward the defense or didn't make sense at all. In a 1986 profile in the *Daily Journal* legal newspaper, a civil attorney said, "At her best, she can be more human than a number of judges I've appeared before. At her worst, she's irrational, unpredictable and doesn't care about the law."

"There's always a skeptical streak of the defense-attorney mentality in her. She will not swallow anything anybody was dishing out wholesale," said longtime CBS-5 reporter Bill Schechner, who walked into court to cover the prelim and found that Conger, his neighbor in Berkeley, was on the bench.

Conger disagreed with any assertions that she was pro-defense. And she was not shy about speaking out on issues that were important to her. In 1985, she and two other judges disqualified themselves from hearing the cases of 158 anti-apartheid demonstrators arrested at UC Berkeley, citing their "feelings about the genocidal racism of South Africa." In 1997, Conger signed a written declaration, siding with her neighbors who supported a court order blocking further expansion of the maternity unit at Alta Bates Medical Center, a half-block from her home. Her letter forced all the judges on the county bench to recuse themselves from hearing the city's lawsuit against the hospital. But Conger would not be cowed. "I do not give up my First Amendment rights and my membership in the community and my concern for my neighborhood because I am a judge. And in no way did I engender this or intend for this to occur," Conger told the *Chronicle*. The suit was later settled.

In 2002, she launched an elder-abuse court after seeing too many elderly people being victimized. In 2006, Conger and another judge threatened to resign from the California Judges Association unless it rejected a plan to require continuing-education classes for judges. "The proposed rule is unnecessary, insulting and unconstitutional," Conger wrote.

She was a longtime member of the association's education committee, having won an award from the judges' group in 2005 for excellence in judicial education. Conger also served on the association's ethics committee. In 2002, she wrote an opinion for the committee stating that a San Diego prosecutor could continue handling the murder trial of a woman accused in the fatal poisoning of her husband despite having been elected as a judge.

When she was off the bench, Conger bred Portuguese water dogs and could often be seen walking them at the Point Isabel Regional Shoreline in Richmond.

If Dolge was concerned about Conger's judicial pedigree, he didn't say so publicly. But it was well known within the DA's office that Conger was no rubber stamp for the prosecution.

On December 11, the prelim began as scheduled at the René C. Davidson Courthouse, overlooking Oakland's Lake Merritt. Hans glanced at the gallery as he made his way to his seat, carrying a boxful of legal papers. But first Conger had to deal with media coverage. Du Bois had no problem with this. "Mr. Reiser has no objection to the press being present throughout these proceedings and no objection to the press having cameras of any sort, moving or otherwise, during the proceedings," he said. It made sense. Hans wanted to make a good impression on the world. Gone now was the guy being chased by reporters and the inmate in jail garb. In his place was a computer programmer in a suit, albeit rumpled, who wanted his kids back and insisted he had nothing to do with his wife's disappearance.

The judge allowed one pool still camera and one pool television camera to be present but barred the media from filming any civilian witnesses. If more than one newspaper or television station wanted photos or footage, everyone would have to share.

Dolge called Ellen Doren as his first witness. Doren made it clear that Nina did not voluntarily just leave her life behind.

On cross-examination, Du Bois pounced, insinuating that like Nina, Doren decided to marry an American man to get into the United States and that the two women led similar lives. Politely, Doren replied, "No. Our home life was very different. Nina was divorced, and I was married."

Du Bois dove into the more salacious aspects of Nina's life, including her affair with Sean Sturgeon. Doren said she never had a chance to see whether his arm had the word "RAGE" cut into it. She said Nina never mentioned to her that Sturgeon was into sadomasochism. Du Bois tried to paint Nina as a woman of intrigue with a shadowy link to Russian intelligence, insinuating that Nina's father worked at the Black Sea resort city of Sochi and that it was frequented by members of the former KGB.

"What you know about Nina Reiser is based essentially—as far as her extracurricular life, her life away from you is based only [on] what she tells you, isn't that right?" Du Bois asked.

"Her life away from me? Yes," Doren said.

In a dramatic moment, Dolge announced that his next witness was seven-year-old Rory. Up until this point, whether the boy would testify was a matter of speculation. "I was kind of on the fence of whether to put Rory on or not," Dolge said later. "If I didn't need him, I wasn't going to expose him to this. But I decided to put Rory on in order to establish that Nina made it to that house."

Heads turned as the little boy walked into the courtroom. Hans raised his eyebrows in greeting as Rory came in, but his son didn't look at him. Conger pulled the microphone down and asked Rory to speak into it to see how his voice carried. The clerk asked for his name.

"RORY," his voice boomed through the microphone. Spectators laughed, and the judge smiled and said, "Well done."

When he got on the stand, Rory looked at his father a number of times before Dolge began asking him questions. At times fidgeting with a plastic cup, Rory said he understood the difference between the truth and a lie.

The boy told the prosecutor that his mother took him and Nio to his father's home on September 3. He said he hugged his father—a comment that drew a smile from Hans—and that his father told him and Nio not to come upstairs.

But Dolge then asked, "Did you hear any kind of argument upstairs?"

"No," the boy replied. It would be a damaging moment for the prosecution and cast some doubt on the DA's theory. Moreover, Rory's testimony conflicted with what he had said during the CALICO interview. In their probable-cause statement, police had said Rory may have heard his parents arguing using "not nice words."

It got even more problematic when Rory said he had given his mother a hug and that she left the house.

"Did you see her go out of the front door of the house?" Dolge asked.

"Yes," he said.

Dolge asked if he could see through the door after she left the house. No, Rory replied, "because the door was made of wood."

Rory said his father took him and Nio to school on Tuesday, September 5, and told them that he would be picking them up after school. Rory knew his mother usually picked them up on Tuesdays. To Dolge, that was the smoking gun. Hans knew Nina wouldn't be picking them up that day.

On cross-examination, Du Bois asked Rory, "Did someone tell you not to look at your dad while you were testifying here?"

"No."

"It's OK if you look at him," Du Bois said.

On redirect, things got muddied up a bit when Dolge elicited from Rory that his parents usually argued "every time my mom would drop me off at my dad's house." Dolge redirected Rory's attention to the day he last saw his mom.

"How do you know she was in the car?" Dolge asked.

"Because I saw her leave."

"Did you see her get into the car?"

"Yes."

"What does your mom have to do to get into the car after she leaves the front door of the house?"

"She walks up the steps and then gets into her car and then turn the car on and then drive away," Rory replied.

Dolge again asked, "Did you see her get into the car?"

"Yes."

"Did you see the car drive off?"

"Yes."

"Where was your dad when you saw that?"

"Somewhere near me."

"Inside the house?"

"Yes."

Conspicuously absent from the proceeding was Nio. She was too young to have remembered exactly what happened on September 3.

Next on the stand was Anthony Zografos. He suggested that Nina's children had been turned against her. "There were occasions when the kids were getting upset at their mom, which is a common thing," he said. "They would use words such as 'You're a liar, you lied to the judge, you want to steal our dad's money,' things like that."

The hearing continued the next morning, December 12. Beverly testified that her son thought Nina was "very neurotic" and that she "projected ailments on Rory that Rory didn't have."

"Did Hans feel that Nina was a liar?" Dolge asked.

"Yeah, I would say that's true," Beverly replied. She noted that her son felt Nina "didn't give the children enough attention and left them with babysitters too much."

During cross-examination, Hans whispered into Du Bois' ear. Having been cued, the attorney then asked Beverly if she

had ever called her son "an inconsiderate slob" and had told
him to move out from her home. She laughed and said yes,
adding that her son then made an effort to clean the house
and their cars.

Also that day, Nina's divorce attorney, Shelley Gordon, testified that the couple's divorce proceedings "were extremely
hostile and acrimonious." In her career, only a few divorces
have been "really, really hostile, and this was one of them,"
she said.

During one court hearing, according to Gordon, Hans had
told Judge Tigar, "Don't look at her eyes. Russian women lie.
You cannot look at Russian women and Thai women because
their eyes lie. You can't tell that they're lying by looking at
their eyes." At a hearing presided over by Judge MacLaren,
Hans kept on talking even after she left the bench.

Gordon said she believed the custody dispute between
Hans and Nina on Labor Day weekend in 2006 had been
worked out. "I didn't call Nina, and I'm sorry that I didn't,"
she said.

Officer Gino Guerrero testified about the cat-and-mouse
game between Hans and police on September 18. When he
recounted how he and Officer Jason Sena followed a taxi and
heard reports that other officers saw Hans running up Snake
Boulevard, Conger interrupted and said, "I'm lost. Is he in the
taxi or is he running up Snake?" she asked. Both Du Bois and
Dolge told the judge that the police thought Hans was in the
taxi when instead he was running up the street.

"The taxi therefore was a red herring," the judge said, nod-
ding in understanding. "A decoy."

As Guerrero testified about how a dozen officers on the
ground and in the plane tracked Hans, the defendant laughed
numerous times. He was reliving the game.

During a break between sessions, Dolge said Hans's move-
ments and behavior were "evidence of a guilty conscience."
But Du Bois said Hans simply didn't like being followed by
police and never intended to flee. "It's sort of silly," Du Bois
told me. "It's an attempt to make a silk purse from a sow's
ear."

On December 14, Hans fired Cheryl Hicks, his family law

attorney. Yet another attorney, Arthur Mitchell, began representing him.

The preliminary hearing resumed on December 20, as Oakland struggled to get through a stubborn cold snap that saw the temperature dip to thirty-five degrees just days earlier. But the heat on Hans was only rising as criminalist Shannon Cavness testified that a bloodstain found on a sleeping-bag stuff sack found in the Honda CRX Hans drove matched Nina's DNA profile.

A bloodstain found on a pillar in the living room of Hans's home on Exeter contained DNA belonging to him and his wife, Cavness said. The DNA profile of the male matched Hans, but only to the degree of one person out of two hundred, presumably because there was a smaller amount of genetic material from the male in the stain.

But the testing linked Nina's DNA profile with such certainty that only one in forty-five trillion women would also match, Cavness said.

The defense drew agreement from Cavness that DNA testing couldn't confirm when bloodstains were deposited. Du Bois suggested in his questioning that the bloodstains could have been degraded over time because of exposure to heat, ultraviolet radiation and moisture in the air. Cavness agreed with the defense attorney that Nina's DNA could have been deposited on the pillar at a different time than when Hans's DNA was left there.

That week, Hans gave his first post-arrest interview, to *Wired*'s Joshua Davis.

"I just keep thinking that I'm stuck in George Orwell's *1984*," Hans said. "The government has taken away my kids, invaded my house, held me in solitary confinement and caused me all sorts of financial problems."

Du Bois told Davis that Reiser was running out of money to pay for his defense. "This is a unique opportunity for someone to buy the company for pennies on the dollar. We welcome all vultures."

A few days before Christmas, Sharanova got permission from Alameda County CPS to take Rory and Nio to Russia for the Christmas holiday. They left the United States on

Christmas Eve, and the children were expected back on January 14. Rory was due back in court on January 16 to answer more questions from Conger directly. Her plan was to close her courtroom before asking him some questions to clear up some discrepancies.

› On January 2, after Officer Jesse Grant testified about Hans's purchase of David Simon's *Homicide*, Du Bois objected to it being admitted as evidence, saying that meant he would have to read it.

"That doesn't follow," Conger said, shaking her head.

After discussing something with his client, Du Bois withdrew his objection and said, "I think we all should read it. There's some good stuff in there."

Conger deadpanned, "I'm sure you could have written it."

To support his change of heart, Du Bois asked Grant if he knew that the book had a chapter about police planting evidence.

Grant said he did not, but under questioning by Dolge, the officer turned the tables on the defense by noting that the book also discussed how hard it was to get rid of a body. Grant could not predict that within weeks, two more people would disappear in what would become the most explosive development yet in the hearing.

On January 16, the proceedings came to a halt even before they began. Jointly, Dolge and Du Bois had some stunning news for Conger: Sharanova had failed to return from Russia with her grandchildren two days earlier. Through a message by e-mail from a Russian attorney, Sharanova said Rory had been seeing a therapist while in Russia and that he was having behavioral problems, including crying and not being able to sleep. The therapist was recommending that Rory stay in Russia because he was traumatized by his mother's absence. Moreover, the Russian courts were seeking legal custody of the children.

Hans wasn't in court that day because traffic problems had delayed a sheriff's bus from Santa Rita Jail. But Du Bois knew that his client would "put a hole in the roof" once he learned that his children were in Russia—and may not be coming back. Du Bois charged that Sharanova was violating a separate family-court judge's order that Rory attend a child-custody hearing in Oakland on January 24. Du Bois said he wasn't sure, though, whether Sharanova could be found in violation of Conger's order that Rory be made available as a witness, as Sharanova wasn't personally told of that order. Conger was also perplexed. "I've never actually had a witness ignore my order to return, so this is something I need to look at."

But Dolge wasn't worried. Outside court, he noted that Rory had already testified and that it could be used at trial. He said he didn't know what the judge wanted to ask Rory. Dolge said later that he had also learned through Ellen Doren that Sharanova didn't want to bring the boy back. Sharanova didn't want the case to stand or fall on Rory. Dolge understood Sharanova's concerns. He knew anyway that in the grander scheme of things, "Rory is not very consequential to the outcome of the case."

On January 18, Conger dropped her request for Rory to return to her courtroom. "I am not inclined to take any action on the non-appearance of Rory Reiser at this time, and it is my feeling that the record as it stands now should remain. And unless and until Rory Reiser returns voluntarily, I will not be requesting further testimony of Rory Reiser," she said. Hans was upset. He believed this was what his mother-in-law had planned to do all along—whisk his kids to Russia, never to be seen again. Du Bois said Nina obtained Russian citizenship for Nio two years ago and had done the same for Rory two months before she disappeared. To the defense, these were signs that Nina was alive and well—and had masterminded one last fraud, by engineering her so-called disappearance and then secretly reuniting with her children in Russia.

On January 23, Sharanova told CPS worker Seng Fong that it was never her intention not to return with the children. But when she learned on January 2 that Rory was needed again to testify, Sharanova said she found it incredible that Rory had become such a key witness. She said it wasn't her intention to violate the court order and apologized—but noted that she was only looking out for the children's best interests. She said she was in the process of obtaining legal guardianship of the children in Russia.

› The February 26 issue of *People* magazine featured the mysterious death of Anna Nicole Smith on its cover. But inside was a three-page spread entitled, "Missing and Presumed Murdered," about Nina's disappearance, complete with pictures. Hans worried about whether the article, which he believed was skewed against him, would affect his chances to get the kids back.

From jail, he continued to barrage Beverly with more requests.

"Did you write that down?" Hans asked his mother in one call.

"Yes," Beverly insisted.

"You don't write that fast," said Hans, not believing her.

While languishing behind bars, Hans kept mostly to himself. He spent a lot of time reading books, including *All the Shah's Men: An American Coup and the Roots of Middle East Terror*, by journalist Stephen Kinzer, and *Invisible Man*, by Ralph Ellison.

› Police found several other books in the Ford Escort that Hans had rented—and later crashed—in Berkeley. One was *Everything Bad Is Good for You: How Today's Popular Culture Is Actually Making Us Smarter*, in which author Steven Johnson opined that video games were so captivating that they stimulated the reward centers of the brain. Another book was *A Feast for Crows*, a fantasy novel by George R. R. Martin. Hans also recalled keeping in the rental car Randall Sullivan's *LAbyrinth: A Detective Investigates the Murders of Tupac Shakur and Notorious B.I.G.* as well as *When Corruption was King: How I Helped the Mob Rule Chicago, Then Brought the Outfit Down*, by Robert Cooley with Hillel Levin.

› Tsegaye Chernet, who had rented Hans the Ford Escort, had received a call from the police shortly after the crash. He had to have the car towed from Berkeley back to his business on Ninety-second Avenue in East Oakland. There, he cleaned the car and filled two garbage bags with paperwork, clothes and a sleeping bag that Hans had left behind. Chernet had the car fixed at a body shop to the tune of nearly four thousand dollars. Neither he nor Iskander, the driver of the other car, had ever gotten reimbursed by Hans. Chernet forgot all about Hans's junk until March 3, when he decided to clean things up a bit. Water had seeped inside because of rain the week before, and Chernet wanted to clean things up. He looked inside and paled. The clothes and sleeping bag seemed to be oozing blood. But a test of the items by the crime lab proved that whatever the substance was, it wasn't blood.

On March 9, after hearing six days of testimony spread over three months—a span of time not uncommon for complex cases due in most part to scheduling issues—Conger told the attorneys to sum it up.

Du Bois referred to "corpus delicti," the Latin phrase for "body of crime," the principle that it must be proven that a crime has occurred before someone can be convicted. "She is missing," he said. "There is no corpus delicti in this case, as we were taught in law school, your honor and I. The corpus delicti of murder is a body that has been murdered, and there is none. One of the problems in making a case where there's a missing person is to show death by a criminal agency, to show death. There has been no showing of death. There has been no showing of criminal agency. Therefore, there's no corpus delicti."

Dolge outlined the prosecution's theory for the first time— that Hans, knowing he had the house to himself, lured his wife to his home and killed her. "He manufactures an argument to get Nina over there," Dolge told the judge. As for Rory's inconsistent statements, Dolge urged Conger to consider Rory's testimony as part of a whole and to accept that he may have been "flat-out wrong" in some of his recollection of key dates. "He clearly is not an entirely reliable witness," Dolge said. "Clearly he's not trying to be intentionally deceptive, but he's a seven-year-old child in extraordinarily difficult circumstances. He's doing the best he can."

Dolge seemed to be making some headway until he accused the defense of cherry-picking parts of Rory's testimony to suit its interests. "The defense wants you to pick, Rory is right when he says this—"

Conger broke in. "No, Mr. Dolge, I think you're asking me to do that."

> Du Bois said there simply was no opportunity for Hans to commit the crime, especially when his son said he saw his mother go out the door and drive away.

> When they were done, the judge ruled that there was enough evidence to hold Hans over for trial, but not before she voiced some reservations.

Even though Nina's body hadn't been found, "There is strong suspicion that an offense has been committed— namely, Nina Reiser is dead," the judge said. "I can see no other reasonable conclusion that can be drawn from the evidence presented other than she has not been heard from since September 3." She also said there was also a reasonable or strong suspicion that Hans could be guilty of the crime.

But Conger said she was not persuaded that Hans had the opportunity to kill his wife at his home. "One of the things that particularly troubles me is your statement that you believe that Mr. Reiser lured his wife there because he was alone at Exeter," said the judge, addressing Dolge. "This is negated by the fact that the children were present. I'm also troubled by the concept under your theory of the case that this occurred, and that all this activity occurred, while the children were left up at the Exeter house alone."

Even so, she said, "I am looking at the totality of the circumstances and I look also at the strongly suspicious activities performed by Mr. Reiser. I am troubled by the missing front seat in the car—[it] is particularly troubling—the books that were purchased, which were left in the car, the actions by Mr. Reiser and the totality of the circumstances, and analyzing all of this I do believe there's a strong suspicion that Mr. Reiser, if not personally was responsible, had some part in the murder of Nina Reiser. Accordingly, I will issue a holding order in this matter." Hans Thomas Reiser, the husband of a woman whose body had still not been found, was going to be put on trial for murder.

Surrounded by reporters afterward, Du Bois said, "There is unquestionable evidence that the client did not commit this crime. The judge had to push the envelope of speculation to reach this judgment." The defense attorney vowed to seek bail for his client. That would be a near impossibility. In Alameda County at the time, defendants charged with murder were rarely, if at all, granted bail.

Dolge wasn't concerned about Conger's doubts, not the least of which was her suggestion that someone else may have participated in the crime. "All I'm concerned with is the results," he said later. "This is just a preliminary hearing. It's not the trial. It's just sort of the gate you have to pass through."

Back in jail on March 15, Hans told his mother during a phone call, "I don't really know what's going on, but I hope that it amounts to the kids coming back and my getting out of jail and this happening soon."

"Hopefully soon," Beverly agreed.

Ramon stayed with Beverly for a while at Exeter. It was difficult for her to live with her former husband, but Hans implored his mother to work with Ramon to try to get custody of the kids.

Two days later, Hans called his aunt, Andree Chicha, an estate-planning attorney in Washington State, and asked her to review a brief that Du Bois had prepared. "Tell me if I'm right to be unimpressed by it," he said. "He wrote this forty-three-page brief, and to me it seems like it actually undercuts his oral argument and, you know, I don't have the objective distance that you do, nor your experience. So if you could screw my head on straight, that would be great." His next question revealed that he may have been weighing his options. "Is there a good book on plea bargaining?" he asked Chicha. She laughed and said she didn't know because she wasn't a criminal attorney but would let him know if she found one.

On March 22, Rory spoke on the phone with Beverly as Sharanova listened in on a different extension. During the call, Beverly mentioned Hans several times, telling Rory to remember that his daddy loved and missed him. She told him that he shouldn't forget his English and that they were waiting for Rory and Nio and that they had kept all of their toys. Beverly asked if he had an e-mail address.

After the call, Rory seemed quite upset. He had problems sleeping that evening, according to Sharanova. The next day at school, his face went pale and he fainted. His teachers told Sharanova that he was unconscious for a short period of time. Sharanova reported the incident to Alameda County CPS. Nio didn't have any reaction after she spoke to Beverly. But the little girl asked if Nina had been found yet. Nio also told her grandmother that when she grew up, she would return to the United States and buy the house that she and her mother used to live in.

On the day of Rory's fainting episode, Hans was formally arraigned. His not-guilty plea on March 23 was pro forma, but in a surprising move, Du Bois requested a trial date within sixty days. Most defendants waived that right to allow themselves time to prepare. Judge C. Don Clay, Du Bois' former law partner, set a trial date for May 7.

"It's his desire to go to trial immediately," Du Bois said outside court. He noted that he would no longer seek bail for Hans because his client's finances would be better spent elsewhere.

Hans felt his chances of beating the rap were good. "Mr. Du Bois is quite optimistic," he told his mother by phone from jail that day.

His mood darkened however, on March 24, when Beverly told him that the kids had asked her two days earlier if Nina had been found—and that Rory, quoting Lavrentiev, Sharanova's husband, had said that he and Nio wouldn't return to the United States until Nina was found. Hans didn't say anything for a full ten seconds, an eternity given the limited time he had on the phone. He seemed rattled throughout the rest of the call, at one point saying, "Mom, this is terrible," and sighing and hesitating repeatedly. Finally, at the end of the call, he said, "Let's hope Nina shows up."

"What? What did you say?" Beverly asked.

"Take care, Mom, OK?" Hans said without answering. He was devastated. He vowed to get out of jail and talk to Sharanova in hopes of convincing her that his children loved him and that he just wanted to be with them and not take them away from her.

CHAPTER 48

›THE PROSECUTION

With a trial date set, it was time for Dolge to pass the baton to another prosecutor, which was the norm in Alameda County. "We just don't have the luxury of doing it vertically," District Attorney Tom Orloff said, referring to when one prosecutor handled a case from beginning to end. By the time Dolge gave his closing argument in the prelim, Orloff had already assigned Deputy DA Paul Hora to handle the trial. "Aside from being a very good trial lawyer, he's also very, very hardworking and has really wonderful organization skills," Orloff said.

Hora's mother, Peggy Hora, remembered when he was just eighteen months old and waiting in line with her at the Bank of America in Castro Valley, California. The toddler was jabbering away, prompting a woman in front of them to turn around and exclaim, "My goodness, he certainly speaks well for two!" The precocious little boy took one look at her and said, "Actually, I'm *not quite* two." And by the time he was three, Hora was already making due process arguments, telling his mother, "But you didn't *tell* me I couldn't do . . ." She knew her son would make a fine lawyer.

But it took Hora a little while to come to that realization himself. After earning a finance degree from Cal State Hayward, he accepted a job as a private building inspector. He would drive all over northern California, checking out roofs at Bank of America branches and at the library at UC Santa Cruz. But Hora came to hate the job. While attending the University of San Diego School of Law, Hora's mother, who later became an Alameda County judge, suggested that he consider a job as a prosecutor. After participating in a summer program at the Alameda County DA's office, Hora got hooked. Being raised by a lawyer almost certainly had its influences, but Hora just as easily could have gone the other way, "running screaming from the law," Peggy Hora said. By the time he was assigned the Reiser trial, Hora had earned a golden reputation after serving fifteen years with the office. An avid hunter and fisherman, Hora helped send the self-proclaimed San Leandro "Sausage King" Stuart Alexander to death row in 2004 for murdering three sausage inspectors at his plant, a massacre that was caught on his own security cameras. Alexander died of a pulmonary embolism at San Quentin Prison a year later. For years, Hora hung a framed "proof of death statement" on his office wall.

Hora's compassion for crime victims was heartfelt. Just because his job as a prosecutor was over didn't mean he would just move on and never look back. After the lone inspector to survive the sausage-plant massacre died of cancer in 2008, Hora went to his funeral.

Now, as he dove headfirst into the Reiser case, Hora girded himself for the long haul. If it meant keeping long hours at nights and weekends and missing dinners—not to mention losing more hair, the balding prosecutor joked—then that's what it was going to take. He wanted to gather every piece of evidence, talk to every witness, get as complete a picture as he could to find out what happened to Nina and to bring Hans to justice. Hora kept a missing-persons poster with Nina's picture on the wall of his ninth-floor office. It was the first thing he looked at when he came in and the last thing he saw before he left. He wanted to do what was right for Nina and her family.

Hora wanted to use the large portrait of Nina and Rory that had hung in her bedroom for trial. He had no other place to put it, so he hung it on his office wall. A passerby who took a cursory glance inside his office saw the portrait and said to colleagues in awe, "Paul must be *really* into his wife and kid."

› When Dolge had the case the past fall, he had called his friend Hora for advice. The two bandied about strategy. Hora ended the conversation by telling Dolge with a laugh, "By the way, don't mention my name." Hora wasn't keen on getting assigned the trial. Based on what little he had heard, Hora thought, "God, I wouldn't want that case. How on *earth* can we ever prove this guy committed the crime?" His concerns remained even as the prelim came to a close and Hans was held over to answer for murder. Although the missing car seat was a "no-brainer," "that gets you to the one-yard line. You still gotta get to the end zone in order to prove the case beyond a reasonable doubt to twelve people," Hora said.

Hora's investigative team consisted of several district attorney's inspectors, all of whom were former Oakland police officers who were no strangers to the dangers of working the streets.

As an Oakland homicide sergeant, Bruce Brock had been assigned the Reiser case from the beginning. Early on in his career, he shot and killed a suspect. He honed his skills as an investigator with stints handling felony assaults and robberies before landing a position in the homicide section, where he was the lead investigator in forty murders. By the time the bespectacled veteran with the bushy mustache retired from the Oakland Police Department, on December 3, 2006, he had spent twenty-four years on the force, just about half his life. But instead of riding off into the sunset or joining a smaller police force like some of his colleagues, the fifty-year-old Brock became a DA's inspector the very next day. He was a natural for the job of being Hora's right-hand man in the Reiser case.

Inspector Craig Chew had only several years on the Oakland police force when he investigated a suspicious car in the city's Temescal District in July 1991. Chew was ambushed and shot five times by a teenage robbery suspect as the officer approached. Despite being injured, the former Berkeley officer managed to return fire, wounding the suspect in the leg. "1L14, 940B, I've been shot!" Chew yelled into his shoulder mike, using the Oakland police code for officer needs help. "I have one down!" The incident earned him a mention—and a reenactment of the ordeal—on the TV show *Top Cops*. Today, Chew still has two bullets lodged in his chest, one of which is only 2 millimeters from his aorta.

Then, in August 1992, just a month after returning to duty, Chew, now a K-9 officer, responded to the on-campus mansion of UC Berkeley Chancellor Chang-Lin Tien for a burglary in progress. Chew shot and killed the intruder, nineteen-year-old People's Park activist Rosebud Denovo, when she lunged at him with a machete in an upstairs bathroom. Denovo, née Laura Miller, and other activists had been upset that the university was planning to build volleyball courts at the park.

Inspector Bob Conner had been assigned to investigate the "Riders" scandal. Conner had to weather accusations by the Riders defense team that he and prosecutors had conspired with police brass to frame the cops, who were accused of framing drug suspects. Conner bled Oakland blue, having served on the force from 1971 to 1994. Along the way, he lost eleven friends on the force, two of whom served in the helicopter unit. But Conner felt no compunction in investigating officers from his former department. To him, it didn't matter if the crooks were dope fiends, politicians or police officers. "If you can't handle criticism, then you have to find another line of work," Conner said.

CHAPTER 49

> THE SECOND CHAIR

Oakland criminal defense attorney Richard Tamor was cooking dinner and enjoying a glass of wine at his home in Alameda when Du Bois called him one night in March. "I've got this case, and I think we can get a lot of publicity out of it," said the voice on the other end. The two lawyers had worked together numerous times, but Du Bois told Tamor that the Reiser case was unlike any other and that the stakes were high. Tamor remembered that back in late September, he had stopped by Du Bois' office and there was Hans, sitting there with his fanny pack on.

Tamor, the former president of the Filipino Bar Association of Northern California, thought the trial would last three months at most. Little did he know that his services would be needed for far longer. But Tamor was up for the challenge. He relished taking a "whole mess" that was a complex criminal case and winnowing it down so it was presentable and manageable. He eagerly accepted cases that would take thousands of hours of work, listening to wiretapped conversations and leafing through hundreds of pages of transcripts. While at UCLA School of Law, Tamor was an editor at the *Law Review*. Now, he had his own firm, Tamor & Tamor, the second half of the nameplate belonging to his civil lawyer wife, Jovita.

Tamor had defended a broad spectrum of clients. There was the man who claimed that his deformed genitals were the reason that he brought lubricant to a meeting with a "girl"—who actually turned out to be an undercover sheriff's deputy. Then there was the member of San Francisco's "Big Block" gang, whom Tamor said got caught in the sights of federal prosecutors who cut deals with lower-level hoodlums to get the big fish.

"I think people in San Francisco ought to question the types of tactics the government is using," Tamor told *SF Weekly* in a story that he has framed in his Oakland office. "No one ever sees the dark side of these prosecutions, the nasty shit that goes on to get these convictions. It's sugarcoated for the public." In a 2002 profile in the newsletter of the Asian American Bar Association of the Greater Bay Area, Tamor was asked for his advice to aspiring law students. "Practice law on your own terms and don't believe people when they tell you that you can't do something," he said.

Tamor didn't mince words, and his quiet, unassuming demeanor in public could fool people. His rise to becoming the second chair of a high-profile murder case capped an improbable journey that few could have foreseen would have led to a career in criminal defense.

In 1972, when Tamor was only three, his father, Hilario Tamor, was murdered by three drunk carjackers in the Philippines. The elder Tamor was stabbed fifteen times before his car was pushed over a cliff with him in it. Aurora Tamor tried to protect little Richard from the details, but when he was eleven, he found the police reports and read them all without his mother knowing. She later told him to become a lawyer so she could hunt down the men who killed his father—and then he could defend her when she did that. The defendants were eventually tried and convicted.

Early in his career, Tamor wanted to be a prosecutor. But as time went by, he realized that he had more in common with defense attorneys. Plus, he had attended UC Berkeley as an undergraduate and still had the "fight the power" attitude in him.

"People may wonder how I could ever defend criminals after having my father murdered," Tamor said. "I think about that sometimes myself. I think had I become a prosecutor I would have let my experience with my father motivate me through anger, and I don't think that's a particularly healthy way to go about things. My father being murdered is a part of me, but it shouldn't and doesn't define me."

Tamor believed he was a better attorney in part because he could view things from the perspective of a crime victim. He felt for Rory and Nio, who was a little older than he was when he lost his father. When he wasn't before a jury, Tamor doted on his three young children and attended Oakland A's games as a die-hard fan.

CHAPTER 50

›LETTERS FROM SANTA RITA

On March 28, Commissioner Rhonda Burgess declared Rory and Nio Juvenile Court dependents, formally removing them from their parents' care and placing them with Sharanova in Saint Petersburg. Sharanova was appointed to act as their educational surrogate and was given authority to travel internationally with her grandchildren. But the commissioner said any visits with Hans would not be appropriate and said that his only contact could be through written letters that were screened by CPS and/or Sharanova.

Hans wrote constantly in his jail cell, whether it was notes to his attorneys or letters to his children in which he asked them if they remembered going to places like the Exploratorium, Whole Foods Market and the water park. He wanted to know if they recalled happier occasions like buying cakes at a bakery, looking for crabs on the beach, sharing a large Italian ice cream, touching the manta rays at the Monterey Bay Aquarium and singing the song about the ants and the butterflies. Hans promised to buy flowers for Nio "when I am free" and to take both of them to Wyoming to get fudge and to see wild buffalo roaming past their car.

Hans gave his children tutorials in his letters, telling them how to calculate percents and explaining to them what friction was. "Take your finger and lightly push a cup on the table, pushing harder and harder until it starts to move," he wrote on April 1. "Do you see how once it starts to move you don't have to push as hard to keep it moving? Interesting and odd, yes? The amount you have to push it before it will start to move is called the 'static friction,' and the amount that you have to push it to keep moving is called the 'dynamic friction.'"

Hans had some advice for his kids while they were in Russia. He counseled them to "act in different ways than you do in America," because "Americans smile in ways that Russians think means someone is a fool. You don't want them to think that of you. Foolish me, I worry you will forget your smiles though. Smile when you watch American movies like an American, OK?" He wrote a smiley face and ended the letter with, "I miss you more than freedom." He then added a P.S. "There are ways in which Russians are much wiser than Americans. Learn them, please." He added another smiley face.

He also urged his children to learn how to make *pelmenyi*, Russian meat dumplings, from Herman, referring to Lavrentiev, Sharanova's husband. "Pelmenyi are like pot stickers, but Herman makes them better. I think he should start a pelmenyi restaurant, because he makes them the best of anyone," he wrote on April 2.

Hans was desperate to receive anything from his children and asked them to draw some pictures or send him a note that said, "I love Papa!" "It would cheer me up, and I will put it on the wall in my cell," he wrote. Instead, Rory scribbled a letter, filled with the misspellings of a child, that said, "From Rory, on my birthday my best preset is Nina." He wrote "Were is Nina?" nine times. The scrawls got progressively larger. He ended by writing, "Too bad papa. You don't mean me anything. You are a lier." Another letter read, "I am not going to America. Only if Irina goes to America for company. I don't want to see you, Hans." Rory only had one thing on his mind. He didn't care about hearing about the water park or restaurants or learning about percents. "I asked you where is Nina. Not about other stuff," yet another letter read. "Tell me where is Nina?"

On April 5, Hans wrote Nio, telling her that he had heard that she was angry at him for "not liking Nina." He wrote, "Niorline, I will never say anything unkind about your mommy to you, I promise. Nina has the most beautiful voice of any woman. Niorline, I hope that when you are grown you will have her voice. You already have her eyes, and I love you for them so much. I taught Nina how to cook, and then she went far past me, leaving me in the dust."

On April 7, Seng Fong spoke with Beverly regarding the stress that resulted when she spoke with Rory on the phone. Beverly was told that she could only have written contact with the children. Fong told Beverly to send letters to her and that she would forward them to the children after the letters were screened. For Rory, Beverly sent an Aladdin picture and a couple of pages from *The Cat in the Hat*. She sent Nio a Little Red Riding Hood connect-the-dots picture. She signed her notes, "Ba Beverly," the term of endearment they used for her.

CHAPTER 51

> STURGEON

That spring, Sean Sturgeon was feeling the pressure. He probably knew more about Hans and Nina than anyone else. He knew he would probably be called to testify at the trial. But Sturgeon just wanted to be left alone. He felt that if Hora called him to the stand, the prosecution would in fact lose the case. He knew that if he was called as a witness, his entire life—as colorful as it was—would distract the jury and become fodder for the media. Nothing could bring Nina back. And how could there be "justice" when the system had already failed her before?

But Hora just wanted to talk to Sturgeon to see what he knew. At that point, no decision had been made as to whether he would be a witness in the case. Hora asked Sturgeon to come down to the DA's office at the René C. Davidson Courthouse for an interview on April 12. Hora told Sturgeon that he needed to know as much as he could about what Sturgeon knew. "I cannot afford to be surprised on the witness stand," Hora said. "I need to know everything." Hora told Sturgeon, "You have to tell the truth." It was the prosecutor's standard admonition to any potential witness.

That's when Sturgeon made a chilling statement. "I killed 8 and a half times," he told Hora, Chew and Brock, who had joined them by then.

"Really?" Hora asked. *Did he just say what he said?* It was beyond comprehension.

"Yeah, I really have."

"What's the half?" Hora asked.

"When I got there, the person may or may not have been dead, but when I left, the person was most definitely dead."

Sturgeon said the killings happened from 1972 to 1995. At least one incident "started" in Alameda County, and the others spanned the state and perhaps some happened outside California or in a different country, he said. But Sturgeon denied killing Nina. He said he had been sexually abused and tortured by a variety of people who were friends or visitors of his mother. As Sturgeon became an adult, he was haunted by what had happened and decided to find and kill the pedophiles who had molested him. He said he owned two guns but had never shot anyone.

Hora, Brock and Chew met Sturgeon that evening at Merritt Bakery, near the lake, where Sturgeon agreed to allow them to search his apartment and to take his guns for safekeeping. They walked the short distance from the bakery to his Lakeshore Avenue home, where a uniformed officer and three other inspectors met them to assist. Sturgeon handed them his keys and told them where his guns were inside. A Winchester 12-gauge shotgun, a .40-caliber Glock semiautomatic handgun, ammunition and spare magazines were turned over to Oakland police for safekeeping.

In a subsequent interview, Sturgeon said, "I will take responsibility for 8 and a half deaths." But he cautioned the investigators, "I won't show anyone where the bodies are or give any names, but I will submit myself to a judge, to a court of law."

Later, Sturgeon said, "Six and a half people was direct vengeance."

"Six and a half?" Hora asked. "Is that what you said?"

"Yeah. Sure," Sturgeon said, adding, "But two people were in self-defense, when I was investigating the six. I sometimes had to deal with some unpleasant people in order to get information."

He gave further details about the "half" victim. He said he was hiking with his abusers as a boy when he came across a little girl. She had been hurt in a fall or animal attack, but Sturgeon felt she was partly responsible for abusing him. Acquaintances would later say that Sturgeon had told them that the girl was the daughter of one of his abusers. Sturgeon said he bit her neck, drank her blood and then hit her in the head with a rock. He left and called her a "half" victim because he wasn't sure if she had died.

The investigators were skeptical. They believed from the beginning that Sturgeon hadn't killed one person, let alone eight and one-half people. They also knew Sturgeon wasn't responsible for Nina's death.

But they still had to pound the pavement and diligently investigate this bombshell claim, if only to eliminate Sturgeon as a suspect. Over the next two weeks, the DA's team focused their efforts almost exclusively on Sturgeon. They drove to Kensington, a small community sandwiched in the hills between Richmond and Berkeley and popular with UC Berkeley professors. They checked out his old home, which Sturgeon said others might well have described as a "hippie commune." After running checks on the many people who had lived there, Hora and Chew interviewed Sturgeon's pastor at All Nations Presbyterian Church after Sturgeon agreed to waive clergy-penitent privilege. From there, they took a number of trips. They drove to Redding to interview Sturgeon's sister and flew to Seattle to interview a former All Nations pastor and his wife. They also tracked down Sturgeon's mother at her home in a remote part of Sonoma County, hidden deep within a redwood forest near the Russian River. It was so dense it felt as if Chew's county-owned Ford Explorer was scraping against the tree trunks.

Hora and his team suspected that what Sturgeon's sister had told them was true—that he came up with this "bizarre story," which was patently false, so that he'd be deemed an unreliable witness whose testimony would be discounted at trial. "And that's the only thing I can think of" as to why Sturgeon was "coming up with all of this stuff," his sister told investigators. But Sturgeon's former pastor told Hora and Chew that he had heard the story about multiple killings as early as summer 2005, a full year before Nina disappeared.

Hora had to disclose to the defense what Sturgeon had told them, because it was potentially *Brady* material, or exculpatory evidence that could prove Hans's innocence. But Sturgeon's statements left Hora with a vexing choice. If he put Sturgeon on the stand, his testimony could be damning enough to help lead to Hans's conviction. But that meant Du Bois would have a go at Sturgeon in court, and Hora knew that the defense could very well divert suspicion away from Hans and instead point to Sturgeon as Nina's killer. Sturgeon seemed to be the perfect suspect. He was an S and M enthusiast and gun-owning confessed serial killer who had been romantically involved with Nina—and regularly loaned her thousands of dollars even after breaking up with her. He was at her door to drop off a load of cash just two days before she went missing. Who might seem the more likely suspect—Sturgeon or a nerdy computer programmer? For his part, Sturgeon insisted to his friends that he didn't kill Nina, and that he was willing to take a polygraph or a "truth serum" to prove it.

As Hora and his team tried to untangle the Gordian knot that was Sean Sturgeon, Sturgeon paid a visit that spring to Shelley Gordon. Nina's divorce attorney was taken aback by the stout man with the haunting green eyes. After speaking to him on the phone, she had expected him to be skinny for some reason. But as he sat in her office, he kind of grew on her. Gordon remarked to Sturgeon that Nina had given her a gift certificate for her birthday in January 2006 for the Soizic Bistro, a French-Asian fusion restaurant at Jack London Square in Oakland. He immediately asked to look at it. He grasped the certificate like it was a sacred object, hungrily looking to see if Nina had written something—anything—on it. He burst into sobs.

> On April 17, Seng Fong wrote Hans with guidelines as to what was appropriate in his letters. "Do not assert any pressure or undue influence on the children. No disparaging comments or remarks. General concern for the welfare of the children is appropriate."

She said his letters would be forwarded to the children. "I will inform the maternal grandmother to read the letters to them or have someone read the letters to them if determined to be appropriate." Fong later reported to Hans that one of his letters had been read to them and that they didn't want to hear from him any more. Hans fretted over which letter had been read to them, whether it was the most boring one or one that made him look bad.

On April 22, Hora and Conner met with an Alameda woman who had spoken to Rory and Nio's one-time Russian-language teacher. The teacher had been talking to Sharanova, who shared some things Rory had been saying while in Russia. "I am only seven years old and already my life has been hell," he said at one point. "He did it with the white scarf," the boy also said later. Rory insisted that the police must search the Exeter home because his mother's body was hidden there. He repeatedly would say, "He hid her in the tiny room; he hid her in the tiny room."

Rory also reported on the day Nina dropped him off at Hans's home, his father sent him and Nio straight to bed that night, instead of being with them and working at his computer until they fell asleep, as was his usual practice.

On April 27, Hans told his parents in a phone call from jail about Sturgeon's confession and noted that Nina wasn't among his victims. "Why would he suddenly confess all this?" Beverly asked. Hans said that Sturgeon had been interviewed by police but told her not to divulge this new twist to anyone. But it was clear that even Hans didn't know what to make of this. He told his mother to wait until "my lawyers and I figure out what the hell this means."

"How come Sean hasn't been arrested?" Beverly demanded several times. Hans said he wasn't sure if he should tell her, at least over the phone. One thing for sure, Hans said, was that this was proof that Sturgeon was a danger to the kids.

On April 28, Hans told Chicha, his aunt, about what Sturgeon had said. "I would like somebody to be saying this to the press, because it seems so obvious to me, so if you could work with my dad on this, that would be great," Hans said.

By month's end, Judge Clay issued a gag order about anything related to Sturgeon. Even the gag order itself was filed under seal.

But it was too late. On May 3, details of Sturgeon's confession appeared on *Wired.com* in a story by Joshua Davis, the same writer who had interviewed Hans after his arrest.

"I have offered to be judged for my crimes," Sturgeon told Davis in an interview. "I take responsibility for what I have done." Sturgeon said that confessing was one of the most difficult decisions of his life. He regretted being a source of distraction in the case and joked that he was not so much a red herring as a "red Sturgeon."

The story left many people following the case shaking their heads and asking themselves what in the world was going on. But the mainstream media, myself included, left the Sturgeon issue alone. I, too, doubted that he could have killed that many people. Until he was arrested or charged, there was nothing to report, especially with a gag order in place. Any of our questions would have been met with, "No comment."

On May 7, Hans's trial was delayed until May 29 because Du Bois was busy on another case. Dressed in a blue blazer and his hair rumpled, Hans reluctantly said, "I guess so," when Clay asked if the delay was acceptable.

Hans was becoming frustrated at his inability to communicate directly with his children. He asked Fong to "arrange for someone to write down what my children say in response to each letter." He repeatedly accused county officials in subsequent letters of failing to provide him with services to "accomplish reunification," the process in which children can visit with parents who are in custody.

He wrote a letter to newly assigned social worker Kelley Rebro, asking that one letter per day be read to the children. He asked Rebro to "record what they say in response so that I may tailor the letters to them and accomplish a meaningful correspondence that meets their emotional needs." He even asked Rebro if she could sing songs he wrote for Nio.

Although Hans's letters were sent by Alameda County officials to Russia, they weren't automatically read to the kids. Their psychologist was tasked with reading the letters to make sure they were appropriate for Rory and Nio, a Russian social worker reported.

> Beverly, meanwhile, was having trouble making ends meet. She decided to rent out a room to a friend, Edie

Okamoto, telling Hans she'd use part of the money to help pay his legal bills. But the funds were apparently slow in coming, because Hans pressed her on the issue in early May. After Beverly balked, Hans became angry and accused her of making excuses.

"If you wanted to come up with the money, you could," he said. "You have priorities, and I'm not one of them."

"That's not true, Hans," she said.

"Which is more important to you, whether I stay in jail or don't? You decide," he demanded. "I mean, Mom, I love you, but sometimes you make it hard. You're the only mother I've got, though."

Beverly was also dealing with the fact that Ramon was still living with her that spring. Hans wanted his parents to get along for the sake of trying to get custody of the kids, but Beverly wasn't optimistic about that happening. Plus, her ex-husband was getting on her nerves. He was running up the electricity bill, and she felt she was always giving up something for him. But Hans felt his mother was insulting Ramon. Hans said his father was helping out a great deal. Beverly disagreed.

"He does things that are impossible," Beverly complained. "No matter what I do for your father, it's not enough."

He continued to call his mother, asking her to make sure letters he wrote to the children were read to them.

On May 17, social services wrote Hans a letter with the bad news: no phone calls or in-person visits with his kids, but he and his mother could continue to write them letters.

On May 28, Hans called his mom from jail and made a cryptic promise: "After this is all over, I'll tell you everything that's happened, and you'll understand that I'm innocent of murder, OK? But I'll tell you after all of this, because it's not a simple story, and after it's all over you'll understand that I don't have any reason to make things up, OK? It'll be easier to believe me when you know I have no motive, OK?" Hora and Brock, convinced that Hans was planning to tell his mom why he killed Nina, later grilled Beverly on this mystifying conversation. "I don't know what to think of the call," she said. She made it clear she didn't have anything that would help the investigation. "You're pumping a dry well," she said, adding, "I don't think Hans did it. You should be investigating Sean."

> In May, Sturgeon called the DA's office with one more revelation: he admitted to inducing a woman to falsely state that she had witnessed the incident on December 22, 2004, in which Hans shoved Nina to the ground. On May 31, Hora and Conner called the woman, who admitted that she had lied because she was Sturgeon's friend and he needed a witness to the incident. She said her so-called eyewitness account was based on Sturgeon's recollection of what he had seen. Sturgeon felt that his testimony would be considered biased because of his attachment to Nina. Sturgeon had passed on his observations to her and instructed her to report them as if she had seen what happened firsthand. "I went with what I was supposed to say," she said, apologizing to Hora and Conner. She added that she had read a story about Sturgeon online, perhaps the *Wired.com* piece, and commented that the article seemed "pretty scary."

The May 29 trial date was bumped to June 11.

CHAPTER 52

> A THIRD SEARCH

Oakland police officers Cliff Bunn, Gerardo Melero and Robert Roche and Sergeants Randy Brandwood and Tim Nolan, along with DA's inspectors Chew, Conner, Brock, Jim Taranto and J. P Williams, drove up to the Exeter home at 9:45 a.m. on June 7. They were armed with a warrant signed by Judge Clay to search the house again. The visit went unnoticed by the media. Brock went to the front door and announced, "Police, search warrant!" He had to repeat this several times. Edie Okamoto, Beverly's friend who had begun living there in May, opened the door. Brock said that they had a search warrant for the house, and Okamoto invited them in. Gone was the black door that police had seized; in its place was a wooden one that matched the outside trim and had set Beverly back by two thousand dollars.

This time, the investigators wanted to seize the two shovel/spades and the pickaxe that they had only photographed during the first search of the Exeter home on September 13. They also wanted to seize bath towels, either the old ones that Hans had reportedly thrown away because his kids didn't like them or the new ones that he had bought to replace them.

In his application for a search warrant, Inspector Brock wrote that he believed the tools "were purchased during the time period contemporaneous to the disappearance of Nina Reiser. I additionally believe that Hans Reiser purchased these tools to be used as instruments in hiding, by means of burying, the body of Nina Reiser. I believe that by recovering these tools it will show that these items were purchased in a time frame that would support that these items were purchased for the disposal of Nina Reiser's body."

As for the towels, Brock wrote that after Hans killed Nina, he used towels "to aid his cleaning efforts to destroy evidence such as but not limited to blood. I believe that if not for the use of these towels, additional evidence of blood would have been found" at the Exeter home or in the CRX.

After they went inside the home, Conner saw what he believed to be bloodstains on the trim and wall area in the living room. Conner knew that Nina's blood had been found on the pillar in the same room. He decided to get a new warrant that would specify a search for blood or other biological evidence. After Clay signed off on it, the investigators removed a piece of window trim, a piece of wood paneling and three large towels from an upstairs hall closet. When Hans called from jail late that night, Beverly told him about what happened. "They did another search?" Hans asked. "Well, that's weird." He paused. For the benefit of his listeners, he said, "I will avoid making any remarks." Beverly told him about the apparent bloodstains. He couldn't resist some dark humor. "I think you need to keep small children out of your house," he cracked. Lest those monitoring his calls misinterpreted him, he added, "Oh no, we love them." He again paused before saying, "I'm not going to make any remarks—I shouldn't have made that remark."

In another call from jail on June 10, Hans told his mother that the purpose of the search was to "apply psychological pressure on you," and she agreed. He recommended that she read *Homicide,* by David Simon, which the police found in the CRX, because it described "all the tactics that they use for pressuring people, including mothers," and "how they plant evidence."

CHAPTER 53

› THE JUDGE

The trial was assigned to Judge Larry Goodman on June 11. The next day, he met with the attorneys for most of the morning in his chambers at the René C. Davidson Courthouse in Oakland, two floors above from where Hans had his prelim. At one point, Goodman emerged and sat down at the defense table. "Judge, this is Hans Reiser," Du Bois said. Hans was wearing a yellow jail jumpsuit, signaling that he was, at least for the moment, no longer in protective custody. Judge Goodman and Hans shook hands and chatted with a genuine bonhomie—something that would be noticeably absent for the remainder of the case.

The judge went on the record and memorialized the game plan: there would be hearings on pretrial motions in June and July, followed by jury selection.

From that first meeting, Hans liked Goodman because he had put him at ease. Hans was in a relatively good mood leaving the courtroom. But that was about to change. At about 5:15 p.m., Hans got on a blue Alameda County sheriff's bus—emblazoned with the phrase "Meet the Challenge . . . Wear the Badge" on its side—for the twenty-seven-mile ride back to Santa Rita Jail in Dublin. After the bus pulled into a sally port, inmate Joshua Cole, twenty-one, began looking through Hans's personal property while waiting to be taken off the bus.

Hans said he told Cole to stop and that the stuff was his.

"It's not yours," said Cole, who continued to look through it.

"Leave my stuff alone," Hans said.

Cole started hitting Hans in the face.

Deputy Benjamin Wilson bellowed several times, "Stop

fighting!" Wilson cleared the bus of all the inmates before removing Cole. The deputy then removed Hans. The two were placed in separate holding cells. Wilson took Hans to see a nurse. Hans had some redness to his left cheek. The nurse gave Hans an ice pack.

Cole declined medical treatment and refused to make a statement.

Hans again came to the attention of sheriff's deputies on June 26. By then, Hans had been transferred from Santa Rita Jail back to the Glenn E. Dyer jail in downtown Oakland, where it would be easier to take him the few blocks to Goodman's courtroom for pretrial motions. It was shortly before 2:00 p.m. when Hans told Deputy Rebecca Lorenzana that he needed to talk to her. Lorenzana asked what the problem was. Hans hesitated. "I don't want the other inmates seeing me talk to you." She took him to a back hallway. Hans told her that an inmate had called another inmate "lazy" and was beaten up for it. A third inmate kept watch as it happened, he told her. Hans said when he asked the injured inmate if he was all right, other inmates told him, "Shut up or you'll be next." The beaten inmate refused to cooperate, and Hans was transferred to another part of the jail for his safety.

> Newcomers to Judge Larry Goodman's courtroom might be surprised by the way he dressed and behaved while off the bench. Unlike other jurists who came to work in suits and ties, Goodman preferred sneakers, blue jeans and comfortable shirts. "That's the judge?" observers unfamiliar with Goodman have said on more than one occasion. His casualness raised some eyebrows, but Goodman shrugged off any criticism. "I do it, number one, because I can. Number two, I've sort of taken a survey of jurors and all the jurors say they like it, it makes them feel more comfortable." Goodman said his informal manner also put victims' families and defendants at ease, to the point that some suspects felt more willing to make deals in their cases.

And while most judges disappeared into their chambers before hearings began or in between sessions, Goodman would often shoot the breeze with his staff, the bailiffs, attorneys, reporters and just about anyone who might be a guest in his courtroom that day. He greeted jurors every day with a smile and a joke or two, and when his eyes twinkled, he looked like an older version of British actor Ricky Gervais, except Goodman had a buzz cut. While court was in session, Goodman preferred to address attorneys by their first names. He told jurors that this was his practice because everyone knew each other and that it wouldn't make the proceedings any less professional, just more personable. He was very media-friendly and worked with reporters to get what they needed, whether it was a good camera angle for high-profile defendants or access to court files.

"I have some good friends in the media—I've been burned by the media. I've been on both sides of it. I know some members of the bench who are scared to death of the media," Goodman said. He said he had learned not to hide from reporters because whatever the issue was, "eventually the media's going to find out."

A native of Columbus, Ohio, Goodman was five when he moved to Castro Valley in Alameda County, where Hora had also grown up. Goodman graduated from Stanford University with a degree in political science. The son of a surgeon and a registered nurse, Goodman tried his hand as an emergency medical technician and an apprentice embalmer before turning to the law. He earned his law degree from the University of San Francisco School of Law and joined a firm in Castro Valley, handling civil and criminal cases before opening his own business-law practice.

Goodman also became interested in politics and served on the steering committee for George Deukmejian's 1982 gubernatorial run. The next year, Governor Deukmejian appointed Goodman, a fellow Republican, as an Alameda County Municipal Court judge. In 1986, the governor elevated him to the Superior Court bench. Hora's mother, Judge Peggy Hora, swore him in, returning the favor after Goodman did the honors for her in 1984.

Goodman acknowledged having some problems checking his temper for the first few weeks as a judge. "Being new, I had

the impression that once you get on the bench, you were supposed to make a ruling right then and there," Goodman said.
Worried, he checked in with a fellow judge, David Hunter,
who told him that there was nothing wrong with saying, "I
don't know" and disappearing into chambers to look something up. "I said, 'Wow!' " Goodman recalled, laughing.

Some defense attorneys initially worried that Goodman's
conservative credentials would make him favor the prosecution. But their fears were allayed when he proved them wrong,
handling one murder case after another with fairness to both
sides and showing respect to the defendants.

At one point, however, Goodman handled seven murder
trials in a row, and it got to him. He was dealing with the same
two attorneys in any given case, plus he was tired of dealing
with juries. One juror who changed her mind about sentencing the defendant to death showed up at Goodman's Castro
Valley home and made off with his golden retriever, Mattie.
The babysitter called the judge's wife, Patty, and admitted, "I
think I made a mistake. This nice lady came to the door and
acted like she knew you. I let her take Mattie." Patty immediately left her job at a San Leandro bank and came tearing
home in her Nissan 300ZX. She happened to see the woman
walking Mattie on the street. She scooped the dog up and
drove straight home, crying with relief.

Goodman spent much of his spare time on boats. After he
took a class with the Coast Guard Auxiliary, he was invited
to go train with the regular Coast Guard. He soon became the
first civilian to be qualified as a coxswain on a forty-one-foot
utility boat—and had his own crew. "I'm kind of anal. Once
I get interested in something, I want to master it," Goodman
said. He would eventually be qualified to pilot any vessel
up to one-hundred gross tons. He and his wife had owned
boats since 1986. Their latest was a forty-two-foot Navigator,
dubbed Katie Marie after their daughter.

Goodman once served as a volunteer "homeland security
maritime specialist," training Alameda County sheriff's deputies for duty on the department's thirty-two-foot gunboat,
outfitted with two Heckler & Koch machine guns that fire
7.62-caliber, NATO-issue, standard military rounds. Because

he was working with members of the same sheriff's office that provided security in his courtroom, Goodman received clearance in the form of an opinion from the court's ethics committee and assurances from the DA, the public defender and members of the private bar that they had no problems with the arrangement. But when a picture of him piloting the boat appeared in a *New York Times* story in 2004, someone—to this day Goodman still doesn't know who—complained. The state Commission on Judicial Performance issued Goodman a private reprimand, and he quit his post on the gunboat. Nevertheless, "To this day, I'm proud of what I did in setting up that unit," Goodman said.

CHAPTER 54

> MOTIONS

In the beginning of July, as the Bay Area baked in temperatures that shot past the one-hundred-degree mark, Du Bois filed what was known as a 995 motion to dismiss the murder charge against Hans. Under California Penal Code section 995, charges could be set aside if the defendant had been "committed without reasonable or probable cause." Du Bois noted that Conger had cast doubt on the DA's theory. He argued that Hans neither had the motive to kill his wife, two years after they had separated, nor the opportunity. Plus, there was still no body.

In a response filed with the court, Senior DDA Mike O'Connor of the law and motion division sniffed that the defense's emphasis on motive and opportunity was the stuff of "Agatha Christie novels" because neither was an element of the crime. As for the missing body, O'Connor likened the situation to when Charles Manson bragged that one of his murder victims was never recovered. "A rule requiring the production of the body would mean that the murderer who successfully destroys or conceals his victim's body would be virtually immune from prosecution," O'Connor wrote, adding, "He can hide the body but he cannot hide his guilt."

Du Bois shot back in another brief on July 16, asking, "So what is a zealous prosecutor to do in order to have his cake and eat it, too?" He said the prosecution was cherry-picking from Rory's testimony by arguing that the boy was right in remembering that he was told to stay downstairs on September 3, 2006—but was wrong when he said he saw Nina leaving Hans's house that same day. The defense could argue that Rory was right about the day he saw his mom leaving—but wrong about the date when he was sent downstairs. "Thus, the people's attempt to partition the reliability of Rory's testimony backfires; their own partly right–partly wrong theory can be used by defendant just as effectively against their killing scenario, as they would use it to preserve their scenario. What's sauce for the goose is sauce for the gander."

On July 18, Hora and O'Connor filed a motion with Goodman asking that Sturgeon's purported confession be excluded from the trial. Hora acknowledged that the defense had the right to present evidence of third-party culpability—the other-guy-did-it defense—so long as it was capable of raising doubt about Hans's guilt. But for this to work under this legal concept, the defense had to show not only that Sturgeon had the motive or opportunity to kill Nina, but that there was also direct or circumstantial evidence linking Sturgeon "to the actual perpetration of the crime." And there was nothing that tied Sturgeon to Nina's slaying, not to mention the eight and one-half others, the prosecutors wrote.

"At present, it is impossible to say whether he is telling the truth and has in fact killed some person or persons unknown, whether he has imagined the killings or whether he is lying for some unknown reason," they wrote.

Moreover, Sturgeon had consulted an attorney and would provide no further details about the alleged eight and one-half killings. If called to the stand, Sturgeon said he would invoke his Fifth Amendment right against self-incrimination. The DA's office would not offer Sturgeon any immunity from prosecution. The prosecutors asked that neither side refer to Sturgeon's alleged confession, regardless of whether he testified. They also asked that their filing—and any responses by the defense—be sealed and that a hearing on the issue be closed to the public.

But in a filing July 27, Tamor wrote that Hans should be allowed to introduce Sturgeon's confession to refute the DA's theory that only Hans had reason to hate Nina enough to want to kill her. There was just enough evidence to point fingers at Sturgeon: he had told friends that he was in love with Nina and that she was like a God to him. Furthermore, he still referred to her as his honey, sweetie and wolf.

Tamor added that Sturgeon had a motive to frame Hans. The defense attorney pointed to Sturgeon's manufacturing of the witness to the December 2004 incident in which Hans pushed Nina.

"Sean Sturgeon's statements, along with other evidence, sufficiently link him to the alleged crime, as to be capable of raising a reasonable doubt of Mr. Reiser's guilt," Tamor wrote. "The inferences that could be made against Sturgeon are just as strong, if not stronger, than those made against Mr. Reiser."

Tamor also said the newfound interest in Sturgeon and the search of his home came eight months after the alleged killing of Nina. It was no surprise that nothing incriminating was found at Sturgeon's home, and Hans should be allowed to cross-examine police officers about the adequacy of their investigation, Tamor argued.

Goodman sided with the prosecution on several fronts. He barred both sides from mentioning Sturgeon's confession and denied the defense's 995 motion as well as its motions to suppress evidence from the wiretaps and Hans's fanny pack. The pretrial skirmishing was nearing an end. But more was still to come.

› In August 2007, Juvenile Dependency Court Judge Stephen Pulido ordered county social workers to ensure the return of Rory and Nio to Alameda County within a month so that they could be evaluated by psychologists. But social workers reported that Russian courts had barred the children from coming back to the United States. Attorneys for the children appealed Pulido's order, and a state appeals court sided with them, allowing the boy and girl to continue living in Russia.

› On Sunday, August 19, a third search was conducted for Nina in the Oakland hills. It wasn't the result of any tip or new evidence. The goal was to look at areas that hadn't been searched before. Search-and-rescue teams with cadaver dogs walked along the Skyline and Huckleberry trails. At one point, one of the dogs alerted on an area twenty feet from the East Ridge trail near Skyline Gate, from where Hans often ran the trails. A second dog showed only mild interest, but a third dog showed strong interest. Their handlers saw nothing out of the ordinary. But just to be sure, search crews dug in the area about a foot and a half deep. There was nothing.

> In Saint Petersburg, a pediatrician and psychotherapist at the American Medical Clinic and Hospital examined Rory and Nio. Doctors said both children showed signs of "attention deficiency." But there was an additional notation for Rory, who exhibited "tearfulness changing to aggression at memories of psychotraumatic situation."

CHAPTER 55

> ONE-YEAR MARK

As the first anniversary of Nina's disappearance drew near, Sturgeon grew morose, thinking of how many lives had been shattered. In a poem, he referred to the tragedy as "Murdersys" and said it would be "OJReiser" if Hans wasn't convicted.

*Two children lost both parents when one murdered the
   other
Grandparents made parents again in their twilight years
The other grandmother grieving
For a son deranged and imprisoned
3 September a personal day of infamy forevermore
Two men once brothers locked in eternal conflict
Right and wrong irrelevant . . .*

Sturgeon was heartbroken. Everywhere he looked, he was reminded of Nina. All he had to do was look outside his front door and there was Lake Merritt, considered the jewel of Oakland. Nina used to run the three-and-one-half-mile jogging path around the saltwater lake, where dog walkers, paddleboaters and crew teams shared space with Canada geese, herons and egrets by day. At night, a necklace of lights circled the urban oasis with the Oakland skyline as a backdrop. Nina loved the pergola and colonnade at the lake's eastern end, a landmark famous for its classical columns and a Spanish tile roof. It was right across the street from Our Lady of Lourdes Church, which Sturgeon and Nina had also visited together. The church sat near the spot in 1772 where a Franciscan priest celebrated the first Holy Mass in what would become Alameda County.

But also whenever Sturgeon would leave his home, he could see the courthouse directly across the lake, a constant reminder that he had lost his wolf and that it would be up to a jury to pass judgment. Never seeing her again and sharing those moments with her, Sturgeon would say later, was his Jobian anguish.

> To mark the year that had passed since Nina's disappearance, a small group of friends gathered at Montclair Park. Ellen Doren carefully adjusted framed pictures of Nina and several candles sitting on a table. "I feel that we don't have closure until there is justice. Not a day goes by that I don't think of her," a tearful Doren told those in attendance. "She is the most caring and giving person I've ever met in my life, and she deserved so much more in her life."

CHAPTER 56

> JURY DUTY

That summer, several hundred Alameda County residents received letters summoning them to report to the René C. Davidson Courthouse in Oakland for jury duty. "Failure to respond to this summons will subject you to a fine, a jail term, or both," the letter warned. Those who actually showed up for civic duty were sent to the jury assembly room on the first floor. Many were excused for hardships, such as medical or financial problems or because they were full-time students or owned their own businesses. The rest filled out detailed twenty-four-page questionnaires with one hundred and fifty questions. Besides the usual queries about their marital status, education, employment and criminal history, there were these inquiries:

> *Do you know or have you ever met or had experience with someone who you would describe as a "computer geek?"*
> *Are you willing to rely on only circumstantial evidence to prove that a person is no longer alive? (For example: if the body of the person alleged to have been killed has not been found?)*
> *Despite anything you may have read or heard about this case, do you believe you can still be fair to both sides?*
> *Have you, a family member or someone close to you ever participated in a divorce proceeding? Have you, a family member or someone close to you ever participated in a child-custody proceeding?*

The attorneys pored over the questionnaires and rejected a number of citizens for cause, meaning they booted anyone whose answers revealed that they were biased, had prejudged the case because of media coverage or couldn't hear the case with an open mind.

Then came the final round of jury selection known as the "big spin," a process normally used for death-penalty cases. Each side had twenty peremptory challenges in which they could reject someone for no reason at all. It was like a high-stakes poker game, with an attorney wanting to conserve his challenges—his cards—while trying to get his opponent to use his. Whoever had more challenges would control the game.

The attorneys had to remember the big picture as they made their picks. Hora wanted jurors who were comfortable with bringing a guilty verdict based only on circumstantial evidence, when there was no smoking gun. Du Bois and Tamor wanted to seat jurors who might view the police with suspicion and remain open to their theory that Nina wasn't really missing at all, that just because she was never heard from again didn't automatically mean that she could be presumed dead, let alone murdered.

CHAPTER 57

> A DEAL?

By fall, the attorneys and investigators had spent countless hours preparing for the trial. There had been three official searches for Nina over hundreds of acres. Only one person could put an end to this charade. The judge felt it was time to offer Hans a deal: tell us where Nina's body is and what happened to her, and you can plead to voluntary manslaughter. While defendants could get three, six or eleven years for the conviction, Goodman told Hans that he would be sentenced to the low term of three years. This would spare the family and children the ordeal of testifying and save taxpayers the cost of the trial. It was a stunning offer, like a lifeline thrown down a well for a man stuck deep, deep inside.

But with characteristic bravado, Hans said he would not reveal the location of her body, despite the impassioned—and repeated—pleas of Du Bois and Tamor, and so any talks fizzled before they even began. After all, Hans thought, everyone and their brother was talking about how there was still no body in the case—and even Judge Conger had cast doubt on the DA's theory. "It was hard to convince him, between the media talking about no body, and then other lawyers talking about it for show, his own lawyers talking about it for show and—probably the worst thing for him was the judge saying, 'Jeez, I don't think this is the way it happened,'" said ADA Rogers. "She disputed our theory of the way it happened. I think she was wrong, but she was sincere. He heard that, I think, and said, 'Well, jeez, if the judge doesn't even think we can get a holding order, then why shouldn't I go to trial?"

For a criminal defense lawyer, the ideal client strictly follows all legal advice. That wasn't happening with Hans by any stretch of the imagination. Legal analyst Steve Clark knew that Hans was a difficult client, but nothing hammered that home more than when he turned down the sweetheart deal. "For a guy that smart to make that dumb of a decision speaks loudly about his arrogance and the kind of person he is," Clark said.

So the attorneys continued with the arduous task of picking a jury. On September 19, the first day attorneys had their chance to actually question potential jurors—known as voir dire—one man made it clear that he didn't want to have anything to do with the trial. "I'm uncomfortable about this," he told Hora. Pressed for an explanation, the man said, "Just this whole show, that's all. You're not going to like what I have to say." He added, "I just don't think I'd be fair." Goodman excused him. Another potential juror got up from a gallery seat and took his place in the jury box. As the process dragged on into late September, Hans at one point had pictures of Rory and Nio out on the table, an apparent attempt to curry favor with prospective jurors.

By October 25, a jury of seven men and five women was chosen to decide Hans's fate. It was an ethnically diverse group that represented a broad cross section of Alameda County. Among their ranks were an Oakland schoolteacher, a former audio technician for Lucasfilm, an account manager at a high-tech firm, an Internal Revenue Service employee who also worked at UPS, a U.S. postal carrier, a lab scientist, a shipping and receiving clerk for a military equipment contractor and two nurses—one employed by Lucile Packard at Stanford University, the other at Children's Hospital Oakland, where doctors had treated Rory and Nio.

PART SIX

>THE TRIAL

CHAPTER 58

> SHOWTIME

Opening statements were supposed to be given on October 29, but the wheels of justice collided head-on with the unstoppable force that was TV "sweeps" month. Each November, networks trotted out new episodes and specials to boost viewing figures and ad revenue. This year, ABC's *20/20* had a special on Hans that would be airing on November 2, a day before Nina would have turned thirty-three. Du Bois worried that the program would influence the jury pool. The attorneys agreed to push back the trial by a week, but there was another good reason to do that: Juvenile Court officials only recently agreed to turn over the thick file for the custody case of Rory and Nio after being ordered to do so by Goodman.

The *20/20* program featured Hans's first televised jailhouse interview. ABC News senior law and justice correspondent Jim Avila had met Hans at Santa Rita Jail on August 31. After shaking hands, the two sat across from each other in a room where the sheriff's office had allowed the TV crew to set up camera and lighting equipment. Sheriff's deputies stood watch nearby, as did Du Bois and Tamor.

If the defense wanted to generate sympathy, the show was a disaster for Hans, who came across as creepy and evasive, speaking in a flat monotone.

He insisted on sharing a song he had written for Rory. His eyes were red and brimming with tears as he spoke. After reading each line, he paused to look up at the camera before continuing.

Where did you go?
Are you trudging through the snow?

He had a similar song for Nio. He asked her where her

smile went and whether it was "lost in the Russian snow." The song ended with, "More than freedom, I love you so."

"Do you think that Nina is alive or do you think she's dead?" Avila asked in the middle of the interview.

Hans blinked and paused for several seconds. His eyes darted to his left, and then down. Finally, he said, "I think I'm the person who doesn't know."

Avila took another tack at the end of their talk. "During this entire interview, we've talked about your kids. We've talked about your family and how much you loved your family. We haven't talked about a woman who has been missing for a year and whether or not you're concerned about that at all."

"Well, I'm very concerned," Hans said, though his demeanor suggested otherwise. "But I'm not going to talk about it before trial." The interview came to an end. Sheriff's deputies snapped handcuffs on him, and he scooped up some paperwork and was led back to his cell.

Avila traveled to Saint Petersburg to interview Sharanova. "Two weeks after Nina disappeared, I tried to get in touch with Hans," she said through a translator. "Not even a single time he answered my calls. I think if a man is not involved in something horrible, he will not be behaving this way."

On November 5, the foyer on the fifth floor of the courthouse outside Department 9 was packed with reporters, sketch artists and the merely curious, all of them eager to partake in *The People of the State of California vs. Hans Thomas Reiser*, docket number 154825. The case had it all: allegations of murder, infidelity, reported ties to the KGB, even links to sadomasochism. But it was what it *didn't* have that made it all the more unusual: no body, no murder weapon and no eyewitnesses. This trifecta was why TV trucks, their antennas stretching high into the sky, lined the streets outside the René C. Davidson Courthouse, an imposing monolith of reinforced concrete with granite walls and terra cotta trim. Built in 1935 and named after a former county clerk-recorder, the structure is sprawled across a city block between Oak and Fallon streets and houses fifteen courtrooms and the DA's office. The movie *True Crime*, starring Clint Eastwood as an Oakland cop reporter, used the courthouse as a backdrop. Local TV, radio, print and wire reporters were joined by crews from *48 Hours Mystery* and *20/20*, as well as veteran sketch artists Joan Lynch and Vicki Behringer, who were staples at all high-profile trials. At the suggestion of *Chronicle* Metro Editor Ken Conner, I launched a trial blog at www.sfgate.com/ZBLS that would be widely read.

But the attorneys emerged from the courtroom that morning and said opening statements would be delayed by a day. Rumors swirled that Hans was upset with his attorneys, which was not a surprise. Du Bois would only say that those involved in the case were "ironing out a few small details." To fill the void, reporters pounced on the defense attorney, asking him if Hans would testify. Du Bois acknowledged that Hans wanted to take the stand, even though that could pose a challenge to his defense. Most defense attorneys tell their clients that it's not a good idea to subject themselves to harsh cross-examination, not to mention there is no requirement that they take the stand. "We are apprehensive to some degree, because we don't know how he will come across because of his intellect," he said. "We are hopeful that he will be able to communicate and that he will vindicate himself when he testifies." He added, somewhat cryptically, "It would be easy if he didn't testify, but it may be that he has to testify."

Du Bois said his client was so meticulous that he could readily identify by memory where key pieces of evidence were amid thousands of pages of discovery, and that had led to disagreements over how the case would be presented.

On November 6, every seat in the courtroom was filled as the five women and seven men entered Goodman's courtroom from a side door. They were followed by four alternates, two men and two women, one of whom was a surgeon. Hans wore a charcoal suit and sat between Du Bois and Tamor.

All eyes turned to Hora as he stood, greeted the jurors and began his opening remarks. Trim and standing six feet one, Hora was the quintessential prosecutor. His eyebrows arched downward, like that of an eagle, yet the intensity of his stare dissipated when it was replaced with a quick grin, especially when he cracked a joke, which was often. He easily won the trust of juries, and he knew he had to get this panel to believe in his case. His goal was twofold: to prove that Nina's life patterns had stopped and that she was therefore dead, and that Hans had killed her.

Hora sketched in the last, irrefutable moments of Nina's life, telling jurors that she bought groceries with her kids on September 3, 2006, and then dropped them off at Hans's home. From there, she "vanished from the face of the earth," Hora said. She never would have let her children be "up for grabs," he said. "She would have never, *ever* abandoned those kids," said Hora, startling some spectators as he shouted the word *ever*.

As he spoke, pictures of Nina, smiling with her children, were flashed on a screen. The portrait of Nina with Rory when he was a baby, the same one that had been hanging on her bedroom wall, sat on an easel. "She would have never, ever let them live a life not knowing where she was," Hora said. "She would never be that cruel." At this point in any other trial, the prosecutor would typically flash grisly photos of the victim from the autopsy or crime scene, in sort of a morbid before-and-after montage. That wouldn't happen here.

Nevertheless, Hora said the evidence would show that Nina was dead. Why would she spend $159.66 at the Berkeley Bowl half an hour before she disappeared? All those groceries "because she was planning to run away?" he asked.

Hora characterized Hans as an angry man fixated on issues surrounding his divorce and the upbringing of Rory. Even while admitting that the case against Hans was circumstantial, the prosecutor said the computer programmer had the motive and opportunity to kill Nina. "Although we don't know it all in this case, as in many cases, we certainly know enough," he said.

But by the end of the case, the jury would see that this was simply a "classic" case of a husband murdering his estranged wife, Hora said, adding, "The mystery has been solved."

Hora beat Du Bois to the punch by bringing up Nina's affair with Sturgeon. "There's no way to sugarcoat it," the prosecutor said, hoping to deflate any use of this subject by the defense. "She shouldn't have done that. It was wrong, but nonetheless it happened."

Hans appeared attentive and frequently whispered to Du Bois as the prosecutor spoke. But some people in the gallery grew restless as Hora read one e-mail after another that Hans had written to his wife and to Supervisor Steele, hoping to paint a portrait of a man filled with venomous hate for his wife. One observer muttered that Hora's opening statement was becoming a filibuster.

Hora continued his remarks the next day by showing surveillance video from the Berkeley Bowl, with fleeting glimpses of Nina and her children. Although we couldn't see their faces, we saw what appeared to be Rory, followed by a stuffed animal falling to the ground and then picked up by Nio. We saw the little girl "hanging on the side of a shopping cart," Hora narrated. Finally, there was a quick shot of Nina, wearing a sundress and flip-flops, pushing the cart out of camera view, not realizing that it would be the last time she went shopping with her children.

After those last indelible images of Nina were seared into everyone's minds, Hora then confirmed that Rory would take the stand, ending months of speculation. He had another surprise when he theorized how Hans may have killed Nina, suggesting that although Hans was relatively small in stature, he had a black belt in judo and was trained in the "art of choking." "When you choke somebody, it's fast, it's quiet and it's deadly," said Hora, a remark that caused Du Bois to smile and shake his head.

Hora wrapped it up on his third day of talking. He played for the jury the telephone call Hans made to his mother on September 23, less than three weeks after Nina disappeared. Despite Beverly's repeated assertions that Nina "didn't deserve whatever it is that's happened to her," Hans essentially gave his mother a list of reasons as to why Nina deserved to be killed, Hora said. The prosecutor told the jury that there was only one simple explanation as to what had happened to her, "and that's that THIS man killed her." Hora walked over and pointed an accusing finger at Hans. Hans turned in his seat to look at the DA but betrayed no emotion.

At the end of the case, Hora said, he will ask jurors to return a verdict of guilty to murder. "Thank you for your patience—I know it was long," he said.

There was no way to tell if Hora's remarks had resonated with the poker-faced jurors. After they were excused for lunch, Du Bois asked for a mistrial on the grounds that wiretap evidence and the contents of Hans's fanny pack shouldn't have been admitted. Goodman denied the motion.

If the courtroom was a stage, Hora seemed to be the master storyteller, even if part of the narrative was missing. Legal pundit Steve Clark said the prosecutor was methodically assembling fragmented pieces of the tale together. "It's like a jigsaw puzzle," he said. "You can't tell what you have until all the pieces are in place."

Legal analyst Dean Johnson wasn't impressed. "It seems to me that after two days of opening statements there is a gaping hole in the prosecution's presentation," Johnson opined. "Namely, how and where does Hora think the murder took place?" Other fundamental questions remained: did Hans have sufficient time to kill Nina, dispose of her body—and then come back to take care of the kids?

CHAPTER 59

> THE DEFENSE OPENS

It was now Du Bois' turn. At half a head shorter than Hora, the bespectacled Du Bois came across as a deft wordsmith, an attorney who peppered his comments with colorful metaphors and witty remarks and whose eyes couldn't hide a glint of mischief. Asked outside court one day how difficult it was to defend someone like Hans, Du Bois replied, "Very difficult."

"In what way?" reporters pressed.

"In every way."

"He's like a Shakespearean actor in court," said J. Tony Serra, a respected defense attorney in his own right. "He can turn anything into wit. Profundity moves through wit."

"I've always had that type of personality from a young age, much to the chagrin of the people who attempted to educate me," Du Bois said. "But I've always felt that between humor and abject sorrow, I choose humor every time, and in an arena where there's so much tragedy, an occasional swath of humor is usually well received by all."

The courtroom was packed with prosecutors eager to see Du Bois at work. Although there were only two hours of court time each afternoon, that was all Du Bois needed to brand Nina as a "master of deception" who could still be alive and was trying to "screw Hans to the wall" by making him appear to be guilty of murder.

"Hans had no opportunity to commit this crime—none," Du Bois said. Instead, he said his client was the victim of a woman whose well-to-do family had ties to the former KGB. Nina was a gold-digging mail-order bride who had been seeking an American husband to gain U.S. citizenship, he suggested.

"This is not Nina—this is the image that the prosecution wants you to have," said Du Bois, pointing to the portrait Hora had placed in front of the jury.

After the couple separated, she had had an affair with Hans's best friend, who has practiced sadomasochism, the defense attorney said. Goodman overruled Hora's objection to this reference to Sturgeon.

Although Hans is admittedly odd, he is extremely smart, blessed with a photographic memory, yet is "devoid of social skills." "Nina is almost the opposite," he said. "Perhaps that is what attracted the two of them initially."

At one point during Du Bois' remarks, Tamor flashed some pictures of porn onto a wall screen. The images were from Craigslist ads that Nina had been viewing shortly before she disappeared. As Du Bois continued talking, however, Tamor fumbled with his laptop computer, and the same pictures kept popping up. Everyone laughed. Whether by accident or design, the defense's point had been made: Nina, apparently, was no angel.

Little Rory Reiser—back from Russia to testify—however, believed otherwise. On November 12, when court wasn't in session, he was interviewed by Hora and Inspector Brock. Rory told them that he didn't love his dad. "First I loved him, now no."

"Now you don't love him as much anymore? Why not?"

"Nina," Rory sighed. He later added, "I know one liar."

"Who is that?" Hora asked.

"Hans Reiser."

"Why is, why is he a liar?"

"He says Nina is in Russia, he first said Nina is in Russia with me, Nio and big Herman. But I never seen her. Lie! How?"

"How, why?"

"Nina isn't, never was a liar. And how can?" Rory began. His next few statements were at the same time chilling and heartbreaking. "He says he did that for our safety. How can we be safe without our mother?" the boy asked Hora. "Do you know how we can be safe? When he all the time hit us?" He added that his father has said "she's a liar, she's a

bad woman, and now he's saying that she's a Russian spy."
Rory said matter-of-factly, "She is a doctor." He drew Hora
and Brock a picture of the symbol of a doctor, a snake coiled
around a staff.

CHAPTER 60

›RORY TESTIFIES

The next day, November 13, 2007, Rory, his frame dwarfed by the walls of Department 9, strode through the door, accompanied by Inspectors Chew and Brock and a Russian social worker. The inspectors held open the swinging half-doors as the saucer-eyed eight-year-old entered the courtroom. Wearing a striped shirt, Rory didn't look at his father as he walked to the stand, but he snuck a few peeks once he got there. The social worker was allowed to sit next to him. Noticing Sharanova in the audience, Du Bois was concerned that she would be signaling to Rory as he testified and asked that she be excluded. Hora countered that he had allowed Beverly to attend the proceedings thus far as a courtesy. The judge said both women were witnesses and would have to stay out of the courtroom until after they were done testifying.

Beverly had some mild words with deputies and left. "I wanted to see the trial," she told reporters later. "I don't think it's fair. Also, I was looking forward to seeing my grandson and now, maybe I won't get to see him at all." It would be the only public flare-up, however mild, on Beverly's part. "I think she was at the center of a tragic Italian opera," McGothigan said. "She doesn't wear emotions on her sleeve." Having been kicked out of the trial, Beverly would now have more time to read *Death in Venice*, by Thomas Mann, in the form of a yellowing paperback that she'd been bringing to court.

The stakes were high. Rory was Hora's first—and most sympathetic—witness. He had apparently lost his mom and stood a good chance of not being with his father ever again. Du Bois sought to take away any tactical advantage the prosecution might have with the boy's testimony. The defense attorney objected to the social worker holding Rory's hand while he testified. But any victory Du Bois may have achieved was short-lived: Goodman, who rarely missed anything that happened in his courtroom, saw Hans apparently making hand gestures to Rory and telling him, "I love you." It had been almost a year since Hans had last seen his son, and that had also been in court, at the preliminary hearing.

Rory's trip back to Oakland had been carefully planned under the provisions of a treaty signed between the United States and Russia on mutual assistance in criminal matters. It was a delicate dance, and Pulido, the juvenile dependency court judge appointed to the bench less than a year earlier by Governor Arnold Schwarzenegger, was still angry that Rory and Nio hadn't returned. But the terms of the treaty were clear: Rory would be allowed passage to the United States without any "restriction of personal liberty." That meant no one could force Rory to appear before Pulido.

Rory confirmed to Hora that he had flown to the United States from Russia over the weekend. Hora asked him a number of questions to make clear to jurors that even though he was young, he could answer many questions accurately. The prosecutor asked Rory what time it was. The boy glanced up at a wall clock and nailed it to the minute. "Ten . . . forty-nine," he said, eliciting laughs. His English now came with a Russian inflection, and the notion that he was now just a visitor to the United States was hammered home when Hora asked how big his bed was. Rory opened his arms several feet wide and said, "About a meter," demonstrating his proficiency in the metric system.

Hora then got straight to the point.

"Have you seen your mom since you've been in Russia?"

"No."

He gave the same answer when the prosecutor asked if his mother had phoned him or written him letters.

"Do you have any idea where she is?"

"No."

"How do you feel about that?"

"Sad."

It was heartfelt testimony, and the jury was riveted. "My

stomach was in a knot the whole time," said juror Kathy Carpenter.

It became clear that as more time passed, his memories about the last day he saw her had faded even more. Rory didn't remember a number of details from that day, besides eating macaroni and cheese and playing computer games.

"Do you remember what happened to your mom?" Hora asked.

"No."

Hora asked the boy if he loved his mom, and he said yes.

"Do you love your dad?"

"At that moment, yes."

Asked to explain, Rory said that he loved his father in September 2006 but that he couldn't say why he felt differently now.

He confirmed that he had written his father several letters over the past year, asking him where his mother was. In one letter, Rory wrote, "I don't want to see you, Hans."

Rory described a picture he drew recently that he said showed "Hans going down the stairs with somebody." "I think here is Nina," the boy wrote on his drawing. Asked by Hora who that "somebody" was, the boy said he didn't know. But then he said that he thought his father might have been carrying a bag down the stairs of his home and that his mother could have been in the bag, curled up like a ball.

Rory got off the stand and got into a ball in the well of the courtroom, prompting the judge and some jurors to stand up and crane their necks to see. He said he was scared by what he saw.

Outside court, Du Bois fumed that Rory's memory "has changed since he's been in Russia." He was perturbed that the boy was no longer saying outright that he saw his mother leaving the house. He accused Sharanova and Russian psychiatrists of brainwashing him to "hate his father."

During court breaks, the investigators did everything they could to make Rory feel comfortable. Inspectors Chew and Brock used a side door to escort the boy in and out of the courtroom, thwarting any photo ops for the cameras waiting in the hallway. At one point, Brock called sketch artist Joan

Lynch over and asked if she could show Rory some of her work. She flipped through some sketches, and Rory seemed thrilled. Lynch said Rory was very perceptive, asking why the faces of the jurors weren't shown. She tried to explain that she was barred from sketching in any identifying characteristics, but that seemed to be a concept that was too hard from him to grasp.

Legal analysts had been speculating as to how Du Bois would handle Rory. Although the attorney had previously questioned the boy, now was when it mattered, in front of the jury. If Du Bois was too aggressive in his questioning, he might be seen as bullying. But if he was too meek, Hans might get upset.

› On cross-examination, Du Bois embarked on a line of questioning to help support his theory that Rory had been brainwashed while in the care of his grandmother. He asked the boy to speak Russian to list what classes he was taking and to say "Where is Nina?" The attorney even asked the boy if it would be better for him to testify in Russian instead of English. Rory said no. Goodman mouthed to Du Bois, "Good try."

To remind jurors that Rory was still Hans's son—even if his love for him had wavered—Du Bois had the boy rattle off all the martial-arts classes he was taking: kung fu, tae kwon do, aikido and judo. Like father, like son.

Rory acknowledged that he had talked to his grandparents in Russia about his belief that "Hans hides Nina." He said he had not been dreaming when he said he saw his father carrying something big down the stairs of his Oakland hills home. "I was not asleep," he said. He denied that Sharanova had told him what to say in court but said Russian social workers told him "Good" after he drew the picture.

As Rory testified, Hans was busy talking to Du Bois. Goodman warned Hans to be quiet, as did his attorney. "Shh!" Du Bois said several times. When Hans continued talking minutes later, the judge said, "Mr. Reiser, I'm not going to admonish you again."

After jurors had been dismissed for the day, the fireworks began.

"I think my client wants to be heard," Du Bois told the judge. "Since I can't finish what I was doing, he might as well be heard. Since he's so insistent—since he can't help but interrupt me while I'm trying to address the court—I'd rather have him get it off his chest."

Speaking so softly that court reporter Annie Mendiola had to ask him to talk louder, Hans said both American and Russian CPS staff had spirited Rory back to Russia now that his testimony was over. In fact, Rory would be back in Russia with his sister and grandmother within days.

"Wait a minute, Mr. Reiser," Goodman said. "You're not just trying your attorney's patience, you're also starting to try my patience."

He continued, "You can have whatever paranoid delusions you want." But the court won't tolerate any of that, said Goodman, describing himself as simply a "lowly trial judge doing a criminal trial," with no jurisdiction over the juvenile court system or any international issues. Hans asked if he could be appointed co-counsel, but the judge said no. Hans looked very troubled as he was led away by deputies.

CHAPTER 61

> SQUABBLING

When the trial resumed after the Thanksgiving break, Hora asked a succession of witnesses the same question: would Nina be the kind of person to abandon her kids? The answer, repeated over and over by her children's teachers and her friends, who spoke in glowing terms of Nina's parenting abilities, was a resounding no.

"I really, truly believe that she was a fabulous mom," Grand Lake Montessori parent Marni Hunter testified. "She had the most infectious smile. A very kind person. I think she was a very wonderful person, and I think the children loved her dearly."

Shelley Gordon also agreed that Nina wouldn't leave her kids. She had stood by Nina's side throughout the divorce proceedings as Hans went through one attorney after another. She had seen firsthand just how much Nina loved her kids. Gordon remembered visiting Nina's house on Forty-ninth Street. The kids surrounded her and were excited to have a visitor. Under direct questioning by Hora, Gordon testified that the Reisers' divorce was "adversarial. It was very hostile, and it just dragged on at a snail's pace." The video-games issue was a "huge bone of contention, pretty much spanning the whole case," she said.

During his cross-examination, Du Bois grew increasingly frustrated with Gordon's habit of adding details to her answers instead of saying just yes or no. At one point, he asked Gordon if Nina would have any stake in Hans's computer company, Namesys.

"I suppose she would have an interest in that. However, I think it's valueless," Gordon said. "If you have an interest in something that's not worth anything, it's not worth pursuing."

Du Bois paused. "Thank you for sharing," he said. Du Bois liked to use that phrase to signal, however subtly, his distaste for padded answers. It was his standard riposte, one that he'd employed at Hans's preliminary hearing and many other trials without any problems. But Goodman wasn't having any of it.

"Bill, stifle yourself," the judge said.

Du Bois protested, saying he was simply trying to cross-examine Gordon on a number of points.

"I understand, but you can do it in a respectful manner," Goodman replied.

Later that day, Gordon described what she believed was the "myopic focus that Hans has on things."

Du Bois wasn't pleased with that answer either and made that clear in his tone. Goodman rebuked him in front of the jury for the second time.

"Bill, if you ask a question and you don't like the answer, it's not her fault," Goodman said.

After the jurors were dismissed for lunch, the squabbling continued, but not before Du Bois asked that Gordon leave the courtroom during the discussion. The divorce attorney smiled sweetly and said she'd be in the hallway.

"This witness is giving the most run-on, protracted, diatribical answers that I've ever heard," Du Bois complained. "I suppose the problem is she's a lawyer. However, she hasn't been responsive. She's been allowed to run on, instead of answering questions yes or no."

Goodman responded that Du Bois was one of the best trial lawyers he knew and therefore shouldn't have a problem controlling a witness.

Reporters teased Du Bois for his use of the word *diatribical* to describe Gordon's answers. During a break, I mentioned to Du Bois that *strategery* happened to be my favorite nonword. Comedian Will Ferrell had used it with great effect to mock President Bush's oratory skills on *Saturday Night Live*. That afternoon, I was astonished when Du Bois purposefully threw in the word *strategery* several times in front of the jury as he was discussing Nina's alleged schemes.

When Beverly Palmer got on the stand on December 3, Hora peppered her with questions as to why she told police in September 2006 that she thought something bad must have happened to Nina. Now, Beverly seemed to be running away from that statement, saying that it was possible Nina could be in Russia. As proof of this, Beverly said Nina had left the kids there before on two occasions, once with a nanny and once with her parents. Beverly acknowledged that she didn't tell police this in the September interview.

"Don't you think there's a difference between Nina making arrangements versus, hmmmm, not telling anybody and just disappearing?" Hora asked.

"She was not with her children," Beverly maintained.

Hora asked Beverly point-blank, "Do you know where Nina is?"

"Do I know where Nina is?" Beverly repeated, her blue eyes widening as she leaned forward. "No."

Before jurors were brought back in after the lunch break on December 4, Hans again complained to Goodman that Rory had been illegally whisked back to Russia by his maternal grandmother in violation of Judge Pulido's order that the boy appear in his court. A livid Pulido was considering sanctions. Hans wanted to attend to issues in Juvenile Court that week in lieu of his criminal trial, but Goodman shot that idea down. "The bottom line is, Mr. Reiser, you're not going to the hearing," the judge said.

When it was his turn to question Beverly, Du Bois asked why neither she nor Hans participated in the searches for Nina. Beverly said they felt "unwelcome," especially because both Sharanova and Doren were angry at them.

"Also, I can't walk through the Oakland hills, which is what they were doing, because I get poison oak, and it's full of poison oak and I get violent poison-oak reactions," Beverly said.

"Does Hans have a similar reaction to poison oak?" Du Bois asked.

"Yes, he gets bad cases of poison oak also," she answered.

Anthony Zografos testified that he searched for his girlfriend but that he never saw Hans do so. Hora pointedly asked him, "Did you get any poison oak?" and he said no.

Zografos cried as Hora played one of his many messages he left on Nina's voice mail. "Everybody wants to see you again. So come back. No matter where you are, call me, I'll come pick you up. OK. It's not too late. Everything will be fixed. Nothing's broken. I love you, and I will talk to you soon. Bye."

One month into the trial, Du Bois finally got his chance to push his theory that Nina simply left her life behind willingly. He suggested in his questioning of Zografos that he really didn't know his girlfriend all that well.

"You and Nina had a relationship of absolute trust, you would say?" Du Bois asked.

"I would say that."

"You trusted Nina, right?"

"I did."

"You think she was looking for other men when she was dating you?"

"I know she wasn't."

"You say that with some authority," Du Bois challenged.

"I knew Nina well."

Du Bois pressed Zografos as to what he meant when he said everything could be fixed. The attorney suggested that perhaps Zografos and Nina had a falling out, and that she had gone somewhere perhaps to clear her head.

Zografos didn't see it quite that way. "Obviously, if something had happened to Nina, she would have assumed that something was wrong," Zografos said. " 'Everything can be fixed' is a generic statement that everything can be fixed. It didn't have a specific meaning."

But Du Bois asked why Zografos said in one of his voice-mail messages to Nina that it was OK if she was taking time off and that she could "take the time you need." Du Bois asked if Zografos was lying to Nina or being insincere when he said that. Zografos said he wasn't really talking to her but simply leaving a message on her voice mail.

"So it's not really a lie if you're talking to voice mail?" Du Bois demanded.

Hora objected, saying that was argumentative. The judge sustained the objection.

"Were you being insincere when you said it was OK to take time off?" Du Bois persisted.

"Asked and answered," Hora interjected.

"Sustained," Goodman said.

Du Bois asked why Nina would be surfing personal ads on Craigslist even as she was dating Zografos.

"I believe this was [out of] boredom," Zografos said. "She was entertaining herself."

"So what you're telling us is, while you're heading over to Nina's house to go to the beach with she and her children—the love of your life—she is bored and going over Craigslist personals?" Du Bois thundered.

"She had told me before that she was doing this for fun," Zografos said. "In fact, she sent me an ad in an e-mail."

"Did you hear my question?" Du Bois said.

"I believe I answered your question," Zografos said calmly.

"Actually not," Du Bois replied. "Let me ask you again—you're saying Nina was bored at the time you were heading to go to the beach . . . and out of sheer boredom was going over half a dozen Craigslist personals while awaiting your arrival?"

"That's what I believe," Zografos said.

Hora brought bankruptcy attorney Darya Druch to the stand next to bolster his argument that Nina was making plans when she vanished and didn't disappear voluntarily. Druch testified that Nina wanted to file for Chapter 7 bankruptcy to wipe out her unsecured debt, including credit-card bills.

"Did you get the impression that she was serious about the process?" Hora asked.

"Yes, she was determined to get it over with quickly," Druch said.

Nina said she was getting a new job by the end of September 2006, and the two agreed that it would be prudent to get the bankruptcy petition filed quickly, Druch said. "She wanted a fresh start," the attorney said.

Nina owed nearly $83,000 on her credit cards, of which $75,000 was joint debt with Hans and the remaining $8,000 was personal debt, Druch testified. Nina listed $62,740 in assets, including a $7,000 bank account. She also reported that she had an interest in her husband's software company, Namesys, "but she didn't think there would be anything there for her," Druch testified. Nina also reported that Hans owed her $15,000 in child support, which is considered a claim, the attorney said.

Ellen Doren wept on the stand on December 12 as she confirmed that she had not seen her best friend since September 2006. She revealed that she saw Rory and Nio in July 2007 in Russia. While all of them visited a tourist attraction, Rory noticed some American tourists nearby speaking English and ran over to them, saying, "Hi, I also speak English," Doren testified.

The little boy then asked them, "Have you seen our mom? Are people still looking for my mom?" Doren recalled. The tourists had no idea what the boy was talking about. Spectators in court, though, knew what Rory meant, and it touched their hearts.

Du Bois tried to grill Doren about Zografos's jealousy and exactly how he managed to get into Nina's e-mail account, but Goodman sustained Hora's numerous objections.

Du Bois was also thwarted in his efforts to question Doren about the feelings of Zografos's estranged wife. Asked by the judge why he was going down this path, Du Bois said, "It's part of a larger puzzle."

"No, it's not relevant," the judge countered.

"I'm just trying to put the two together, judge," Du Bois said of his intent to try to explain disparate accounts.

The judge later rebuked the defense attorney for editorializing at one point. "We don't need you to comment on the evidence, thank you," Goodman said.

Du Bois got into more trouble when he tried a back-door approach to get Doren to say that Rory had unequivocally seen his mother leave Hans's house on September 3, 2006.

Hora objected, and Goodman grew furious.

"Mr. Du Bois, if you comment on the evidence that's not before the jury one more time, I'm going to find you in contempt, and that's the end of it," Goodman thundered in front of the jury. Unfazed, Du Bois tried to interrupt and referred to something Rory had said.

"I DON'T CARE what Rory testified to at this point," the judge continued, glaring at the defense attorney. "I know what you're doing, and you know what you're doing, and I don't appreciate it." Du Bois again opened his mouth in a futile attempt to explain. "Mr. Du Bois, I'm warning you for one more time, and it's going to cost you money. The objection is sustained."

Incredibly, Du Bois tried once again.

Goodman's face hardened. "In chambers!" The judge barked to the attorneys, pointing his finger. The three disappeared for several minutes.

A chastened Du Bois and Hora then returned.

"Next question," Goodman said simply.

"I never got mad at Bill," Goodman said later. "Bill's one of my best friends. He's a great lawyer. Sometimes you have to appear mad to control the situation. You play to the jury. The best control you have in the courtroom is when the jurors like me better than anybody else. If they think I'm upset, then they're going to ask what the lawyer is doing to make the judge upset."

Dr. Peter Koltai, the ENT surgeon who performed Rory's adenoidectomy, told the jury that he found Nina to be "really charming and very professional. She clearly had an accent. I, not having been born in the United States, I asked her where she was from. She told me she was an ob-gyn doctor that was trained in Russia, that she was from Saint Petersburg. I told her I had been to Saint Petersburg, what a beautiful city it was. It was a comfortable interaction, nothing out of the ordinary, except for the fact that she was from Russia."

He said his philosophy for treating children was simple: "Do what's right for the kid. You'll always come out OK."

Hora asked why he didn't stand down when Hans threatened to sue him.

"I felt that I was being manipulated and I was being threatened. I really don't like that," Koltai said, turning to look straight at Hans. "I find that really negative, and I respond negatively to that, like [when] someone confronts you like a bully. I was right, simple as that. I was right. I was doing what was right for this child."

The doctor said he was taken aback by Hans's behavior. "I assumed I was talking to a rational human being, a father," Koltai said. The doctor added that he recited a list of Rory's problems, but "Hans was not interested." Koltai again fixed his gaze on the defendant.

Hans spoke vigorously to Du Bois as the doctor testified.

Koltai said he finally performed the surgery on October 28, 2005. After the operation, Rory's ears functioned normally. The surgery confirmed that Rory had a "huge adenoid pod" and had something equivalent to a "huge Swedish meatball" up his nose, he said. Nina was delighted with the results.

Du Bois didn't help his case much when he asked the doctor about a telephone conversation he had with Hans.

Hans had a "very cold affect, this strange, monotonal voice on the phone. It was bizarre—and keep in mind, I've been in this business for a very long time—I've never had a parent call and say, 'Don't operate on my child or I'll sue you,' especially with a kid that clearly needed help," Koltai said. "It was so out of the ordinary. It was hard not to remember."

He said his conversation with Hans "almost gave me the chills."

Willy Cahill, who ran Cahill's Judo Academy in San Bruno, took the stand next. Cahill was an eighth-degree black belt who had coached U.S. Olympic judo teams in 1984 in Los Angeles and in 1988 in Seoul. Hans had earned his first-degree black belt from Cahill in 2004. Under questioning by Hora, Cahill confirmed that judo teaches the art of choking and throwing.

Hans didn't have any temper-control problems, Cahill said on cross-examination.

Du Bois asked if Cahill confronted Hans after his wife vanished. Hora objected, saying that was hearsay. But the judge said that was only a question.

The defense attorney asked Cahill if he had asked Hans if he had killed his wife. Hora objected on the same grounds. The judge overruled the DA again.

"What did he say?" Du Bois asked.

"*That's* hearsay," Hora said.

"Sustained," Goodman said.

There was a pause as Du Bois looked at some papers.

"Want me to answer that?" Cahill said.

"No, don't answer that," Goodman said politely.

> Cahill filled in the blanks later. The judo master said Hans came into the dojo at least once after Nina had disappeared. "Everybody was surprised, because he was already in the papers," Cahill said.

He asked Hans, "Hey, how long have I known you?"

"About ten years," Hans replied.

"So as a friend, I want to ask you . . ." Cahill began.

"I know what you want to ask me," Hans said.

"Did you kill your wife?" Cahill asked.

"No, I didn't do it," Hans said.

Most students warmed up before training sessions. But Hans always came late, jumped into his *gi*, or judo outfit, and immediately started fighting. His philosophy was to fight hard and fast, to ensure that his opponent would lose. "He was good, but he was just a little different," Cahill said, noting, "He liked to choke people. He was good at that."

Another one of Cahill's students, Artem Mishin, took the stand. Mishin, who had driven Hans from court on September 18, 2006, the day the police had tailed them, denied that the two had been engaging in countersurveillance and gave a number of innocent explanations for their behavior.

Mishin said he had been looking for any scratches or marks—and not tracking devices—on his precious BMW M3 because it was parked in a "questionable neighborhood in Oakland." That may have been taking it too far. Although arguably no place was immune from crime, the area where Mishin had parked his car was relatively safe. If it was true that Mishin was unfamiliar with Oakland, as he had testified, he very well may not have known which neighborhoods were safe and which weren't. Still, Hora could relate to Mishin's concerns. The prosecutor had owned a BMW M5 until recently and knew that many owners of M-series cars were very particular about their rides. They considered themselves part of a club, often acknowledging each other on the road with a nod.

Mishin said Hans was helping him navigate that day. He said he had driven slowly at times because he was busy chatting with Hans and may have turned his head to speak to him. And as for their detour off San Pablo Avenue, Mishin said they had decided that there wasn't any place to eat in that area and had made some turns to go somewhere else.

The prosecutor ended his direct examination of Mishin by asking him if he had joked with Hans when he first saw him.

"Yes, I did," Mishin said, suddenly looking uncomfortable.

"Do you remember what you said to him?" Hora asked.

"I called him Scott," Mishin said as he rubbed at his eye and explained he was referring to Scott Peterson, who was convicted of killing his wife, Laci, and their unborn son.

CHAPTER 62

> O.G.

Arthur Gomez had on a red jail jumpsuit as he testified that he had met Hans while both were incarcerated at Santa Rita Jail on February 13, 2007. Hans had introduced himself as Thomas, his middle name. The two were in the dayroom, where inmates eat and play cards, when Hans suddenly rushed up to a television set as a KTVU Channel 2 news story came on about a body having been found in the Oakland hills. Hans was glued to the screen as reporter Kraig Debro began his report. But then Hans immediately lost interest and seemed relieved when Debro said the body was that of an African American man, Gomez said.

Vince Dunn, a black juror sitting in the front row, looked at a fellow African American juror sitting next to him. Dunn and the other juror, the IRS-UPS worker, shared a chuckle.

Hora asked Gomez why he was coming forward with this information when he wasn't promised any leniency for his own domestic-violence case.

"I've had my share of domestics," Gomez said. But for someone to lose a life, "that's just the ultimate if you want to take someone's life," Gomez said as Du Bois unsuccessfully tried to object.

Gomez told Du Bois that he considered his client "a wuss." The inmate added, "I was just introduced to him. I shook his limp hand." Hora, seated at his table, laughed. So did jurors.

"O.G. Is that what you are? O.G.?" Du Bois asked.

Gomez agreed.

Du Bois then asked if "O.G." stood for "old gangster."

"No, original gangster," Gomez said.

Hora laughed again. More chuckles from the jury.

Hans "gave you no respect?" Du Bois asked. "In fact, he actually offended you by the way he was acting?"

No, it offended him that Hans was in jail for "what he was arrested for," Gomez said.

So when someone's arrested in a domestic-violence situation, except when you're involved, it offends you? Du Bois had asked.

"No, when death is involved," Gomez responded.

"But you don't know if there's a death involved," Du Bois pressed.

Gomez maintained that based on Hans's actions that day, that's the conclusion that Gomez and other inmates drew.

There was a little bit of show-and-tell when Hora called Inspector Brock to the stand. Brock testified that in May, he and Hora had inspected the CRX that Hans had been driving. The car was being stored at A & B Auto Co., a tow company in East Oakland. Hora showed pictures of the car with its front passenger seat missing. As Brock testified, two other DA's inspectors brought in a replica passenger seat from another Honda CRX.

Brock said he found the replica seat at Pick-N-Pull, a salvage yard on San Leandro Boulevard in East Oakland. The seat came from a 1989 Honda CRX Si model, one year newer than Hans's Honda. As Brock showed jurors the rail and runner system on the replica seat, the judge invited jurors to stand up and watch. Some courtroom observers wondered why the replica seat was brought in at all. But the implication was clear: Hans had removed the seat and washed the floorboard to remove incriminating evidence—including, perhaps, Nina's blood.

It would be the last image jurors would have in their minds before the Christmas break. "That does it for the year," Goodman told the jury. "We're getting there," he said, noting that they had heard from thirty witnesses and seen one hundred and twenty-nine exhibits—one hundred and thirty if you count the replica car seat—during twenty days of trial.

Goodman gave his standard admonition to the jury not to discuss the case with anyone or read or view media accounts of the trial or do their own independent investigations.

Any contact with jurors could prove disastrous and potentially lead to a mistrial. Shortly after the case began, author Stephen Elliott, a trial regular, had made what he thought was an innocuous greeting to a juror on a BART train. The juror, a sixty-five-year-old gun enthusiast, reported the incident to Goodman. The judge ordered Elliott into his chambers and told him not to do it again. One day, I noticed one of the alternates walking around Montclair, where he lives, and studiously avoided any contact. Tamor spotted one of the female jurors at Easter Sunday Mass and—for a split second—wondered where he had seen her before.

On December 19, 2007, Hans turned forty-four while behind bars, one of five hundred inmates biding time at the Glenn E. Dyer jail. It was the second birthday he had while in custody.

CHAPTER 63

> TWO VIDEOS

When the trial resumed, on January 14, 2008, Hora replayed for the jury snippets of surveillance video from the Berkeley Bowl. One could see the kids, but only the tops of their heads. On cross-examination, Du Bois asked Officer Shan Johnson how he could be so sure that it was really Nina and her kids.

As court ended that day, Hora was troubled. *How could Nina have possibly been at the store for more than an hour without being on tape?* He asked Brock to retrieve the CDs containing the Berkeley Bowl surveillance footage from the Oakland police evidence room. That evening, Hora put the first CD into his computer. Just forty-five seconds later, he stared at his screen in shock. There was Nina, as plain as day, buying food at the counter. He picked up the phone. "Bruce, you gotta get up to my office. You're not going to believe it!" Brock arrived and both men just gaped. Hora immediately played the rest of the CDs and found even more footage. Johnson saw the new images the next morning before court began. Although police had first obtained the CDs twelve days after Nina disappeared, an Oakland police officer who had been assigned to review several CDs of footage had missed it. Now, here she was in full color, some sixteen months later.

As Hora prepared the new video before jurors arrived, Hans gazed intently at the footage. Hora asked Johnson on the stand, "Were you surprised when you saw them?"

Johnson smiled and said, "Yes, sir."

On one video, Nina wore a white sundress while being assisted at the checkout counter. Nio and Rory were walking around in the aisle until Nina hoisted them both into her shopping cart. From another camera, the three were seen browsing in an aisle. In the foreground was a sign reading, "Cheese Island." At one point, there was a clear shot of all three of them, the last video of Nina and her kids together.

On cross-examination, Du Bois, not wishing to dwell on the last recorded moments of Nina's life, asked few questions about the new footage. But the attorney did elicit revelations from Johnson that fruit from a cherry or plum tree had been stuck on the tires of Nina's minivan when it was found abandoned on Fernwood Drive.

A leaf like that from a cherry tree was found on the floorboard of the Honda hybrid used by Hans, Johnson said, citing a plant expert consulted by police. The fruit could be found growing on Fernwood and not near Hans's home on Exeter Drive higher up in the hills, Johnson testified. That suggested that the two cars had both been on Fernwood at some point, the officer said. But Johnson acknowledged that the source of the leaf could not be confirmed and that no leaves had been found in Nina's minivan.

There were two more videos shown to the jury that day.

The first, shot by investigators, showed Officer Eugene Guerrero reenacting how Hans spent thirty-two minutes walking to his CRX after being dropped off by Mishin on September 18.

Hans spent time waiting at street corners, talking on the phone and looking around "in all directions," looking for people in cars or on foot, Guerrero testified. "He's not walking the entire time," the officer said.

"He did not know that he was being followed," the officer said. In fact, he was "cleaning himself, making sure he wasn't followed," said Guerrero, who said he had been tailing suspects since 1991. "I'm 100 percent confident" that Hans didn't know he was being tracked, Guerrero said.

As Hora got ready to play a second video, Brock turned around in his seat and gave me a knowing smile. I knew what was coming. The prosecutor began playing on the wall screen the NBC footage showing Hans running away when confronted by reporters on September 18, 2006. Then I came into view, chasing after him. I didn't think anybody would recognize me, because all they could see was my back. But juror Giacomo "Gino" Giordano immediately looked in my direction.

"The guy who's chasing him, he's not one of your units?" Hora asked Guerrero.

"No," the officer replied.

The prosecutor asked the officer if he knew who it was that was following Hans, and Guerrero replied, "He's sitting in the back, the gentleman in the blue shirt. I believe his name is Mr. Lee."

I felt my face grow hot as the jury, the attorneys, Guerrero and Goodman all looked at me and laughed. Hans turned in his seat to look at me and was chuckling, too. The sketch artists drew pictures of the screen that was showing the video of me chasing Hans. And as this was all happening, I was blogging this on my laptop computer for the *Chronicle*. It was all too surreal.

"Let the record reflect that the witness has identified the *Chronicle*," Du Bois said, smiling.

It seemed as if Oakland homicide lieutenant Ersie Joyner, who had believed that a video of Hans acting nervous would play well in court, had been granted his wish. But so much for that old reporters' credo: just cover the news, don't become the news.

> On January 23, the jury got to hear from Hans's other attorney, Richard Tamor, when he cross-examined Oakland police criminalist Shannon Cavness. Juror Vince Dunn smiled in surprise as Tamor—and not Du Bois—peppered her with rapid-fire questions.

Cavness confirmed that it was impossible to determine when bloodstains were left on something. Tamor directed her attention to bloodstains found on a pillar in Hans's home. Cavness had testified the day before on direct examination that DNA samples matching both that of Hans and Nina Reiser were found in the bloodstains.

"You can't tell us whether those mixtures in this case were deposited at the same time. You can't tell us whether one DNA sample was deposited days before the other DNA sample, isn't that right?" Tamor asked.

"That's correct."

"You can't tell us if DNA sample 1 was deposited even years before DNA sample 2?"

"That's right. I have no way of dating a DNA sample."

"And the other thing about DNA, isn't this true, is you can't tell us exactly how it was deposited?"

"That's correct."

Tamor then elicited an acknowledgement by Cavness that she had, in fact, made a mistake while swabbing the bloodstains on the pillar. She said she should have taken two samples instead of one on an area of the pillar where blood was seen.

"That's a mistake?" Tamor asked.

"I'll admit that I should have taken at least two samples."

"If you had to do it over, you would have swabbed it two different times, right?"

"At least two distinct areas, yes."

"And isn't it generally accepted in the forensic community that what you do is you swab them separately when you see two distinct bloodstains like that?"

"Yes."

"And you didn't do that in this case?"

"No, I didn't," said Cavness, adding that she had believed the blood came from a single source, "which is a mistake on my part."

Tamor suggested that Nina may have drooled on a sleeping-bag stuff sack found in the defendant's car, accounting for her DNA being found in a bloodstain on the sack.

On January 28, Du Bois filed a motion for a mistrial on the grounds that Goodman had made "inaccurate, intemperate, unfair remarks" while chastising the defense attorney in front of jurors in December. If the judge declined to unring the bell by asking jurors to "specifically disregard" those remarks, then the defense wanted him to remind the panelists that they were the "sole, exclusive judges of the facts in this case." It would be up to the jury, the defense wrote, to determine whether in fact Nina hugged her son "and as he testified at trial, left the house and walked up the outside stairs to her van, and as he testified at the PX got in her van and drove away."

Erin Morasch, an internal auditor and security manager with Patelco Credit Union, testified that Nina had an average of thirty-five transactions each month but that all activity stopped after September 2006. In the days and weeks before she disappeared, Nina registered her car with the state Department of Motor Vehicles and paid for her utilities and her next month's rent, Morasch said. She last used her debit card at the Berkeley Bowl, and her last Patelco check was dated August 28, 2006, and made out to Adventure Time. Her account was now "dormant" and had a balance of about forty-five hundred dollars, Morasch said. His testimony added to the growing mountain of evidence that Nina's life had ended.

In contrast, there had been unusual activity with Hans's account around that time, the auditor said. There had been a dramatic increase in cash withdrawals after Nina disappeared, including his hopscotching from one branch to another to make withdrawals, he testified.

"It's uncommon for members to drive from branch to branch to branch to withdraw cash," he said. "I mean, usually you don't want to inconvenience yourself. You just take it out when you need it. My experience as a fraud investigator is it looks like a fraud pattern."

As CPS worker Seng Fong testified on January 29 about the series of child-custody hearings and the fact that his children were now in Russia, Hans grew increasingly agitated. As Hora wrapped up his direct examination, Du Bois started to address Goodman, only to be interrupted by Hans. "Shh!" Du Bois said loudly to his client. Hans raised his hand, as if someone, if not the judge, would call on him, and began speaking loudly as jurors were present.

"Mr. Reiser, please," Goodman warned. "I'm as tolerant as I can be this afternoon, and I'm starting to lose my patience. Talk to your lawyer in a low tone."

Du Bois told the judge that his cross of Fong would take a while and suggested that he start fresh the next day. Du Bois also noted that his client had some concerns that he wanted to address outside the presence of the jury.

After the jury filed out of the box, Hans said he didn't want to stipulate that the issue of his children's custody was on appeal, as the judge had said in open court. Addressing the judge directly, Hans said, "It's still an issue whether the U.S. courts have lost jurisdiction over the children completely."

"That's right, and what I said was it's still subject to appeal, who's going to end up with the kids," Goodman said.

"That implies that the U.S. appellate courts have the power," Hans replied. Wagging his finger at the judge, he added, "That doesn't apply."

"Mr. Reiser, you point your finger at me again and use that tone with me, you're going to have a serious problem," the judge said. "The bottom line is, is there any court of any jurisdiction in any country in this world who's said who's going to have custody of the kids in the end, to your knowledge?"

Hans hesitated a bit and then said, "The U.S. courts [don't] have the power to compel the kids to return."

"That's not what I asked you," Goodman said. "Has it been settled in any court who's going to have custody of the kids in the end? Is it not still subject to litigation?"

Hans said, "I'm hesitant to characterize the actions of the Russian court."

Hans then began complaining about the way the trial was proceeding, leading Du Bois to remark that what his client was saying sounded an awful lot like a *Marsden* motion, in which a defendant seeks to discharge his or her appointed counsel. Problem was, Du Bois hadn't been appointed by the court but had been retained by Hans himself, the judge noted.

"You can fire him at any time you want, but that's not going to stop the trial from going forward," the judge said. Hans responded that he believed he was allowed a delay of sixty to ninety days if he got a new attorney, but the judge said that only applied before the trial began.

"Change your lawyers now, nothing's going to stop. I told you that," the judge said. "We're not stopping this trial for sixty to ninety days. That's not happening. You fire him, we go tomorrow with whoever you have."

Hans continued with his grumbling. The judge said, "You know, Mr. Reiser, you can do whatever you want to do.

You have the right to represent yourself. Call any lawyer in Alameda County and say, 'You want to do my trial?' "

Hans said he couldn't phone people while in jail.

"Then you got friends who can make calls for you," the judge replied, growing more exasperated.

Hans retorted, "So you're not offering me a realistic alternative?"

"I'm telling you how it's going to be. This is becoming absurd, Mr. Reiser," the judge continued. "You've got two of the best attorneys. If you want to fire him, if you want to represent yourself starting tomorrow, go for it. Other than that, you get Mr. Du Bois, you get Mr. Tamor. They're doing a fine job. We'll see everybody at ten tomorrow morning."

Du Bois later confirmed that as far he knew, both he and Tamor were still on the case.

On the morning of January 30, Hans continued with his complaints, and the judge wasn't in the mood. "You can put on the record whatever you want. You can disagree all you want. I'm going to put you on notice. I'm going to start admonishing you in front of the jury, and it's not going to do you any favors. I'm tired of you disrupting the courtroom and believing you're in charge of the courtroom. You are not."

During the trial, Du Bois and Tamor spent many long hours on Saturdays with Hans in jail, listening to his complaints. Almost invariably, the three would get into disagreements over trial strategy.

Hora, meanwhile, spent his weekends at his office at the courthouse. That was on top of a backbreaking schedule during the week, especially on the days before key witnesses testified. Hora would get up at his home on a tree-lined street in Contra Costa County while it was still pitch-black outside. He would hop onto Highway 24, drive through the Caldecott Tunnel, which cut through the hills between Berkeley and Oakland, and be at his desk in Oakland by 4:30 a.m. He would spend the whole day preparing for the next day's witnesses, toiling in his office long after other prosecutors had left. Some nights he wouldn't get back home until 11:00 p.m. He would sleep, shower and come back and do it all over again. At lunch, he'd be back in the office and not running two laps around Lake Merritt like he usually did every other day. Hora would be lucky if he had time to work out at the 24 Hour Fitness on Webster Street—the same one Hans had visited. "I felt like I was campaigning for president," Hora said of the grueling hours.

But on February 2, the prosecutor had another reason to burn the midnight oil: he and his wife, Jamie, welcomed their new baby boy, Joseph. It was almost a repeat from what happened in December 2003. As Hora was preparing for the "Sausage King" trial, Hora's wife gave birth to their first son, Tommy. "It tests your true grit, whether or not you've got enough to do it," Hora said. "There were times when my wife said, 'Hey, you know, no more trials, OK?'" The prosecutor could laugh about it later, but his wife almost certainly had not been in a joking mood. "You know, you're never home," Jamie Hora told him at one point. "Your kids don't even know you. Your baby doesn't know you. Your baby's not going to see you."

› When the trial resumed, two days after Joseph's birth, Tamor greeted the prosecutor, saying, "Hi Paul, how are you doing? Getting enough sleep?"

"Sleeping great," Hora replied earnestly. As jurors filed in, a few gave him an extra smile or two. Hora responded in kind.

DA's Inspector Frank Moschetti, a retired Oakland police officer who served on the Contra Costa County search-and-rescue team, told the jury on February 7 that despite three searches for Nina in the Oakland hills, she had not been found. Much of the terrain was steep, and the brush was dense, he testified. "That is the proverbial needle in a haystack, and Nina Reiser was the needle," Moschetti said.

On cross-examination, Du Bois asked Moschetti if it was possible that the searches failed to turn up Nina because police had operated on the wrong premise. "If she wasn't killed at all, and just left the area, you wouldn't find her?" Du Bois asked, and Moschetti agreed.

CHAPTER 64

>A MOTHER'S GRIEF

The hallway outside the courtroom was busier than normal on the afternoon of February 11. Nina's mother, Irina Sharanova, was going to testify as the last witness for the prosecution. Sharanova was originally supposed to have been on the stand right after Rory, but scheduling issues arose. It was just as well that the jurors would hear from her now. Prosecutors liked to start strong and end strong, and Hora managed to "bookend" his case with Rory and Sharanova, even if it wasn't by design.

"Do you speak English?" Hora asked after Sharanova got herself settled on the stand.

"A little," Sharanova said in English, with a smile. A Russian translator sat next to her. Hans had doubts as to whether the translator would be interpreting accurately. He had often thought about writing a novel about a character in a police state who relied on an interpreter only to suspect that the interpreter could very well be an intelligence agent.

Sharanova bit her lip and paused after Hora asked her how many children she had. "One daughter," she said.

"Are you OK to continue?" Hora asked.

Sharanova nodded yes and put on her glasses. She dabbed at her eyes with a tissue.

Asked if Hans and Nina were in love at the start, Sharanova said, "I can only speak about Nina, and I know she was in love."

The Reisers visited Russia shortly after Rory was born. Sharanova began weeping and dabbing at her eyes after Hora brought out the framed portrait of Nina and Rory, the same one he had shown to the jury before.

"What did Nina think about her kids?" Hora asked.

Sharanova again grew emotional. "She loves them and she loved them. From day one, they were beautiful children, very smart children," she said.

Sharanova said she spoke to her daughter frequently, about a couple times a week in 2006. "We were very interested in the children and how they were doing, their accomplishments, what was going on with Nina, Nina's work and how the money situation was for them," Sharanova said.

Hora asked if Nina had talked to her about things that were going on in her life, and Sharanova said yes. "She was telling me everything," Sharanova said.

"How close were you?" Hora asked.

Sharanova paused and looked down several times. "We were very close," she said. She tried to regain her composure and sipped from a cup of water.

Hora asked Sharanova if Nina had discussed that she wanted to become a licensed doctor in the United States. "Yes. She tried several times and she continued to and she would have succeeded," Sharanova said.

"She said that in 2006, she absolutely had to pass the exam. She had to get a job, because she couldn't anymore borrow [money] and Hans wasn't helping her and wasn't giving any support to the children," she said.

That year, Sharanova and her husband wired Nina eight thousand dollars from a Latvian bank. Sharanova said she also gave her daughter an additional two thousand dollars.

On her second day on the stand, Sharanova testified that Hans had commented to her in 2003 that he didn't want a "smart wife." Hora asked if Hans had said other negative things about Nina to her, and she said yes. "Our communication was limited due to the linguistic barrier, but nonetheless Hans tried to show us and tell us that Nina was a bad wife and that she was not doing the things that a good wife [should be] doing."

Hans also said that Nina "was bringing up the children the

wrong way. He did not like that," Sharanova said. "He didn't want the children to speak Russian." When Sharanova asked him why not, "he would say that Russia is not a sufficiently developed country. He didn't want them speaking in that language," she said.

Hora asked Sharanova about Nina's relationship with Zografos. At that point, they had been together for more than a year, and "she trusted this man," Sharanova said. "There were certain plans that they were building. Anthony was looking for a house and was inviting her to live with him."

Hora asked if Nina had shared any negative things about Zografos, and Sharanova said, "Yes, he was jealous."

Sharanova said her daughter was reluctant to move in with Zografos "because she was afraid that it was going to put her in a financially dependent situation. Also, she didn't want to be emotionally dependent on Anthony."

"Did you offer her any advice?"

"I told her first of all she had to become independent herself financially and then decide who she was going to share her life with."

"How did she react to that?"

"With understanding."

"Did she ever express any fear of Anthony, that she was afraid of Anthony?"

"No, she would smile and say, 'Men, a lot of men are jealous.'"

Nina returned to the United States on July 23, 2006, but not before her stepfather suggested that she just stay in Russia, Sharanova said. Crying, Sharanova said her husband told their daughter, "Nina, Nina, just forget about it. Let's just come home."

"What was Nina's response?" Hora asked.

Wiping away tears, Sharanova said Nina told them, "I have children. I have a house, and I want to live in the United States."

As for their divorce, Nina said that "there was very little that wasn't completed yet" and noted that "the sole question was with money because Hans owed her a great deal of money for all the years that he did not offer any support for his children," Sharanova testified.

Nina discussed filing for bankruptcy and wanted her mother to come to the United States to help with the kids as she studied for her medical licensing exams, Sharanova said.

Hora asked why Sharanova sought custody of the children. "I don't want the children to be with the killer," she replied. There was no visible response from the defendant when she said this.

Hora asked how the children were doing. Sharanova smiled and said, "Very well."

Did she envision living the rest of her life raising her grandchildren? Hora asked. "Was that something you planned on doing?"

"No," she said.

Hora transitioned to an issue that was critical with the defense. "Have you or anyone you know attempted to influence Rory or influence his testimony?"

"No," she said. "We don't want to traumatize the child."

"Was he traumatized?" Hora asked, and she said yes.

"What do you base that opinion on? How do you know that?"

"The boy talked a great deal, and I cannot repeat what he said without tears," Sharanova said as she began to cry. "He cannot listen to songs where the word 'mama' is mentioned. He talks about how he did not manage to say to mama how much he loved her. And he was always talking about, always interested about who's working for mama and how one could find mama, that's all he could talk about. And in addition to that, the relationship with his sister has been very—there's a disconnect between the relationship between him and his sister. The first months we were together he would very often hit his sister."

Sharanova said she told Rory that he shouldn't do that because his sister is a little girl. Rory would say that "Papa—" Du Bois objected at this point, saying it was hearsay, perhaps triple hearsay. The judge said subject to a motion to strike, he'd allow it at this point.

Sharanova said that Rory replied that "Father told him to do that so that she would not grow up to be a liar like his mother." A look of astonishment crossed Hans's face.

Rory has been seen by psychologists in the United States and in Russia, Sharanova said. Asked what he had been told about his mother, Sharanova said, "Mama has disappeared. Papa is with the police because he doesn't want to answer questions that have to do with her disappearance."

Du Bois repeatedly tried to object but was shot down by the judge. At one point, Goodman called for a sidebar. When the attorneys emerged from chambers, Goodman said, "Objection overruled."

In testimony that startled spectators, Sharanova said Rory had recalled an incident in which Nina "couldn't scream because Hans covered her mouth with a scarf." Sharanova said she asked the boy what kind of scarf and pressed him for more details, but he said, "I don't remember." Sharanova said Rory also discussed a room in his father's house that "no one ever entered. If Hans hid Nina then he would have had Nina in that room," Rory told Sharanova.

Hora put a series of pictures of Nina and her children on the screen for the jury as Sharanova narrated. There was a photo of a smiling Nina in 1998 at the time she met Hans. There are pictures of her with her children at her old home on Jordan Street in Oakland and on her most recent home, on Forty-ninth Street in Oakland. There was a picture of Nina and Rory wearing frog hats and a picture of them in the Crimea in July 2006. There was one showing Nina carrying an inner tube while at Lake Tahoe and another of her family at a summer house in Russia. One female juror appeared to get misty-eyed.

In one picture, Rory appeared to have something on his nose. Was it chocolate or food? Hora asked. "No, not food," Sharanova said. "He fell off a tree and scraped his nose." Jurors laughed.

The last picture shown to jurors was one showing a smiling Sharanova with her grandchildren at Nina's Oakland home in April 2005.

Sharanova said she went to Nina's home in October 2006

and recovered her possessions, including her jewelry. Sharanova said she was wearing her daughter's earrings and two of her rings at the moment.

Hora began to wrap it up.

"Since September 3, 2006, when you talked to Nina on the phone, have you ever received another phone call from her?" Hora asked.

Sharanova shook her head and said, "Nyet." The translator said, "No."

"Since you saw her in July 2006, have you seen her since then?" Hora asked.

She shook her head again.

"Since September 3, 2006, have you received any letters, any e-mail, has she made any contact with you at all?" Hora asked.

She shook her head.

"Based on your spending your entire life knowing Nina, was she the kind of daughter that would do that to you? Just disappear and not contact or call you?"

"No. That would have been impossible."

"Would she have been the kind of mother that would have left her kids up for grabs and abandoned them?" Hora asked.

Du Bois interjected at this point, saying that "absolutely misstates the evidence. The children have, in fact, have been in this witness' custody. They have never been up for grabs."

The judge demurred, saying that was a decision left to a family court judge.

But Du Bois said, "Not up for grabs." The children would have been put into the custody of either their father or one of the grandparents. "They were never left up for grabs," the defense attorney said.

Hora said, "They would have been from her point of view."

"Yeah, overruled," the judge said.

On cross-examination, Sharanova confirmed that she had written an e-mail to Hora in which she said that Rory "saw Mom leave the house that day." Du Bois asked twice if that was the case, and Sharanova said yes.

Du Bois pressed Sharanova as to what kinds of conversations she had with Rory about Nina. Sharanova said that to avoid traumatizing him, she never brought up the subject. She said she'd ask him questions only if he brought it up first.

Things got testy as Du Bois asked more questions about what she meant in her e-mail to Hora. She stiffened. "I think it's very clear in this letter. I can't add anything to it," she said.

Du Bois asked Sharanova if she was being honest when she told a family court judge that she wanted to take her grandchildren to Russia for a three-week vacation.

She answered with another clipped "Yes."

On her second day of cross-examination, as Du Bois asked some of the same questions as before, it was clear that Sharanova had reached her limit. Through the translator, Sharanova said it appeared that he believed the answers she gave the day before were "insufficient." With a flash of anger, she asked coldly, "Would you like me today to repeat my responses for a third time?"

Her comment drew audible gasps in the gallery. Juror Vince Dunn turned his head and opened his mouth in surprise.

Du Bois' voice and tone changed dramatically. "That is not necessary," he said. He added, "And what I said was your responses weren't being adequately translated."

Dunn mouthed, "Translated?" and gave a look of confusion before shaking his head in apparent disagreement with Du Bois. Dunn, an Oakland schoolteacher who bore a passing resemblance to Cedric the Entertainer, was one of the more animated jurors on the panel who served as the Greek chorus of sorts during the trial. His facial expressions at any given time seemed to match the reactions of trial watchers. Dunn was also well-known for his unbridled joy of the catered lunches and restaurant trips given to the jury.

As the cross-examination continued, Du Bois didn't do himself any more favors when he snapped at Sharanova, "Is that a nyet?"

"Why did Nina apply to marriage agencies in 1998?" he asked her.

Sharanova's eyes reddened. "Every girl dreams about princes. Maybe that's why."

"Why would she use a marriage agency to find a prince?"

"It's one of the ways of finding a prince," Sharanova said evenly.

Du Bois asked, "Did something happen in Nina's life which caused her to reach out to the possibility of men in other countries?"

"Only love," Sharanova responded.

Du Bois was about to ask another question, but Sharanova added under her breath: "Unfortunately."

Asked if she would describe Hans as lovable, Sharanova said for the first two years, Hans tried to be "attentive and sufficiently warm," she said. "And then he started showing signs of disdain. He started treating us like servants who for some reason owed him something."

Du Bois sought to pit Rory against his grandmother by suggesting that she was the one who was lying.

Why would Rory say that she and her husband told him that "Hans hid his mother and that Hans did something bad to his mother?" Du Bois asked.

Sharanova said the boy has a vivid imagination and that this may have been said in the presence of social workers.

Du Bois asked why Rory reported that Sharanova told him not to say that she had talked with him about the case.

"I cannot explain it," she replied. "I don't have an answer for that."

When Du Bois said he had no further questions, Sharanova sighed as she left the stand with the interpreter.

And with that, Hora said, "The people rest," bringing to an end three months of testimony from fifty-seven prosecution witnesses in a murder trial with still no body, no weapon and no eyewitnesses—but strong circumstantial evidence pointing directly at the defendant.

CHAPTER 65

› DEFENSE BEGINS

The defense began its case on February 19, 2008, as the first in a series of wintry storms made its way toward northern California and filled the air in the Oakland hills with the smell of wet eucalyptus. First on the stand was Greg Silva. Only days earlier, Hans's divorce attorney had warned Du Bois that if Hans waived attorney-client privilege, the DA could potentially get a warrant for Silva's files. The attorney feared that Hans's own e-mails, diatribes and letters would rain on the defense's parade.

Silva, who had succeeded Cheryl Hicks as president of the Alameda County Bar Association, testified that he had deposed Nina over the course of several days to see how she had been handling Namesys's finances.

"I wanted to follow up on our theory that some of the money that was generated by Namesys, as I believe it was, had been diverted to other purposes other than the business purpose itself," Silva said.

Sturgeon had access to the company's bank accounts with Hans's permission, Nina told Silva during her deposition. She reported that her affair with Sturgeon began less than a year after he was given access to the accounts and that Hans knew about it from the very beginning, Silva testified.

Du Bois asked Silva what happened to "all that money," referring to the $1.2 million earned by Namesys in 2002, but Hora successfully objected on the grounds that the defense had not properly laid a foundation.

"Did you investigate whether Nina was embezzling money from Namesys?" Du Bois asked.

"I was in the process of investigating," Silva said.

Silva became uncomfortable when Hora asked him to read a letter he had written to Hans on August 23, 2006. Silva cited attorney-client privilege, but the judge ordered him to read it. In the letter, Silva expressed disappointment that Hans had canceled an appointment. Not being able to respond to discovery requests by a due date could open them up to paying attorney's fees and being sanctioned. "It will reflect negatively on you in the eyes of the court," Silva wrote. "Additionally, we cannot object to any of their demands if we do not respond on time. We have obtained at least two extensions on your behalf. Your refusal to cooperate is only hurting yourself, Hans, especially with this contempt-of-court motion in front of the court."

On redirect, Silva confirmed that Hans believed Nina and Sturgeon together stole money from Namesys and that his client felt Sturgeon was suing him for money that was actually his own. As Du Bois stood at the lectern, Hans waved at him to get his attention and said something that was audible but indecipherable. Goodman warned Du Bois, "Calm your client down before he's removed from the courtroom."

CHAPTER 66

> A FATHER'S EXPLANATIONS

Ramon Reiser took the stand next. There was no mistaking where Hans got his genes. When Du Bois asked about Hans's childhood, Ramon rambled on and on without answering the questions directly. Instead, he went on tangents that included references to a light switch, a flashlight, enzymes, airplanes and banks, exasperating Du Bois and prompting multiple objections by Hora.

Du Bois asked Ramon if he had ever driven a car without a seat, and he said he had, many times.

"We do it in our family routinely. We don't repair old cars. We drive it until they fall apart. We do not put new seats in it."

A female alternate juror put her hand to her mouth to suppress a laugh as he described a series of cars he drove—including a 1956 Volkswagen Beetle and a Rambler—with seats that were missing or broken. The alternate would later be discharged from the case, not because of her giggling but because of scheduling conflicts.

Ramon testified that Hans and Nina "looked to everybody like the perfect couple," and Nina "had more smiles than anyone I've seen." But she appeared to be projecting happiness while at the same time hiding problems inside.

During a midmorning break, when mostly everyone had cleared out, Ramon did one-armed push-ups in court. When the jurors returned, he gave more convoluted responses that drew smiles from jurors and the judge.

Ramon testified that he worked in security in Russia. He was robbed at one point by a "superbly conditioned crack addict," he noted as reporters exchanged bemused looks.

He said he warned Hans that "however alert he was, that if

he picked up on anybody he thought was following him, that they were not likely going to be police."

"Why was that?" Du Bois asked.

"You can't pick up on any competent police officer unless he was lucky with surveillance," Ramon said, adding that he believed his son was instead at risk of being hunted down by the former KGB or "Russian Mafia groups within California that I have met in Seattle." Goodman scrunched his eyebrows in confusion.

"Move to strike," Hora said. "Irrelevant and non-responsive."

"Sustained," Goodman said.

Ramon also said he feared his son was being tracked by the Russian Mafia or the "techno-geek S and M crowd."

"What!?" Du Bois asked, giving what would become his trademark perplexed look—a Rumsfeldian squint through rimless glasses, his mouth agape in disbelief.

"Those who are highly sophisticated . . . who are into S and M, part of Nina's . . ."

Hora objected, and the judge struck the last part of the answer, just as Ramon seemed poised to talk about Sturgeon.

CHAPTER 67

>"I WON'T SUE YOU"

Ramon stepped down and was replaced on the stand by Beverly Parr, his one-time paramour and ex-wife's friend. Du Bois made it clear that Parr, a psychiatrist from Southern California, wasn't being called to render a medical opinion. But the two then launched into a discussion of Asperger's disorder, a mild form of autism characterized by an inability to read social cues. The two cited the *Diagnostic and Statistical Manual of Mental Disorders, Fourth Edition*. Otherwise known as *DSM-IV*, the text was generally considered by psychiatrists as the bible of their profession.

Parr said she believed Hans's behavior was consistent with someone with Asperger's disorder. But she qualified herself—repeatedly—by saying that she never examined or diagnosed him clinically. Hora grew frustrated as Du Bois went down a list, ticking off symptoms and asking questions—many of them leading—in hopes of bolstering what would be known as the "geek defense"—Hans may be a nerdy computer scientist devoid of social skills, but he was no murderer.

Hora wasn't buying it. On cross-examination, he tried to trick Parr by asking her what her diagnosis of Hans was, but she wouldn't bite. But the eagle-eyed prosecutor soon gained the upper hand when he asked to see the note Hans had given her just before she went on the stand. He even put it on the projector so jurors could see it on the screen. It read, "It is OK to do the Asperger's diagnosis. I won't sue you. Hans." Hora had knocked Parr off-balance. Faltering, Parr made reference to the outdated *DSM-III* instead of *DSM-IV* and soon afterward spoke of Alzheimer's instead of Asperger's.

Hora began setting a trap for the frazzled witness. Could

people be socially inappropriate, selfish and conceited without having Asperger's? Yes, she replied each time. Could someone with Asperger's have children? Yes again.

Could someone with Asperger's premeditate murder and have the intent to kill?

"I don't see why not," she admitted. She had been ensnared, with no way out.

On the second day of cross-examination, Hora came back with a theory of his own, that Hans showed the classic signs of having narcissistic personality disorder.

Parr bobbed and weaved, refusing to agree with Hora that Hans showed signs of having the disorder. She noted that most of the people she had treated with narcissistic personality disorder were lawyers, not computer scientists. That remark drew guffaws.

Hora asked Parr if she knew the name of the file system that Hans created.

"ReiserSF," she said, transposing the letters.

"He named it after himself?" Hora asked.

Parr paused.

"Well, is his name Reiser?" the prosecutor demanded. "Did he name it after himself?"

"Uh, Hans Asperger named the disorder after himself. It's nothing unusual in medicine or maybe other fields to name a disorder after yourself," Parr replied. Hans, the defendant, grinned broadly.

If Parr thought she had scored any points, she was wrong. The prosecutor began reading from the *DSM-IV*'s definition of narcissistic personality disorder:

> *Individuals with this disorder have a grandiose sense of self-importance. Individuals with Narcissistic Personality Disorder believe that they are superior, special, or unique and expect others to recognize them as such. Individuals with this disorder believe that their needs are special and beyond the ken of ordinary people. They are likely to insist on having only the "top" person (doctor, lawyer, hairdresser, instructor) or being affiliated with the "best" institutions, but may devalue the credentials of*

*those who disappoint them. Those who relate to individu-
als with Narcissistic Personality Disorder typically find an
emotional coldness and lack of reciprocal interest. Arrogant, haughty behaviors characterize these individuals.
They often display snobbish, disdainful, or patronizing
attitudes. For example, an individual with this disorder
may complain about a clumsy waiter's "rudeness" or
"stupidity" or conclude a medical evaluation with a condescending evaluation of the physician. Vulnerability in
self-esteem makes individuals with Narcissistic Personality Disorder very sensitive to "injury" from criticism or
defeat. Although they may not show it outwardly, criticism
may haunt these individuals and may leave them feeling
humiliated, degraded, hollow, and empty. They may react
with disdain, rage, or defiant counterattack.*

It was a masterful stroke. The description seemed to paint
Hans to a T. As Hora read each sentence, he asked Parr if he
had read correctly from the *DSM-IV.* She reluctantly agreed.
He also asked her repeatedly, "Ever see this in Hans?" She
hesitated or parsed her answers.

"I know many people . . ." Parr began at one point.

"Ma'am," the judge interjected. "Answer yes or no."

"How about a father who insists that his son is gifted, is
brilliant, is a genius, is inadequate in school because he's
smart and is bored? He's in first grade but should be in third
or fourth? A father who sees his son like that, is that a trait of
narcissism?" Hora asked.

"I'm not a specialist, but it could be," Parr said.

On redirect, Du Bois tried to repair the damage, only he did
so by asking more leading questions. Hora made his distaste
clear. He thrust his arms out at a 45-degree angle, palms raised
up in a "What gives?" gesture. But he didn't say anything.

"What does *this* mean?" Goodman asked Hora, mimick-
ing the gesture.

"I'm sorry, it's just a gesture," Hora said.

"*This* doesn't have meaning," said the judge, again jutting
his arms out and provoking waves of laughter.

› During the lunch break, Parr was visibly exhausted. She had only two hours of sleep the night before. She worried that the media had portrayed her in such a way that she appeared to be disrespecting those with autism. Drained, Parr tried to catch up on some rest by lying down on some chairs in the court hallway, next to Beverly. Nearby, Ramon highlighted passages from a text.

CHAPTER 68

> DRINKING THE KOOL-AID

On February 25, the geek defense continued in earnest as the defense showed the jury a video of Hans giving a talk about his Reiser4 file system two years earlier. Appearing heavier and his hair longer than it was in court, Hans answered questions while giving a PowerPoint presentation. A stem-winder it was not, especially to nontechies. One of his slides was entitled, "Need to match rather than mold structure" and included bullet points that read, "Boolean algebra effective for when user's fragmentary knowledge is unstructured," and "For large scales, ignoring known structure is better than requiring knowing it—no Web search engine uses relational algebra."

The jury also watched a video of private investigator Ed Torres lying down inside the CRX that police had impounded. To bolster its claim that Hans threw out the seat to make it more comfortable to sleep in, the defense had Torres demonstrate that it was possible for Hans to have lain down—with knees bent—with the seat removed. The video was taken by fellow PI Clarick Brown, a former Berkeley police officer who had crossed to the other side and now did defense work. Torres was paid one hundred dollars for his trouble.

The defense brought another PI, Warren Levicoff, to the stand to hammer home the possibility that Nina was alive after secretly faking her disappearance. It was not unheard of for people to change their names and create a whole new life for themselves. There was only one problem with this theory: barring those who were spirited off by the government and relocated under witness protection programs, weren't the bulk of identity shifters suspects in something to begin with?

Undaunted, Levicoff testified that Nina could have walked across the border to Canada or Mexico before journeying to her native Russia with a fake passport. Or she could have made it to Russia after beginning a clandestine trip on a fishing boat or other private vessel. Or she could have gone to a Russian Embassy in the United States or another country with her birth certificate, reported that she had lost her passport and asked for replacement travel documents. Barring that, someone like her could go to a "sleazy neighborhood" and track down someone who created forged passports, Levicoff said. For the defense, anything was possible, especially if it sowed the seeds of reasonable doubt in the minds of jurors.

To curtail the speculation, Hora drew an admission from Levicoff that he hadn't been paid to look for the missing woman. After jurors left for the day, Du Bois complained to Goodman that Hora had made an unfair inference by asking the question. Hans was indigent, and taxpayers were paying for the fees of defense experts like Levicoff, Du Bois reminded the judge. Du Bois noted that the court hadn't authorized funds for the defense "to look around the world for anybody."

On February 26, after jurors were dismissed for the day, Goodman denied the defense's motion for a mistrial on the grounds that he had improperly rebuked Du Bois in front of the panel in December. The judge said he would instruct the jurors not to take any cues from him. The judge also denied the defense's requisite motion for a judgment of acquittal, saying, "Based on the evidence before me at this time, I think there is enough evidence sufficient to sustain a conviction."

The next day, Hans's family law attorney, Cheryl Hicks, testified that she had taken his personality into account before opting not to have him take the stand in Juvenile Court proceedings. Du Bois wanted to explore this issue further, but the judge sustained Hora's objections. Du Bois protested vociferously, prompting the judge to retort, "No, Mr. Du Bois. I'm really getting tired of you arguing with me every time I make a ruling." Spectators knew Goodman meant business whenever he didn't address attorneys by their first names.

"May we be heard?" Du Bois asked, referring to an in-chambers discussion.

"You don't need to be heard with that kind of tone," Goodman snapped. "You don't need to be heard with that kind of disrespect."

The bickering continued after the jurors were dismissed for lunch. "You know what?" said a stern Goodman, addressing Du Bois. "I think you're beginning to drink from the same Kool-Aid. You're starting to see ghosts where there are no ghosts."

Child psychologist Michael Fraga testified on February 28 that Rory could easily have mixed up his accounts of his parents' dealings around the time Nina disappeared, especially if police and prosecutors had confused him through their interviewing techniques.

"It would appear, from the transcripts, that the techniques used in the interviews or the way he was interviewed fostered confusion and resulted in many instances of variable responding," Fraga said. "In other words, different answers to events, circumstances and individuals."

Fraga added that he was "surprised and saddened by the techniques that were used and the various players to elicit information" from Rory. Short of a major event like a car crash, the chances that a young child can recall with any specificity the date of any given event is "highly improbable," he said. Fraga added that children's discussions with adults about traumatic events could lead to altered memories, nightmares and drawings such as the one Rory had drawn.

Fraga agreed on cross-examination that he had never examined Rory in person, had never testified as an expert witness on children's cognition or written papers on the subject, and usually testified on behalf of the defense. Hora also sought to destroy Fraga's credibility as a witness, suggesting that he was a "for hire" psychologist and eliciting his acknowledgment that he had been convicted of selling cocaine to an undercover federal agent and forging U.S. Treasury checks in separate cases in the 1970s. Du Bois tried, without much success, to object to Hora's barrage of questions and termed one of them as "complex, compound, unintelligible and leading."

CHAPTER 69

›HANS TAKES THE STAND

The Reiser trial was a full-time venture for many spectators, whether they were physically there in court or logged on from their computers, following along online. As the trial progressed, my blog drew more and more hits. What began as a slightly haphazard venture, consisting of a brief overview of witness testimony, became a near-transcript of the proceedings—and everything going on around it. Gavel groupies, judges, legal experts and even the trial attorneys themselves regularly checked the blog to review each day's testimony. It was extremely time-consuming on my part, but I wanted to give the full flavor of the courtroom scene. And that meant taking note of every time Tamor's cell phone went off— prompting merciless needling from those who read it on the blog—and transcribing every e-mail read into the record. On a couple of occasions, some entries didn't get posted until very late. That was when my laptop froze or lost what I had saved, forcing me to start all over again from raw notes. No matter when I posted, though, each entry would get the blogosphere buzzing. The online comments ranged from the thoughtful to the downright crazed.

There would be even more fodder for thought when Hans took the stand, on March 3. Every news agency was in attendance for the big day. TV trucks ringed the courthouse with their masts fully extended skyward. Cameras weren't allowed in the courtroom, so reporters and photographers jammed the hallway outside. The media mob surrounded Du Bois as he arrived at court that morning. Asked about Hans's mood, Du Bois said, "I think his mood is similar to John Glenn's mood when his space capsule was reentering the earth's orbit, and he saw that the tiles that were heat-deflecting were burning off the front of it. He experienced moments, he said, of 'nervous apprehension.' "

With Alameda County sheriff's deputy Sheri Moss sitting next to him, Hans took his place on the stand. The strange guy who had avoided eye contact and creeped people out was gone, replaced by a confident man answering questions as if he was on a TV talk show. Instead of a monotone, Hans, clad in a dark blue blazer and a white buttoned shirt, modulated his voice. It seemed as though Hans wanted people to like him.

Hans said after Nina dropped off their kids on September 3, 2006, the two discussed the children and their divorce proceedings for about an hour. He said he had told her he didn't want to continue paying her one thousand dollars a month in child support. He asked her for legal custody of the children, but she said no. He said he had wanted to continue talking to his wife, but she cut him off, saying, "Hans, I have to go," he testified. Rory gave her a "squeeze-hug," and she walked out the door, got into her minivan and drove away, he said.

"Did you ever see her again?" Du Bois asked.

"No, I did not."

Hans, like his father did before him, gave long-winded answers and ended up forgetting what Du Bois had asked him in the first place. Hans also offered to provide explanations for his answers, frustrating Du Bois. The attorney told his client to limit his responses or at least to "stop answering" if he lost sight of the question. "I'm laying the foundation," Hans said at one point, prompting Goodman to crack a smile in amusement.

Hans admitted that he had loved Nina "but not enough to marry her, and that was a mistake." He added, "I think Nina loves attention and needs to be loved, but does not herself love." But then again, most romances are a waste of time, "if you look at them with excessive logical analysis," he said. A female juror in the front row looked at a fellow juror as he said this.

Even so, Hans described his wife as a great cook and a perceptive woman with "the most beautiful voice" who was "a step above all the other ladies that I dated."

On his second day on the stand, Hans said Nina spent thousands of dollars on jewelry, clothing and a top-of-the-line laptop computer at a time when Namesys was suffering financial problems. He described how his accident at the French gym made it impossible for him to sit in chairs for a couple of years and also led him to sleep in cars to keep his legs elevated. He also explained why he withdrew thousands of dollars from ATMs shortly after his wife disappeared and why he had carried thousands of dollars in cash on him. He simply was trying to make payroll for his Russian programmers, and it was much easier to pay them in cash.

Du Bois then steered the conversation toward Sturgeon. Everything went smoothly until Hans began talking about Sturgeon's involvement in S and M. Hora repeatedly objected. After the jury was dismissed for lunch, the attorneys had a spirited discussion. Du Bois said he wanted to show the jury that Nina wasn't the "perfect mother" if she indeed had lived with Sturgeon. Hora countered that in photos of Nina's house, he had never seen "leather whips, chains, handcuffs or anything else." What a woman does in the privacy of her bedroom and the privacy of her adult life has nothing to do with this case, Hora said. All this did was "to just trash her again," Hora fumed.

Goodman agreed with the prosecutor, prompting Du Bois to walk outside and tell waiting news cameras, "I think it's fundamentally unfair for this jury not to know that the woman, for two years, lived with a sadomasochist who was also a drug abuser, and she's not just a goody two-shoes that takes her kids to Adventure Time or to little Kindergyms."

Hora saw Du Bois on the TV news at home that night and was infuriated that his adversary was spouting off on things that Goodman had specifically excluded. The prosecutor used his cell-phone camera to record the clip. Although Hora had no reason to believe that jurors were ignoring Goodman's warnings to not discuss the case with anyone and to avoid all media reports on the trial, they could still be inadvertently exposed to those comments through their spouses, friends or coworkers. The next morning, Hora asked for a gag order, and the judge—whose openness with the media was long heralded—obliged. Goodman, while acknowledging that he was aware of the "high level of attention that this case has been given by the news media," ordered that none of the attorneys, investigators and anyone working on the case would have contact with the press. The judge cited the landmark Supreme Court ruling in the case of Dr. Sam Sheppard, the doctor wrongly convicted of murdering his wife in a case that inspired the movie and TV series *The Fugitive*. Sheppard successfully argued that media coverage had prevented him from receiving a fair trial.

Hans wasted no time in attacking his wife's character. On March 6, his third day of testimony, he said Nina had "worked" Ben Denson, the Oakland police officer who had told her to get a gun to protect herself from Hans. "She'll just look people in the eyes and she'll smile and she'll say these words of flattery and I'll be thinking, 'This is just too over the top. It won't work,' but it does," he said.

In similar fashion, Nina once saw a "wonderful old man shaped like a bowling ball," Hans said. "She walked up to him and stroked him on the tummy and said, 'There's nothing but muscle here,' and he just beamed, and he just loved it. And that was Nina."

For his part, Hans did acknowledge that he had been a "patronizing asshole" for making the comment at the party for Grand Lake Montessori parents. But he said that what he meant to say was that men, in general, didn't have a *financial* need for a wife or kids and that unlike other guys, he truly had good intentions in starting a family. If Hans thought he had gained any ground with that explanation, what he said next eviscerated it. All in all, he said, marriage is "altruistic in the financial sense. It's a lot cheaper to hire a housekeeper." That comment raised eyebrows among jurors and those in the gallery.

Hans tried to salvage himself after the midmorning break. There was no question pending when he said from the stand, "I just want to say I don't think I can be psychologically happy without a wife and children."

When it was time to actually start asking questions, Du Bois held up the same framed picture of Nina and Rory that

Hora had shown the jury. "Is that the public image that Nina projected?" Du Bois asked.

"That was the image that she learned was wanted from her, and she responded to that," Hans said. "She was actually more interested in being respected as a doctor than as a mother." Motioning to the picture, he said, "That's my dream, not hers. And I was such an egotistical asshole that I thought that after I got her pregnant, then she would have changed her mind and made it her dream, and it didn't."

Du Bois next turned to Hans's curious behavior in jail when he saw the TV news report about a body in the Oakland hills. Du Bois asked Hans why he had been interested in the story.

"Because I care about my wife," Hans replied.

When asked how he felt when his children were taken away from his custody, Hans began tearing up and weeping. He paused and shook his head. "I can't say . . ." he said before pausing again. "My kids love me so much," he said, adding that they had this "pure, uncomplicated love" for him.

"So when they were taken by the police, did this affect the way you conducted yourself?" Du Bois asked. Hans said yes.

Du Bois turned to the fact that Hans's Treo cell phone had its battery removed when it was found in his fanny pack. Hans said he might have turned off the phone "because I have the battery in reserve." He said he also kept a spare battery in his fanny pack and that he had taken the battery out of his cell phone before to change the battery. He said he had kept the battery in his phone since then.

Turning to his jaunts to distant locations, Hans testified that he had driven to Reno because he had gone through there at some point in the past and "had a fond memory of it." Plus, Reno was "on the way to Yellowstone," which he had also visited before. He said he spent a night sleeping in his vehicle in the parking lot of the Sands Hotel, where he could park for free. He also enjoyed the buffets during his Reno stay. Hans may have thought his explanations made perfect sense, but the confused looks on jurors' faces proved otherwise.

If there was anything Hora could have used while Hans was on the stand to prove that the defendant was egotistical, it would have been the conversation he had with Du Bois on his fourth day of testimony, on Saint Patrick's Day.

Hans said that things were actually improving between him and his wife at the time of her disappearance.

"Can you explain what you mean by that?" Du Bois asked.

"She was making an effort to be nice," he said.

"What's that?" Du Bois asked, and Hans repeated his answer.

"How about you?" Du Bois asked, setting his client up for an easy spike.

"Well, I liked it that she was making an effort to be nice," Hans said. A male juror in the front row looked at a fellow panelist in the second row.

"Did you make an effort to be nice? Is that within your vocabulary of activities?" Du Bois asked, trying mightily to drop his client a hint.

"Well," Hans said. There was a long pause. "I was still pursuing the deposition, which is inherently not nice."

Du Bois tried once again. "I'm asking you whether you made any effort to improve the way you conducted yourself with respect to Nina while things were getting better."

Hans gave a small shrug. There was another pause before he asked his attorney, "You mean outside the courtroom?"

"I mean in your life," Du Bois said, repeating his question again. "This is a yes-or-no type answer."

"Yes, the answer is yes," he said. By now, Hans had proven that getting a straight answer from him—let alone the "right" answer as most defendants gave their own attorneys—would be like trying to squeeze blood from a turnip.

After twice saying that he believed Sturgeon had engaged in money laundering—and twice eliciting objections from Hora that were sustained—Du Bois asked Hans, "What, if anything, might you have done that could have caused Nina to disappear?"

"Um, I opened the door," Hans replied matter-of-factly. He later suggested that she fled the area after he confronted her and told her that "embezzlement was a serious crime, that forgery was a crime, that she committed perjury."

He said that after she left his house, he reheated some tri-tip roast and spaghetti for dinner. "Actually, it was an unusually, uh, poor dinner. Well, I mean it wasn't anything criminally wrong with it. It just wasn't such a great dinner." When he put his kids to bed that night, he sang "Bathtub Blues" to them.

As for his sudden interest in cleaning in early September 2006, Hans said he didn't want to incur his mother's wrath after she returned from Burning Man. He said he washed down his driveway because it hadn't been cleaned for eight years and that he sprayed the CRX with a hose because milk had spilled in it a week earlier. The water didn't drain out the bottom of the car because it didn't have a hole in it like the 1991 Plymouth Laser he once owned, he testified. Hans noted that he had tried to dry the CRX by driving fast around corners and opening the doors. He said he also tried scooping up the water with his hands and with a container. But the only thing that worked was a siphon pump, he said.

He acknowledged that he had given Adventure Time employees a wrong cell-phone number, transposing two digits by mistake. "I know it's not very stereotypical, but computer-science people aren't necessarily all that good with addition, subtraction and remembering numbers," said Hans, who moments earlier had been able to recite from memory the license plate number of the plain-wrap minivan that Oakland police had used to follow him.

Hans confirmed that he called Nina's cell phone at 5:04 p.m. on September 5, 2006, but didn't leave a message because he didn't want to be accused of telephone harassment. He recounted an incident in which he had called her five times to remind her about returning Nio's dress and was accused of telephone harassment in a temporary restraining order. "It made me look bad in court," he said.

As for his strange behavior behind the wheel, Hans said he had driven erratically "because Nina was missing." Goodman scrunched his brow in confusion. Asked by Du Bois what he meant by that, Hans said, "Well, why is Nina missing and did somebody cause her to be missing, and what does this mean and it's a good time to be paranoid."

On his last day of direct examination, on March 18, Hans told jurors that it was possible Nina could have left blood in his home as a result of slicing her finger on a cutting board or "popping a blood vessel in her nose," both of which occurred in the summer of 2006. He noted that it was a Reiser family tradition to gather around the couch and sympathize with whoever had suffered some bleeding. As for his DNA being present on the post, he said, "There's no possibility that I have not touched the post in the last thirty years of living in that house."

Hans said he threw the passenger seat from the CRX in a Dumpster near Tom's Hardware and Auto near the Bayfair Mall in San Leandro. Hora looked at the jury and smiled as Hans said this. Hans said this was near Hegenberger Road, the road that leads to Oakland International Airport. A male juror, a postal worker and former San Leandro resident who knew his way around, shook his head vigorously. Hans corrected himself and said it was actually near Hesperian Boulevard. Asked by his attorney why he threw out the seat if it was in good condition, Hans replied, "Um, that was not a seat that you would miss with the depths of your heart." He said he went to Manteca because it reminded him of small towns and that he swung by a storage center because "I didn't want my car to be seized." He added that he had contemplated actually sleeping in the storage locker, where he would put his "worldly possessions."

Hans said he didn't throw out the two murder books because he hadn't finished reading them. Plus, he said he had an "arrogance of innocence" at the time.

Hora grinned again when Hans admitted that he had not been forthright when he testified that he usually didn't remove the battery from his cell phone. Hans may not have known it, but he had just all but fashioned for himself a giant noose.

He wrapped up his testimony on direct by insisting that he still worried about what happened to Nina. "I'm still interested in Nina's interaction with the kids. I'm still concerned about Nina. To this day, I'm concerned about Nina," he said.

And with that, Du Bois said, "I have no further questions."

CHAPTER 70

›HORA VS. HANS

After the lunch break, Hora wasted no time.

"Let me begin by asking if you're willing to admit, here and now, that when you [previously] testified you willfully concealed the fact that you routinely removed the battery from your cell phone after Nina disappeared?" Hora asked.

"Yes, and I feel badly about that," Hans said.

"And that was a willfully false or deliberately misleading statement of a material fact, do you agree?" the prosecutor asked. Legal experts in the audience knew where Hora was going.

"Yes," said Hans. He later added that he had told his attorneys that he wanted to come clean "because I felt it was deceptive of me." He still apparently had no idea what damage this seemingly grand gesture would cause.

Hans complained several times during his cross-examination that the prosecutor was asking him to draw a legal conclusion. Hora asked Hans to explain what he meant when he said he didn't want to contradict Mishin's testimony about why they drove erratically.

"Can you give me a nice, simple, well-defined, complete question without any references to other questions?" Hans demanded.

"What was the contradiction?" Hora asked.

"OK," Hans said. "Can you give me a sentence in which you use the word 'contradiction' so I can understand it?"

"What was the second part of the reason for the erratic driving besides going to the bar?" Hora repeated.

"Um, I prefer not to answer that," Hans said. "But I will do so if directed by the judge."

After Goodman told him to answer, Hans acknowledged that he didn't want his car seized. "I don't have a great deal of desire to give the government all of my possessions, not my underwear, not my car, definitely not my children."

Hora shot back, "And not information about where Nina is?"

Hans gave the prosecutor a withering look and said, "Your question is ridiculous."

It was high theater in the courtroom, with a veteran prosecutor pitting himself against a highly intelligent computer programmer who believed he could hold his own. Onlookers were enthralled as they watched this verbal judo unfold. But it got even more dramatic as Hans shot back rapid-fire answers to Hora's point-blank questions about what happened the day Nina disappeared. Jurors moved their heads back and forth during the most dramatic moment yet in the trial, as if they were watching a ping-pong game.

"Was there an argument?" Hora asked from a lectern.

"We talked about the divorce," Hans said. Hora asked the question again.

"I would say there was a negotiation," Hans said. His voice remained calm, but his eyes darted between Hora and Du Bois. Hans would get no help now. He was on his own.

"Were there raised voices?"

"No."

"Was there a sudden quarrel?"

"No."

"Did your passions get aroused?" Hora wanted to see if Hans would admit that he had snapped and lost control and killed Nina in a spur-of-the-moment unpremeditated act, which would argue against first-degree murder and could lead the jury to convict him instead of a lesser offense, such as voluntary manslaughter.

"No. Well, maybe not. We cared about what we were discussing."

"Were you as calm speaking to Nina that afternoon as you are here now this afternoon?"

"That's a good way of putting it."

"You had no reason to be upset with her, right?"

"We were in the middle of an acrimonious divorce."

"Did you strike her?"

"No, I did not."

"Did you apply any physical force?"

"No."

"Did you assault her? Did you touch her?"

A pause. "Probably not."

"Did she provoke you in ANY manner whatsoever that afternoon, provoke you to attack, assault or hit her?"

"No. We did, however, have a contentious divorce that we did discuss."

"She didn't provoke you in any fashion whatsoever to an act of violence?"

"That's correct."

"So you certainly didn't kill Nina in any fashion?"

"That's correct."

"And you certainly didn't kill Nina in a sudden quarrel?"

"I certainly didn't kill Nina. I did not murder Nina."

Hora recited a litany of legal terms, asking Hans if he had committed murder, voluntary manslaughter or involuntary manslaughter. He said no on all counts.

"I didn't commit any form of manslaughter or murder."

"Have you studied up on the various forms of homicide, in your homicide research, after Nina disappeared?"

"Yes."

"So you know there's a different level of punishment for different grades of homicide?"

"Yes."

"And you know voluntary manslaughter carries more serious punishment than involuntary manslaughter in California?"

"Yes."

Hora went through more scenarios, but Hans gave the DA no reason to mitigate the killing down to anything less than murder. It was all or nothing.

"Did Nina fall down the stairs that afternoon?"

"No, she did not."

"Did she fall on her head?"

"No, she did not."

"Did she trip or fall?"

"She did not experience any injury or fall that I witnessed."

"Did she have a heart attack?"

"No."

"Did she happen to drop dead in your house?"

"No."

"Did she bleed?"

"No."

"Did you accidentally hit her?"

"No, I did not."

"Did you accidentally choke her?"

"Did not."

Hora asked if Hans had researched instances of accidental killings.

"You're asking for a legal conclusion," Hans said again.

"Your research is all I'm asking."

"I think there's also negligent manslaughter."

"I'm not going there," said Hora, reminding Hans that he was only discussing accidental killings. The DA then asked if it was possible that Hans had accidentally killed Nina without negligence.

"I already told you I didn't kill Nina Reiser."

"Did she inflict harm on herself?"

"No, she did not."

"Did she commit suicide or attempt suicide?"

"No, she did not."

"Did you see anybody else strike her that afternoon?"

"No, I did not."

"Did you see anybody else strike her or assault her?"

"I saw a squeeze-hug," Hans said, referring to the embrace between Nina and Rory.

"Did Nina hit you?"

"She did not."

"Did she apply any physical force to you at all?"

"She did not."

"Did she touch you?"

"I believe she did not touch me."

"You guys did not kiss or hug?"

"No, we did not."

"So you have absolutely had no need to defend yourself from her that afternoon, is that true?"

"That's correct."

"So you didn't kill her in self-defense?"

"That's correct."

When Hora asked Hans about his judo skills, he tried to downplay it by commenting that when he got his black belt, he was in his forties. At that age, martial-arts instructors kind of "find an excuse" to award older students their black belts, he said. The judge, himself a second-degree black belt in tae kwon do, Kenpo Karate and White Tiger kung fu, scrunched his brows in confusion. Now fifty-eight, Goodman had started his martial-arts training eight years earlier.

› Hora asked Hans to read a number of e-mails he had written to Nina. Like many witnesses on the stand who were asked to read documents while on the stand, he went a mile a minute, prompting requests for him to slow down. He did that all right, only he would read. Each. Word. He. Wrote. Like. This. Hora asked what he meant when he wrote in a June 2005 e-mail to Nina, "Those who anger slowly, cool slowly."

Hans said only, "What the words said."

Hora was no less relentless on the second day of his cross-examination, on March 19. The prosecutor began by grilling Hans about his claim that his old Plymouth Laser had a hole in the bottom.

"Did you just take a hose and start squirting water in it and discover that water could drain out of it?" Hora asked.

"You know, I don't remember," Hans said.

"This was not one of the Reiser family traditions, hosing down the inside of the car and removing the seat?" Hora asked, riffing off Hans's testimony a day earlier that it was a Reiser family tradition to sit on the couch to comfort people who got hurt.

"You are correct," Hans said.

Hora asked Hans to demonstrate how he threw away the passenger seat of the CRX. He got up from the stand and walked to the replica seat, which was still in the courtroom well. Sheriff's deputy Sheri Moss rose from her seat to watch. After Hora warned him not to throw the seat onto the table, Hans decided to mimic grabbing the seat and heaving it away into a Dumpster.

Hora grilled him on the specifics about how, when and where he had discarded the seat and then steered the conversation to the two books about murder that he had purchased. Hans mentioned something about interrogation methodology, and the prosecutor asked him to explain further.

"You know, this is really a better question for Mr. Du Bois," Hans said.

"Mr. Reiser, Mr. Reiser, just answer the question," Goodman said.

"If you were·to ask me a different question . . ." Hans began.

"I didn't ask you—" Hora started.

"I wish to object to the question," Hans said. His insouciance stunned observers. It evoked comparisons to when murder defendant Susan Polk, representing herself on charges that she killed her husband, Felix, in Orinda, California, tried to hijack the proceedings in similar fashion. I had sat through Polk's trial, enduring months of her incessant bickering with the prosecutor.

Back in what seemed to be becoming the Court of Hans Reiser, Goodman spoke sharply to the defendant. "Mr. Reiser, you don't get to object to the question. The lawyers object to the question. You can answer the question," he snapped.

"May I request that my lawyer object to the question?" Hans asked.

"Answer the question," Goodman directed.

Hans finally answered that he wasn't familiar with the interrogation methods. Hora thundered, "Then how did it scare you? What was the reason you wouldn't talk to the police?" Hans had no substantive answer.

Hora asked if police surveillance of him had been foremost in his mind after his wife disappeared. Hans said yes, then added, "And Nina and my kids."

But when Hora asked what Hans had done to try to find his

estranged wife in the days after she disappeared, he paused and admitted, "Nothing."

Later, as Hora pressed him as to when he removed things from the CRX, Hans seemed to be throwing out times at random. "Are you just making things up?" Hora demanded.

Hora continued to press Hans for details, prompting him to complain, "You are asking ridiculous powers of memory here." At various points, he complained about the way he was being cross-examined, accusing Hora of adding to his testimony and bluntly telling the prosecutor, "Asked and answered" and even "You're being evasive."

Hans said he was paranoid of being followed by the police after Nina disappeared. "I was probably driving around trying to figure out if I was being followed by the police," he said.

"So what?" Hora demanded. "So what if you're being followed? What's the big deal?" The prosecutor threw his arms into the air.

"Have you ever been followed by the police?" Hans asked. "It kind of freaks you out."

"What should you do if you're being followed by the police?"

"I don't know."

"Run from them?"

"Um, they did attempt to stampede me into—I had a feeling they were trying to stampede me into a chase scene."

Hora asked Hans if he thought the best approach if he were being followed by police, when his wife is missing, is to "run and hide from them . . . ?"

"I can see how this could be seen as inconsiderate and insensitive to the police and everyone else."

Hora wasn't impressed. He shrugged.

Hora asked if Hans was in fact innocent, why did he try to hide his purchase of the two murder books?

"I am not consistent with my thinking," Hans said.

"That's a hallmark of lying, isn't it?" Hora asked.

"It's a hallmark of real people," Hans volleyed.

That afternoon, Hans listed all the places where he had spent the night, from hotels to campgrounds to inside the CRX or Ford Escort. Hora asked if Hans had kept all his hotel receipts, and he said no. "Does that mean I don't have all the receipts?" Hora asked. Smarmily, Hans responded, "You're being very logical." Hans again lavished the prosecutor with faux praise moments later: "You know, you're making a real good argument! I'm inclined to believe you!"

Hans confirmed that he had removed the hard drives from his computer. Asked when he had done so, Hans said he could give only an estimate, maybe sometime between September 7 and 15, 2006. He wasn't sure if it was day or night when he did this. Hora asked why Hans was saying things he knew weren't precise, and he replied, "Because I'm a fool." Hans appeared to be making light of his response.

Hora told him sternly, "This is a murder trial, right? You've got to get this right. This isn't a time to be loose or flip about the process. You're under oath. You have to tell the truth, OK? You understand that?"

"Yes, I understand," Hans said.

Hans then revealed that he no longer had the hard drives—he had given them to his attorney. Mouths opened and all eyes turned to the defense table as a slack-jawed Hora asked, "Which attorney, Mr. Du Bois?" Hans replied in the affirmative and said he didn't want the police to go through his computer.

"What were they going to see on the hard drive that you didn't want them to see?" Hora demanded.

"I don't think that anybody would particularly want the government going through their hard drive," Hans said.

On the third day of cross-examination, Hora gave Hans a copy of a search warrant and asked him to read it. Hans began speaking quickly, and both the judge and Annie Mendiola, the court reporter, told him to slow down.

Hans did just that, but he again decided to speak in slow motion. He went even further when he listed all the computer parts that the police had been seeking, saying "comma" for each comma. If that wasn't obnoxious enough, he even threw in a "slash" for good measure.

As maddening as that might have been, Hora didn't let his emotions show. The prosecutor was content to let Hans's antics speak for themselves. Returning to the issue of Hans's computer, Hora asked Hans if he knew where those hard drives went after he had given them to his attorney.

"No," Hans said. But he added, "I kind of suspect you'll get them in a short period of time."

"What good are they now after seventeen months!?" Hora demanded.

Some trial watchers were convinced that Du Bois had purposefully withheld evidence from the prosecution and would face sanctions. But the defense attorney said later, "We are under no obligation to turn over material that we had unless we were going to use it. We never were going to use it until it became an issue as to where they had gone. And so as it became an issue, we made them available."

The prosecutor twice asked why Hans chose to go to Manteca in search of a storage locker. Twice, Hans replied, "Why not?" An incredulous Hora asked how Hans would have shut the roll-up door or gone to the bathroom in the locker. What, was he going to set up an entire home office inside?

"The truth is, you were never going to live in the storage locker—you were simply looking for a place to hide the car," Hora said.

"That's not true," Hans retorted. "That's kind of like saying I was never going to live in my car. Same logic would apply. And it's been proven that I lived in my car."

Hora was about to ask another question, but without prompting, Hans added, "And a storage locker is better than a car." An annoyed Hora raised his voice and told Hans, "There's no question! So this isn't a chance for you to just talk."

Hans continued to sass around on the stand, engaging in back-and-forth exchanges with Hora and delivering long, meandering answers to yes-or-no questions. His mind-numbing testimony was becoming a long slog.

A frustrated Goodman told the attorneys to meet with him in chambers. When they came out, the judge dismissed the jury early for lunch and then spoke directly to Hans, who was still on the witness stand. "Your attitude to the court is disrespectful. Your attitude to this court is condescending. I will no longer tolerate it. You are not in a position to control this court. You are not in the position to control the questioning or the actions of your counsel. Now Mr. Du Bois is going to talk to you about that over the recess. I would urge you, most strongly, to follow his advice if you continue to be on the witness stand."

Hans leaned forward into the microphone and said, "Apologies" as the judge stalked off the bench.

Hans needn't have apologized to Hora. "When he would say ridiculous things and would do his outbursts, et cetera, et cetera, it just kept getting better and better for me," the prosecutor said later. "It was the gift that kept on giving."

While his son was on the stand, his father waited in the hallway, highlighting passages from books by Robert D. Hare. One was *Without Conscience: The Disturbing World of the Psychopaths Among Us*. Ramon also carried with him another book, cowritten by Hare, called *Snakes in Suits: When Psychopaths Go to Work*. Ramon had made it a point to show that book to the investigators who came out to interview him in Birmingham. The elder Reiser's activities outside the court became the subject of much speculation online, with a number of commenters convinced that he was posting vitriolic rants on my trial blog—during the court proceedings—against anyone who dared to speak ill of his son. I never saw him working on a laptop in the foyer.

After lunch, Hans continued to quibble and disagree with everything Hora said. The tediousness of it all prompted one woman in the audience to say in disgust, "Say yes for once in your life."

Hora next confronted Hans with his cell phone records and asked if he had called Nina shortly after 5:00 p.m. on September 5, 2006. Hans insisted on poring over his records before answering. Hora was convinced that Hans was stalling for time so that he could think up a lie.

"OK," Hora said after waiting some more. "I'll tell you what line it is. Line 2, on page 3."

Hans was becoming flustered. "It would have taken less time for me to just find it. I actually was already there," he said peevishly, shaking his head. "At 5:04 p.m. this says I called Nina."

"Why did you call her?" Hora asked.

"Wait a minute!" Hans cut in.

"Why did you call her at 5:04?" the DA repeated.

But Hans was busy researching something else. "I'm sorry?" he asked.

"Why did you call her at 5:04 p.m. on September 5?" Hora asked for a third time.

"To find out if the whole thing had been settled with respect to the kids being picked up."

"What did she say?"

"I didn't speak to her."

"So you didn't know if the kids ever got picked up?" Hora asked.

"Uh, that's correct."

"So they were just dangling in the wind, as far as you know? You had no idea if they got picked up or not?"

"That's correct. However, I assumed I would get a phone call." He said he didn't leave a message because he didn't want to be accused in court of having harassed her.

Hora wanted to show how ridiculous that answer was. "Because if you left a civilized, respectful, ordinary, reasonable message on her voice mail, someone might listen to it and say you harassed her?" he asked.

Hans conceded that he never called her again to see how the children were doing or whether they had been picked up.

"I just didn't care about it very much," Hans said in a response that caused audience members to gasp. He added, "I'm an inconsiderate asshole." This self-deprecating remark had already become a catchphrase in his trial.

To drive the point home, Hora asked, "How many times did you call her after September 5, 5:04 p.m.?"

"None," he said.

Hora noted that Hans had called Nina twenty-six times in August 2006. The prosecutor's line of questioning was powerful in its implication: why would Hans bother calling Nina when he knew she was already dead?

No jurors were present on March 26 when Goodman denied the defense motion for a mistrial, this time on the grounds that Hora had improperly cross-examined Parr, the psychiatrist. The judge then angrily shot down claims he had intimidated

Hans a week earlier with his warning to behave. Du Bois initially accused Goodman of having rebuked Hans in front of the jury. But Du Bois was mistaken; the panel had already gone for lunch that day. The defense attorney then asserted, "It was in front of the client, and it intimidated him."

Goodman erupted, saying, "Oh COME ON, Mr. Du Bois. Don't even start there about how I intimidated your client. There's no way. For you to suggest that I somehow intimidated him is so disingenuous, it's insulting to me."

Goodman said that if Du Bois didn't realize that Reiser had been "acting like a lawyer," then "I'm disappointed in you."

There was more bickering between Du Bois and Goodman during the fourth and final day of cross-examination, on April 1. Hora pressed Hans for details as to how Nina's blood may have been deposited in his home. Hans gave rambling answers, prompting Hora to cut in. Hans complained that the prosecutor was forcing him to give answers based on "false precision."

Du Bois joined in when jurors had been dismissed for a break. But once again, Goodman chastised the attorney for his "disrespect to the court," including mischaracterizing what the judge had said or challenging the judge in front of jurors. In truth, Goodman had given Du Bois a lot of latitude, from allowing him to come in late to shrugging it off when his cell phone rang.

"This is not the way you normally practice law," the judge told Du Bois. "We've tried a bunch of cases together. I don't know what the motivation is; I don't know why this is happening. I'm beginning to get tired of it."

Goodman said he understood that Hans was a "difficult client," and that's why he allowed Du Bois to meet with his client in a holding cell near the courtroom—which was technically in violation of sheriff's policy—as well as at the jail housed on the tenth floor of the courthouse. At one point during this discussion, Hans raised a finger from the stand. Deputy Sheri Moss told him no. The judge said he wanted the record to clearly show that "we aren't in any way infringing on his right to due process, equal protection or anything else. I have an obligation to control the proceedings in this court.

You're making it real difficult for me to do that." A chastened Du Bois later joked to me that he had been "torn to shreds and sprinkled in the jury box."

When the courtroom fireworks ended, the trial resumed. Hans told the jury that he had removed the trim assembly, near the back of the CRX, to get rid of a bad smell. He said the smell remained after he used a siphon pump to remove the water he had sprayed inside the car.

He didn't specifically identify the smell but said it would be consistent with what could happen if children threw or spilled some milk and Lucky Charms cereal in the car. Observers wondered grimly if Hans in reality had wanted to mask the unmistakable smell of death.

Hans testified that he had also wanted to trace the car part onto a piece of plywood and put futon material onto the part as a "construction project" to make the seat more comfortable.

But when Hora asked what Hans had done with the trim assembly, he acknowledged that he had thrown it away, maybe in some kind of "trash receptacle," possibly in Oakland or San Leandro, between September 15 and 17, 2006. His account of what he had done with the car part was vaguer than his description of how he heaved the passenger seat into a Dumpster.

On April 2, Hans's ninth day on the stand, Du Bois began his redirect examination, and that was when the attorney produced a yellow manila envelope with the two missing hard drives inside. Du Bois brought over the computer that police had seized, and Hans put the hard drives in it. They fit perfectly. During a court break, Hora immediately made arrangements to have the hard drives analyzed. The clock was ticking. He had no interest—or time—to press the issue of not having gotten the hard drives sooner.

Hora may have felt jammed for time, but Hans was in no such rush now that he could be back in control of the discussion. Jurors got noticeably restless as they realized they were in for more drudgery. They might as well have been thinking, *Do we really need to know why corn starch is preferable to talc as a foot powder? Or why Hans was so good at building decks? Or why it was more fun to debug somebody else's code*

than one's own? Du Bois tried to steer his client back into
what was important. Hans said he knew that his kids loved
Nina. He tried to impress on the jury that he was devoted to
them as well.

"Under no circumstances would you have done anything
whatsoever to deprive those children of their mother?" Du
Bois asked.

"No," he said.

Hans wept for the second time in his trial as he described
the shock he felt when CPS removed Rory and Nio from his
care. "Logically and legally and [with] all the abstractions
and all the facts, there is no reason for what they did. It was
terrible."

Du Bois had to repeatedly ask his client whether his behavior changed after his children were taken away. In what some
legal pundits believed was a stretch, Du Bois tried to tie that
feeling of desperation to Hans's decision to throw parts of the
CRX away.

"Was your decision to put the seat in the Dumpster affected
by the feelings you had after the kids were taken away on the
8th?" Du Bois asked.

"Well, the level of frustration was there," Hans replied.

Asked about his removal of the rear trim assembly in the
Honda, Hans said, "Well, not only did I not have my kids, but
I didn't have a home, and this way I could make something
that would make the car a bit of a home."

Du Bois showed the jury pictures of Hans's home and
its proximity to neighbors' homes, suggesting that neighbors couldn't have missed seeing a body being carried out
of his house in a bag, as Hora had intimated through Rory's
testimony.

On April 3, Tamor again took over questioning, this time
of DNA expert Keith Inman, who opined that the traces of
Nina's blood that were found in Hans's home and car could
have been left as a result of intimate contact. He also testified that a scratch found on the pillar at the same spot as the
bloodstain was made after the blood was deposited on the pillar. Inman, who had worked at police departments and labs
throughout California, testified that it appeared that someone

may have tried to "wipe or swipe" away some of the blood before it dried completely. This was a startling statement, one that seemed to score points for the prosecution. But Inman then bounced squarely back into the defense's corner when he stated that some of the blood could have been deposited as a result of someone grabbing the pillar and falling, or from a cut, wound or nosebleed.

Under cross-examination, however, Hora elicited an admission from Inman that it was likely that Nina's blood had gone "flying through the air" before hitting the post. Hora would later tell jurors that what Inman described "sounds like violence" and that the defense's DNA expert turned out to be one of the prosecution's best witnesses.

On Hans's final day on the stand, on April 7, it became abundantly clear that Du Bois had completely lost whatever control he had of his client. Du Bois all but begged Hans to answer questions "without going into more detail than we need to have." During another exchange, Hans sharply told his attorney that he was trying to answer his question. "If you would not interrupt me, I'll get to it," Hans said. At one point, Du Bois even told Goodman he wanted his own client's answer to be considered nonresponsive.

As Hans launched into a rambling monologue as to why scientists used data to communicate, Hora asked to strike the whole thing, and Goodman agreed.

"Why do you want to strike it?" Du Bois asked the judge.

"Because you know what, Bill?" Goodman said. "It's taking up a long time. Under 352, I can do that," he said, referring to a section in the evidence code. "If it's more prejudicial and time-consuming than probative in helping the jury reach a conclusion, then we don't need to hear it."

After more back and forth, Goodman erupted. "Mr. Reiser, enough! I've had it with your answers that don't answer anything."

Du Bois asked point-blank if Hans killed his wife, and he said no.

"How do you know that Rory's dream of you carrying a package with Nina in it down the stairs on September 3 is false?" Du Bois asked.

"Because Rory would never be afraid of me carrying anything down the stairs," Hans said in another comment that raised eyebrows. He added that Rory "loves me and he trusts me completely, and there's no way prior to CPS coming in and getting a hold of him that he's afraid of me."

He confirmed that the night after Nina disappeared, he took his kids into the Oakland hills and brought a flashlight to look for deer. Asked if the moon was out, Hans said, "I don't remember." With no question pending, however, he said, "I remember the owl."

Du Bois turned anew to the sleeping bag, and Hans agreed that he had used the stuff sack in the past as a pillow during camping trips. It was a reasonable explanation, until he once again put his foot in his mouth when he described how Nina was "pissy" during a trip to Big Sur.

"You should never go on a vacation with a woman at that time of the month. It's better to stay home and work through the weekend than to go on vacation at that time of the month. You'll have more fun," he said.

A female juror in the front row who worked at a fertility center—and had thought Hans seemed to be a likable guy when he first took the stand—shook her head in barely disguised disgust. He had lost quite a bit of sympathy with that remark, even if he wanted to float the theory that this was how Nina's blood ended up on the sleeping-bag stuff sack. But he didn't get it, because he added, "The next time a woman brings a box of tampons on a camping trip, I'll turn around." The defense also suggested that Nina's blood got on the sack as a result of "intimate contact."

The trial was delayed a week to allow the sheriff's computer forensic technician Kyle Ritter to examine the more than two million files and fifty million lines of text on the hard drives.

Anyone who expected a smoking gun was sorely disappointed. On April 14, Ritter testified that he had found nothing incriminating on the hard drives, even after looking up search terms including "murder" and "kill my wife." He cautioned that he had not been able to go through all the contents of the drives during a preliminary four-day review and that a more thorough analysis would take at least a month.

Hans then got back on the stand to make some more points. He said the "whole thing is silly," referring to the case itself as well as the issue over his hard drives. He pointed out that he could have easily withheld the fact that he had turned over the drives to Du Bois. As the attorney continued with various and sundry more questions, it became clear that the two of them were quarreling once again.

"I have no further questions, but is there anything else you feel you must say before you get off the witness stand?" Du Bois asked.

Hora objected, and the judge sustained the objection.

"I'd like to have my children called to the stand," Hans said with no question pending.

"Your honor," Hora complained.

Du Bois began conferring with Tamor.

"I wish to change my attorney," Hans said loudly at that point. He said he wanted his former divorce attorney, John Fuery, to ask him questions. But Du Bois asked a few more questions before quitting. Hans clearly wasn't pleased. The judge had to tell him twice to step down and then asked Du Bois if the defense rested. "No, it does not rest," Hans sputtered.

After the jury was then sent home for the day, Hans again demanded that Fuery come to represent him. Goodman told him that closing arguments would go on as scheduled the next day, and Hans cut him off.

The judge exploded. "Mr. Reiser, I have about had it with you. You are rude. You are arrogant. There's not enough words in the English language to describe the way you are. You have been trying to make a mockery of these proceedings. You have mocked the court reporter. You have mocked the prosecutor—oh you don't remember?" Goodman asked with indignation as Hans shook his head in protest. "When she asked you to slow down, you said, 'Oh. O-K. I'll. Talk. Slower.' You are not in control of this courtroom. You are not in charge of these proceedings. If you want to ask Mr. Fuery to come in tomorrow, we'll see if he's willing to come take up your defense. You're not going to have a continuance."

"May I make a record?" Hans asked.

"No, you may not," the judge growled. "You have your lawyers. I'm tired of hearing you talk." Goodman warned him again that "if you continue to disrupt this courtroom, I will have you removed from this courtroom."

Hans continued to mutter complaints about Du Bois as he was led out of court.

CHAPTER 71

> CLOSING ARGUMENTS

The portrait of Nina and Rory was again front and center on April 15 as Hora began his closing argument. When he first spoke directly to jurors at the beginning of the trial, Hora had to carefully craft his words, saying only what he believed the evidence would show. Now Hora could let loose, legally speaking, by arguing his case to the panel as he weaved together the last moments of Nina's life. "We don't know everything that happened to Nina Reiser. We don't know everything that Hans Reiser did to her, but we know enough," said Hora, delivering his summation with the use of PowerPoint.

Nina disappeared off the face of the earth on September 3, 2006, and hasn't been seen for 591 days, he said as the number, written in red, appeared on a slide that was projected on the courtroom wall. The next slide read, in smaller text, "And counting." It was a powerful visual: after the first few weeks, months maybe, it could be argued that Nina was still out there somewhere. But as more and more time passed, with no sightings of her at all, no letters or contact with family, missed birthdays and holiday gatherings, it only strengthened the DA's theory that she was dead.

Hora quickly sought to dispel any notion that Hans could get off scot-free without Nina's body. He cited an appeals-court ruling in the Charles Manson case: "The fact that a murderer may successfully dispose of the body of the victim does not entitle him to an acquittal. That is one form of success for which society has no reward."

Hora said the jury had three questions to decide: Is Nina dead, did the defendant kill her and was it murder or manslaughter?

If their answer to the first question was no, "then he goes home," Hora said, motioning to Hans. Although Hora never said so explicitly to the jury, looming in observers' minds was the fact that if Hans went free and direct evidence later tied him to Nina's murder, he could never be tried again.

"Is Nina dead?" Hora asked. "Yeah, she's dead. No doubt she's dead. Let me tell you why. Number one, first and foremost—and I told you this when I gave my opening statement—is Nina, from what we know about her, was the kind of mother that would never abandon those kids. She would never do that. There's a bond between mother and child. I've seen it; you've seen it. It's powerful. It's sincere. That's not to say that one out of a million people do leave their kids. Yeah, it's happened, but by and large, unless you know something about this woman that nobody else does, there's no way," said Hora, shaking his head.

Hora showed a picture of Rory and Nio on a beach with their backs to the camera. "Think about what it would do to little children who were what, six and five at the time she vanished? Can you think of anything more cruel to do to two little kids? Night after night after night?" Hora said, his voice betraying emotion. "They go to bed, wondering where their mother is. Does my mother love me? Why would my mother leave me? Does she hate me? What happened to her? Is she hurt? Is she gone? Is she coming back?" Hora asked plaintively, skillfully taking on the personas of Rory and Nio. "That's child abuse! She wouldn't do that to those kids. It's vicious. It's cruel to do that to kids."

Nina also would not buy a week's worth of groceries, pay her next month's rent, write a check for child care, study for a U.S. medical licensing exam, negotiate a salary for a new job and take steps to file for bankruptcy or take leftovers home if she planned "to be on a plane to Siberia that afternoon," Hora said. She was thinking about the future, not "planning on a getaway," he said.

Nor would she leave behind all her possessions, including her Honda Odyssey minivan, her cat, her driver's license and money, Hora said. After 591 days of complete invisibility and silence, "The only reasonable inference from all the evidence is that Nina is dead," he said. He acknowledged that although this was a case built on circumstantial evidence, "It's powerful, it's convincing, it's persuasive and it's the truth."

As for the second question that jurors must answer, Hora said, "He behaved like she's dead. He behaved like he killed her. The evidence showed that he killed her." This, even though no one knew how he killed her, whether it was by strangulation, stab wounds or something else, he said.

Hora reminded jurors that Hans didn't call Nina after telling Doren that he needed to speak to his lawyer. "The mother of his children [is] missing, he doesn't even bother to pick up the phone and dial her number once? *Not once!*" Hora roared with indignation, the veins in his neck bulging. "That's absolutely mind-boggling!" Hans knew a phone call would be a waste of time, said the prosecutor, his voice softer now.

"And what does the defendant do when he gets the call from Ellen?" the next slide read. "Let's wash off the driveway!" said Hora, his sarcasm obvious. "*What!?* You got time to hose off the driveway and you don't have the time to call the mother of your kids, once? He's a little more concerned now. Now he knows they know," Hora said as juror Vince Dunn repeatedly nodded, albeit almost imperceptibly.

On the second day of his summation, Hora scoffed at Hans's explanation that he had thrown out pieces of the CRX and hosed it down because of his kids' messes. He pointed out the similarities in where Hans had stashed his CRX and where Nina's minivan had been found. Both were parked on streets alongside Highway 13, within jogging distance to the Exeter home. He also noted that both Hans's and Nina's cell phones were found with their batteries detached.

"This is probably the most incriminating circumstance in this case. Nobody walks around with their cell phone battery intentionally removed—nobody. Who even thinks of removing their cell phone battery to hide their location and remain undetected? Someone who is familiar with technology—the defendant," Hora said, pointing at Hans. "It's that unique. It's a signature."

Hora turned to how Hans admitted to lying about the fact that he routinely removed his cell-phone battery. The prosecutor said the judge would be giving them an instruction that says, "A witness who is willfully false in one material part of his or her testimony is to be distrusted in others. You may reject the whole testimony of a witness who willfully has testified falsely as to a material point." That was why right out of the gate, Hora had forced Hans to admit that he had lied while on the stand.

Hora asked the jury to convict Hans of either first- or second-degree murder. But the prosecutor wasn't done. After the defense had its chance to give its closing argument, Hora would have the last word.

⟩ That afternoon, a packed gallery watched as Du Bois stated the obvious in pointing out that his client was a "difficult person to communicate with" and a "difficult person·to relate to." In contrast, Nina is "easy to like and likable. She is a pleasure to look at, a pleasure to be around, apparently, and projects very well," he said. "In a beauty contest, Mr. Reiser would lose, hands down. His hope is that you will not regard this case as a beauty contest."

Du Bois said he hoped the jurors would bear in mind an old adage that "old lawyers like me remember," which is that when the law is in your favor, argue the law and when the facts are in your favor, you argue the facts. And when neither the law nor the facts are in your favor, "you pound the table and throw a lot of dust in the air." Du Bois needled Hora for the number of times he raised his voice "almost to a screaming point, in an attempt to bolster evidence." Du Bois said he hoped not to do that.

Du Bois drew chuckles as he compared his client to the duck-billed platypus and showed them a stuffed animal of the odd creature. The attorney said his client is the "duck-billed platypus of criminal defendants, the duck-billed platypus amongst some of his peers, the duck-billed platypus amongst normal people." Yet he must get "the same consideration under the law," he said.

Du Bois brushed off any suggestions that Nina had been in the passenger seat of the Honda CRX, much less the car itself. What was Hans planning to do, use her to drive in the commuter lanes? Du Bois asked. Some of his actions could be interpreted as those of a guilty man, but some of his conduct was a "product of his own platypusian personality, as you will see," Du Bois said as a female juror in the back row shook her head. Goodman's wife, Patty, sitting in the gallery, nearly burst out laughing as Du Bois said "platypusian."

"He has to be one of the least attractive people," Du Bois said, showing jurors the stuffed playtpus again. "And she is a doll. She projected beautifully; he's just a difficult person to get along with on a social basis, let alone on an intimate basis."

Based on Rory's testimony, "There's direct evidence that Hans Reiser had no opportunity to commit this crime. Zero," said Du Bois, whose goal was to cast enough reasonable doubt to convince at least one juror not to convict his client.

Hans's actions are "equally consistent with being a self-centered, self-important, selfish, inconsiderate slob as it is with his having anything to do with Nina's disappearance," Du Bois said. Hans says "incredibly obnoxious things at times. He's such an easy person to dislike. He comes across so lousy, so self-centered. He gives the impression that he doesn't care about who's asking the questions. He only cares about his answer. Even when the judge is talking to him, he's still talking. He doesn't get it. That doesn't mean he killed anybody. The evidence shows he's not a violent person and has never has been in a fight."

As court ended for the day, former Alameda County Public Defender Jay Gaskill, whose blog on the trial was a must-read, wrote that Hora's closing reminded him of the "if it walks like a duck, quacks like a duck and had feathers like a duck" line of argument. "So you can imagine my surprise when Bill Du Bois opened his own argument this afternoon by comparing his client to a duck-billed platypus," Gaskill wrote. "You just can't make this stuff up."

Du Bois' platypus metaphor drew laughter and scorn. Juror Kathy Carpenter said her late husband was a criminal defense attorney and that she appreciated the importance of a vigorous defense. But she said Du Bois was "awful" and that she felt embarrassed for him. "The worst thing he did was the platypus," she said.

At home that evening, Patty Goodman decided to pull a prank on Du Bois. She went online to the Wikipedia entry for platypus, imported the text and picture of the animal into a Microsoft Word file and printed it out—but not before mischievously adding a sentence of her own: "The male platypus kills the female after it has two offspring." There was no way to tell that anything had been added to the entry because the text was all the same.

The next morning, when Du Bois and Tamor stopped by Goodman's chambers before Du Bois resumed his closing argument, the judge asked Du Bois, "Did you really research the platypus thing?"

"Yeah, why?" Du Bois asked.

"Patty didn't look very hard—she found this," Goodman said, handing Du Bois the Wikipedia printout. Patty had highlighted in yellow the phrase about the platypus killing its mate.

Du Bois paled. Goodman thought the attorney was going to have a stroke right then and there.

"Have you shown this to Paul?" Du Bois demanded.

"No, I think you should be the first one to get it," Goodman said.

Du Bois looked stricken as he continued to read the article. Finally, the judge let him off the hook and told him it was all a joke.

Crisis averted, Du Bois continued his summation by once again going back to the trusty platypus. This time, he showed jurors a picture of the real thing. "This is what they actually look like," he said. "But you get the idea."

Du Bois groused that the prosecution was unfairly conjuring up images of the Scott Peterson case by emphasizing the fact that Hans had twice been found carrying thousands of dollars in his fanny pack—once when he was detained him for a DNA sample and the second time when he was arrested. Peterson, too, was carrying a large amount of cash when he was taken into custody for killing his wife, Laci, and her unborn son.

Du Bois said police and prosecutors had cherry-picked certain points to make Hans look guilty. "There's a shading that happens," Du Bois said. "Sometimes, shading can be the difference between life and death."

He went back to the platypus. "Did you know that the platypus is the only mammal that lays eggs?" Du Bois asked, smiling. "I was trying to think recently how a platypus could even evolve. It must have been a genetic mistake. That's why it reminded me of . . ." Du Bois trailed off but turned his head and gave a disdainful look at his client. Some laughter wafted through the courtroom.

Du Bois referred to the testimony by inmate Arthur Gomez that Hans rushed up to the TV in jail when a news report came on about a body being found in the Oakland hills. The prosecution wants you to infer that "he got up only because he's guilty. 'Oh darn, they found Nina's body,'" Du Bois said. Instead, "He got up to see what was going on, *whether* it was Nina's body, because he's interested, vitally interested in not being convicted of this crime he didn't commit."

Du Bois said, "I just know this is one of the great screwjobs of what happened to Hans Reiser. It's easy to screw a platypus." He also remarked, "I don't know how they stay away from predators. They must taste terrible."

And had Hans called Nina's cell phone over and over, asking, "Nina, where have you been? I was so worried about you," then the prosecution would just say, "He's just trying to throw you off, making those calls to Nina," Du Bois intoned, using a deep voice to represent the government.

Behind the scenes, Du Bois had refused to concede that Nina was dead, despite Tamor's insistence that he do so. Tamor said later that he didn't want to "argue what is inarguable" and risk losing any more credibility with the jury.

In front of the jury, Du Bois continued to raise the possibility that she was still alive. But if Nina was in fact dead, then others could have killed her, Du Bois said. Oakland police failed to conduct a proper investigation of Sturgeon, and they failed to look into whether there had been any "sexual trysts" between Nina and men she may have met through online Craigslist ads, he said.

"Not one of them was contacted by the Oakland police—that would be inconsistent with the theory that they ultimately wanted to bring," Du Bois said.

Hans's paranoia is consistent with someone with Asperger's, and just because he's "acting funny" doesn't mean he's guilty, Du Bois said.

Du Bois referred to Hora's closing when the prosecutor argued to jurors that they could disregard all of Hans's testimony because he lied on the stand. The defense attorney told jurors that if they use that standard, then they should also reject testimony by Sharanova, who had been "lying on multiple occasions while testifying under oath" about never having coached Rory before he testified.

As for blood evidence, "You can't convict a man on murder based on the prosecution's suggestion that perhaps the sleeping bag picked up on this very weak sample from something that was on the floor of the car," Du Bois said. "There's no evidence, none." Police are liable to find blood in one's home during a meticulous search "because people leak. Human beings leak in their houses. It's not uncommon to find their DNA," Du Bois said as Hora grinned from his table.

On the third day of his closing, Du Bois spoke in a courtroom that had been rigged with a television pool camera in advance of the verdict, and cables snaked through the gallery and into the hallway. He described Nina as "someone who has contacts across the world, in Eastern Europe" and was "as comfortable in Europe as she is here." He pegged Sturgeon as someone who had an "equal motive or greater motive to do harm to Nina than Hans Reiser."

The prosecution has tailored the circumstantial evidence to make Hans look bad no matter what the situation, he said. "So if it's clean, we can infer guilt," Du Bois said of the CRX. "If it's dirty, we can infer guilt. If he made a phone call to his wife only once, we can infer guilt. If he made many, you can infer guilt" on the grounds that he was trying to throw people off, Du Bois said.

He repeated several times of his client, "He's an eccentric," and he read from the Wikipedia entry for eccentricity. He ended by telling jurors that there was no evidence that Hans murdered Nina or even that she was dead—but if they were convinced he killed her, they should convict him of nothing more serious than voluntary manslaughter.

› That afternoon, Hora began his rebuttal argument. He had been waiting the entire trial for this moment. Retired stockbroker Ron Hora, clearly proud of his son, sat in the audience, much as he had at various key points in the trial. Peggy Hora, the prosecutor's mother, followed along on my blog. She had to "mightily resist the temptation" of responding online whenever her son was criticized, which had happened from time to time.

Hora told jurors that the platypus was actually one of the few venomous mammals in existence. He noted that the male platypus has a spur on the hind foot that delivers venom capable of causing severe pain to humans. Many jurors chuckled at this irony. He derided the "platypus nonsense" and other defense arguments as "nonsense, lies and his baloney." "His excuses about all the things that he did," Hora said. "Odd by itself just doesn't cut it."

Of course the police looked at Sturgeon and Zografos early on in the investigation, Hora said. "Everyone was a suspect. I mean, she's missing. Darn right they're suspects!" Hora said. But in the end, the police focused on "one guy, sitting over in the chair, right over there in the chair," Hora said, motioning to Hans. At that point, the defendant looked up and turned around in his seat, as if to see who the DA was referring to.

On April 22, the second day of his rebuttal, Hora put a large jigsaw puzzle made of foam core board onto an easel next to a picture of Nina. The puzzle was broken up into twenty-five segments. Each piece had some circumstantial evidence written on it, like "Hide & Seek," "Defendant's Perjury," "Cell Phone Batteries" and "Nina's Last Location." One by one, Hora removed the pieces of evidence, gradually revealing a picture of Hans at his first arraignment, and put the interlocking pieces together on the picture of Nina. Ultimately, there were two pieces missing: "Location of Body" and "Method of Murder." It was a powerful visual, modeled after a similar demonstration by Placer County prosecutors in their no-body case.

Hora said the last place anybody saw Nina was at Hans's house, "not Sean's house, not some boyfriend's house, not Anthony's house, not some Craigslist house. It's at *his* house. *His* house. That's the last place on *earth* she was. That's a big deal. Don't overlook what a small, simple fact that is, how important, how powerful it is. *His* doorstep."

Hora scoffed at Hans's testimony that he went out looking for deer. The prosecutor was convinced that Hans, scared that he may have been spotted in the hills by a witness, had made up that story as an alibi. But he didn't say that outright to the jury. He was confident that the panel could see that Hans had been weaving more fiction than fact while on the stand. Hora reminded jurors that Beverly had said neither she nor Hans had gone looking for Nina in the woods because of poison oak. "Uh, he's got time to look for deer in the hills, he doesn't have time to look for Nina, doesn't have time to make a phone call?" Hora asked.

Hans was so cold and callous that he wanted to trash Nina in a press release, Hora said. "You killed Nina—isn't that enough!? And you want to publish a press release on what a piece of garbage she is?" he roared.

Hora played a recording of part of the interview he had conducted with Rory on November 12, 2007, just before trial began.

"And I bet you have a mom and a dad, too, right?" Hora asked.

"No."

"You don't have a mom and a dad?"

"Not anymore."

"Why not?"

"Nina . . ."

"Nina. Do you know where Nina is?"

"No."

"How's that make you feel?"

"Sad."

"Yeah, I know, it is sad. Tell me, what was your favorite thing about Nina? What did you like best about her?"

Rory paused. "Everything."

"Mm-hmm. And you miss her?"

"Yes."

Hora stopped the recording. "*That's* murder—when you realize what you've done to your son and you've stolen their mother," Hora said as Du Bois shook his head.

Hora next put onto the screen a picture of one of the books that Nina had in her minivan when it was found abandoned. It was the 1942 classic *The Runaway Bunny*, by Margaret Wise Brown, with pictures by Clement Hurd. Hora read the book in its entirety as each page and picture flashed on the screen.

The story was about a little bunny who insisted on running away. He described to his mother all the different ways he imagined he could escape from her. It didn't matter if the bunny turned into a fish, a bird or a sailboat—his mother would similarly transform herself, turning into a fisherman, a tree or the wind. Each time, she would think of some way to find her son, proving that she would go to the ends of the earth for him. The little bunny finally realized that any plans to leave would be futile, and the bond with his mother was strengthened.

There were lumps in the throats of many who witnessed Hora's storytelling. It was not hard to imagine Nina, from beyond the grave, desperately seeking to reunite with her little boy. The prosecutor had practiced reading the story many times on his laptop. Each time he did, he couldn't get through it without becoming overwhelmed with emotion.

Hora then put a picture of a smiling Nina on the screen. "A man who commits manslaughter realizes that mothers are going to miss birthday parties, and he shows remorse," he said. "Rory's birthday was September 28, remember? The day he's running away from Henry Lee on that tape we have in evidence."

Hora said, "Watch this—this is the last birthday party Nina ever got to go to." As he had earlier in the trial, the prosecutor played part of the videotape taken by Zografos at Rory's sixth birthday party, in September 2005. It showed Nina jumping around with the kids on mats and the children happily eating cake. The video then went into slow motion as

Nina, looking every bit the perfect mommy-hostess, leaned in and softly kissed Rory, wearing a party hat, on the side of his head. The scene then froze and faded to black.

"That's murder," Hora said sharply. "She would have never left those kids, never. This was murder. I ask that you find him guilty of first- or second-degree murder." He paused. "Thank you very much for your enduring patience." Hora was done. He hoped the jury would look at all the facts and circumstances as a whole, and not bits and pieces that, taken individually, could seem inconsequential or lead to innocent interpretations. Many observers agreed that his argument was a pitch-perfect combination of outrage at Hans and a heartfelt plea for justice for Nina and her children. But would the jury see things the way the prosecutor did?

CHAPTER 72

> THE VERDICT

That afternoon, the seven men and five women made their way to the deliberation room. They picked Gino Giordano, an account manager at a San Jose technology firm, as foreman, in a nod to his calm demeanor and his proven ability to lead a group. Although most jurors dressed casually, the bald Giordano always wore a shirt and tie.

The jury asked to see only one piece of evidence. It was Hans's July 10, 2006, e-mail to Supervisor Steele in which he had complained about being falsely accused of domestic violence—and chillingly asked, "Does inaccurate punishment damage the psychology of those punished and increase the likelihood of later real domestic violence?" It was a telling sign to Hora. After reading this e-mail to jurors during his closing argument, he had told them, " 'Keep this up, keep screwing with me—especially when it's not justified, and the end result could be real domestic violence.' That's in July 2006. That's what's on his mind."

On the afternoon of April 28, the third full day of their deliberations, jurors signaled that they had a verdict. It has been said that if a jury comes back within an hour, the defendant is almost certainly guilty. If the jury deliberated for a week or more, it was a telling sign that there was some discord and that there could be at least one holdout juror. But three days—after a five-month trial? Du Bois had a bad feeling. Still, anything was possible. Word quickly spread: the verdict would be read at 3:00 p.m. Spectators filled the hallway outside Department 9. When the doors opened, they crammed the courtroom, which now seemed to carry an electric charge.

Hans, clad in a white shirt with its collar askew, a red tie and his usual dark blue blazer and slacks, looked pensive. The twelve jurors and three alternates filed into the jury box. At 3:10 p.m., Giordano handed the verdict forms to the bailiff, who handed them to Goodman. Time almost seemed to stop at that point. There was absolute silence as the judge spent fifteen interminable seconds reviewing the verdict form, his face betraying no emotion. Goodman then took the unusual step of polling each of the jurors to make sure that it was his or her true and individual verdict.

Finally, Goodman handed the forms to court clerk Fil Cruz. She stood and read aloud: "We, the jury in the above-entitled cause, find the defendant Hans Reiser guilty of a murder." Reiser bowed his head and closed his eyes briefly. But Cruz was still reading. "We, the jury, fix the degree of the above offense as murder of the first degree." Hans did not appear to blink, his eyes as wide as his mother's were at times when she testified. Tamor sat back in his seat. Hans would be spending twenty-five years to life in prison. Everyone following the case was stunned. At most, everyone expected second-degree murder. But in the end, most agreed that Hans had talked himself into first-degree murder.

Goodman had wanted to avoid the possibility that Hans would lash out at jurors if he had polled them after the verdict was read, as it was usually done by most other judges. Now that the jury had rendered its decision, Goodman ordered deputies to take Hans to the jail upstairs. As he stood, the defendant, looking crestfallen, said, "I've been the best father that I know how." In an instant, that statement blew away any shred of doubt. Hora knew those were the words of a killer, someone trying to explain why he murdered his wife and, in doing so, left two innocent children without parents. It mirrored what Sturgeon had told the prosecutor nearly a year ago: "Hans is a threat to any who get between him and [the] children. He is even a greater threat than before because a way he can salvage his unbelievable pride is to state that everything he did—he did in order to save his children."

Hora's mother was stopped at a red light in her Audi convertible in downtown Walnut Creek when she got a call from a retired sheriff's sergeant soon after the verdict was read. When Peggy Hora heard the word *guilty*, she screamed so loud the pedestrians crossing the street in front of her jumped, wondering who this crazy lady was. When she heard that it was first-degree murder, she kept screaming, "You're kidding!"

The prosecutor told reporters afterward that the lack of a body wasn't an insurmountable challenge for the jury. "We have a body," he said. "We just don't know where it is." Both sides were asked if Hans would be afforded any leniency if he divulged where Nina's body was.

"We'll have to talk to the prosecutor about that," Du Bois said. "I mean, that would have to be something the prosecutor would have to participate in."

Hora said, "There are no scheduled discussions, and so the only discussion that I'm looking forward to is the discussion about when the sentencing date will be."

McGothigan was at work when he learned, possibly from my blog, that a verdict had been reached. Soon after, Beverly called. "She was distraught, more than I'd ever heard her," he said. McGothigan rushed home, grabbed his old copy of William Blake's *Songs of Innocence and Experience* and drove to Beverly's house, where they sat together in the living room. Beverly's housemate, Edie Okamoto, sat on the stairs. "Words fail me at a time like this, so I'll leave it to the masters of the language to express my thoughts," McGothigan told Beverly before reading Blake's "The Little Girl Lost" to her.

> *In futurity*
> *I prophetic see*
> *That the earth from sleep*
> *(Grave the sentence deep)*
> *Shall arise and seek*
> *For her maker meek;*
> *And the desert wild*
> *Become a garden mild.*
> *In the southern clime,*
> *Where the summer's prime*
> *Never fades away,*
> *Lovely Lyca lay.*

McGothigan noticed the similarity of the name Lyca to Nina. But no one knew where Nina lay. Back in Russia, Rory and Nio wrote "Where is Nina Reiser?" on paper boats that floated in a lake.

The jury, however, knew enough without Nina's body, said legal pundit Steve Clark. Putting Hans on the stand "back-fired badly because not only did the jury not like him, but he filled in the blanks for the prosecution. There was nothing left for the jury to consider," Clark said.

Juror Vince Dunn said the panel was struck by the lack of sympathy Hans had for the mother of his kids. "He was always making her the bad person," Dunn said. "He just focused on his belief that she was unfit, a thief, not a good mother, on and on and on, but everybody else was talking about what a nice person she was."

Dunn said he and his fellow jurors "all came to the conclusion that there was so much circumstantial evidence" and that "all the evidence pointed to him as the culprit."

Juror Kathy Carpenter agreed, adding, "His ego was so huge. It was so damning, his testimony. When he gets up there and says, 'I perjured myself,' I mean—how ridiculous?"

Hora said later that he wanted to force Hans to "explain the unexplainable" under cross-examination. "I wanted to make sure that I put the screws to him, made him confront those specific questions and give specific answers to the unexplain-able. And the end result was he gave ridiculous, absurd answers, which is another way of saying he lied." Hans had done himself no favors by insisting that he take the stand. And by doing so, Hans ended up being Hora's Exhibit A.

Hora said later that his grilling of Hans was "probably the biggest deal for me in terms of cross-examination. I've never cross-examined a guy for so long that was as smart as he was, in an arena where there was so much pressure, where it was live-blogged every day, it was going to be on TV, it was going to be in the newspapers—every move I made was going to be watched. Every move he made was going to be watched. And that adds pressure to what was already an enormously demanding, an intense trial."

On April 29, the day after the guilty verdict, legal analyst

Michael Cardoza appeared on KTVU's popular *Mornings on 2* news program with host Ross McGowan. Cardoza, a former Alameda County prosecutor who now worked as a defense attorney, dismissed speculation that Hans would reveal where Nina's body was, especially if the DA didn't offer anything in return. "How does it benefit the district attorney?" Cardoza asked. "How does it benefit the family to know how he disposed of the body? You're going to take it from twenty-five to life what, down to a second, fifteen to life? No. You want to tell where the body is, tell where the body is. If you don't, they've got the first-degree conviction. They'll live with that. They will not bargain that away."

Hans was led back into court a couple of hours later. He had ditched the suit and was now back in his familiar red jail garb. There was no jury to impress now. Goodman set a July 9 date for sentencing. Du Bois told reporters afterward, "My client went all-in in a table-stakes game of the murder trial. And he lost, despite my best efforts to improve his hand."

CHAPTER 73

> BREAKING NEWS

The judge received a flurry of motions that summer, all of which underscored the continuing acrimony between Hans and his attorneys as the parlor game continued. On June 30, Du Bois filed a brief opining that Hans "may be mentally incompetent as a result of a mental disorder or developmental disability." Tellingly, the filing continued, Hans was "unable to understand the nature of the criminal proceedings or to assist counsel in the conduct of the defense in a rational manner." Hans was still resisting the advice of his lawyers, but to what end?

The next day, as the state Franchise Tax Board filed papers suspending Namesys as a corporation, Hans fired off a motion of his own, again seeking that John Fuery, his former divorce attorney, represent him because Du Bois "has a deep bias against me." Fuery then filed a motion on July 3 saying that Hans was indeed competent and that his behavior "is normal under the circumstances" in light of the stress he was experiencing. But by that Fourth of July weekend, Hans's reluctance to cooperate would be eclipsed by a stunning turn of events.

A procession of unmarked law-enforcement vehicles left Santa Rita Jail in Dublin on the warm afternoon of July 7, two days before Hans was to be sentenced. Inside the cars were members of the Oakland police Tactical Operations Team, what the department called its SWAT team. They were escorting a caged police van with a shackled Hans on board, sitting in the backseat with Du Bois. Hora sat in the middle row. Brock and other DA's inspectors were among those who took part in this most unusual journey, one that required them to get Goodman's permission to release Hans from jail.

Under a blistering sun, the caravan headed west on Interstate 580 and then north on Highway 13 before exiting at Park Boulevard, near where Hans had parked the CRX. The cars wended their way up Snake and Shepherd Canyon roads, made a sharp right at Aitken Drive and then veered left onto Evergreen Avenue. Had they taken the next right turn, they would have ended up right at Hans's house. Instead, they continued to the next street, Skyline Boulevard, and made a right turn. Within moments, they converged at the Skyline Gate parking lot of Redwood Regional Park at Pine Hills Drive, culminating a twenty-seven-mile trek that was all but unthinkable until just three days earlier. On the Fourth of July, when most people were firing up the barbecue and gearing up for fireworks displays, Du Bois, Tamor and Hora had met with Hans at Santa Rita Jail and, after several hours, finally persuaded him to reveal where he had buried Nina. In exchange for doing that—and so long as he told police how he had killed her and waived his rights to any appeal—he would be allowed to plead guilty to second-degree murder and get a sentence of fifteen years to life in prison. It wasn't that much different from spending twenty-five years to life in the joint—especially as the parole board tended to frown on releasing any murderers—but it was still a tangible difference.

Hans had refused to divulge Nina's location from the very beginning. Not after desperate pleas from Nina's family and friends. Not when Rory repeatedly asked him, "Where is Nina?" Not when presented with an unbelievable three-year deal in exchange for pleading guilty to voluntary manslaughter, and certainly not while he was on the stand. Only now, after being convicted of murder, was he willing to cut a deal.

Now, they just had to find Nina's body. After the vehicles had assembled at the parking lot, the officers continued driving 250 yards up the East Ridge Trail, a dirt fire road, after breaking off a lock on a gate. The cars came to a stop near a junction to a foot path. Hans was led out of the van in shackles. He breathed fresh air, away from the confines of the jail, for the first time since his arrest. He was joined by Du Bois, Tamor, Hora, Lieutenant Ersie Joyner, Sergeant Tim Nolan and Sergeant Caesar Basa from homicide and Inspectors

Brock, Chew, Conner and Mike Foster. Hora and the inspectors were dressed in khaki pants or blue jeans and blue shirts. Hora wore a Nike baseball cap.

The SWAT officers included Roland Holmgren, still doubling as the department's public information officer; Robert Roche, a decorated Marine Corps veteran who had been involved in several fatal shootings as a cop and was among the officers who had listened to Hans's calls in the wire room; and Sergeant Michael Reilly, who had been shot at while investigating the killing of a fellow officer. Wearing police raid jackets, blue jeans and stern expressions, the tactical officers had seen their share of danger and weren't about to take any chances today. This was a convicted murderer they were escorting out in the free world. They last thing they wanted was Hans running loose through the woods.

But Du Bois resented what he thought was a police convention, with officers armed to the teeth with AR-15 semiautomatic rifles and "every kind of gun you could imagine. There was no chance of him escaping without being shot." Brock wanted Hans shackled and chained as he led them to Nina's body. Du Bois balked at that, too, and the disagreement got so bad that at one point Hans went back to the van and demanded, "Take me back to Santa Rita. I'm not going to do this."

"At no time were the police helpful or did they induce the conduct of Hans Reiser to find the body," Du Bois said later. The attorney gently encouraged him to do what he came out here to do. Hans sat in the van for a while.

The stalemate was avoided when Du Bois volunteered himself to literally be the "ball and chain." He told the police to handcuff him and Hans together. If he takes off, "just shoot him!" said Du Bois, who may only have been half joking. Du Bois took off his jacket, and an officer handcuffed the attorney's left hand to Hans's right. The two made a striking pair, with Hans, his hair mussed and looking like an unmade bed in his red jail jumpsuit and Du Bois, clad in dress shoes, dark slacks and a blue dress shirt with several buttons undone. There would be no chance of Hans escaping, especially in the woods. "You ever try to run away with somebody handcuffed to you? Pretty hard," Holmgren commented later.

The group walked north on the foot path for about two hundred yards until Hans indicated that they would be going down a steep deer path off the trail to the right. It proved to be a tough trek that sunny Monday afternoon as the temperatures crested eighty degrees. Du Bois adjusted his pants and mopped his brow as he and his client maneuvered gingerly down the steep hill under the watchful eyes of the SWAT team, their AR-15s visible. Joyner, whom Du Bois had known since he was a young beat cop, helped the attorney negotiate through the brush. The officers busted through bushes, broke branches and used tree trunks to steady themselves as they made their way down.

Hans came to a stop after traveling forty yards down the path. He looked around for a long while. The officers grew exasperated. It seemed like he was stalling. Hans commented that he wanted a cherry tree to be planted as a memorial for Nina. Incredulous and angry, an officer insisted that they didn't need Hans anymore. "We know where it is now. We'll bring the dogs in!" he shouted.

Finally, Hans, his face covered in light stubble, crouched down and looked into some bushes. He got up, went further down the hill and stopped. "She's right up there," he said. "We just passed her."

The group took a hard look and found an area where the hillside had been disturbed. Brock and Joyner grabbed some shovels and began digging. "If you dig down two feet, you're going to hit Nina's toes," Hans said. He told them that she was inside a black trash bag that was itself in a duffel bag. And sure enough, after digging for a long while, the very first thing the shovel hit was a cloth strap. Hora immediately thought of Rory's drawing.

Nina had been found, 622 days after she disappeared. Hans had buried her four feet below ground on a sloping part of the hill carpeted by red-barked madrones, bay laurel and lichen-covered manzanita. It was less than half a mile from Hans's home, just a minute's drive. Looking downhill and facing east, one could look through the trees and see Mount Diablo in Contra Costa County. The site, between Redwood Regional Park and the Huckleberry Botanic Regional Preserve, was only two hundred yards behind the nearest house. One could easily hear the traffic passing by and bicyclists chatting on Pinehurst Road further down the hill, but no one would have ever come across her body. She was buried in crumbly, silty shale that was millions of years old. Had it not been for Hans leading officers to the body in the overgrown brush, it might have gone unnoticed for quite some time more. This was far from where one would find any hiker or jogger. "You had to know where she was buried to find that," Holmgren said. "The person who put the body in there is most likely the person responsible for committing that crime."

> Inspector Chew, wearing gloves, began clearing away dirt by hand as the smell of decomposition filled the air. Goodman showed up at the scene at one point. Sergeant Justin McComas, Deputy Jintapa Piyamanothamkul and Investigator Charles Brewer from the Alameda County coroner's bureau arrived. McComas ordered a halt to the excavation. The Special Operations Recovery Team, forensic anthropologist Dr. Chuck Cecil and the county crime lab were summoned to the scene, which was blocked off by yellow police tape. News helicopters began circling overhead, and neighbors craned their necks skyward, wondering what to make of the spectacle. Several news stations carried the search live with "Breaking News" crawling across TV screens.

Hans and Du Bois, meanwhile, slowly advanced back up the hill with ropes, and Hans was taken back to jail. Hans was very saddened, but he didn't want to lose it in front of everyone. He told Du Bois, "I'll cry when I get back to my cell."

Du Bois said the police were acting like cowboys and that they had been pointed in the opposite direction of where Nina was found. "They would have once again failed," Du Bois said. "They never in a million years would have found this location because it was so cleverly located." The initial searches for Nina were based on the theory that she had been left no more than fifty feet from the road. There had been no suggestion that she had been buried.

During an all-night effort, investigators carefully exhumed

Nina's skeletal remains from the makeshift grave as bright lights illuminated the scene. They found remnants of the same dress she had been wearing the day she disappeared and a yellow metal ring with a clear stone. The body was wrapped in two tarps, secured with straps and put onto a Stokes basket. Members of a search-and-rescue team, many wearing miner's-type hats with lights on them, helped bring the litter up the hill. At 12:15 a.m. on July 8, the body was gently placed into a coroner's van.

CHAPTER 74

> A GRIM TASK

Nina's remains were brought to the coroner's bureau on Fourth Street in downtown Oakland, just half a block from where Hans had run away from me nearly two years earlier. Coroner's investigator Phillip Abrams placed the ring and cloth evidence into a locked cabinet.

Dr. Thomas W. Rogers, a board-certified forensic pathologist under contract to the county for some thirty years, had seen it all: victims of drug wars, murdered police officers, rape-killings, the slaughter of innocents. The white-bearded Rogers charged eight hundred dollars per autopsy and had conducted about five hundred autopsies—half of the total—during the fiscal year 2007–2008 in Alameda County. His bill to county administrators in that period came to a little more than four hundred thousand dollars, a grim testament to his busy workload. Rogers also performed autopsies across the bay in San Mateo County and had testified in hundreds of criminal cases. But most of the time, his autopsies were conducted long before any jury would come to pass judgment.

At 8:55 a.m., Nina's autopsy got underway. Dr. Rogers opened up a blue body bag and peered at the remains. They were of a white female. There was very little left of the body, as it was almost skeletonized, and nearly all the soft tissue had decomposed, ravaged by time. The bones were mixed with dirt, dried plant material and winged insects. The entire remains were X-rayed. No bullets were found.

He found tattered clothing, a bra with a tag that read "Victoria's Secret" and bikini-type panties.

Dr. Rogers removed a skull from a plastic bag. The jaw and teeth and three pieces of the U-shaped hyoid bone were found. A broken hyoid bone could be consistent with manual strangulation, but there were no signs of trauma. Similarly, petechial hemorrhaging, tiny pinpoint red marks in the eyes as a result of burst capillaries, would also suggest strangulation. But the left eye was gone because of decomposition. The right eye—with a brown iris—was still there, but too much had deteriorated for any meaningful analysis.

As Dr. Rogers examined the neck, he found a necklace with a blue pendant. Also recovered was a watch with a white-metal band and a black face—and a gold ring with four green stones resembling a butterfly, which Nina's mother gave her when the two last saw each other, in July 2006 in Russia. Sharanova had described this last gift to the jury.

When Dr. John Berk wasn't running his family dentistry practice in Castro Valley, he had the grim task of positively identifying those who would never smile again. As a forensic odontologist, Berk performed many of the dental identifications in Alameda and Contra Costa counties. Berk often testified in court, describing how he helped provide closure by putting a name to a body that was burned beyond recognition or how a bite mark on a suspect matched the victim who lived to tell about it. On this day, the coroner's bureau was abuzz with activity, and there was a sense of urgency in the air. But Berk needn't have worried about a rush to judgment. He took a look at the teeth and then consulted Nina's dental records. They were a match. The body that had been discarded like trash, left rotting in the hills as her family plunged from hope to the depths of despair, was that of Nina Reiser. To kill her was bad enough. But to hide her body made it even worse.

Hora called Sharanova that morning in Russia to deliver the grim news. Although grateful, Sharanova began the mourning process all over again. First there was the heart-wrenching uncertainty, not knowing where Nina was. And now, with her daughter's fate sealed, her grief was renewed, as fresh as it was when she first heard Nina was missing. Never had Sharanova expected to outlive her only child.

The prosecutor then joined Joyner, Oakland police public information officer Holmgren and now-Assistant Chief Jordan at a press conference at Oakland police headquarters.

Holmgren, dressed all in black as if in mourning, made no mention of his unique role a day earlier but confirmed that Nina had been positively identified.

Joyner expressed his condolences to Nina's family and hoped that the department could "offer some sort of warmth and closure to the unanswered questions that they may have in regard to where her body had been located for all this time." Joyner said all the evidence showed that Hans acted alone.

Hora explained that the decision to allow Hans to plead guilty to second-degree murder "would not have happened without the support and the desire of Nina's family. After going through this horrible trial that the family had to go through, and having to go through all the speculation that Nina had run away, and that the family was somehow involved in hiding her or secreting her away, and then having to live in the future with people saying that they've seen Nina, they've sighted Nina, and not having to worry about appeals and all that uncertainty, and where their daughter is and where she was and what happened, that's all solved for them now. And so ultimately, this was done for the family."

CBS-5 reporter Simon Perez asked Hora, "In reducing the sentence, aren't you sending the message to defendants that they're better off withholding the truth, so you can cut a better deal afterwards?"

Hora responded that the case was unique and defended the proposed deal, saying law enforcement had sent the message that "if you commit murder, you're going to be found guilty of murder, with or without the body, truth or lie. It doesn't make any difference. In the end, we have to do what's right as a prosecutor's office. And doing what's right at the beginning, during or after the trial doesn't make any difference. And what's right in this case, thankfully the jury saw the truth. They found the defendant guilty of first-degree murder, and that gave me the opportunity to still offer the defendant a conviction of murder, not manslaughter, but murder, and I'm also able to end the speculation and help the healing process."

Hora ended by saying, "Now the family gets to pick the burial site, not the defendant."

Back at Santa Rita Jail that evening, Hans chatted with

J. D. Nelson, his former middle-school gym classmate who was now a sergeant and public information officer for the Alameda County sheriff's office. Hans told Nelson that he didn't remember him from school.

Nelson, who had grown up in a different part of the Oakland hills, commented to Hans that there were many places where bodies could be hidden.

"Well, yeah," Hans agreed, as if that was self-evident.

"You gotta feel a lot better now, right?" Nelson asked, referring to the recovery of Nina's body.

"You know, sergeant, I just got tired of lying," Hans replied. With no hint of irony, he added, "It's not my personality to lie."

CHAPTER 75

› THE JUDGE SPEAKS

On July 9, the original date of Hans's sentencing, Goodman delivered an unusual statement from the bench, saying he wanted to clear up some misconceptions for the public. He acknowledged the hard work of the jury and said the first-degree verdict gave the prosecution the leverage it needed to be able to find Nina's body. "The court is absolutely convinced that without that verdict, Mr. Reiser would have made no effort whatsoever to assist in locating the body," Goodman said. He likened repatriating Nina's remains to the great lengths taken by the government to bring home the bodies of citizens who were killed overseas.

He also noted that the difference between fifteen years to life and twenty-five years to life was meaningless. "There is no guarantee whatsoever that after fifteen years or twenty-five years, whichever sentence is imposed, that a person would be released," he said, pointing out that the state Board of Prison Terms will decide whether Hans is paroled.

Juror David Turner, the former Lucasfilm audio technician, said he understood the need for closure but noted, "I think a lot of money was wasted, for sure." In the end, "That's our system. It's the best we have."

Du Bois withdrew his motion claiming that Hans was incompetent. He denied any suggestions that Hans would be getting any break. "Actually, Mr. Reiser is not being treated leniently," Du Bois told reporters. "He's serving much more time than he would have had he been more rational."

On the same day Goodman was giving his primer on the criminal-justice system, Dr. Rogers examined Nina's bones again after they had been cleaned. Her remains were arranged on a metal table, with the skull in pieces on one side and her foot bones at the other. He found no evidence of "incised defects"—marks on the bones caused by a sharp implement like a knife—or gunshot wounds or old or new fractures. In his thirteen-page report, Dr. Rogers summarized his findings: "Skeletal remains without abnormalities." And as for cause of death, he could only say this: undetermined. Now that it was officially confirmed that Nina was dead, Dr. Anthony Iton, Alameda County Health Officer, signed her death certificate on July 24.

CHAPTER 76

> THE CONFESSION

On July 31, Hans told Deputy Probation Officer Sindy Guinn-Begley at Santa Rita Jail, "I didn't want to kill her. I wanted things to work." He said he had heard an audio recording of himself speaking and realized that his voice sounded "very egotistical" and that "I sound very impressed by myself." He said he was glad Sharanova had Nina's body. "I felt that she was wondering what had happened. I'm sorry that I lied to her during the trial," he said. "I deeply regret that. I'm very sorry for the pain I've caused. I tried to protect the children and probably just made it worse. I'm very sorry. I haven't yet met anyone who thinks I've done the right thing." He declined to provide specifics about how he killed her.

But that changed on August 21.

"The time right now is 1522 hours, which is 3:22. My name is Inspector Bruce Brock with the Alameda County district attorney's office," Brock said into a recording device. "And I am in Department 9 of the courthouse here and I am in the presence of Deputy District Attorney Paul Hora and Mr. Hans Reiser and his attorney, which is Mr. William Du Bois." Brock gave Hans the standard Miranda warning. Hans was all set to begin but then told Brock and Hora that he wanted to go off the record to protect the "interests of an innocent party." He was reluctant to contradict what Rory had said about seeing Nina leave the Exeter home that day. He didn't want to call Rory a liar. Hora told Hans to just tell the truth. And with the tape recorder back on, he finally did, matter-of-factly revealing what had happened that day as best as he could. His remarkable statement, lasting an hour and twenty-two minutes, would never be played for a jury.

Nina arrived at his home at 2:20 p.m., twenty minutes late. The two discussed their divorce. Nina said she was willing to let Hans have Namesys but refused to share legal custody of the children. The two quarreled as the children were downstairs. Rory was playing video games.

According to Hans, Nina discussed a "falsified ailment" and said she didn't believe in it herself. She "conveys to me that there's going to be more of this Munchausen by proxy disorder stuff and that I will be unable to do anything about it. And uh, this, uh caused me to become enraged and um, I killed her. And I shouldn't have done that. I'm very sorry that I did it."

Hans said he struck Nina in the head, but it didn't knock her out. So based on his version of events, as her vision dimmed and she faded into unconsciousness, Nina's last moments were face-to-face with her husband as he squeezed the life out of her. *He had to protect the children.*

"I placed my hands on both sides of her neck, and in the most unsophisticated chokehold that any judo instructor would completely despise you for ever using, I choked her," he said with no hint of emotion. "And this is the kind of choke that people who have no martial skills at all would employ, and um, and yet it uh, was completely painless for her. It's the least painful way to die."

Whether that was true for Nina would never be known, as she will never be able to give an account of what happened. But in typical strangulation cases, forensic pathologists have testified that it takes at least a minute—several minutes, on average—to choke someone to death. It is an excruciating way to die, certainly not as quick as being stabbed in the heart or shot in the face. Many prosecutors choose to demonstrate this in graphic fashion by setting a timer and then squeezing on a Styrofoam head, grimacing as pieces break off and stopping only after the buzzer sounds after what seems like an eternity.

Hans said the attack began near the front entryway and ended when he killed her on the wooden stairs leading to the upper floor. Nina put up a struggle but didn't say anything as he killed her, he said. He cut the ring finger on his right

hand on her tooth. She bled from her nose but never said anything or cried out. To hear Hans tell it, Rory and Nio were still
downstairs and never heard or saw a thing as Nina's life ebbed
away. She would never see them grow up, get married or have
families of their own.

Now, Nina's body lay near the front door. Hans was a
newly minted murderer.

Hans knew he had to act quickly to hide what he had
done. He tried to wrap her body with two trash bags from the
kitchen, but they weren't large enough for her to fit into them.
He put her inside a duffel bag and carried the deadweight up
the stairs to his mother's bathroom, which featured a custom-
made granite sink and puffy white clouds painted on the
walls. Now that Nina's body was out of the way, he went back
downstairs and used bath towels to wipe off some specks of
blood on the wall near the front door. He backed Nina's minivan into the driveway and threw the groceries from the back
into the passenger area. But then he couldn't find her keys.
So he drove the CRX as close as he could to the house and
stashed the bag with Nina inside into the back. He parked it
on a street some distance away from Exeter. After returning
home on foot, he checked for more signs of blood in the house
and fed the kids.

That night, when Rory and Nio were in bed, he drove
the CRX with Nina's body and parked it not far from where
four streets—Skyline Boulevard, Shepherd Canyon Road,
Pinehurst Road and Manzanita Drive—all came together
in one spot at the top of the Oakland hills. He walked on a
trail that curved up along the incline that paralleled the 8200
block of Skyline. It was the same path that connects to the
East Ridge Trail that investigators would eventually take
from the opposite direction. Hans cut to the left and went
down the deer path as it dropped precipitously down the
brush-covered slope. He knew the area well, having hiked
there plenty of times. But it was more difficult to navigate in
the night in the fog-ribboned hills. Hans had a flashlight and
used it sparingly, not wanting anyone to see him. He began
digging with a shovel as the moon—very nearly full and illuminated—hung in the sky. It was a lot of work, and it would

soon be daylight and he would need to tend to the kids. He walked back home.

On the morning of September 4, as dawn broke and Bay Area residents slept in to enjoy their Labor Day holiday, Nina's body was stiff from rigor mortis in the back of Hans's CRX. He became relieved when he found Nina's keys in the house. He removed the battery from her cell phone, threw a mountain bike into her minivan and then parked it on Fernwood Drive. He stashed the keys in some ground cover nearby and rode the bike back up the hill before leaving it on Gunn Drive, several streets below Exeter and where there used to be a tunnel for the railroad. Hans had planned to go back, clean Nina's vehicle and move it again, but, he said, "You guys picked up the minivan one day too early."

After moving the CRX to Aitken Drive, one street below Exeter, he resumed his grotesque task, continuing to dig as the kids slept and the moon shone brighter than the night before. Finally, the grave was big enough. He went to the CRX, drove it back to the top of the hill where the five streets converged, tugged the bag along the path and put it into the hole. He covered it with dirt. Finally, by the early morning hours of September 5, Nina's body was completely buried.

Hans said he put the dirty bath towels into plastic bags and "threw them in various people's garbage cans throughout Oakland," all places he was familiar with, including a trash container in a park near where his CRX was found.

As for getting rid of the evidence, Hans said he threw out the passenger seat because he was concerned that there were "faint traces" of blood on it. "I really threw it into a Dumpster," he said. He tossed the CRX's rear trim assembly into a trash bin near a school on Redwood Road in the Oakland hills. "I think that everything I threw away had no blood on it, and I was just being paranoid." He said he had gone to Reno so that he wouldn't be hounded by the police and that he didn't throw out any evidence there.

He said he had gone to Adventure Time, thinking that they didn't have his cell-phone number, and ended up giving them the wrong number because of "simple error." He laughed.

At the end of his statement, Hans said, almost as an

afterthought, "Um, you know, Nina was wonderful in so many ways. I'm so sorry."

"Thanks for your cooperation this afternoon, Hans," Hora said.

"Thanks, Hans," Brock said. "The time right now is 1644 hours, and we'll be going off tape."

The remarkable confession was a coda to a most extraordinary case. The lies that had come out of Hans's mouth and washed over the jury during his eleven days on the stand, all of that had now come down to this. No longer was he a duck-billed platypus, a social klutz or, as Du Bois had put it, a "nerd among nerds." The curtains had finally come down on the Hans Reiser Show. His new avatar was that of a stone-cold killer—a murderer—whose kids would never see their mother—nor him—again.

"The day that Hans led them to Nina was probably the worst day for me," Montclair parent Marni Hunter said. "For the last two years, not only did he ruin Nina's life and the children's and his own, but he took all of us through two years of drama and pain. And that's not OK."

Du Bois emerged from the trial battered and bruised. "It was the hardest trial I ever had. It was the most exasperating representation I've ever undertaken. It had almost no redeeming qualities," he said. Du Bois had taken the case because it fascinated him and he knew it would draw headlines. In retrospect, "The loss that we took, money, and the irascibility of the client, certainly rendered the publicity a nonfactor. It certainly wasn't worth it—and the publicity wasn't that good."

Du Bois said he and Tamor were "sort of sucked into the case step by step. Before we knew it, we were face-to-face with the prospect of the client testifying against our adamant advice. By that time, it was the rule, that client wouldn't follow our advice, it wasn't the exception. From the first day he walked into my office up until we dug up the body, he never followed my advice."

Some people wondered if Du Bois knew he was defending a guilty client from the beginning—or whether Hans had actually confessed early on to his attorney, with those admissions remaining confidential because of the attorney-client privilege. But Du Bois said Hans never told him what really happened until after the trial. Had Hans taken the deal that had been offered to him before it started, he would have done his time by May 2009.

Although Hans certainly had his backers in the beginning, the trip to Nina's body all but eroded any support that may have remained. The condemnations were quick, and some were laced with humor. "Reiser kills wife. Great, like geeks needed another reason to repel women," someone posted on Twitter, the popular micro-blogging service that burst onto the scene just two months before Nina was killed. (Had the fateful day of September 3, 2006, taken a different turn, Hans might well have taken to "tweeting" about how his latest file system was the best—but whether he could keep each post to under one hundred and forty characters would be a matter of conjecture.) Others cracked that there should be T-shirts emblazoned with "You're about to experience chaos" or an annotation that *Wired* reporter Josh Davis had found in the 80,496 lines of the Reiser4 source code: "Death is a complex process."

On August 25, the First District Court of Appeal in San Francisco ruled that the question of whether Pulido, the juvenile dependency court judge, had the power to order Rory and Nio back to the United States from Russia had been "rendered moot" now that Hans had been convicted. "The controversy before us has become an abstract proposition," Justice Henry Needham wrote. The conviction "makes it extremely unlikely the minors will return to this country under the provisions of the treaty," the justice noted.

On August 28, just short of the two-year anniversary of their mother's murder, Rory and Nio filed a lawsuit against Hans in Alameda County Superior Court, alleging wrongful death, negligent infliction of emotional distress and loss of love, society, companionship and advice. Each child asked for more than seven million dollars in compensatory and punitive damages. Hans responded with numerous motions, attacking the process and making it clear that a quick resolution would not be forthcoming. "Liability is fairly clear given the guilty plea, but, nevertheless, as you saw from the trial, [the children's attorney] is going to rue the day they decided to engage Hans in litigation," Tamor told me. "They'll prevail eventually, but it will be a long, painful journey getting there." And assuming Rory and Nio will prevail, it is doubtful that their father would ever be able to pay. The children would forever be collateral damage in a tragedy not of their making.

CHAPTER 77

› SENTENCING

Judgment day was August 29, 2008. The gallery was packed, and many of the trial jurors sat in the front few rows. Beverly was there to watch her son, whose hair was now grown out and curly, making him look like Art Garfunkel or Gene Wilder. But this time there was a new face: Sturgeon. His hair dyed red, Sturgeon remained standing in the gallery, glaring at Hans, before a deputy shouted at him to take a seat. Hans never turned around. "I wanted to be in his face, looking him in the eyes, and say one word: 'Nina,'" Sturgeon said later.

But things didn't start on time. Hans was led into Goodman's chambers and then into the stairway, where he met with his attorneys.

"What's going on, Paul?" a reporter asked Hora.

"There's never a rush to justice," Hora said, grinning. The audience's collective unease inched up a notch. Spectators wondered whether there had been yet another twist that would nix the sentencing.

Finally, at 1:00 p.m., Goodman took the bench. He led Hans through a formal waiver of his appeals. Hans said he was willing to take a polygraph to say that he believed his wife suffered from Munchausen by proxy syndrome and was making up illnesses for Rory. That didn't go anywhere.

Goodman asked Hans to formally state whether he believed he had received effective assistance of counsel. Hans replied that they had advised him to take fifteen years to life instead of twenty-five years to life, which might constitute "good assistance of counsel" if those sentences "are the only choices available."

"All right," the judge said.

"So that's a yes?" interjected Hora. "I'm taking that as a yes."

"Is that correct, Mr. Reiser, I could assume that's a yes?" the judge asked.

"Well, it's a narrowing of the meaning of the yes, but yes," Hans said.

"Don't play word games with me, Mr. Reiser! Is it yes or not?" snapped Goodman, who was incredulous that Hans was still parsing things on his day of reckoning.

"Yes, your honor," said Hans, still sounding reluctant.

His hair unkempt, Hans appeared withdrawn and frequently looked down at the table. When asked by Goodman if Hans wished to make a statement, Du Bois said, "Probably. May I speak to him on that subject?" Du Bois told Hans, "Try to be as brief as possible—succinct, to the point, as brief as you can."

The bailiffs did not allow Hans to stand, and so from the defense table, Hans said, "I wish to humbly apologize to society for my crime. Every human life is sacred, and I took the life of a human being, and I am very sorry for that. I don't think that I'll ever be able to make up to society for what I've done. But I'll try to the extent that I can."

He said he had set up a trust fund for his children and said money could be sent to his mother's home on Exeter Drive.

"I'm very sorry that I deprived Anthony of a life living with Nina, deprived the two of them of their happiness together," Hans said. "And I'm very sorry that I deprived Irina of her daughter, because I knew how much she loved her." He paused to control his emotion. "And I'm very sorry for the terrible harm that I've caused my children. And if I'm able to I'll try to contribute to society while in prison."

Hans turned to Du Bois. "Is there anything else I should add?" He then said, "Oh, I'm very sorry for the time that I've wasted of all these people who've worked very hard to convict me of my crime. And I admire the district attorney and the police for their skill and their dedication—and your honor as well. Thank you."

"Anything else?" Goodman asked.

Du Bois looked up. "He didn't say anything about his lawyers," he deadpanned. Hora grinned.

As promised, Goodman sentenced Hans to fifteen years to life in prison, meaning the earliest he could seek parole is in 2021, when he is fifty-eight years old.

Juror Vince Dunn had earlier criticized the deal, even calling it blackmail. "It just doesn't seem right to me that that can happen in America," he said, shortly after the body was recovered. "I thought the jury had the last say." But now, Dunn had changed his mind, agreeing with his fellow jurors that it would provide closure.

Although Beverly attended the sentencing hearing, she did not address the court. Instead, she penned a letter. "I believe that Hans Reiser has already suffered the worse punishment he could, which is the loss of his children whom he dearly loves," she wrote. "If he is paroled, he will be able, by being free to use his gifts, to make a contribution to society. He has a unique mind and is very gifted in the sciences and will once again be able to create something of value to mankind."

Sturgeon wrote to the court, "I pray that Hans comes to seek and know the salvation from sin which faith in Christ offers. Nina has her wings now and is keeping heaven's gardens well fertilized, watered and feline-haunted."

Sharanova and her husband also wrote a letter. It ended by saying, "Nina will always stay in our memory a kind and loving daughter and mother. Our hearts are crying out, 'Nina, come back to us!' We agree with the verdict. A murderer, Hans Reiser, who took away his children's mother and caused parents to lose their daughter, should suffer the harshest punishment. He shall stay in prison for the rest of his life. He shall never disrupt Rory and Niorline's life again. They [will] grow up in a loving family just like Nina did and not in a family that is trying to manipulate them while hiding the indifference in their hearts."

CHAPTER 78

> AFTERMATH

On September 5, 2008, almost two years to the day after he murdered Nina, Hans was sent to San Quentin Prison, located on the edge of San Francisco Bay. The prison's reception center is where all convicted murderers are first sent for processing. Hans was designated as California Department of Corrections inmate G31008. He was classified as a high-security, Level 4 prisoner and shared his cell, measuring four by nine feet, with another inmate.

Despite having waived his rights to appeal, Hans challenged his conviction and sentence that fall. His claims were nothing short of bizarre. In a handwritten motion, he accused Du Bois of having "oxytocin excess" because people who have too much of the so-called love hormone "enjoy betraying others." "He has much in common with persons I was in conflict with during my divorce and identified with them to an extent that biased him against me enough that he wanted to betray me," Hans wrote. "He hates me."

He suggested that Du Bois led him to believe that he would only get a three-year sentence if he led police to Nina's body and accused the lawyer of basing jury selection in part on Chinese astrology. "It is a logical necessity that either I am delusional, or he is delusional," Hans wrote of Du Bois. Reporter David Kravets couldn't resist writing on *Wired*'s *Threat Level* blog that he "covered the trial gavel to gavel for six months and knows the answer to that question."

Hans complained that he was repeatedly denied access to the law library or to his legal papers and that at one point guards made him sweep the floor when he pressed them on the issue. Hans gave a number of other reasons for his appeal, saying he wanted to explore "anything else that may help me get out of prison and reunited with my children" and get his "life situation improved."

He would not get any help from Goodman. "The request is denied," the judge wrote in response to Hans's request for what is known as a certificate of probable cause, which is required for an appeal to move forward. Hans had already waived his rights to an appeal, and anyways he had filed his paperwork too late, the judge noted.

Hans continued to write letters from behind bars, including long missives to his mother-in-law in which he asked if she would agree to mediation in the wrongful-death suit and insisted that he had only wanted to remedy the Munchausen by proxy situation. As usual, he pined for his kids. "My dream is to buy a gingerbread house from Hotel Europa for the kids and get them an account to buy desserts at the Europa Hotel bakery," he wrote Sharanova that fall. "I know it's a silly dream, but as soon as I can earn money, I will do it if it's OK with you."

It was not OK, evidently, as Sharanova wrote an e-mail to Kathy Siegel, the Alameda County deputy public defender representing Rory and Nio, and asked that Hans's letters stop. "It appears Mr. Reiser is engaging in a form of harassment against the caregiver and the family, perhaps in an effort to discourage the family from proceeding with the wrongful-death action filed against Mr. Reiser," Siegel wrote. Judge Morris Beatus agreed and slapped Hans with a restraining order that barred him from contacting Sharanova, her husband and the children by phone, letters or e-mail, through at least November 2011. "The restrained person's letters to the caregiver disturb the peace and tranquility of the children's placement," Beatus wrote in the order he issued on November 13, 2008.

On December 29, 2008, Hans wrote me a letter from San Quentin. He again asked to be polygraphed so that people would believe him when he said Nina was a threat to their children. "I defended the children from harm," he wrote. "I think people know deep down that I defended a child from real danger, and they don't want to consciously know it, and a polygraph would force them to consciously know it." In his usual discursive fashion, he had a number of requests for me, asking that I read Dr. Schreier's book on Munchausen by proxy syndrome. He also put *Anna Karenina* on my list of must-reads, saying Tolstoy's tragic love story "is a book that most educated women read, and every man would be wise to read before marriage." Hans wrote that he only read it "after my conviction, unfortunately." He said he was as good a husband as Mr. Karenina was.

> Goodman, Hora, Du Bois and Tamor continue to handle criminal cases.

Goodman celebrated twenty-five years on the bench and was feted at a party in January 2009 at Pier 29 Restaurant in Alameda. A veritable who's who of the Alameda County legal community was there, including key players in the Reiser case like Du Bois and Chew.

A picture of Hora accompanying Hans and police to Nina's makeshift grave is attached to the wall in the prosecutor's new office at the Wiley Manuel Courthouse. Hora now contentedly works in the same cattle-call courtroom where Hans had made his first appearance. With a set nine-to-five schedule, Hora now has more time to spend with his family. He has a number of mementos from the trial. A box containing a five-inch-tall vinyl toy platypus named Burnum sits unopened on the prosecutor's shelf, an anonymous gift that came through the mail. (An online description reads, "When close enough he will sting his opponents with his venomous heel spurs to incapacitate them.") Someone else had given Hora a huge stuffed-animal platypus, but it's at home, where the newest addition to his family plays with it. And on his laptop computer is a picture of Du Bois with his client sitting next to him in court. But instead of Hans, Brock had Photoshopped a platypus into the suit.

Peggy Hora said she understood all the joking behind the scenes. "When you deal with the macabre every day, when you deal with incredible pain every single day, you need the release of humor. It can be seen by other people as disrespectful or inappropriate, but when you're on the inside, we can get pretty wicked sometimes because you have no other way to release the stress of dealing with it. Otherwise, you'd go home and open a vein."

The trial marked a big shift in how the public came to regard Hora and his mother. Shortly after the verdict, Peggy Hora was sitting on assignment as a judge in a San Francisco courtroom. An attorney appearing before her asked, "Are you any relation to Paul Hora?"

"That's my son," she said with pride. It had now come full circle. For years the prosecutor had been referred to as Peggy Hora's son. Now, she was known as Paul Hora's mother. "He has totally come into his own," she said. For a while, she had to fend off assumptions that she had helped her son when he was in law school or that he asked for her advice during the trial. "He proved himself on his own," she said.

> On January 6, 2009, Hans was beaten up by a group of inmates after he returned from the morning meal at the prison dining hall. A prison staffer set off an alarm, and guards came running to the first tier of what is known as the Badger section housing in the south cell block. They found Hans with cuts and bruises to his face, but when they asked what happened, he simply said, "I fell down." From his days at Santa Rita Jail, Hans had learned not to snitch. But by not fighting back and standing up for himself, he was already pegged as weak. The guards later learned that Hans had been eating with and hanging around black inmates, breaking another unwritten convict code: stick to your own kind. But among the different cliques in prison, from gang-bangers to drug addicts to hardcore skinheads, it wasn't like there was a club for computer geeks.

Hans wouldn't be tested again behind the brick walls of San Quentin. On January 28, as part of the standard transfer process, he was sent to Mule Creek State Prison, population 3,862, in Ione in Amador County, forty-one miles southeast of Sacramento, California. He was assigned a six-by-nine-foot cell with another inmate at the prison, ensconced in an octagon-shaped, 866-acre parcel of land in oak-studded foothills in the state's Gold Country. Eligible prisoners can work at the prison's coffee-roasting plant, textiles program, a laundry and a meat-processing plant.

Beverly, who was never able to pay her son a visit at San Quentin, made a two-hundred-mile round trip to see him at Mule Creek in March 2009, her first visit since his sentencing. That same month, the Oakland Police Department hosted the fortieth annual California Homicide Investigators Association conference at the Silver Legacy Resort Casino in Reno, where Hans had said he'd enjoyed the buffets. Hora and Brock were there to give the lead presentation—an overview of the Reiser case.

Also in March, Hans proposed the creation of a company that would be held in trust for Rory and Nio. As an employee, Hans would tutor his children via teleconferencing and then turn the company over to them when they turned eighteen. In a filing on March 15, 2009, he reiterated that he had defended his children from harm but added, "It should have been the government that did that." When told by the children's attorney, Irene Pertsovsky, that she had not conveyed his idea to Rory and Nio, Hans then accused Pertsovsky in a filing of displaying "sexual bias and other prejudice to the detriment of her clients. She does not care about their actual welfare, I feel."

By spring, Hans seemed to be acting abnormally while behind bars. He was moved through a succession of cells over a month's time because of his "uncleanliness and personal hygiene," including the fact that he didn't flush the toilet, Mule Creek corrections officers reported in May 2009. He also seemed forgetful, confused and lost things that had been given to him only minutes earlier, guards said. It was bitterly ironic that Hans was experiencing these problems at the exact time when he would have been released had he taken the deal for voluntary manslaughter. In a court filing in June 2009, Hans denied that there was anything wrong with him, saying his fellow inmates were "violent predators with anger management problems" and, like lawyers, were "con artists" who were making up falsified ailments in him, just as psychologists had done with Rory.

Hans had to find his place in the pecking order and earn what counted as respect from behind bars, but that, too, was difficult. He reported being hassled because his typing was too loud and because he had the light on while his cellmate was trying to sleep. Hans claimed that guards told him to simply fight it out with his "cellies." "I killed someone. It was horrible. I have had enough violence for this life. Please let me retire from that field," he wrote in a court filing. In another filing, in January 2010—numbering 342 pages—Hans blamed the system for the murder. "If the Alameda County courts followed the law, I never would have killed Nina. I never would have needed to. It is not hard to prove ailments have been falsified if a trial is fair, especially ailments." He added, "Everyone wants me to say I just lost it and killed Nina. They mean well, but I had to force myself to kill; I did not want to do it. If I had been motivated by malice or greed, that would be indicative of murder, but I wanted to protect Rory."

In spring 2010, Nina's mother traveled back to Oakland with her grandchildren and formally adopted them. They promptly returned to Russia.

Two bouquets of flowers tied upside down from a tree branch on a deer trail signal visitors that they are approaching Nina's makeshift grave in the Oakland hills. A single sheet of paper with nine color photos of Nina bears a handwritten message, "In Memory of Nina." A vase, placed by a trial-watcher, remains in the hole where she once lay. The flowers inside are withered.

Nina is now buried in Saint Petersburg, Russia. "Her children will be able to come and talk to her, rather than in the dirt of the Oakland hills, and I believe that Nina's name was cleared," Doren said. She said of Hans, "He cannot lie anymore and he cannot make a mockery of jurors and the people."

Amid all his lies and obfuscations, a complaint Hans had made about Nina years before her murder was chillingly prophetic, although he probably didn't intend for it to turn out quite the way it did: "I would like to say that the children should be taken away from her, and I would certainly benefit from having someone else raise them, but I know that they love her and it would hurt them deeply."

ABOUT THE AUTHOR

HENRY K. LEE is a reporter at the *San Francisco Chronicle*, where he covers crimes, courts and aviation. He has appeared on television and radio programs across the country, including CNN, HLN, MSNBC, the Fox News Channel and Court TV. He lives with his family in Oakland, California.